Approaches to the Bible

VOLUME 2

A MULTITUDE OF PERSPECTIVES

Approaches to the Bible

The Best of Bible Review

VOLUME 2
A MULTITUDE OF PERSPECTIVES

EDITED BY
HARVEY MINKOFF

BIBLICAL ARCHAEOLOGY SOCIETY
Washington, DC

To my parents, wife and children–
links in the chain of tradition.
H.M.

Hershel Shanks/general editor
Suzanne F. Singer/managing editor
Judy Wohlberg/production manager
Carol R. Arenberg/special projects editor
Laurie Andrews/copy editor
Sean O'Brien/special projects assistant
Designed by Sharri Harris Wolfgang, AURAS Design, Washington, DC

Library of Congress Cataloging-in-Publication Data
Approaches to the Bible: the best of Bible review / edited by Harvey Minkoff.
p. cm.
Includes bibliographical references and indexes.
Contents: v. 1. Composition, transmission, and language.
v. 2. A multitude of perspectives.
1. Bible–Introductions. 2. Bible–Study and teaching.
I. Minkoff, Harvey. II. Bible review.
BS475.2.A66 1994
220.6 94-21126
ISBN 1-880317-21-4 (set)
ISBN 1-880317-16-8 (v. 1)
ISBN 1-880317-17-6 (v. 2)

4710 41st Street, NW
Washington, DC 20016

Contents

PART IV

Sociology and the Bible

PART V

Linguistics and the Bible

PART VI

The Bible as Literature

PART VII

Structuralism and the Bible

PART VIII
Feminism and the Bible

Foreword

If we have learned anything from publishing *Biblical Archaeology Review* and *Bible Review,* it is that there is a tremendous need, one might say thirst, for up-to-date, first-class biblical scholarship for a lay audience. And that audience is much larger than even we suspected.

Articles from these two magazines are now so widely used in study groups, in college, university and seminary classes and in church and synagogue religious schools that it is no longer remarked upon. But when articles are used in this way, they tend to lose some of the sweep and depth that characterize them when they are carefully arranged and understood as a developing whole.

We first sensed this in the case of *Biblical Archaeology Review,* which prompted us to compile the two-volume set entitled *Archaeology and the Bible: The Best of BAR* (1990). Volume 1 covered "Early Israel," and volume 2 covered "Archaeology in the World of Herod, Jesus and Paul." These volumes have been so successful and so widely adopted for classroom use that we decided to compile another collection of articles, this time from *Bible Review* (or *BR*, as it is known to its friends).

Approaches to the Bible: The Best of Bible Review is the result. Edited with flair and erudition by Harvey Minkoff (see his introductions to the various sections), this series also consists of two volumes, the first subtitled "Composition, Transmission and Language" and the second subtitled "A Multitude of Perspectives."

Even we were surprised at how neatly these articles could be grouped into a comprehensive whole, an overview of various approaches to the biblical text. Just glancing at the intriguing titles, the articles beckoning to be read, impresses us with the importance and excitement of approaching the Bible from a variety of perspectives.

I venture to suggest there is no more readable or comprehensive introduction to the greatest, most inspiring, most influential collection of books ever written—what we call the Bible—than you will find in these pages. The reader will be introduced not only to the latest scholarship, but also to an even-handed presentation of different and sometimes conflicting points of view—

all designed to deepen an appreciation of the many levels on which the Bible can be read and studied.

This is an exciting venture, and I envy those who are coming to it for the first time. We hope you will find it a never-ending source of enrichment.

Hershel Shanks
President
Biblical Archaeology Society

A Multitude of Perspectives
A General Introduction

"Turn it this way, turn it that way, everything is in it," one sage in the Talmud said of the Bible. Indeed, for centuries, believers and skeptics, scholars and guileless readers have turned the Bible every which way, for all sorts of reasons, and discovered a wide range of meanings in it. Readers with different religious, cultural and academic motives have mined the Bible for insights into theology, history, archaeology, sociology, linguistics, literature and politics.

The word Bible comes from the Greek word *biblia,* meaning "books." But despite the implied unity of a single bound volume, the Bible is a collection of histories, laws, prophecies, rituals, narratives, poems and short stories written by different authors at different times under varying conditions. In fact, one of the key questions addressed or implied in these studies is whether the Bible is a unified work with a single, consistent theme or an accidental accretion of texts, the value of which is different from the purpose intended by the compilers. In other words, is the Bible, from Genesis to Revelation, a coherent statement of God's plan for the world, or must we be satisfied to discover a nugget of ethical gold here or a historical gem there and discard mounds of associated rubble?

Even the phrase "Genesis to Revelation" raises questions. The Hebrew Bible, the Jewish Holy Scripture, ends with Chronicles, thus encompassing a different message from the Christian Bible, in which Chronicles ends the "Old Testament." Changing the Hebrew Bible to the Old Testament changes a completed story with an open-ended promise of redemption into part one of an entirely different story of salvation. Members of various faith communities, reading ostensibly the same text, come away with entirely different impressions, messages of personal comfort, inspiration and guidance.

How, then, do we get at the meaning of a book—or books—written two to three thousand years ago, in Hebrew, Aramaic and Greek, in milieus very different from ours? How can we know what this material means?

The scholarly answer is that we cannot interpret the Bible until we learn more about the life, language and ideas of the biblical world; only then can we hope to comprehend what "son of man" or "Sheol"—or God—meant to a distant people long ago. In fact, some scholars argue that the main value of reading the Bible today is that it initiates efforts to recapture the past. Others believe that modern readers who engage the Bible empathetically can derive a personal sense of the longing, hope and promise, as well as the literary merits, of this ancient text.

These approaches are not necessarily mutually exclusive, or even sequential, although to many they are one or the other or both. Historical critics do not always reach conclusions favorable to believers. The lessons of modern psychology and politics may cast doubt on, or even contradict, biblical culture and theology. And people hoping to find a personal relationship with the word of God or to evaluate one of the world's great books as literature may ignore questions of historical accuracy.

From its inception in 1985, *Bible Review (BR)* has provided an open forum for all these approaches to the Bible by bringing first-rate scholarship to lay readers as well as scholars. As a nonconfessional publication, *BR* publishes discussions of the background, context, structure, language and meaning of the Bible; *BR* is not a pulpit for any particular interpretation, but all of the authors believe that studying the Bible is important.

In volume one of this set, the articles focus on the composition, transmission and language of the text. In this volume, we explore various approaches to reading the Bible, from theology to literature, from abstract scholarship to political activism. Each section begins with a theoretical and historical overview; the articles that follow show how a specific approach applies to a particular book or crucial biblical passage. The cumulative effect of these articles, which are based on diverse assumptions and arrive at diverse conclusions, is reaffirmation that these texts, written thousands of years ago in a small area of the eastern Mediterranean, still command center stage in the drama of contemporary life.

Harvey Minkoff

PART I

Theology and the Bible

Theology and the Bible
Introduction

First and foremost, the Bible is a religious text, the holy scriptures of various faith communities. For almost three millennia, people have looked to biblical texts as the word of God. In the Bible, they have found rules for daily living, solace from life's pain, assurance of their immortal souls, the record of a divine hand in history and a promise for the future. In short, the Bible has been the defining text of Western civilization and Judeo-Christian culture. It permeates art and literature, still demands our attention and engenders intense attachment in some and revulsion in others. Even enthusiastic admirers of the classical world do not look to the *Iliad* as a model of conduct; and ardent contemporary feminists do not bother excoriating or revisioning the *Odyssey*.

The very fact that the Bible is the sacred text of two major religions, Judaism *and* Christianity, is an indication that there is more than one religious interpretation of the text. The composition of the Bible, the process by which diverse sagas, poems, laws, oracles, visions, proverbs, royal records, short stories, biographies and letters came to be held sacred and then, much later, to be considered a single book, lends itself to multiple interpretations and various theologies. In this respect, the New Testament is easier to characterize than the Hebrew Bible, because the authors of the New Testament were all concerned with validating Jesus as Christ and explaining what that meant. Whether biography, narrative, vision or letter, the books of the New Testament are unified in intent. They were written over a period of a century or so by members of the Christian community for the edification, guidance, support and comfort of those who were, for the most part, already members of that community. Even so, the theological message is interpreted differently by various Christian communities, and the function or incorporation of theology in specific biblical books is a matter of debate.

The texts of the Hebrew Bible were composed over a much longer period of time by a wider range of authors for far more diverse reasons. Even the question of what to call the community of readers is a theological one. Some see a straight line from the patriarchs–through Abraham, the first Jew, the Exodus of the Jews from slavery in Egypt, the giving of the Ten Commandments at Mount Sinai, the reign of Jewish kings, the preaching of Jewish prophets, the Exile of the Jews in Babylonia, the establishment of the Second Jewish Commonwealth, the modern Jewish Diaspora–to modern Jews in Israel and around the world. Others emphasize the distinction between the people of the Bible and Jews of today; they refer to the Hebrew slaves in Egypt, the Israelite kingdom and prophets and the Jews at the time of Jesus. The theological implications of this contrast are immense. In one case, the Hebrew Bible is the story of God's relationship with the Jews; in the other, it is the developing revelation of God's redemption of humanity.

Little wonder, then, that the question of what to do with the Jewish Bible has been a major theological controversy for Christians from the very beginning. In the second century, Marcion founded a sect in Rome that discounted the Jewish Scriptures and purged Christian documents of all Jewish elements. When the orthodox church declared Marcion a heretic, the church fathers reaffirmed the importance of the Hebrew Bible, which was reinstated as the "old" testament that was fulfilled in Jesus; and, according to some interpretations, the "old" covenant was superseded by a "new" Christian covenant. During the Renaissance, however, Hebrew was on a par with Greek and Latin as a learned language for humanistic studies, and Christian Hebraists, trained mostly by Jewish tutors, eagerly explored postbiblical Jewish works of law, liturgy, grammar, philology and Kabbalah. According to James L. Kugel, a contributor to *The Hebrew Bible and Its Interpreters*, "Christian Hebraists generally assumed as axiomatic the continuity (just as some modern scholars have assumed the discontinuity) between biblical and postbiblical Jewish civilization...Jewish tradition was, at least initially, consulted as a kind of 'native informant' for all matters touching on the Bible."[1]

The new field of biblical scholarship unavoidably became a battleground in the religious wars that subsequently tore apart the Christian world. All sides mustered the latest scholarly insights as doctrinal ammunition. By 1787, Johann Philipp Gabler called for "proper distinction between biblical and dogmatic theology," and academics took up the threads of humanistic biblical studies, emphasizing history, philology, archaeology and literature. Nonetheless, as John J. Collins argues in the same volume, the objective history of Israelite religion and early Christianity soon became blurred as historical scholars tried to answer dogmatic questions. The goal of biblical theology was defined, in the words of G. E. Wright in *God Who Acts*, as "history interpreted by faith."[2]

In "Must 'Biblical Theology' Be Christian Theology?" Rolf Rendtorff describes the dangers of scholars speaking for the text.[3] In Germany, biblical scholarship became entangled with Nazi politics, because the Old Testament was of Jewish origin. Scholars defending the validity of the Hebrew Scriptures within the

Christian church claimed that after Jesus the Old Testament became a Christian book, thus repudiating the Jewishness of the Old Testament and denying that the Hebrew Bible had any meaning or significance outside Christianity. In this context, they declared, the Old Testament foreshadows the New Testament, Old Testament characters prefigure New Testament characters, and the promise of the Old Testament is fulfilled in the New Testament.[4]

The implicit, and often explicit, denigration of Jewish Scriptures has been repudiated by recent Christian scholars. Catholic spokesmen, for example, have publicly rejected the notion that God's covenant with the Jews was superseded. But the question of what to do with the Old Testament still dogs Christians. Apparently, Henry O. Thompson believes, a large number of Christians simply ignore the Old Testament except for a few stories from Genesis, Psalm 23 and scattered quotations. But he believes the Hebrew Bible "adds depth and dimension to our understanding and words to live by. It gives examples of faith that we have not yet equalled, let alone surpassed."[5]

Why, then, is the Bible, in particular the Hebrew Bible, seldom looked to for guidance today? One answer offered by Simon Greenberg is that many adults have childish memories of the Bible. Genesis, for example, is identified with "stories told to six and seven year old children in both Christian and Jewish religious schools." Greenberg adds that because "very few students continue their religious studies long enough to be exposed to a more mature understanding...it remains in their minds, even after they grow up, as a collection of mildly interesting fairy tales."[6]

Another reason people tend to ignore the Bible today is that values are shaped by the larger society in which the Bible is largely ignored. Conservatives may quote a passage that seems to support the established order; radicals may look for allies among the prophets who condemned corrupt leaders; feminists may find fault with sexist attitudes; psychologists may recoil at the admonition not to spare the rod. All of these attempts to use the Bible to reinforce a single point of view come up against the age-old philosophical conundrum—is something right because God does it, or does God do something because it is right? Certainly, some acts demanded or performed by God in the Bible offend modern standards of morality. Does this reflect badly on God or on modern morality? This question is taken up in Ronald S. Hendel's essay, "When God Acts Immorally."

CHAPTER 1

Ecclesiastes
Odd Book In

James L. Crenshaw

One stumbling block in the path of biblical theologists is the Book of Ecclesiastes. Rather than justice for widows and orphans or the promise of everlasting life, the theme of Ecclesiastes is existential nihilism–futility, oppression, ignorance and death. How does this negative message square with the rest of the Bible?

Many scholars believe that Ecclesiastes was included in the canon because of the epilogues, which may or may not have been part of the original composition. The injunction in the epilogues to "fear God and keep his commandments" encapsulates traditional piety but runs counter to the rest of the work. Crenshaw suggests that "Israel had an ancient tradition of skepticism that surfaces time and again, if only for brief moments." Anyone attempting to fit the God of Ecclesiastes into the image of a just and loving God concerned with the well-being of the righteous must ignore "the stated inability of humans to discover what the deity actually does or to benefit from divine activity." Traditional theologists have tried "to remove the sting" from the message of Ecclesiastes, but Crenshaw labels these efforts "refusal[s] to hear unaccustomed sounds within religious traditions."

Sooner or later, Crenshaw maintains, "even devout worshipers encounter life's ambiguities." The author of Ecclesiastes faces the reality of chance, tedium, monotony, inequity, stupidity, callousness, death and oblivion and encourages people "to live as fully as possible." The author, Crenshaw says, speaks "what was true for him. That honesty ought to earn him a special place in history, for the willingness to question revered beliefs is rare indeed."–Ed.

One book of the Hebrew Bible stands out like a sore thumb–Ecclesiastes, an alien book that denies human access to revelatory insights. The deity in Ecclesiastes is indifferent to human behavior and dispenses rewards and punishments regardless of merit. The author, a radical thinker who calls himself

Qohelet, questions everything regardless of its source and gives credence to nothing but what he or she can see or hear.

At first glance, Ecclesiastes seems like a hodgepodge of narrative genres—royal experiments, anecdotes, autobiographical narratives, poetic metaphors and allegories, maledictions and benedictions, sayings, existential observations, reflections and disputes. The book begins with a superscription apparently attributing authorship to King Solomon—"The words of the Preacher [Qohelet], the son of David, king in Jerusalem" (Ecclesiastes 1:1).[1] It ends, 12 chapters later, with two quite different epilogues, one (12:9-10) sympathetic ("The Preacher sought to find pleasing words, and uprightly he wrote words of truth"), the other (12:11-12) cool and dismissive ("The sayings of the wise are like goads...My son, beware of anything beyond these"). The opening superscription is followed by an introductory poem (1:3-11) about the meaninglessness of everything natural and human:

> Vanity of vanities, says the Preacher,
> Vanity of vanities! All is vanity....
>
> Ecclesiastes 1:2

> What has been
> Is what will be,
> And what has been done
> Is what will be done;
> And there is nothing new
> Under the sun.
>
> Ecclesiastes 1:9

> There is no remembrance of former things, nor will there be any remembrance of later things yet to happen among those who come after.
>
> Ecclesiastes 1:11

A concluding poem (11:7-12:7) about old age and death precedes the epilogues:

> [I]f a man lives many years, let him rejoice in them all; but let him remember that the days of darkness will be many. All that comes is vanity.
>
> Ecclesiastes 11:8

> [T]he almond tree blossoms,
> The grasshopper drags itself along and desire fails;
> Because man goes to his eternal home,
> And the mourners go about the streets.
>
> Ecclesiastes 12:5

This poem ends the same way the introductory poem begins. Together they make a thematic envelope for the book:

> Vanity of vanities, says the Preacher;
> All is vanity.
>
> Ecclesiastes 12:8

The introductory poem is followed by a royal experiment (1:12-2:26), in which the author tests wisdom and folly, sensuality and achievement, fame and fortune, and concludes that none of them brings lasting satisfaction:

> I the Preacher have been king over Israel in Jerusalem.
>
> Ecclesiastes 1:12

> I said to myself, "I have acquired great wisdom, surpassing all who were over Jerusalem before me; and my mind has had great experience of wisdom and knowledge." And I applied my mind to know wisdom and to know madness and folly. I perceived that this also is but a striving after wind.
>
> For in much wisdom is much vexation,
> And he who increases knowledge increases sorrow.
>
> Ecclesiastes 1:16-18

> I said to myself, "Come now, I will make a test of pleasure; enjoy yourself." But behold, this also was vanity.
>
> I said of laughter, "It is mad,"
> And of pleasure, "What use is it?"
>
> Ecclesiastes 2:1-2

> I made great works; I built houses and planted vineyards for myself; I made myself gardens and parks, and planted in them all kinds of fruit trees. I made myself pools from which to water the forest of growing trees.
>
> Ecclesiastes 2:4-7

> I also gathered for myself silver and gold and the treasure of kings and provinces; I got singers, both men and women, and many concubines, man's delight.
>
> Ecclesiastes 2:8

> Then I considered all that my hands had done and the toil I had spent in doing it, and behold, all was vanity and a striving after wind, and there was nothing to be gained under the sun.
>
> Ecclesiastes 2:11

> Then I said to myself, "What befalls the fool will befall me also; why then have I been so very wise?" And I said to myself that this also is vanity. For of the wise man as of the fool there is no enduring remembrance, seeing that in the days to come all will have been long forgotten. How dies the wise man? As the fool! So I hated life, because what is done under the sun was grievous to me; for all is vanity and a striving after wind.
>
> Ecclesiastes 2:15-17

The royal experiment thus ends on a note of despair that life offers only fleeting pleasures.

Another memorable section (3:1-22) begins with the well known poem about a time for everything. The author laments that it is impossible to discover the right occasion for particular words or deeds:

> For everything there is a season, and a time for every matter
> under heaven:
> A time to be born, and a time to die;
> A time to plant, and a time to pluck up what is planted;
> A time to kill, and a time to heal;
> A time to break down, and a time to build up;
> A time to weep, and a time to laugh;
> A time to mourn, and a time to dance;
> A time to cast away stones, and a time to gather stones together;
> A time to embrace, and a time to refrain from embracing;
> A time to seek, and a time to lose;
> A time to keep, and a time to cast away;
> A time to rend, and a time to sew;
> A time to keep silence, and a time to speak;
> A time to love, and a time to hate;
> A time for war, and a time for peace.
>
> Ecclesiastes 3:1-8

The remainder of Ecclesiastes consists of collections of proverbs (7:1-12, 10:8-11,14). Here are some of the better known ones:

> A good name is better than precious ointment; and the day of death, than the day of birth.
>
> It is better to go to the house of mourning than to go to the house of feasting; for this is the end of all men, and the living will lay it to heart.
>
> Ecclesiastes 7:1-2

> Dead flies make the perfumer's ointment give off an evil odor; so a little folly outweighs wisdom and honor.
>
> Ecclesiastes 10:1

> Cast your bread upon the waters, for you will find it after many days.
>
> Ecclesiastes 11:1

> As you do not know how the spirit comes to the bones in the womb of a woman with child, so you do not know the work of God who makes everything.
>
> Ecclesiastes 11:5

Qohelet laments the powerlessness of victims, warns against overzealous piety, observes that all work is for naught, notes that chance frustrates all purposeful effort and acknowledges the ever-present threat of death. This somber message persists through various repetitions, refrain-like phrases and favorite expressions: Everything is *hebel*–futile or ephemeral, a vanity. All effort is like shepherding (or pursuing) the wind. Human effort is of no avail. Death cancels every gain. God does not distinguish between people and animals at the moment of death. Qohelet urges his readers to seize the moment in spite of the fact that pleasure is fleeting and that Sheol (the netherworld) is a dark and permanent home.

QOHELET THE PREACHER displays the opening words of Ecclesiastes: "The words of the Preacher, the son of David, king in Jerusalem. Vanity of vanities! All is vanity." This wood engraving by Stefan Martin is based on a drawing by the American artist Ben Shahn (1898-1969). The title "Rex" suggests that the artist pictured the author of Ecclesiastes as King Solomon, to whom the work has been attributed by tradition. *Photo: Courtesy Bernarda Shahn*

How did a book with such radical ideas get into the Bible? Why was it accepted into the canon? We don't really know. The epilogues go a long way toward nullifying the skepticism of the rest of the book by ending on a traditional note: "Fear God, and keep his commandments; for this is the whole duty of man" (12:13).

Perhaps attributing the book to David's son, Solomon, facilitated its acceptance into the canon. After all, Solomon has a great deal of authority. On the other hand, the stratagem did not work in many other instances. (In fact, attributing authorship to ancient worthies was so common at this time that we have a special word for such writings–pseudepigrapha–which means falsely attributed writings.)

My opinion is a little different. There was an ancient tradition of skepticism in Israel that surfaces for brief moments in the canonical texts. For example, when Israel was overcome by the Midianites, the Angel of the Lord appeared to Gideon and declared, "The Lord is with you, valiant warrior." Gideon responded, "Please, my lord, if the Lord is with us, why has all this befallen us?" (Judges 6:12-13). Job, too, expresses despair and doubt: "Why does God place light on the sufferer/ and give life to the bitter in spirit?" (Job 3:20). In Proverbs, we read of the impossibility of gaining wisdom: "Who has ascended to heaven and come down?/ Who has gathered the winds in his fists?" (Proverbs 30:4). Perhaps this tradition of skepticism accounts for the acceptance of Ecclesiastes into the canon.

Two other books of the Hebrew Bible are attributed to King Solomon–Song of Songs and Proverbs. According to rabbinic tradition, Song of Songs was written in his youth, Proverbs in middle age and Ecclesiastes in old age. Another work attributed to Solomon, the Wisdom of Solomon, was included in the Septuagint, a third-century B.C.E. translation of the Bible from Hebrew into Greek. Jews and Protestants have relegated the Wisdom of Solomon to the Apocrypha; Catholics consider it deuterocanonical.

Modern critical scholars agree that Solomon did not write Ecclesiastes. Besides the superscription in Ecclesiastes 1:1 ("The words of the Preacher, the son of David, king in Jerusalem"), an extensive literary passage, from 1:12 to 2:26, begins with the statement, "I the Preacher have been king over Israel in Jerusalem" (1:12). Incidentally, note the use of the equivalent of the English past perfect tense, *hayiti* (I have been). Later rabbinical commentators speculated that Solomon must have been deposed before he wrote Ecclesiastes; they speculated wildly about the reasons for such punishment.

The first epilogue, that these are wise sayings "given by one Shepherd" (12:11), may also refer to Solomon; "shepherd" was a common metaphor for royalty in the ancient world. We have already noted the literary passage I call a royal experiment (1:12 to the end of chapter 2), which identifies the author as someone who has been "king over Israel." The author adopts this genre, called a royal fiction, which was common in early Egyptian writings and Sumerian wisdom literature. Royal fictions impart important teachings as insights of supreme rulers. This practice was especially fashionable in the Hellenistic and late Roman periods. Today we recognize royal fictions, but in ancient times the entire book may have been ascribed to the "son of David" on the basis of this attribution.

In the rest of the book, the speaker drops the royal pretense and addresses pressing problems from the perspective of an ordinary citizen who has no means of redressing wrongs. In the royal fiction, the author reinforces his arguments about the futility of human endeavor by means of royal ascription; the king, of course, could afford to experiment with various modes of life without worrying about the consequences and without suffering from scarce resources. Nevertheless, he concludes that "All is vanity and a chasing after wind" (2:26).

The enigmatic Hebrew title *qohelet*, usually translated "preacher," is derived from the root *QHL* (assembly). The Greek title, Ecclesiastes, is a translation, also based on a root meaning assembly (as in *ecclesia*, the Greek word for church). Perhaps Qohelet echoes the repeated appearances of this root in 1 Kings 8:1,2,14. There we read that Solomon assembled (*yaqhel*) the governing body of Israel and later summoned the entire assembly (*qehal*) of Israel for the purpose of dedicating the newly constructed Temple. Perhaps the title

Qohelet in Ecclesiastes was intended to suggest the teacher's function as an assembler of the people, just as Solomon had assembled the people to dedicate the Temple. Perhaps the title was less than flattering, referring to Solomon's habit of collecting (or assembling) wives and concubines. Another possibility is that the title Qohelet refers to the assembly or collection of aphorisms.

The language, grammar and syntax of Ecclesiastes all seem indicative of a late composition (probably no earlier than the fifth or fourth century B.C.E.), but scholars disagree about this. Some of the sayings may well have appeared at a much earlier date, possibly during the flowering of culture in the eighth century B.C.E.[2] There is a great deal of scholarly debate and disagreement about the implications of some linguistic peculiarities in the text. Perhaps the language of the book is in the vernacular or colloquial speech. Sociological analysis of the particular combination of ideas in Ecclesiastes (a discipline still in its infancy)[3] suggests to some that the book dates from the middle of the third century B.C.E.

How are we to understand the several voices within the book[4] and the numerous tensions and contradictions in Qohelet's thought? One theory is that different voices speak in different parts of Ecclesiastes–a narrator, Qohelet, who speaks in the first person, a younger person, the "I," who investigates life's futility in 1:12-2:26, and an implied author (not Qohelet), who is responsible for the entire book. The narrator remains in the background, emerging only in the second epilogue (12:12) to tell his son about the strengths and weaknesses of Qohelet, the ancient wise man whose teachings cause weariness and sting like the jabs of a shepherd's goad.

A more traditional explanation of opposite points of view in Ecclesiastes is that they are unreconciled contradictions in Qohelet's mind.[5] Scholars who read the book this way see it as a kind of diary in which the author reflects about life at various times and the disparities as evidence of Qohelet's changing perceptions. Consequently, although in his youth he may have denied the possibility of life after death, in old age he accepted the likelihood of an afterlife; and although he once dismissed judgment, he later came to believe that God would bring everything into the light of day. The trouble with this explanation is that the book doesn't read like a diary; contradictions sometimes interrupt the natural flow of Qohelet's thought. Furthermore, the explanation of multiple voices as the evolution of one person's ideas overlooks the possibility that later editors made changes in the text, perhaps softening Qohelet's dark vision and bringing it into line with conventional wisdom.

In my opinion, the two epilogues offer the key to understanding Qohelet. The author of the first epilogue commends his teacher, Qohelet, for sharpness of vision; the author of the second epilogue adopts a detached, if not hostile, attitude toward Qohelet, warning him against writing more books–and summing up what really matters–fear of God and keeping the commandments. This summary has little to do with Qohelet's experience of reality. The double imperative–to fear God and keep the commandments–is also out of synch with Qohelet's concept of divine indifference. Someone, it seems, refused to allow Qohelet's judgment to stand.

Scholars must also reckon with the possibility that glosses, later changes, have entered the text. My own investigations show only a few additions. For example, the superscription (1:1), "The word of the Preacher, the son of David, king in Jerusalem," is redundant and was probably a late addition; the real introduction is 1:12, where Qohelet declares, "I the Preacher have been king over Israel in Jerusalem." Another late addition is the thematic envelope, "Vanity of vanities, says the Preacher; all is vanity," in 1:2 and again in 12:18, both times in the third person. Elsewhere Qohelet writes in the first person, which suggests that these famous words may have been a gloss. (Other glosses occur in 2:26a, 3:17a, 8:12-13, 11:96; perhaps 5:18 [5:19 in English versions] and 7:26b.)

Seven times Qohelet exhorts his reader to pursue pleasure wholeheartedly (2:24a, 3:12,22a, 5:17, 8:15a, 9:7-9a, 11:7-12:1a). But each time, the exhortation occurs in a context that qualifies the advice by reminding us of the necessity of accepting one's lot, the brevity of life and our inability to know the future.

Although the case has been made that Qohelet is a preacher of joy,[6] I cannot accept that reading because it undermines the integrity of the book as a whole. The somber message of the futility of life runs through Qohelet's teaching like a scarlet thread. Qohelet seems overwhelmed by the prospect of toil, oppression and darkness. In my view, the initial refrain (1:2), that everything is utterly futile and absurd, which is repeated in shortened form in 12:8, colors everything, even Qohelet's advice to make the most of life while one can. The initial refrain sets the tone for all of Qohelet's teaching. The assertion that life is futile and that we can only shepherd the wind (2:26) admits no exception; everything is futile and absurd, including Qohelet's experiments with pleasure. Death cancels out every gain; reality is absurd; merit has nothing to do with who enjoys life and who does not.

Qohelet's exhortations to enjoy life must, therefore, be understood against the background of thoroughgoing pessimism. The first exhortation (2:24a) is undercut because God arbitrarily decides who can do what, thus, "all this is futile, absurd and shepherding the wind" (2:24-26). The second exhortation (3:12) occurs in much the same context. God gives human beings a special prize but keeps them from taking advantage of it because they are ignorant and incapable of changing things; hence one should enjoy life, for God has a way of instilling fear in all people (3:12-14). The third exhortation (3:22a) follows the dire declaration that no one knows his destiny, and human beings, like animals, die and return to dust. The fourth (5:17) emerges from a reflection on grievous evil and vexation, and the fifth (8:15a) follows a discussion of inequities. The sixth (9:7-9a) is a response to man's ignorance of God's fundamental disposition toward human beings. The final exhortation concludes with a declaration of the ephemeral quality of youth. The exhortation to enjoy life is again overshadowed by a stern warning: "But know that for all this activity God will bring judgment on you!" (11:9-10).

In short, Qohelet encourages people to live as fully as possible while youth lasts, but he has no illusions that daily existence has lasting value. Life still is best described as utterly futile. The shadow of death, the role of chance, the tedium, the monotony, the inequity, the stupidity, the callousness, the inevitability of oblivion—these were Qohelet's daily fare.

Groping for a positive approach to Qohelet's teaching, one scholar claims that Qohelet's God was just and loving, a God who ensured justice for the virtuous.[7] But maintaining this thesis requires that we overlook the stated inability of humans to understand what the deity does or to benefit from divine acts:

> Then I saw all the work of God, that man cannot find out the work that is done under the sun. However much man may toil in seeking, he will not find it out; even though a wise man claims to know, he cannot find it out.
>
> Ecclesiastes 8:17, cf. 9:1

In the final poem, despair swells to a crescendo (12:1-7). Here Qohelet draws together everything from the preceding lessons—the tenuous affirmation of life that, even for the privileged few, ends in cold winter and, finally, death. The opening thought, "a generation dies," with which Qohelet burst into consciousness, returns, this time with a solemn funeral procession and thoughts about an eternity of dust, devoid of the animating principle, God's breath.

Most interpreters of Ecclesiastes try to remove the sting from Qohelet's words, just as they have tried to silence Job's dissenting voice through various interpretive strategies.[8] Their refusal to hear unaccustomed voices within religious traditions robs them of authenticity, for, sooner or later, even devout worshipers encounter life's ambiguities and are forced to ask hard questions about things they once believed.

In my view, skeptics like Qohelet convey a heightened sense of justice and a vision of a better world; they should not be faulted for lack of faith. Qohelet describes life as he sees it. He may not have a prophetic conscience or feel the joy that comes with the conviction that God communicates his will in specific statutes, but he says what is true for him. That honesty ought to earn him a special place in history, for the willingness to question revered beliefs is rare. If there is a time for everything under the sun, then Qohelet's dark words will one day be heard above the clamor of those who would lighten them.

Afterword

Ecclesiastes may have been troubling to the ancient rabbis, but Daniel Pawley of Northwestern College believes the book speaks directly to people in the 20th century. In his article, "Ecclesiastes–Reaching Out to the 20th Century," he explains:

Scores of contemporary artists and writers have used Qohelet's words as springboards for their own. They may truly be called children of the Preacher. The American novelist Thomas Wolfe, for example, wrote in his last novel, *You Can't Go Home Again*:

> I am not given to dogmatic judgments in the matter of literary creation, but if I had to make one, I could only say that *Ecclesiastes* is the greatest single piece of writing I have ever known, and the wisdom expressed in it the most lasting and profound.[1]

Ecclesiastes was number one on Wolfe's list of influential books, ahead of Shakespeare, Milton and Tolstoy....

Ernest Hemingway was another of the Preacher's children. To Hemingway, Ecclesiastes was the stuff of life, the permanent, unchanging human commentary. Hemingway regarded the Preacher as "a better writer." Hemingway's most durable novel, *The Sun Also Rises*,[2] begins with the following epigraph:

> One generation passeth away, and another generation cometh;
> But the earth abideth forever.
> The sun also ariseth, and the sun goeth down,
> And hasteth to the place where he arose.
> The wind goeth toward the south,
> And turneth about unto the north;
> It whirleth about continually,
> And the wind returneth again according to his circuits.
> All the rivers run into the sea;
> Yet the sea is not full;
> Unto the place from whence the rivers come,
> Thither they return again.
>
> Ecclesiastes 1:4-7
>
> You are all a lost generation.
>
> Gertrude Stein

Shortly after his controversial novel was published, Hemingway explained that his point in writing the book had been to contrast the permanence of the natural world with the impermanence of his own superficial, pagan generation. Hence the juxtaposed quotes from Ecclesiastes and Gertrude Stein, one of Hemingway's literary mentors.

Reexamining the quote from Ecclesiastes in this epigraph, however, I believe reveals a deeper truth–the simple recognition of *what is*. As a realist, Hemingway is interested in what is. Not what was, or what shall be, or what should be. But what is. The emphasis is on the present, the touchable, discernible, present reality. From start to finish, Hemingway focuses on what is.

Throughout the Preacher's impressive themes and thinly spun narrative, the focus remains, penetratingly, on what is. At the end of the book, we realize that what we have read is a transcription of reality—a transcription that sounds much like Hemingway or some other modern writer. The language and vocabulary are simple, the meanings straightforward, the implications down-to-earth and everyday. No high-minded spirituality, no promises of immortality, no false hopes—just a straight, honest examination of human beings and the world in which we move.

Theologian Paul Tillich explains the Preacher's appeal to modern authors by characterizing him as the forerunner of existentialist philosopher-poets. Because many modern writers are existentialists who believe that meaning must be created or imposed by man in an otherwise meaningless universe, they find great resonance in Ecclesiastes. Tillich writes:

> The spirit of the Preacher is strong today in our minds. His mood fills our philosophy and poetry. The vanity of human existence is described powerfully by those who call themselves philosophers or poets of existence. They are all children of the Preacher, the great existentialist of his period....[3]

As a purely realistic statement, Ecclesiastes provides a marvelous counterweight to the history, prophecy and spiritual promise elsewhere in the Bible. Where David praises, the Preacher sulks. Where Daniel prophesies, the Preacher says "Don't pay too much attention to what will be. Think about what is." Where John promises, the Preacher negates. And where the Gospels say "accept," the Preacher says "analyze."

No one really knows how Ecclesiastes came to be accepted into the sacred canon, but its existence suggests that a "backside" to biblical truth indeed exists. Perhaps the Bible should be likened to a two-sided coin. On the "heads" side are the positive truths of grace and salvation. On the "tails" side are the harsh truths of doubt and unbelief. As believers, we tend to focus only on the heads side; as skeptics, we see only the tails side. Perhaps we should acknowledge, as the original creators of the canon may have intended, that belief and skepticism exist in all of us, and that we should be willing to stand the coin of truth on edge so that we can see both sides simultaneously. ***BR** 6:5 (1990), p. 34*

CHAPTER 2

When God Acts Immorally

Ronald S. Hendel

The Bible is called the "Good Book." But many people think God does not always act morally. If God is good, they ask, how can this be? Perhaps, one shudders to suggest, God is not good after all.

In the 18th century, Thomas Paine, an influential supporter of the American Revolution, attacked the Bible in his essay The Age of Reason *as "barbarous... vindictiveness...wickedness that has served to corrupt and brutalize mankind." And more recently, the television comedian Steve Allen, in* On the Bible, Religion, and Morality, *finds in the Bible a God who commits atrocities and a Jesus who is disrespectful even to his own mother.*

To test "these dangerous and murky waters" once again, Hendel examines "a well known problematic moment in the Bible"–God's apparently unmotivated rejection of Cain's sacrifice. In this episode, God seems "arbitrary and capricious," hardly positive qualities. Various explanations have been offered for God's behavior. One common theory is that Cain is evil, the son of Satan, and his sacrifice, therefore, is inferior and not sincerely offered. The problem with this explanation, says Hendel, is that nothing in the text supports it. A second suggestion is that the story is an allegory in which Cain represents self-love and Abel represents love of God; others claim that Cain represents farmers, and Abel shepherds. Again the weaknesses of this theory are lack of textual support and lack of historical evidence of a conflict between farmers and shepherds in early Israel. A third explanation is that God's will is beyond the limits of human understanding. Hendel finds in this answer "an unwillingness to engage the passage seriously" and an inability to reconcile a seemingly capricious act with God's "reasonable and straightforward" behavior elsewhere in the story. A final explanation is that God does act capriciously and arbitrarily in this instance. In Freud's words, God is "a projection of the childhood memory of the father," an explanation that does nothing to counter the charge that God's behavior is immoral.–Ed.

The Bible is often called the Good Book. And usually, this good reputation is warranted. From the Bible we learn basic moral precepts, such as "love your neighbor," "honor your father and mother" and "you shall not murder."[1] The Bible urges us to envision a peaceful world, a time when people will beat their swords into plowshares and practice war no more.[2] Rather than becoming complacent with prosperity, we should advocate justice for widows, orphans and the oppressed.[3] Rather than taking pride in our dutiful practice of religion, we should let justice flow like a river, righteousness like an ever-flowing stream.[4] The Bible challenges us to be good, to act morally and to put ethical ideals into practice in our daily lives. Any book that advocates such profound morality certainly deserves to be called a good book.

But, when we read the Bible closely, goodness seems to fade in and out of view. Many characters in the Bible—including God—sometimes act in ways that seem to transgress the moral code the Bible espouses. This conflict within the Bible (both the Hebrew Bible and the New Testament) creates a dilemma. If God is good, how can he (she?) seem bad sometimes? If biblical heroes and heroines are supposed to be holy, why do they sometimes do immoral things?

Should we ignore problematic passages and concentrate on the good ones? Or should we try to harmonize the good with the bad? Perhaps—to take an extreme view—the Bible is really just a bad joke or the product of a devil instead of God.[5]

Since the 17th and 18th centuries, when critical reason became the order of the day, many people have questioned the morality of the Bible. A particularly powerful example is Thomas Paine's *Age of Reason*, which appeared in 1793. Paine, a hero of the American Revolution, turned his critical eye from the crimes of King George to the apparent crudity and cruelty in the Bible. He thought the biblical portrayal of God was rather pathetic:

> Whence could arise the solitary and strange conceit that the Almighty, who had millions of worlds equally dependent on his perfections, should quit the universe and come to die in our world because they say one man and one woman had eaten an apple?[6]

Paine condemned killing and violence in the Bible; these stories, he argued, simply fostered brutality and reflected a demon god:

> When we read the obscure stories, the cruel and barbarous executions, the unrelenting vindictiveness with which more than half the Bible is filled, it would be more consistent that we called it the work of a demon than the word of God. It is a history of wickedness that has served to corrupt and brutalize mankind: and for my own part I sincerely detest it, as I detest everything that is cruel.[7]

Paine found that the Bible often failed to live up to its proclaimed lofty moral level. He considered the Bible an obstacle to morality rather than a moral guide. In order to be good, he argued, humans ought to set aside their blind allegiance to the Bible and rely instead on the moral insight with which God has endowed each of us. Ironically, Paine's methods and goals were much like those of the biblical prophets, who also criticized moral complacency.

In a recent book on the Bible and morality, these questions have been taken up again. Steve Allen—as unlikely a Bible critic as Paine—took a break from his work as a television comedian to write a rousing critique of the Bible. His book, *On the Bible, Religion, and Morality*,[8] was begun in hotel rooms during his business travels, and perhaps credit should be given to the Gideons for providing Allen with reading material. Allen's book is not as eloquent or rousing as Paine's manifesto, but it is written in a modern idiom with all the enthusiasm of a convert to a newly discovered cause.

Allen treats a wide range of subjects in alphabetical order, from "Abel" to "Zechariah." Each discussion ends with a familiar diatribe, in which he locates and criticizes the moral flaws in a biblical passage. His sharpest criticisms are aimed at modern fundamentalists who refuse to acknowledge the moral shortcomings of the Bible. These fundamentalists are "trapped in an intellectual prison" that Allen hopes to demolish.

Although Allen's political and educational aims might be praiseworthy, his idea of the Bible is misleading and one-sided. Surely there is more to the Bible than a God who commits atrocities and a Jesus who is disrespectful even to his mother (see, for example, the articles on "God" and "Jesus"). Allen's book is disappointing because he spends so much time criticizing the Bible that he never gets around to trying to understand it.

Nonetheless, as Paine and Allen pointed out, the Bible *is* sometimes morally problematic, and it is good for us to be reminded of this. Responding to moral problems is a difficult challenge, as many readers of the Bible have discovered. To test these dangerous and murky waters once again, let's examine a well known problematic moment in the Bible—God's rejection of Cain's sacrifice:[9]

> In the course of time, Cain brought from the fruit of the earth an offering to Yahweh; and Abel too brought from the firstborn of his flocks and their fat. Yahweh paid heed to Abel and his offering, but He did not look with favor on Cain or his offering. Cain was much distressed and his face fell.
>
> Genesis 4:3-5

Why does Yahweh reject Cain's offering? No good reason—in fact, no reason at all—is given in the text, which simply states, "He did not look with favor on Cain or his offering." Steve Allen's complaint is legitimate:

> I've always felt sorry for Cain. The poor fellow had toiled from dawn to dusk to raise food...but that wasn't good enough for the capricious Yahweh. Any child who has had a parent favor a sibling's Christmas gift and had his or her own go unnoticed will understand how Cain felt.[10]

Cain naturally feels hurt when his gift is rejected by God. Why should Yahweh reject Cain's offering? It is certainly easy to feel sorry for Cain. It seems

IN "THE DEATH OF ABEL" by French illustrator Gustave Doré (1832?-1883), nature reacts to the murder with horror—lightning rends the clouds; twisted shrubs on the hillside recoil; even a snake slithers away.

that Yahweh acts arbitrarily and capriciously, favoring Abel over Cain for no apparent reason.

If this is so, many disturbing questions come to mind. Most of us assume that God, if he (she?) exists, is good. This seems axiomatic. When God acts, we assume it is with forethought and to further a just cause. But if God is good, how can God also be capricious? Doesn't he abide by an impartial moral standard? If God "knows good and evil,"[11] certainly one would expect his decisions to reflect this moral sense. Then why does he favor Abel over Cain? Over the years, commentators have proposed various answers to these questions. None of the responses is completely satisfactory, but they bring certain aspects of the problem into focus.

1. *Cain is evil.* Although Cain does not commit any evil act before he murders his brother Abel in Genesis 4:8—an act motivated by jealousy over God's preference for Abel—many commentators have suggested that Cain was already evil when he offered his sacrifice. According to this interpretation, Yahweh, who can look into a person's heart, perceived Cain's inherent immorality and rejected his sacrifice. If so, Yahweh is absolved of the charges of partiality and immorality, because he was guided by moral concerns. If Cain was evil before Genesis 4:3-5, then Yahweh was morally justified in rejecting Cain's offering.

The problem with this explanation is that there is nothing in the text to support it. Some postbiblical writers claim that Cain was the son of Satan (and Eve).[12] This would certainly lend support to the argument that Cain is inherently evil. But this interpretation is nowhere supported in the text and is obviously motivated by the kind of moral problem we are addressing. If Cain was the son of Satan, then Yahweh is off the hook. But this explanation does not satisfy those concerned with the actual text.

More subtle support for this position can be mustered if one squeezes additional meaning out of the description of Cain's offering. In Genesis 4:3, we are told that "Cain brought from the fruit of the earth an offering to Yahweh." This description seems straightforward and does not appear to cast blame on Cain. But some interpreters believe blame is implicit in the contrast between this verse and the description of Abel's offering in Genesis 4:4: "Abel too brought from the firstborn of his flocks and their fat." The phrase "Abel too brought" seems to place his offering on the same level as Cain's. But the word "firstborn," according to some commentators, indicates a qualitative distinction between Cain and Abel's offerings. Cain brought his gift "from the fruit of the earth," while Abel brought his "from the firstborn of his flocks." The important difference is not between grain and livestock, but between *any* grain and the *firstborn* of the flock.

Although I think this explanation is overly subtle, it is an ancient and still popular solution to the problem.[13] If Cain's sacrifice was inferior, then one can understand why Yahweh preferred Abel's sacrifice. And yet there is a problem with this interpretation. Why would Yahweh reject an agricultural offering? Even if it did not come from the "first fruits" of the harvest, the offering should still have been acceptable.[14]

A variation on this argument is that Yahweh preferred Abel's offering because the aroma of burnt meat was more appealing to him than the aroma of burnt grain.[15] But this does not absolve Yahweh of blame for rejecting Cain's offering. Out of courtesy, if for no other reason, Yahweh should not have shown favoritism.

2. *The story is an allegory.* Another ancient and widely accepted explanation is that the story is an allegory. According to this interpretation, the story is impossible to understand literally and, therefore, must mean something other than what it says. Proponents of this idea say that Cain and Abel are allegorical

symbols of ethical or social principles. The reasoning behind this interpretation usually goes something like this. When the Bible says something contradictory, offensive or impossible to understand, this is a sign that the passage should be understood symbolically. This principle was first stated by the third-century Christian theologian, Origen:

> [If] the logical coherence and the smooth flow of the historical narrative were automatically evident everywhere, we would not believe that it is possible to find some other sense in the Scriptures besides the obvious one. For this reason the Word of God has arranged the insertion of certain offensive features, of stumbling blocks and impossibilities amid the law and historical narrative.[16]

God's seemingly arbitrary rejection of Cain's offering is an example of such a stumbling block, and so symbolic meanings have been proposed for the characters and actions in the story.

The most common allegorical interpretation in ancient times was that Cain and Abel symbolize Evil and Good. If God chooses Good over Evil, he acts morally, and the reader is exhorted to choose good over evil as well. The earliest allegorical interpreter whose works on Genesis have survived is Philo, a Jewish philosopher who lived in Alexandria, Egypt, in the first century C.E. Philo believed that Cain was a symbol of the corrupting principle of self-love; Abel represented the ennobling principle of the love of God. At the beginning of the story, when Eve conceives Cain and Abel, Philo comments, "Now both these views or conceptions lie in the womb of the single soul."[17] Philo reads the story of Cain and Abel as a cautionary tale warning us to guard against self-love, which can overwhelm the love of God and lead our souls to misery. Similar interpretations were offered by early Jewish and Christian commentators; for example, Saint Augustine regarded Cain and Abel as symbols of the morally corrupt City of Man and the holy City of God.[18]

More recently, biblical scholars have changed the tenor of the allegorical interpretation of Cain and Abel somewhat. Many modern interpreters agree that obscurities or impossibilities in a biblical narrative should be interpreted symbolically,[19] but they tend to prefer historical, rather than ethical, allegory. A widespread modern interpretation is that Cain symbolizes "farmers," and Abel symbolizes "shepherds."[20]

In the story, Cain is indeed a farmer and Abel is a shepherd, so this interpretation has a certain appeal. But to see the conflict between the two brothers as an enactment of some ancient or symbolic enmity between shepherds and farmers is far-fetched. As other modern scholars have pointed out, there is no reason to think that the ancient Israelites considered farmers evil; nor is there any evidence of a historical conflict between farmers and herders.[21]

In a variation on this theory, Cain is a symbol of the Kenite tribe, a neighbor of Israel that may have been involved with copper smelting and metalwork.[22] The problem with this hypothesis is that there is no reason to think the

Israelites considered the Kenites evil. On the contrary, Kenites are portrayed in the Bible in a positive light. Moses' father-in-law, who helps to establish a judicial system for Israel,[23] is identified as a Kenite in two biblical passages;[24] the righteous Jael who slew a Canaanite general was a Kenite,[25] and Saul shows mercy to the Kenites, "for you showed kindness to all the Israelites when they left Egypt" (1 Samuel 15:6). Although Cain's name in Hebrew (*Qayin*) suggests a connection with the Kenites (*Qeni*), it is far-fetched to interpret Cain's relationships with Abel and Yahweh as symbolizing Kenite relationships.[26]

3. *God's will is mysterious*. In a third interpretation, God's rejection of Cain's offering is a symbol of another kind. Rather than symbolizing an ethical or social conflict, God's seemingly arbitrary choice highlights the mysterious nature of God's will and the limits of human understanding. To these interpreters, inability to understand a passage in the Bible is a sign of human finitude. God's will is mysterious, and we should be humble before that mystery.

This theology of God's inscrutable will may be appealing because it is an easy way to avoid addressing the difficulties in this passage. Couldn't one make the same argument for any problematic passage in the Bible? One senses here an unwillingness to engage the text seriously, or perhaps an attempt to avoid subjecting God or the Bible to criticism, whether justified or not. Certainly elsewhere in the Bible Yahweh's decisions are subject to dissent and criticism, particularly by Abraham and Moses.[27] Why exempt Yahweh from criticism here? And yet this interpretation, which finds in God's inscrutable will a sufficient response, is the one chosen by two very important modern interpreters of Genesis, Gerhard von Rad and Claus Westermann.

Gerhard von Rad, in his commentary on Genesis, mixes his interpretation with some fine theologizing:

> Writers have looked diligently for the basis of [God's] preference, but it lies neither in the ritual nor in Cain's attitude. Nothing of that kind is indicated. The only clue one can find in the narrative is that the sacrifice of blood was more pleasing to Yahweh. Obviously the narrator wants to remove the acceptance of the sacrifice from man and place it completely within God's free will. He refrains from making the decision for Abel and against Cain logically comprehensible ("I will be gracious to whom I will be gracious, and will show mercy on whom I will show mercy," Exodus 33:19).[28]

Westermann also solves the problem on a lofty theological note:

> When it is narrated that God regarded the sacrifice of one brother and not of the other, then it is saying that one experienced commendation from God and the other rejection. When such an experience as the brothers had is traced back to a divine action, then this is a sign that it is something immutable. It is fated by God to be so. God's disregard for Cain's sacrifice does not go back to Cain's attitude nor to a sacrifice that was not right nor to an incorrect way of offering the sacrifice. It is saying something about the immutable; it happens so.[29]

One senses the fervor of von Rad's faith in God's free will and the grace that transcends human understanding as well as the strength of Westermann's conviction in the immutability of God's decree: "It is fated by God to be so." And yet, one also senses that the story of Cain and Abel has somehow been forgotten. Von Rad and Westermann both use the story as an occasion to expound their theologies, rather than the theology of the text. Indeed, if God's will is mysterious and immutable, why does he change his mind when Cain complains that his punishment is too harsh? (Yahweh marks him to protect him from murderers who may attack him in his wanderings.)[30] In this part of the story, Yahweh acts reasonably. If Yahweh is a moral and understandable God elsewhere in the story, why does he act capriciously with regard to Cain's offering?

4. *Yahweh is capricious and arbitrary*. If none of these approaches seems to solve the problem, then it may be worth considering the possibility that the most obvious interpretation is correct. Yahweh does act arbitrarily and capriciously. Not many modern biblical scholars have pursued this line of reasoning,[31] but some well known writers in other fields have taken the idea seriously. The most famous modern scholar to consider the problem of God's ambivalent character is Sigmund Freud.

Freud is such a looming presence that it may be difficult to assess his interpretation calmly. Moreover, his ideas about the nature of God are often embedded in theories of historical origins that are now considered untenable.[32] But he had a clear idea of the ambivalent character of God. According to Freud, God is a projection of a childhood memory of the father, and God's ambivalence is a projection of the child's mixed feelings about the father:

> [The] god-creator is undisguisedly called "father." Psychoanalysis infers that he really is the father, with all the magnificence in which he once appeared to the small child.[33]

Elsewhere he says:

> The child's attitude to its father is colored by a peculiar ambivalence....[I]t fears him no less than it longs for him and admires him. The indications of this ambivalence in the attitude to the father are deeply imprinted in every religion.[34]

If God capriciously rejects Cain and his sacrifice, this can be explained in Freud's interpretation by the nature of the concept of God. Although the child may feel that the father's decisions are arbitrary, the father remains an object of love, respect and awe. God's decisions are inexplicable and unmotivated because, in a child's view, that is how a father sometimes acts. The childhood memory of the father gives God a warrant to act arbitrarily, show favoritism and punish capriciously.

Whatever one thinks of Freud's theory of religion,[35] his description of God's fatherly outbursts is remarkably apt for Yahweh's occasional outbursts in the Bible, particularly in the J source.[36] In a fascinating recent book called *The Book of J*, Harold Bloom boldly links Freud's theories and J's description of Yahweh. Bloom observes that "in one of the greatest of ironies, Freud is J's descendant and is haunted by J's Yahweh."[37] Whether or not J's Yahweh animates Freud's theories of the psyche and religion, there is a curious equivalence between Yahweh's character in the J source and Freud's concept of God.

In an extension, or transformation, of Freud's idea, Bloom argues that J's Yahweh is a "grand character" who embodies the dynamism and irony of J's view of reality: "Nothing in J is quite what it seems to be...since Yahweh is for J just the name for reality."[38] Elsewhere Bloom describes J's Yahweh as "pure will, as well as willfulness."[39] Perhaps Bloom is thinking a bit allegorically here, with Reality or Pure Will as the symbolic meaning of Yahweh.

Even if Bloom's perception of J's Yahweh is colored by exuberance and irony, there is something to be said for this approach to the moral problem of Yahweh's rejection of Cain's offering (the story is attributed to J). Yahweh is "at once all-too-human and totally incommensurate with the human,"[40] a paradoxical yet familiar deity. This somehow corresponds to our experience of life and our expectations of God. In other words, if God's nature were uniform and predictable, then he would be a poor match for the complexity of the world.

In later writings in biblical Israel, the "fit" between God and the world becomes increasingly difficult. By the time of the Book of Job, as Paul Ricoeur has noted, the "ethicization" of God was so complete that a moral crisis was inevitable.[41] If God is wholly good and wholly powerful, then there can be no justification for undeserved suffering. And yet Job, who is blameless, suffers. The crisis of faith in the Book of Job culminates in what Ricoeur calls Job's "tragic wisdom...that triumphs over the ethical vision of the world."[42] If Job's final understanding is in some sense tragic, and if his God is somehow "tragic," then perhaps we can consider J's vision of Yahweh in a different light. Perhaps J's morally complex Yahweh has some advantages over simpler conceptions of God.

If J's Yahweh is sometimes unpredictable, even arbitrary, there still remains the possibility of a moral order. Elsewhere in the J source, Yahweh acknowledges the existence of moral principles even when he does not adhere to them. Abraham and Moses both argue with Yahweh over ethical matters (Abraham in connection with the destruction of Sodom and Gomorrah and Moses in connection with God's threat to destroy Israel after the Israelites made the golden calf at the foot of Mount Sinai),[43] with the result that Yahweh alters his decisions.

This is far different from the situation in Job, where Job resigns himself to God's indomitable will. J's Yahweh even argues with himself over moral matters. He wonders if he is right to hide his intentions from Abraham before the destruction of Sodom,[44] and he even has an inner struggle about the rightness of destroying all humanity in the Flood, which he decides he will never do again, implying that he ought not have done it in the first place.[45]

A God who is sometimes capricious, who sometimes makes mistakes, who doesn't always do the right thing, is God of a world where morality can exist. Yahweh may not always live up to the ethical standards in his laws and exhortations, but at least there is hope that next time he will. Perhaps it is this possibility of morality in the world—even though it is often thwarted—that gives J's Yahweh a moral quality and makes his failings forgivable.

But even this last interpretation—that Yahweh does sometimes act capriciously—does not explain the moral basis of Cain's jealousy or the murder of Abel. Nor does this explanation preclude the existence of morality. Perhaps this interpretation is best because it acknowledges that immorality exists—even in God's thoughts and deeds in the Bible[46]—and that, as Yahweh tells Cain in the next verse, life is a continuous moral struggle. Yahweh exhorts Cain: "Sin is crouching at the door; its desire is for you, yet you can master it" (Genesis 4:7). Yahweh may not be a wholly good God, but he has a moral sense, and his advice to Cain is valid. Yahweh is not ethically perfect, but he is a good God nonetheless.

Perhaps the Bible, as some critics have argued, is not completely good. I would agree that moral lapses should be challenged. And yet, after the criticism has been examined, the Bible still has moral virtues. It may not be a wholly Good Book, but perhaps it is a good enough book. The moral dilemmas and possibilities in the Bible stimulate our moral sensibilities and shed light on the moral complexities of the Bible, our world and ourselves.

Afterword

The disparity between biblical mores and contemporary morals has been the subject of widespread commentary and debate. Among his "Eight Questions Most Frequently Asked about the Book of Esther," Carey A. Moore of Gettysburg College includes "Isn't the story immoral? Doesn't the festival of Purim commemorate the massacre of innocent women and children?" He offers the following answer:

Certainly many critics have claimed and more than one scholar has opined that Queen Vashti, who refused to appear before King Xerxes (Ahasuerus in Hebrew) and was deposed for her refusal, is the only decent person in the story. The other major characters are deceitful and cruel, their hands covered with blood. Vashti at least had the good sense—and decency—not to degrade herself by appearing before a bunch of drunken, reveling men. (Some ancient Jewish exegetes interpreted Esther 1:11—where we are told that Vashti was ordered to appear "wearing the royal turban"—to mean that she was to appear wearing *only her royal turban*, i.e., naked!)

Ingenious efforts have been made to explain away the embarrassing fact that 75,000 people, including innocent women and children, were massacred on Adar 13, the date Haman had fixed for the massacre of the Jews (Esther 9:16). Recently Robert Gordis has argued that, despite more than 2,000 years of universal agreement on the matter, Mordecai's royal edict in Esther 8:11 *did not* grant Jews permission to kill innocent noncombatants. Rather, the phrase "along with their women and children" in 8:11 referred to *Jewish women and children*, not the women and children of their enemies.[1]

This explanation is comforting perhaps in that it explains away a vengeful and vindictive phrase incompatible with Judaism, but Gordis' interpretation is probably not correct. For one thing, the destruction of enemy men, women and children is perfectly consistent with the principle of *peripety*, the sudden reversal of fortune, which is a basic rhetorical theme throughout the Book of Esther. In Esther 3:13, Haman decrees the annihilation of "all the Jews—men and boys, women and children." The sudden reversal occurs in Esther 8:11, where the Jews are given permission "to defend themselves" by slaughtering their enemies, "those who were hostile to them, along with their women and children." It seems unlikely that the last phrase refers to Jewish women and children, who may now defend themselves against their enemies.

The author of Esther, like many people today, might argue that Haman had initiated a war of extermination against the Jews, a Holocaust if you will, that demanded an exceedingly strong response. From time immemorial, when it comes to the survival of a nation or a people, winning is evidently everything. Some philosophers and theologians may decry the axiom "All's fair in love and war," but historians know, and the average person suspects, that, for better or worse, men nearly always play by that rule. The Allied bombing of Dresden or the dropping of atomic bombs on Hiroshima and Nagasaki are now perceived by many Americans as immoral—now that we have the luxury of reexamining our conduct in a war we won long ago. Both Judaism and Christianity decry murder and assassination, but I suspect that many decent, law-abiding Jews and Christians devoutly wish the assassination plot against Hitler had succeeded.

But when all is said and done, many Jews are probably as embarrassed by the vengeful, bloodthirsty, measure-for-measure retaliation of Esther 8:11 and 9:16 as Christians are embarrassed by the cry of the Crusaders who, when attacking a certain "infidel" city where "innocent" Christians lived, cried "Kill them all! God knows his own!" In any event, the festival of Purim is less a celebration of the destruction of the enemy than the deliverance of the Jews (Esther 9:21-22), an important distinction to remember. ***BR** 3:1 (1987), p. 16*

In "Why Christians Should Bother with the Old Testament," Henry O. Thompson of the Unification Theological Seminary also addresses the issue of morality. A summary and personal perspective follow:

From time to time, Christians question the use of the Old Testament, the Hebrew Scriptures or the Tanakh, in Christian life or worship. Some ask why, since we have the New Testament, we should bother with the Old. Of what use is the Old Testament now that we have a *New* Covenant? Some Christians are embarrassed by all the wars and killing in the Old Testament.

This is an old debate. As far back as the second century, Marcion, founder of an early Christian sect in Rome, tried to eliminate the Old Testament and limit the scriptures to portions of the New Testament. The church leaders declared Marcion a heretic because the creator in Genesis is also the God of Jesus. But even today there are those who follow Marcion's example and dismiss the Old Testament.

For many other Christians, the Old Testament is simply there. They may know that it tells about some old kings. They may be familiar with the 23rd Psalm. Occasionally, at Christmas and Easter, they hear certain Old Testament words, such as "Emmanuel," meaning "God with us." For the most part, Christians do not reject the Old Testament; they simply ignore it. There is much in these ancient books that can easily be ignored—such as the lengthy genealogies or the rule against mixing two kinds of cloth or detailed instructions for sacrifices in the Temple, which was destroyed 2,000 years ago. This, of course, is true of the New Testament as well. At least I have not seen anyone walking around with only one hand because Jesus said, "If thy hand offend thee, cut it off. It is better to go to heaven maimed than to go to hell in one piece" (Matthew 5:30). But there is much in both scriptures that should not be ignored.

Some Christians consider the Old Testament merely the forerunner of the New; they search the Hebrew Scriptures for predictions of Jesus. Does the

Old Testament predict the coming of Jesus? Well, yes and no; but mostly no. The prophet Isaiah mentions someone to come, a descendant of Jesse (Isaiah 11:1). But his words of hope were addressed to his own people. Suppose we were in trouble and someone said, "Don't worry. In 800 years, God will do something." We might attack him for joking about our problems. We would not be comforted. God was concerned with Isaiah and with his people. Personally, I take that to mean that God is concerned with us today and indeed with people in every generation.

In another sense, the predictions in the Old Testament are true. The prophets reminded people that God did not bring only their fathers up from slavery in Egypt. "He brought you up from Egypt" (Deuteronomy 5:3, 16:6; Judges 2:1). The people of Isaiah's time were reliving history, making that history their own. God spoke to a later generation through earlier events. The words of Isaiah and Jeremiah applied to the first Christians, and they apply to us today.

The words of the Bible, Old Testament or New, speak to people today. For me, this is one thing that makes the Bible the word of God. At a given moment, a biblical passage may be meaningless, but at another time, the same passage may be meaningful. The words have not changed. My situation, outlook or need has changed.

We see this reapplication of truth in the way the prophets interpreted the Exodus story. They called upon people to apply the Exodus story to themselves. American black slaves did the same. They found comfort in the words of God to Pharaoh, "Let my people go" (Exodus 5:1). The freedom movement of Hebrew slaves in Egypt is important in contemporary liberation theologies of Latin America and Africa. There is even a growing liberation theology for the poor in America that is powerfully reinforced by the words of Hannah, Samuel's mother, in 1 Samuel 2:4-5,8:

> The bows of the mighty are broken,
> And the faltering are girded with strength.
> Men once sated must hire out for bread;
> Men once hungry hunger no more.
> ....
> He raises the poor from the dust.
> Lifts up the needy from the dunghill.
> Setting them with nobles.
> Granting them seats of honor.

The same ideas are repeated by the Virgin Mary in the Magnificat (Luke 1:52-53): "He has put down the mighty from their thrones and exalted those of low degree. He has filled the hungry with good things and the rich are sent away empty." Jesus was also inspired by Isaiah and echoed his words in Luke 4:18:

> He has anointed me to preach good news to the poor. He has sent me to proclaim release to the captives and recovering of sight to the blind, to set at liberty those who are oppressed.

Returning now to Marcion's argument that we should take the New Testament just as the fulfillment of the Old, we run into a practical problem. If we eliminate the Old Testament from the New, there is not much left. It is not simply that the New Testament quotes directly from the Old but that the Old Testament is the very *raison d'être* of the New. Cut the vine from the root and the plant dies.

But more is at stake here than understanding the New Testament. The Old Testament should be preserved for its own sake. Consider the creation stories in the Old Testament, which are largely ignored in the New Testament. Quite apart from the beauty and majesty of the first chapter of Genesis, the idea of God as creator is essential for understanding the world as God's world and for understanding ourselves and all people as children of God and stewards of God's earth.

The New Testament spans a mere century in time. The Old Testament begins at the beginning of time and ends a few centuries before the birth of Jesus. This sweep of history reminds us that God acts in history and that God is Lord of history. The Communist dialectic—the mechanistic, deterministic, reductionist unfolding of economic laws—cannot stand in the face of the Old Testament view of history. Communists, like the ancient Greeks, believe in fate. In contrast, the Hebrews experienced God in history.

The historical perspective adds depth to our lives. In the words of the old saying, those who do not learn from the mistakes of the past are doomed to repeat them. The Chinese communists keep the memory of the way things were alive—the filth, the rats, the vices of the old regime. Israelis keep the memory of the Holocaust alive—Hitler's slaughter of six million Jews and millions of Gypsies, Slavs, handicapped people and others. Thanksgiving reminds Americans of the Pilgrims who came to this country seeking religious freedom. The United States recently celebrated the 200th anniversary of the Constitution. We live in history. Traditions add meaning to our lives.

From the Old Testament, we learn principles of living. In Genesis 50:20, Joseph responds to his brothers' fears: "You meant it for evil, but God meant it for good." From this we learn that there should be no revenge in human relationships. When sickness or trouble threatens to overwhelm us, the story of Job reminds us that God is with us, even in difficult times. The prophets of Israel stand in judgment of our society as they did in biblical days with ringing cries, "Let justice roll down like waters and righteousness like an everflowing stream" (Amos 5:24). Or consider Micah's eloquent summary of the Law: "What does the Lord require of you but to do justice, and to love mercy, and to walk humbly with thy God" (Micah 6:8). And then there is the word of the Lord to Jeremiah proclaiming the possibility of everlasting renewal and return: "I will make a new covenant with you and my law will be written upon your hearts" (Jeremiah 31:33). Or to put it another way, "As people think in their hearts, so are they" (Proverbs 23:7). The basic principle of religion echoes in

Deuteronomy and Leviticus: We should love God and love our neighbors as ourselves (Deuteronomy 6:5; Leviticus 19:18).

Important as these principles are, they also remind us that the ancient Hebrews did not live on an abstract philosophical level. They lived life—real life—in the raw. When King David was convicted of sin, he did not retire on a large pension. He repented before God and begged forgiveness. Although the people rejected Samuel's leadership, he continued to pray for them. In the psalms, the whole spectrum of human existence is described. Psalm 23 reminds us of God's care in good times and bad. Psalms 22 and 31 praise God in the face of suffering and disgrace, both personal and national. In the Book of Daniel, when Shadrach, Meshach and Abednego are about to be thrown into the fiery furnace and burned alive, they say "Our God is able to deliver us. But even if he does not, we will not bow down to your idol" (Daniel 3:17-18).

The Old Testament adds depth and dimension to our understanding and words to live by. It gives examples of faith that we have not yet equalled, let alone surpassed. As the well known archaeologist Lawrence E. Toombs once said, "I cannot understand people who say, 'Go *back* to the Bible.' We have not caught up with it yet." ***BR*** *5:1 (1989), p. 12*

PART II

The Bible as History

The Bible as History
Introduction

The great eleventh-century scholar Rabbi Solomon ben Isaac, known by his Hebrew initials as Rashi, begins his comprehensive and authoritative commentary on the Bible with the observation that if the Torah is "the Law," it should rightly begin with Exodus 12, the first chapter containing commandments, or laws. The book of Genesis, he says, proves that the purpose of the Bible is not only legal and juridical, but also historical. The Torah "illustrate[s] the power of God's works," the role of God in history as validation of divine commandments.

The idea of the Bible as "sacred history" is supported by evidence in the text and is widely accepted by scholars. The historical agenda of the Bible is summed up in this passage from Deuteronomy (4:32ff.):

> Inquire about bygone days that came before you, ever since God created man on earth, from one end of heaven to the other: has anything as grand as this ever happened, or has its like ever been known? Has any people heard the voice of God speaking out of a fire, as you have, and lived? Or has any god taken one nation out of the midst of another by acts, signs, and portents...as the Lord your God did for you in Egypt before your very eyes?...Therefore observe his laws and commandments....

The overall structure of the Bible is chronological, from the creation of the world, through the prehistory of the Hebrew people, the ups and downs of the United Monarchy and Divided Kingdom, the Exile and return, to the life of Jesus and the ministry of his disciples. In fact, even books like Ruth and Esther, which are grouped together in the Hebrew Bible because of their liturgical function, are distributed chronologically in Christian Bibles. Moreover, historical references abound in the legal codes and prophetic speeches. Malachi begins (1:2-3):

> I have loved you, said the Lord. But you asked, "How have you shown love?" Esau is Jacob's brother, says the Lord, but I have chosen Jacob and rejected Esau. I have made his hills a desolation, given his land to the beast of the wilderness.

When the Israelites ask Samuel to appoint a king to rule over them, Samuel declaims (1 Samuel 12:7ff.):

> Stand before the Lord and I will cite against you all the kindnesses that the Lord has done to you and your ancestors. When Jacob had come to Egypt, your fathers cried out to the Lord and he sent them Moses and Aaron, who brought them out of Egypt and settled them in this place. But they forgot the Lord their God, so he delivered them into the hands of Sisera...and the Philistines...and the king of Moab, who made war upon them. Then they cried to the Lord...and the Lord sent Jerubbaal and Bedan and Jephthah and Samuel to deliver you from your enemies.

Even observance of the Sabbath, which logically commemorates the Creation, is given historical significance in Deuteronomy (5:12-15):

> Observe the Sabbath day and keep it holy...Remember that you were a slave in the land of Egypt and the Lord your God freed you from there with a mighty hand and an outstretched arm. Therefore, the Lord your God has commanded you to observe the Sabbath day.

Even though the Bible appeals to history and the biblical community accepted it as history, there are still questions about how modern historians should approach biblical material. Some scholars ascribe considerable historic value to the Bible and use it as a basic text for reconstructing the story of the past. Others are more circumspect and use modern historiographic techniques to illuminate the Bible.

The history of Israel from the eighth century B.C.E. on can be reconstructed by parallel, interrelated biblical accounts and official records of Assyria, Babylonia, Persia, Greece and Rome. These sources focus on different aspects of events, but kings, treaties and wars mentioned in the Bible can often be found in other sources as well.

But little or no mention is made of Israel in extrabiblical documents before the eighth century B.C.E., including the significant eras of Joshua, David and Solomon. For this reason, academic "histories" of ancient Israel simply retold the biblical story. Dates were computed from internal evidence, such as genealogies and lists of dynastic succession. In the 17th century, for example, Archbishop Ussher dated the Creation to 4004 B.C.E. As more was learned about the ancient world, texts and artifacts were used to validate biblical accounts. Abraham became a nomad, Solomon an oriental potentate, and evidence of destruction at archaeological sites proved that the Israelites invaded Canaan.

Scholars agree that the narratives of Saul, David and Solomon in the books of Samuel, Kings and Chronicles incorporate records and contemporaneous traditions, especially the administrative details of taxation and military organization and the names of court and Temple officials. But scholars also understand that the Bible is not simply a historical chronicle or a description of ancient life for its own sake. Even when dealing with verifiable events like the royal history of Judah and Israel, biblical authors drew attention to the significance of these events in the divine plan for mankind; aspects of the story that are not relevant to this purpose are ignored.

So, although some modern historians consider the Bible the beginning of historical writing, they also realize that there is an editorial point of view and a romantic element in biblical narrative. David and Solomon are idealized, despite the obvious failures that led to the breakup of their kingdom. Idealization is even more pronounced in the portraits of Moses and the patriarchs.

Most scholars now use modern methods of historical research to corroborate historical events in the Bible. Close examination of the text reveals that earlier traditions are sometimes quoted for effect, and certain words take on different nuances in different contexts. Roland de Vaux, for instance, shows that the Abraham stories were originally distinct from the Jacob stories, but as the Israelite nation evolved a unifying mythology, the two traditions were combined.

Theories of social history have also been brought to bear in biblical studies. Adherents of this school argue that traditional history was concerned exclusively with great men and wars and ignored the lives of common people—their diet, jobs, health, family structures, entertainment and popular culture. Using this approach, social historians have concluded that the Bible is the product of an upper-class male political and religious establishment in the royal court and Temple; this elite group was concerned with organized rituals, formalized liturgy and standardized literary models. Even prophets like Isaiah and Jeremiah, who are usually considered populist reformers, were officials of the national cult. And they too omitted or suppressed working-class values, folk religion, and manifestations of heterodoxy, like women's rituals. The details of folk culture, fertility cults, the significance of amulets and other elements of folklore, have been brought to light by modern archaeologists.

Social historical studies do not always illuminate biblical texts, but they do add to our understanding of the larger social environment. For instance, Lawrence E. Stager shows how studies of population density, agricultural techniques and pastoral economies may explain why six tribes responded to Deborah's call for military aid and four did not.

CHAPTER 3

The Separate Traditions of Abraham and Jacob

Roland de Vaux

Most biblical scholars subscribe to the documentary hypothesis, the theory that the Pentateuch is a combination of material from several sources (usually four). But they disagree about which material should be attributed to which source and, even more, about the significance of the composite origin of the Bible. De Vaux turns to the "history of tradition" to resolve some of these disputes.

The time of composition of a particular text may be inferred, de Vaux argues, from assumptions that underlie the text. The author of Genesis, for example, assumes that Israel is a single nation with a common religion. At the time Genesis was written, the Israelites believed they were descended from and worshiped the God of Abraham, Isaac and Jacob. The stories of the patriarchs in Genesis confirm the origins and history of the promise of a national homeland. God tells Abraham (Genesis 12:7), "To your descendants will I give this land," and Joseph's last words (Genesis 50:24) are, "God will return you to the land he promised to Abraham, Isaac and Jacob." "This link," says de Vaux, "presupposes that the end, that is, the existence of Israel as a people settled in Canaan, was known."

The Israelite people was composed of disparate groups, de Vaux says, and in Genesis, the bond among them was mythologized into a genealogy. Before that, however, there were separate traditions. "Each group forming part of the people of Israel had its own special traditions and above all its own ancestor, whose story was told and who was remembered in the group's cult of the 'god of the father.'"

Evidence of these separate traditions can be found in the association of the patriarchs with different geographical sites. Abraham is associated with Hebron and Mamre, Isaac with Beer-Sheva and the Negev, Jacob with Shechem, Bethel and Transjordan. Ethnographically, Abraham is related, through Lot, to the Moabites and Ammonites; Jacob, through Esau, is related to the Edomites. Finally, the traditions have different central themes. The Abraham-Isaac cycle focuses on family continuity; the Jacob-Esau cycle focuses on the conflict between herdsmen and hunters. De Vaux concludes that differences of origin and conception imply that the Abraham-Isaac cycle and the Jacob cycle were originally independent of each other.–Ed.

The further back the historian goes into the past, the more difficulties he faces. The most intractable problem concerns the first ancestors of Israel, the patriarchs Abraham, Isaac and Jacob, whose "history" is told in Genesis 12-35. The history of Joseph, which is told in the rest of Genesis (except for Genesis 38 and 49), belongs to the following period, the sojourn in Egypt.

Despite the enormous amount of work that has been done during the past two centuries in the field of literary criticism, in connection with the Pentateuch in general and Genesis in particular, the conclusions that have been reached are far from unanimous, and the foundations on which literary criticism has been based have been called into question time and again. The theory that is most frequently encountered is based on the documentary hypothesis, according to which the Pentateuch can be traced back to three or four main sources—the Yahwistic source (J), the Elohistic source (E) and the Priestly source (P). The fourth is Deuteronomy, which is designated (D). There is general agreement about how, at least in broad outline, the text should be divided among the first three sources.

The smallest share in the compilation of the Pentateuch is attributed to P. The priestly writers, it is argued, touched up and completed certain accounts and inserted lists, genealogies and the details of births and deaths and the ages of the patriarchs, thus providing a chronological framework for the narrative. According to this theory, only two long passages were written in full by the priestly authors. The first is Genesis 17, which describes the covenant with Abraham—the promise of numerous descendants and of possession of the land of Canaan—and the institution of circumcision. The second passage, Genesis 23, is a description of how the cave of Machpelah was acquired for the tomb of the patriarchs.

Most of the stories are believed to be combinations of material from J and E. The first evidence of Elohistic material is found in Genesis 15, where the covenant with Abraham and the promise of many descendants and possession of the land are described. This chapter is, of course, parallel to Genesis 17 (P).

The literary composition of Genesis 15 is, however, complex, and to some extent, the other patriarchal narratives are also characterized by combined material from two sources. The Elohist's share is most apparent in certain repetitions of incidents or language called doublets: Abraham and Sarah in Egypt (Genesis 12:10-13:1, J) and Abraham and Sarah at Gerar (Genesis 20:1-18, E); Hagar and Ishmael in the wilderness (Genesis 16:1-14, J) and Hagar and Ishmael at Abraham's house (Genesis 21:8-21, E); Abraham and Abimelech (Genesis 21:22-34, E) and Isaac and Abimelech (Genesis 26:12-23, J). Elohistic material can also be found in short passages in Genesis that have no equivalents in J: Jacob building an altar at Bethel (Genesis 35:1-7); the birth of Benjamin; and the death of Rachel (Genesis 35:16-20). Finally, there is general agreement among scholars that Genesis 14, where Abraham's victory over the four kings and his meeting with Melchizedek are described, does not come from any of these three sources.

Even granting the existence of these sources, there are still many unanswered questions about the inner unity and nature of the material from each source and about the period and the environment in which they originated. The only way to find satisfactory answers to these questions is to study Genesis along with material from these sources in other books of the Pentateuch. All that can be done here is to summarize the most probable conclusions and apply them to the patriarchal narratives.

No serious problems are posed by the P text, which was the work of priests of the Temple of Jerusalem and was edited at the end of the Exile (late 4th century B.C.E.) or soon after the return. It is, however, possible that material from earlier traditions was incorporated into P.

Most likely, the Yahwist (J) was a single author, probably a Judean at the royal court during the reign of Solomon. More important for the historian are problems raised by the Elohistic source. Most scholars agree that the elements attributed to the Elohist were inserted into the earlier Yahwistic material, with which they sometimes merged and sometimes competed.

According to one widespread opinion, these Elohistic elements are derived from an oral or written source independent of J. There is less agreement about the period and the environment in which this source originated, the predominant view being that it became established during the eighth century B.C.E., that it was a compilation of material from various traditions that were prevalent in the north and that it was connected with the prophetic movement. From Abraham on, E runs parallel to J.

Certain scholars, however, do not accept the existence of a parallel and independent Elohistic source. The arguments against a separate E source are based on the fact that distinctions between J and E are often less than striking and that some of the fragments attributed to E seem to be additions or corrections to the J text reflecting lofty moral and religious ideas. According to these scholars, the existence of a parallel and independent E source cannot be proved. J, they argue, was probably revised, completed and corrected orally and edited by adding these traditional E variants.

There are several convincing arguments in favor of this theory. Admittedly, there are many uncertainties in the distribution of texts regarded as common to both J and E. And one should keep in mind that the classical documentary theory is still hypothetical. But, in my opinion, the consistency of words and ideas in the elements ascribed to E (and the fact that they are parallel to words and ideas in J) tip the balance in favor of the documentary hypothesis.

But we may still agree that there was an independent tradition common to and prior to both J and E. Even if this is true, however, literary criticism of the Pentateuch can go back only as far as the period when the tribes were settled in Canaan and regarded themselves as a people united by ties of blood and a common faith. They were, they believed, a single people descended from Abraham. They worshiped one God, who was the same as the God of Abraham, Isaac and Jacob. They inhabited one country, which was the land promised to Abraham, Isaac and Jacob. This threefold unity is proclaimed throughout the Pentateuch. How did the authors arrive at this conviction, and what is the significance of this unified tradition? To answer these questions, it is necessary to leave the sphere of literary criticism and enter the sphere of the history of traditions.

Whether or not we accept the existence of the Elohist, we cannot dispute that the Yahwist used material from an extant tradition. This tradition could only have been found in or disseminated from sanctuaries where the tribes worshiped the same God together. The basic article of faith was that this God had delivered their ancestors from Pharaoh's oppression and had led them to Canaan. Memories of the Exodus from Egypt, combined with memories of taking possession of the land, were part of this primitive tradition, which also included–contrary to the opinion of certain scholars–memories of Sinai, which was the seminal encounter with God and the cornerstone of their faith.

We are bound to ask, however, if stories of the patriarchs might have been integrated into this tradition at a late stage, because there is a remarkable break between Genesis and Exodus, that is, between the end of the story of the patriarchs and the beginning of the story of the Exodus from Egypt. No account of the intervening period has been preserved, and the editors of the Pentateuch did not try to fill in the gap.

In its present form, the story of the patriarchs is linked to the stories of the Exodus and the conquest of the Promised Land by the theme of the promise. In other words, the settlement of the Israelites in Canaan is the fulfillment of promises to their ancestors that they would have many descendants and a land of their own. This theme also unites the various patriarchal narratives, which are set within a framework of the announcement made to Abraham, "It is to your descendants that I will give this land" (Genesis 12:7), and Joseph's last words, "God will be sure to remember you kindly and take you back from this country to the land that he promised on oath to Abraham, Isaac and Jacob" (Genesis 50:24). This link suggests that the existence of Israel as a people settled in Canaan was a given at the time of composition and that the history of salvation, beginning with Abraham and ending with the conquest of Canaan, was already firmly established.

In their earliest forms, the narratives of the promises must have included fulfillment of those promises. The promise of posterity, for example, had to be followed by the birth of a son, as in Genesis 18, and the promise of land had to be followed by an account of taking possession of that land, as in Genesis 12:7, 13:15, 28:13. In its final form, the link between promise and fulfillment is extended to include the time in Egypt, the Exodus and the conquest. The long delay in the fulfillment of the promise was said to have been explained to Abraham by God (Genesis 15:13-16).

Any reconstruction of the stages by which this tradition became the common property of the whole of Israel must remain purely conjectural. Each group that became part of the people of Israel had special traditions, and, above all, a particular ancestor whose story was told and retold from one generation to the next. Each ancestor was remembered in a cult of "god the father," which was specific to each group. When several groups later became united, three patriarchal figures, Abraham, Isaac, and Jacob, emerged from the multiplicity of early ancestor figures. The bonds between the composite groups were then expressed as a genealogy, which showed that the descendants of Abraham, through Isaac and Jacob, were all "sons of Israel."

The multiple prehistory is evident in the many traditions that refer to each patriarch. The great cycle of Abraham traditions (Genesis 12-25:18) and the cycle of Jacob traditions (Genesis 25:19-34) spring to mind.

It is more difficult to distinguish a cycle of Isaac traditions because the story of Isaac is, in the first place, included within the story of his father, Abraham (Genesis 21, 22, 24), and the story of his sons, Jacob and Esau (Genesis 25:19-28, 27, 28:1-9, 35:27-29). Only in Genesis 26 is Isaac the central figure; but even here, the stories are about Isaac's relationships with the people of Gerar, and they are all duplicated in the story of Abraham: the testing of Rebekah (Genesis 26:1-16; cf. Genesis 20:2-18); the matter of the wells (Genesis 26:15-25; cf. Genesis 21:25-31); and the alliance with Abimelech (Genesis 26:26-33; cf. Genesis 21:22-32). These passages may be remnants of an earlier, independent Isaac cycle, various elements of which were integrated into, or duplicated in, the story of Abraham after a genealogical connection had been established between them. Thus, Isaac became the link joining Abraham to Jacob.

The *geographical* associations, however, are clearly independent of each other. The Abraham tradition is, above all, associated with Hebron and Mamre, whereas the tradition of Isaac is firmly attached to Beer-Sheva and the neighboring well of Lahai Roi.

It is also possible that there never was an Isaac cycle. After all, the narrative of Genesis 12-25 is essentially a family story focused on the issue of posterity. The announcement of Isaac's birth (Genesis 18:1-15) is the central episode in the Abraham cycle. The story of Isaac's marriage (Genesis 24) may be regarded as the conclusion of this group of narratives, at which point the continuation of the tribe, which is the main theme of this cycle, is assured, and Abraham can die in peace (Genesis 24:1, 25:11, J). If everything that has to do with Isaac is removed from the Abraham cycle, very little remains.

An Abraham-Isaac cycle is the earliest traditional body of narratives we can trace back, and it seems futile to try to go back any further in history. In this case, the events attributed to Isaac in Genesis 26 may be regarded as attempts to enrich the figure of Isaac by borrowing from the Abraham cycle rather than remnants of an independent story cycle. The Isaac elements strengthen the established link between the cycles of Abraham and Jacob. The fact remains, however, that the traditions connected with Abraham and Isaac are all associated with the south of Palestine, the Negev, Hebron and Mamre, Beer-Sheva and the well of Lahai Roi, and Gerar; these traditions, therefore, clearly originated in the south.

The Abraham and Isaac traditions are also connected with another story of a different origin, the story of Lot. The germinal idea of the Lot story, the destruction of Sodom and Gomorrah, can be found in a popular tradition about a natural disaster south and southwest of the Dead Sea (Genesis 19). It is possible that the memory of an ancient geological disaster is preserved in the tradition of Lot, but in terms of literary genre, the story is much closer to the flood myths than the patriarchal narratives. Just as the flood was explained as a punishment for man's sins, the destruction of Sodom and Gomorrah was regarded as punishment for the perversity of the inhabitants (see, for example, Genesis 13:13, 18:16-32).

The origin of the Moabites and Ammonites (Genesis 19:30-38), which has been added to the story of the destruction of Sodom, is from a tradition that originated in Transjordan and was incorporated into the story of Abraham. Lot was Abraham's nephew (Genesis 12:5); Abraham and Lot shared the land between them (Genesis 13); and God saved Lot from the disaster that destroyed Sodom because of Abraham (Genesis 19:29). Originally, the Israelites may have been related to their "cousins" in Transjordan. In this way, the family focus in the story of Abraham was extended to include relationships between different peoples, suggesting that the story went beyond the boundaries of Palestine.

The story of Jacob and Esau (Genesis 25:19-34, 27, 32-33), like the story of Abraham and Isaac, is also a family story. But in the Jacob-Esau story, interest is focused not on descent from father to son but on the relationship between rival brothers. The twins Jacob and Esau fought with each other even in their mother's womb (Genesis 25:22). The name Jacob means "supplanter" (Genesis 27:36). Jacob in fact deprived his brother of his birthright as the firstborn son (Genesis 25:29-34) and of his father's blessing (Genesis 27:1-40). Jacob only pretended to be reconciled to Esau in order to deceive him (Genesis 32:4-22, 33:1-17). Jacob was a cunning man and his mother's favorite, whereas Esau was stupid and his father's favorite.

The focus in this cycle of stories is transcended by the conflict between two social types represented by Jacob and Esau. Jacob is a peace-loving herdsman who succeeds by skill and intelligence rather than force, whereas Esau is a nomad who lives by hunting and pillaging (Genesis 25:27, 27:39-40). The

"THE LORD SAID TO ABRAM, after Lot had separated from him, 'Lift up your eyes and look from the place where you are, northward and southward and eastward and westward; for all the land which you see I will give to you and to your descendants forever. I will make your descendants as the dust of the earth; so that if one can count the dust of the earth, your descendants also can be counted. Arise, walk through the length and the breadth of the land, for I will give it to you.' So Abram moved his tent, and came and dwelt by the oaks of Mamre, which are Hebron; and there he built an altar to the Lord" (Genesis 13:14-18). British explorer Colonel Sir Charles W. Wilson identified the site where Abraham pitched his tent as the great oak tree known as "Abraham's oak." This illustration by Harry Fenn and J.D. Woodward is from Wilson's 1883 travel book, *Picturesque Palestine. Photo: Land of Judea, Ariel Publications*

point is that nomadic hunters, who were the first inhabitants of the land, had to give way to herdsmen.

The story of rival brothers has also been modified by the addition of another element. Esau was also called Edom, the ancestor of the Edomites. The story conveys a message beyond the rivalry between herdsmen and hunters. It highlights the contrast between the fertile land of Palestine where the Israelites lived and the mountainous, desert land of Transjordan inhabited by the Edomites.

The story of Jacob and Laban (Genesis 29-31), which was originally independent of the story of Jacob and Esau, is also a composite narrative. On one level, this is a family story about the time Jacob spent with his uncle Laban, his marriage to Laban's two daughters and his flight. On this level, the Jacob-Laban story is a continuation of the previous narrative (Genesis 31:50). This story is followed by an account of the treaty between Jacob and Laban

(Genesis 31:43-54), which is both a family agreement that safeguards the position of Laban's daughters and a political pact that establishes the frontier between Jacob and Laban (Genesis 31-52). Clearly, this treaty was not between individuals but between two peoples, the Israelites (or their ancestors) and the Arameans.

A third group of stories connects Jacob with the sanctuaries at Shechem and Bethel. There is no mention of Esau or Laban in these stories, in which Jacob dreams and erects a monument, a *massebah*, at Bethel (Genesis 28:10-22, JE), sets up an altar and a stele, also at Bethel (Genesis 35:7-14, E), and buys a field and erects an altar at Shechem (Genesis 33:19-20, E). The two sanctuaries are brought together in a cultic passage (Genesis 35:2-4, E), in which Jacob's family buries the images of foreign gods under an oak tree near Shechem and makes a pilgrimage to Bethel to erect an altar there.

In Genesis 32:29 and 35:10, Jacob's name is changed to Israel, and in Genesis 33:20, Jacob erects an altar at Shechem to "El, God of Israel." These are the first references in the Bible to Israel, and they are often interpreted as the collective name that reinforces the bond between the tribes believed to have descended from a common ancestor. "Israel," however, is also a personal name that seems originally to have been the name of the ancestor of a special group with which the group of Jacob became united. In fact, the change of name and the rather clumsy etymological explanation of the name Israel seem to be of secondary importance in the account of Jacob's struggle with the mysterious being at the ford of the Jabbok (Genesis 32:23-33). This story can be traced back to a very old legend adopted in the Jacob cycle. In the second reference (Genesis 35:10), the change of the name Jacob to Israel is linked with an appearance of God at Bethel (Genesis 35:9-13). This passage has, correctly, been attributed to P, but it is possible that verse 10 is a very early element from E (the Elohistic source).

Geographically, the Jacob traditions can be divided into two groups. The stories about Jacob and Esau and the treaty with Laban take place in a small area of Transjordan, primitive Gilead and the lower course of the Jabbok (Peniel, Mahanaim and Succoth). In one tradition, it is possible that Jacob's tomb is located in Transjordan (Genesis 50:10). The stories about Jacob at Shechem and Bethel and the Jacob-Israel narratives take place in central Palestine. The Transjordanian tradition is very early and was probably added later to enrich the Jacob cycle, which originated in central Palestine at Shechem.

Shared stories going back to the remote past facilitated the merger of the two groups. At the time of the patriarchs, in the region of Shechem where Israel first lived, there were also clans of the house of Jacob (Genesis 34) who were of the same stock and who practiced the same cult of El associated with the "god of the father" at Shechem and Bethel.

A little light can be shed on this obscure early history by considering the status of the "tribes" of Israel at this early date. Above all, they had not yet become separated into individual tribes with distinct names, and their relationships with each other did not become stable until after they had become settled. Before that time, they were disparate groups vaguely related by blood, a common landscape and similar social and religious practices.

Despite much uncertainty, we can be sure of one thing. The geographical area in which the cycle of Jacob stories is set, central Palestine and central Transjordan, is different from the locations of the Abraham cycles, namely southern Palestine (in the case of Abraham and Isaac) and southern Transjordan (in the case of Abraham and Lot).

The Abraham and Jacob traditions are also different in form and theme. The Abraham cycle is, above all, a story of family and continuity. The ethnological element, Abraham as the ancestor who personifies the group that descended from him, is secondary and is important only in the stories of Ishmael and Lot's daughters. The family element is still present in the Jacob cycle, where the emphasis shifts to the relationship between brothers rather than father and sons. But in the Jacob tradition, individuals also—or perhaps only—represent groups. The rivalry between Jacob and Esau, for instance, is emblematic of the rivalry between herdsmen and hunters or, in the blessings in Genesis 28, between peasants and nomads. Jacob and Edom are personifications of the Israelites and Edomites. The treaty with Laban involves the Israelites and the Arameans. Generally speaking, the

12 sons of Jacob and the events surrounding their births can only be explained in terms of the 12 tribes of Israel.

The central themes of the Abraham and Jacob cycles are also different. The theme of the Abraham cycle is promise, whereas the theme of the Jacob cycle is blessing. After wrestling with God, Jacob receives a blessing, not a promise (Genesis 32:27-30), and this blessing from God explains his superhuman strength (Genesis 32:28) and his success in his dealings with Esau and Laban. The theme of blessing is repeated in different forms in this cycle. Jacob receives his father's blessing (Genesis 27); Laban is blessed because of Jacob (Genesis 30:27,30); and the dying Jacob blesses Joseph's two sons (Genesis 48).

These differences in location and conception suggest that the Abraham-Isaac cycle and the Jacob cycle were originally independent of each other. The patriarchal traditions are very complicated. Scholars have concluded that certain elements might have been preserved throughout the long period of oral transmission of the stories, but all they can say for sure is that the memory of origins may be one of these elements. This is the most that can be said from studying just the biblical text.

This article is an edited version of an excerpt from The Early History of Israel *by Roland de Vaux (English translation, Darton, Longman & Todd Ltd., 1978). Published in the U.S. by Westminster Press. Reprinted by permission.*

Afterword

Biblical history and historiography have widespread ramifications. George W. Ramsey of Presbyterian College reviews the place of history in biblical studies in his comments on In Search of History: Historiography in the Ancient World and the Origins of Biblical History,[1] *by John Van Seters:*

"History" has long been an important category in biblical interpretation because much of the Bible recounts events in which the activity of God was perceived. Some interpreters have gone so far as to say that the biblical faiths, Judaism and Christianity, take history more seriously than other religions. In the pages of the Hebrew Bible, according to many scholars, we have the first real historical accounts in the ancient world. Chief among the candidates as the first real history are several blocks of material that are usually dated around 950 B.C.E., a period of "enlightenment" during the reign of Solomon: the history of David's rise (1 Samuel 16-2 Samuel 5); the court history of David (2 Samuel 9-20; 1 Kings 1-2) and the sections of the Pentateuch usually ascribed to the Yahwist, or J, writer.

John Van Seters agrees that Israel was the first nation in the ancient Near East to write history. He does not mean that Israel was the first people to think "historically." Nor does he mean that Israel was the first people to think of its God as an active participant in historical events. Van Seters takes as his starting point a definition formulated by the Dutch historian Johan Huizinga: "History is the intellectual form in which a civilization renders account to itself of its past." Van Seters argues that the Israelites were the first to integrate a broad variety of material into a complex, unified narrative that communicated to the nation a sense of its identity. He does not, however, believe that this kind of writing appeared in Israel until about 550 B.C.E.

Across the ancient Near East there were historiographical genres such as king lists, chronicles, annals and royal inscriptions, which recorded and interpreted the past; the first half of Van Seters' book is a useful survey of this material. But by itself, historical consciousness was not enough to produce history writing. According to Van Seters, history writing emerged only when someone composed from the assorted historiographical genres an orderly story of the past, which gave a people a sense of who they were. This happened first in Israel in the sixth century B.C.E., then in Greece in the fifth century B.C.E. Van Seters pleads for biblical scholars to give more consideration to a comparison of Israelite and Greek historiographical techniques, and he devotes much attention to Herodotus, who took an assortment of disparate materials and genres and composed a unified narrative for the Greeks. Van Seters does not press the case for direct continuity between Greek and Israelite culture too hard (although he does speculate briefly about some contact via Phoenicia).

His goal is the modest one of convincing biblical scholars to consider the techniques Herodotus used to compose a unified narrative, as well as the more common model used by biblical scholars, a communal process of evolving traditions, when they hypothesize about how the narratives in the Hebrew Bible took shape.

In Van Seters' estimate, the first historian in Israel was the anonymous figure called the "Deuteronomistic historian" who composed the narrative now found in the books of Joshua, Judges, 1 and 2 Samuel and 1 and 2 Kings. The evidence that this block of material is a unified composition was persuasively presented by the German scholar Martin Noth in 1943. Noth demonstrated that a chronological framework underlies this material and that a theology derived from the Book of Deuteronomy perfuses the corpus (thus the label Deuteronomistic History). This Deuteronomistic theology is expressed in stock phraseology at a number of points in the biblical narrative: Israel, as the chosen people of Yahweh, is obligated to Yahweh and to the laws of the covenant established at Mount Horeb (Sinai); Israel's obedience to these laws will lead to peace and prosperity, whereas disobedience will bring punishment. Noth argued that the Deuteronomistic History (Joshua, Judges, 1 and 2 Samuel and 1 and 2 Kings) and a new introduction (Deuteronomy 1-4) and conclusion to the Book of Deuteronomy (Deuteronomy 31-34) were composed about 550 B.C.E. The purpose of the Deuteronomistic History was to demonstrate to the Israelites that their apostasy was the reason for their downfall as a nation. Noth believed that the Deuteronomist, the author of the History, made considerable use of older sources, such as the story of David's rise and the court history of David; in these sections the Deuteronomist contributed mainly editorial touches.

Van Seters affirms Noth's basic thesis, but he believes that the Deuteronomist deserves more credit for originality than Noth gave him. Van Seters says it is difficult to identify earlier sources in the final text, and he is critical of efforts to reconstruct hypothetical stages in the development of the material prior to the final version, an approach scholars call tradition criticism.

Van Seters, in fact, believes that the Deuteronomist originated much of the material in his history, just as Herodotus seems to have done (according to at least one school of interpretation). For example, in Van Seters' judgment, the Deuteronomist created the stories of Joshua's conquest as a narrative expression of the Deuteronomic theme that Israel should remain pure and obliterate everything un-Israelite. For the period of the Judges, Van Seters thinks the Deuteronomist perhaps knew some assorted histories, out of which he constructed the present narrative. In 1 Samuel 1-7 (the childhood of Samuel and the capture of the Ark by the Philistines), he observes, it is "scarcely possible...to recover earlier stages in the tradition...if they ever existed." About Solomon's reign, Van Seters says, "The whole presentation is a rather elaborate reconstruction by the Deuteronomist based upon very little prior material." The theme of divine election and rejection of kings throughout the monarchical period Van Seters labels a "literary artifice" of the Deuteronomist. Such stories as the establishment of golden calves in Dan and Bethel by Jeroboam I (1 Kings 12:26-30) and the discovery of the book of law in the Temple during Josiah's reign (2 Kings 22:3-20) he regards as pure fiction.

Van Seters' treatment of the court history of David, however, differs most sharply from recent scholarship. The court history, dating from the time of Solomon, is frequently cited as a high water mark in Israelite historiography and a primary source for the Deuteronomist. Van Seters argues that the portrayal of David as "a moral and spiritual weakling" in the court history is so different from the Deuteronomist's portrait of an ideal David that he could hardly have incorporated the court history into his work. Far from being a product of the tenth century B.C.E., the court history is a *post-Deuteronomistic addition* to the Deuteronomistic History, a product of the post-Exilic period in the sixth century. Consequently, Van Seters argues, the court history can not be Israel's first history writing. ***BR** 4:2 (1988), p. 4*

CHAPTER 4

The Song of Deborah

Lawrence E. Stager

Roland de Vaux's theory that Israel arose from the merger of independent tribes is supported in the Book of Judges, which presents a picture of shifting tribal alliances. One such alliance, Stager argues, is implied in the Song of Deborah, "one of the two or three oldest passages in the entire Bible." Composed, perhaps, in the immediate aftermath of the Israelite victory over the Canaanites, in the Song of Deborah, six tribes answer the call for assistance, and four refuse, a total of ten instead of the expected twelve. Stager proposes that archaeological, ecological and sociological studies of the Israelites can reveal the reasons for the behavior of various tribes.

Archaeological evidence indicates "a dramatic increase in the number of permanent settlements in the central hill country" at the time. For example, the population in the territory of Ephraim and Manasseh quadrupled between 1200 and 1100 B.C.E. putting a strain on food resources. To increase the amount of arable land, the practice of terracing hillsides was developed. This technique is mentioned in the Song of Deborah in connection with the tribe of Naphtali. The six tribes that answered Deborah's call lived mainly in highland villages that tended to be "economically independent, isolated and self-reliant."

In contrast, the four tribes that refused to fight had developed "economic entanglements with non-Israelites," either maritime trade or pastoral arrangements. Unlike the highlanders, herder tribes were dependent on Canaanite farmers and townspeople for many food products and handicrafts; seafaring tribes may have worked for Canaanite shipowners and may have been reluctant to join in the fight for economic reasons.–Ed.

The Song of Deborah (Judges 5) is one of the most powerful poems in the entire Bible. The story, retold in a prose version, with many variations, in Judges 4, concerns the deliverer (Judge), Deborah, and her reluctant general, Barak, who do battle against an alliance of Canaanite kings. The events take place after the Exodus from Egypt and before the institution of the monarchy, a time we call the settlement period–in biblical terms, the period of the Judges.

From the prose account in Judges 4, we learn that the kings of Canaan are led by Jabin, who is identified as the king of Hazor (Judges 4:2,18,12). Jabin's commander is a man named Sisera (Judges 4:2). Deborah, the war leader, who lives and judges in Ephraim, summons Barak of the tribe of Naphtali and tells him to muster 10,000 men and engage Sisera in battle at Mount Tabor. Barak replies that he will respect her summons only if Deborah goes with him. Deborah agrees but declares that the glory of victory will be denied to Barak personally. The enemy commander, Sisera, will be delivered not into Barak's hands, but into the hands of a woman (Judges 4:4-9). Barak musters 10,000 men from the tribes of Naphtali and Zebulun on Mount Tabor, and Deborah goes with him.

Seeing Barak's troops at Mount Tabor, Sisera, the Canaanite commander, orders 900 chariots and all his men to the Wadi Kishon, which courses from Mount Tabor through the plain of Megiddo. There the Canaanites prepare to meet the Israelites.

Deborah then gives the signal to Barak: "Up! This is the day on which the Lord will deliver Sisera into your hands: The Lord is marching before you" (Judges 4:14, NJV).[1] Barak charges down the slope of Mount Tabor and triumphs gloriously. Sisera alone escapes. "Sisera leaped from his chariot and fled on foot" (Judges 4:15, NJV).

Sisera arrives at the tent of Heber the Kenite, a friend of King Jabin, and begs for water. Heber's wife, Yael (also translated Jael), does better and gives him milk. Sisera falls asleep, exhausted (Judges 4:17-19). Yael then takes a tent peg and a mallet and, while Sisera sleeps, she kills him by driving the tent peg through his temple (Judges 4:21). When Barak arrives in pursuit, he finds that Yael, a woman, has already slain Sisera (Judges 4:22).

The poetic version of the episode–in Judges 5–is much more cryptic and difficult to follow. This archaic poem was composed long before the prose version. In the New Jewish Version (NJV) translation of the poem an unusual footnote informs the reader, "In many parts of this poem the meaning is uncertain." This is surely true. Few passages in the Bible have presented more grist for the scholarly mill than the Song of Deborah. But many passages are of soaring beauty and moving drama, as is apparent in these excerpts:

> Hear, O kings! Give ear, O potentates!
> I will sing, will sing to the Lord,
> Will hymn the Lord, the God of Israel.
>
> O Lord, when You came forth from Seir,
> Advanced from the country of Edom,
> The earth trembled;
> The heavens dripped,
> Yea, the clouds dripped water,
> The mountains quaked–

Before the Lord, Him of Sinai,
Before the Lord, God of Israel.

In the days of Shamgar son of Anath,
In the days of Jael [Yael], caravans ceased,
And wayfarers went
By roundabout paths.
Deliverance ceased,
Ceased in Israel,
Till you arose, O Deborah,
Arose, O mother, in Israel!
....
Then did the people of the Lord
March down to the gates!
Awake, awake, O Deborah!
Awake, awake, strike up the chant!
Arise, O Barak;
Take you captives, O son of Abinoam!

Then was the remnant made victor over the mighty,
The Lord's people won my victory over the warriors.
....
Then the kings came, they fought:
The kings of Canaan fought
At Taanach, by Megiddo's waters–
They got no spoil of silver.
The stars fought from heaven,
From their courses they fought against Sisera.
The torrent Kishon swept them away,
The raging torrent, the torrent Kishon.

March on, my soul, with courage!

Then the horses' hoofs pounded
As headlong galloped the steeds.
....
Most blessed of women be Jael [Yael],
Wife of Heber the Kenite,
Most blessed of women in tents.
He asked for water, she offered milk;
In a princely bowl she brought him curds.
Her [left] hand reached for the tent peg,
Her right for the workman's hammer.
She struck Sisera, crushed his head,
Smashed and pierced his temple.
At her feet he sank, lay outstretched,
At her feet he sank, lay still;
Where he sank, there he lay–destroyed.

Through the window peered Sisera's mother,
Behind the lattice she whined:
"Why is his chariot so long in coming?
Why so late the clatter of his wheels?"

The wisest of her ladies give answer
She, too, replies to herself:
"They must be dividing the spoil they have found:
A damsel or two for each man,
Spoil of dyed cloths for Sisera,
Spoil of embroidered cloths,
A couple of embroidered cloths
Round every neck as spoil."

So may all Your enemies perish, O Lord!

Judges 5:3-31 (NJV)

Scholars agree that the poetic version of the story is extremely old, one of the two or three oldest passages in the entire Bible. It was composed in the 12th century B.C.E.[2] George Foot Moore[3] considered it the "only contemporaneous monument of Hebrew history" before the Israelite monarchy.[4]

All kinds of intriguing questions can be and have been raised about this poem and its prose counterpart–textual questions, literary questions, historical questions, theological questions, moral questions, etc. But I would like to focus on one specific aspect of the story. Scholars have long noted that not all of the tribes of Israel answered Deborah's call. Indeed, only six tribes responded; four others stayed home.[5] I propose to examine the social organization of the Israelites that permitted the acceptance and refusal of the call to arms. In so doing, I believe we will better understand the social texture of Israelite society at the time of Judges.

My synthesis will encompass a number of methodologies and sources of data, providing an example of what could be called social archaeology of the Bible. This synthesis incorporates archaeological discoveries, ecological and sociological studies, as well as some textual analysis of the biblical accounts.

In the later prose account (Judges 4), Barak musters troops from his own tribe, Naphtali, and the tribe of Zebulun. None of the other tribes is mentioned, either as providing troops or as staying away. In the poetic account, however, the poet dramatically recalls both the tribes that answered the call and those that declined to participate. First, five tribes that responded affirmatively are listed:

From *Ephraim* came they whose roots are in Amalek;
After you, your kin *Benjamin*;
From *Machir* [*Manasseh*] came down leaders,
From *Zebulun* such as hold the marshal's staff.
And Issachar's chiefs were with Deborah;
As Barak, so was *Issachar*–
Rushing after him into the valley.

Judges 5:14-15 (NJV)

Then the poet describes four tribes that refused the call:

In the divisions of *Reuben*
great were the searchings of heart.

Why did you sit beside the hearths [or sheepfolds]
listening to pipings for the flocks?
In the divisions of Reuben
great were the searchings of heart.
Gilead remained camped beyond the Jordan.
And *Dan*—why did he linger by the ships?
Asher remained at the seacoast
And tarried at his landings.

Judges 5:15-17 (NJV)

Then the poet mentions Zebulun again and adds Barak's tribe, Naphtali, bringing to six the number of tribes that responded affirmatively:[6]

Zebulun is a people that mocked at death,
Naphtali—on the open heights.

Judges 5:18 (NJV)

To what extent the story of this Canaanite-Israelite war is historical has been much debated. But whether or not it is historically accurate in every detail, the poet, in order to achieve verisimilitude, must have grounded the story in a setting and circumstances that seemed plausible to the contemporary audience for whom the poem was intended. In other words, it must have been plausible to the listeners (assuming the poem was first recited orally) that Ephraim (Deborah's tribe), Benjamin, Machir (later called Manasseh), Zebulun, Issachar and Naphtali answered the call and participated in the battle, while Reuben, Gilead (or, as it is also called, Gad), Dan and Asher did not. Recent archaeological evidence (see map on p.54), shows that this was indeed plausible—and we can now understand, I believe, why some tribes were more willing than others to answer Barak's muster.

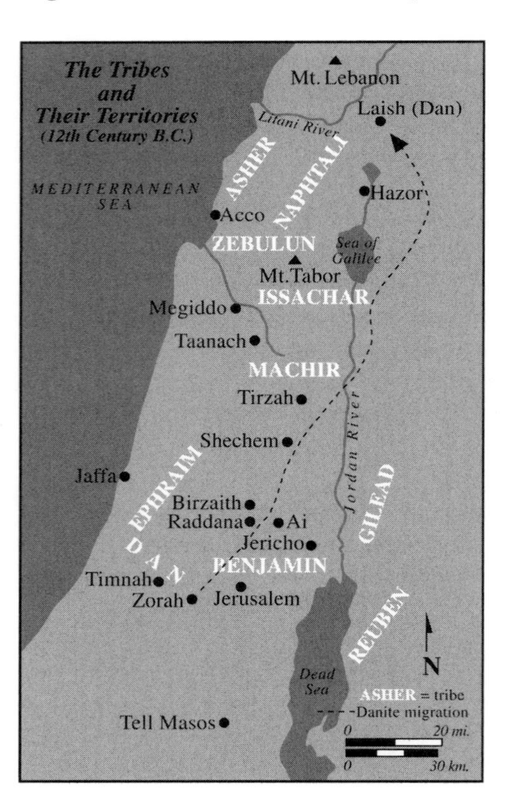

At the beginning of the period archaeologists call Iron Age I, or Iron I for short (Iron I extends from about 1200 to 1000 B.C.E.), there was a dramatic increase in the number of permanent settlements in the central hill country of ancient Palestine. It is hard to avoid the conclusion that most of these settlements belonged to Israelites who settled in the highlands of Canaan.[7]

The contrast with the preceding archaeological period (the Late Bronze Age, 1550-1200 B.C.E.) is striking. Archaeological surveys and excavations have identified some 27 sites in the central hill country from the Late Bronze Age. In this same area, which became known as the tribal territories of Ephraim and Manasseh, archaeologists Adam Zertal, Israel Finkelstein and others have found at last count 211 sites dating to Iron I, nearly an eightfold increase.[8]

Although fewer in number, the settlements in the Late Bronze Age were larger (and thus more urbanized). The Iron Age settlements, by contrast, were often small farming villages. The median size of the Late Bronze settlements was approximately 12 acres, the Iron I settlements, a little more than 2 acres. The difference is substantial. Of the more than 200 Iron Age sites in Ephraim and Manasseh, 85 percent were newly founded settlements; that is, most early Israelite villages were established on previously unoccupied sites.

An overall eightfold increase (23 times in Ephraim; 4.4 times in Manasseh) of settlements in the central hills is such a dramatic increase that it can hardly be ascribed to natural growth in the highland zone itself. More in keeping with natural growth would be doubling the population in this same area from Iron I to Iron II. Obviously, a new population moved into the central hill country from about 1200 to 1100 B.C.E. This is entirely consistent with the biblical record. In Joshua 17:16, the tribes of Ephraim and Manasseh complain that they are confined to the highlands, while the Canaanites live in the lowlands. In 1 Kings 20:23, Arameans refer to the God of the Israelites as the "god[s] of the highlands" (*elohei hariym*).

The Israelite habitation in the highlands is also reflected in the Song of Deborah itself, where the poet frequently refers to the Israelites going down against the Canaanites:

> There they recited the triumphs of Yahweh,
> The triumphs of his village tribesmen [*przn*] in Israel.
> Then the kindred [literally "people"] of Yahweh went down against
> the gates...
> Then the fugitives went down against the nobles,
> The kindred of Yahweh went down against the warriors.
>
> Judges 5:11,13

The Israelites not only "went down," but they also did battle "against the gates." In an earlier verse (Judges 5:8), we read that the Israelites "did battle with the gates." The "gates" undoubtedly represent the fortified–that is, walled–Canaanite cities in the plains. In these cities the area most vulnerable to attack was the city gate, as we know from several archaeological examples.[9]

The early Israelite villages, by contrast, were rarely, if ever, fortified with free-standing fortification walls. Instead, they built houses in contiguous

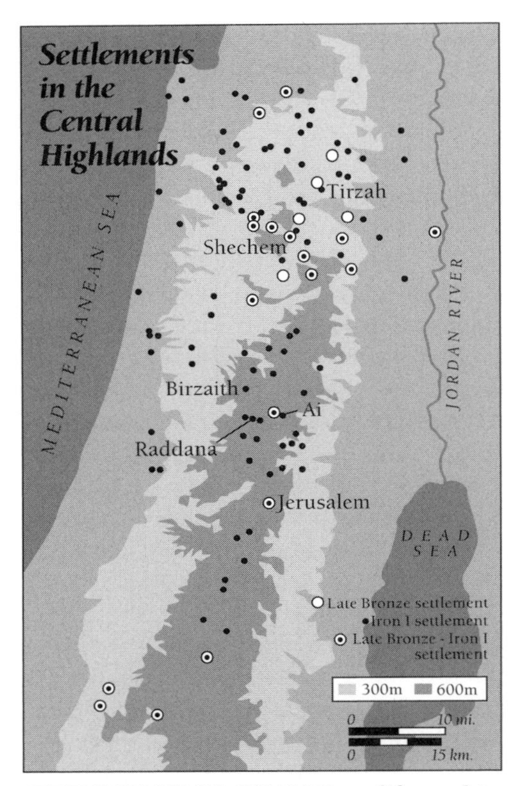

SETTLEMENTS IN CANAAN proliferated in the early Iron Age, especially in hilly terrain 600 meters or more above sea level. Since this map was drawn, archaeologists have discovered many more Iron I sites in the hill country. *Map: Courtesy Douglas Esse*

arrangements on the village perimeter; these contiguous houses formed a kind of wall that afforded limited protection against attack. Most villages, however, relied primarily on hilltop positions and surrounding terraced slopes for defense against attack. The leading protagonists among the "kindred of Yahweh" were the inhabitants (*perazon*) of the tribal villages (*perazot*). In Ezekiel 38:11, this land of unfortified settlements is described as a place where the quiet people dwelled securely, even though their villages were without walls and had "neither bars nor gates."

The hill country was a far less hospitable environment for the primitive agriculture in which these early Israelites engaged than was the low country to the west, which had sizable tracts of arable land. In the hill country, only a few plateaus and valleys were arable initially. Much of the hill country was covered with forests, and the rocky slopes of the hills resisted cultivation and were subject to erosion. Nevertheless, population pressures on this limited environment soon prompted the Israelite settlers to try to expand their food supply.

The Israelite immigrants devised new strategies for increasing the agricultural productivity of the woodland hills. Extensive deforestation was one result. Joshua speaks of it in the previous biblical passage cited:

> The highlands are not enough for us [complained the tribes of Ephraim and Manasseh]. Yet the Canaanites living in the lowlands all have iron chariots [and therefore we cannot dispossess them of the land]...Joshua replied: "...True, [the hill country] is a woodland, but you will clear it and possess it to its farthest limits."
>
> Joshua 17:16,18

Once the forests had been cleared, the Israelites created agricultural terraces on the land. This technological advance in a very real sense opened up the highland frontier to the Iron Age farmers and dramatically altered the attractiveness of the hill country to incoming agriculturalists. The carrying capacity of the land (the maximum number of people who can live on the agricultural produce of a certain area) was increased far beyond anything that had been known there in the Late Bronze Age.[10]

Terracing transformed the natural slopes into level steps—artificially flattened surfaces, or "fields"—suitable for farming. Terrace soils were anchored in place by retaining walls built of dry-laid stones. The terrace walls, which were usually built on the natural contours at right angles to the slope, countered soil erosion and, to a lesser degree, induced sedimentation.

Terracing was a highly successful adaptation to the highlands. But the accompanying new mountain ecosystem was just as fragile as the natural ecosystem, perhaps more so. Without regular maintenance, the terraces deteriorated rapidly. The combined weight of collapsed walls and unconsolidated earth sometimes caused devastating landslides, leaving in their wake denuded hillsides that could not be restored by nature alone.

AGRICULTURAL TERRACES at Khirbet Raddana, about ten miles north of Jerusalem, cover the same hillsides where Israelites once worked the land. The terraces, held in place by dry-laid stone retaining walls along the outer edges of natural limestone terraces, hold the soil in place and create level areas for farming. The technique of terracing transformed the economy of the struggling Israelites, enabling them to become self-sufficient and independent. ***Photo: Joseph Callaway***

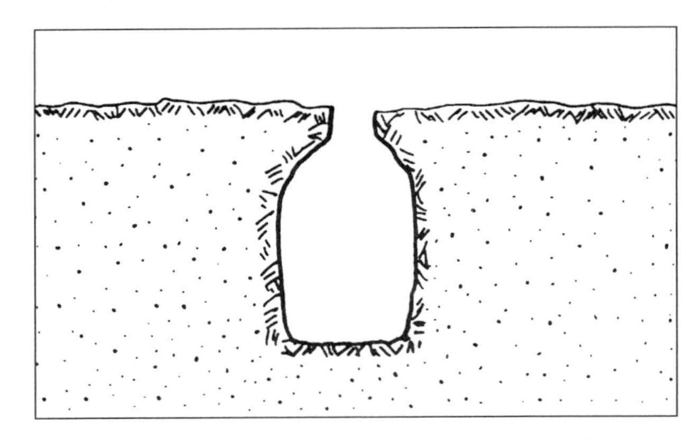

HOUSEHOLD CISTERN. Bell-shaped cisterns were carved from bedrock beneath the floor in Iron Age I houses at Ai. The pioneering Israelites introduced cistern building to the area. ***Drawing: Courtesy Lawrence E. Stager***

The agricultural terraces that can be most accurately dated by archaeological evidence are on the slopes just outside and below the Iron I villages of Ai and Raddana. These small, hilltop villages sustained by terrace farming were typical of the many new settlements in the hills. The highland villagers were already well advanced in the techniques of terrace agriculture when they established settlements *de novo* on hilltops and laid out terraced plots on the slopes below. These terraced fields are referred to in the Song of Deborah in Naphtali's *meromei sadeh*, traditionally translated "high places of the field" (Judges 5:18).

Two other technological advances were perhaps not as important as scholars sometimes suppose. I refer to the lime-plastered cisterns for water storage and the gradual ascendancy of iron over bronze. William F. Albright first offered a technological "explanation" for the Iron I settlement pattern in the hill country. These hill people, whom Albright correctly identified with the early Israelites, were able to establish new settlements in formerly uninhabited areas "thanks to the rapid spread of the art...of constructing cisterns and lining them with waterproof lime plaster instead of the previously used limy marl or raw lime plaster."[11]

Most scholars have found Albright's formulation compelling, especially when combined with the technological advantage that supposedly came with the introduction of iron tools and weapons into the hill country about 1200 B.C.E. With a superior edge on iron axes for cutting down forests, the highlanders supposedly were able to increase agricultural production.[12] With iron quarrying tools, they supposedly were able to cut tunnels through the rock for irrigation and hew out large reservoirs for water storage.[13]

Since Albright developed his hypothesis, however, cisterns lined with waterproof plaster have been discovered from earlier periods—at Late Bronze Taanach and Hazor (1550-1200 B.C.E.) and much earlier at pre-pottery Neolithic 'Ain

Ghazal (7000-6000 B.C.E.), east of the Jordan River. But the important point is that lime plaster was not really necessary to waterproof most of these Iron Age cisterns in the hill country because the bedrock of this region—Cenomanian limestone intercalated with chalks and marls—is impermeable. True, most residential compounds had one or more bell-shaped cistern beneath the floor of the house or courtyard, but they were not always lined with lime plaster. For example, none of the cisterns at Ai or Raddana was lined with lime plaster. At other sites, lime plaster was necessary as a "waterproofing cement," but local geological conditions must be considered before conclusions can be drawn about the need for waterproofing cisterns with plaster.

As for iron tools, iron did not come into common use in Palestine until the tenth century B.C.E. Even from this later period, most of the iron artifacts have

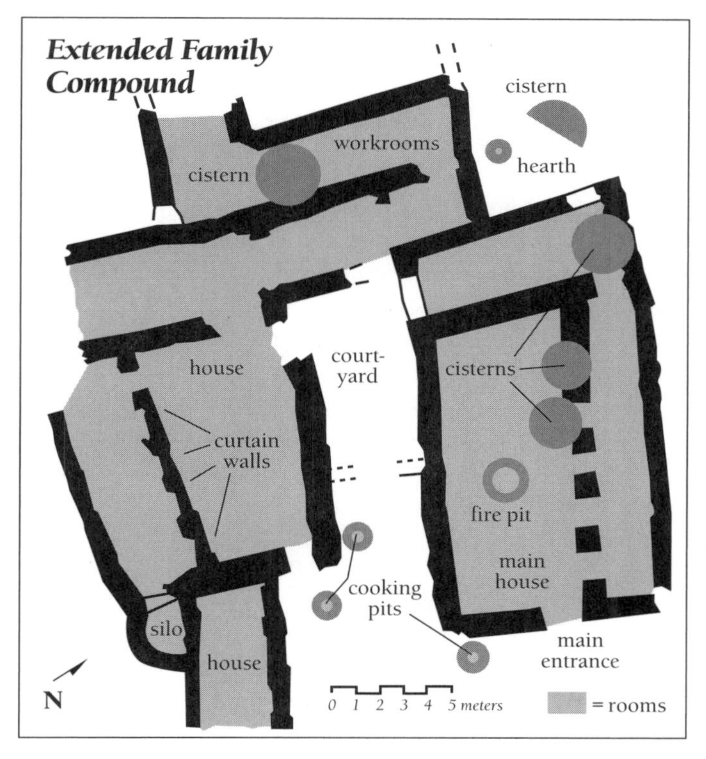

A MULTI-FAMILY COMPOUND at Khirbet Raddana, about four miles west of Ai. The largest room of the main house is separated from a long narrow room by a row of four pillars that once supported a second story. To the left of the largest room is a courtyard. The drawing shows cisterns under the bedrock floors capped by large rocks. In workrooms behind the three-house cluster, family members made tools from metal melted in the hearth in the far north workroom, upper right, where archaeologists discovered daggers, chisels, spearheads and axe heads.

been found at sites outside the hill country. Moreover, some of the early iron tools were inferior to bronze in hardness. In short, slope terracing was the crucial technology for the highland villagers. Lime plaster and iron tools were not.

A standard house in the Iron I period was a small rectangular building with two to four rooms entered from an exterior courtyard. (This house plan became even more popular during the Israelite monarchy.) To the right or left of the doorway were piers, or rows of pillars, often with low, thin curtain walls between them; some of these low walls had built-in mangers or troughs, where animals could feed (see box, pp. 60-61) the narrower side room(s). A broadroom, running the width of the building, formed the back end of the house. In the so-called four-room house, the central room is usually depicted in modern drawings as an open courtyard flanked on three sides by one or two stories of rooms. It seems clear, however, from the position of the pillars and, in one instance, ceiling timbers found in the central room itself, that pillared houses (whether two, three or four rooms) were designed to take a second story; thus a four-room house may, in fact, have had as many as eight rooms. It is, therefore, better to use the term "pillared" rather than the number of rooms to designate this building type.

At Ai the ceiling beams were 5.2 feet above the floor.[14] These beams would have been a constant headache to inhabitants more than five feet tall, but human comfort was probably not a primary consideration in building the side rooms, many of which were designed and used as domestic stables—for sheep and goats, donkeys and cattle, especially the "fatted" or "stall-fed" calf known from the Old and New Testaments (for example, I Samuel 28:24; Psalms 50:9; Amos 6:4; Luke 15:23-27).[15] At other sites—for example, Atar Haro'a in the Negev—ceiling heights were between 5.8 feet and 6.5 feet, far more compatible with human stature of the period, and allowed for ample clearance.

These Iron I dwellings are so small that they could have housed only a nuclear family—a father, mother and children. However, these houses—for example, those at Raddana, Ai and Tell Masos[16]—were built in clusters. The clusters or compounds typically included two or three individual houses, either completely independent or linked to each other by one or two common walls. Each house, nevertheless, had a separate entrance, usually approached through a shared open courtyard. These compounds were separated from one another by streets, paths or stone enclosure walls. Each compound probably housed multiple or extended families.

Modern ethnographers, although describing a family unit in a 20th-century Arab village, probably accurately describe the family relationships in an Israelite dwelling compound of the 12th century B.C.E. In the Arab village built at the site of ancient Bethel, an ethnographer described the *za'ila* (joint family) as follows:

> It consists of the father, mother and unwed children as well as the wedded sons and their wives and children, unwed paternal aunts and sometimes even unwed paternal uncles. In short, this unit is composed of

> blood relatives plus women who were brought into the kinship through marriage. Large as it may be, this unit tends to occupy one dwelling or a compound of dwellings built close together or often attached to one another. It is an economic as well as a social unit and is governed by the grandfather or the eldest male. The joint family normally dissolves upon the death of the grandfather. The land, which until then had been held by the grandfather, is divided among the heirs, and the male children separate, each to become the nucleus of a new za'ila.[17]

Authority over the household resided with the *pater familias* who, in the case of a three-generation family, would be the grandfather. Sometimes, even after their father's death, married brothers and their families would continue to live in the same compound as a single household working together cooperatively; in this case, the older brother would usually become the head of the household.

The architecture of the Iron I agricultural villages reflects the social structure referred to in the Bible. The individual male (*geber*) with his nuclear family lived in a single dwelling. The compound housed the extended household (*bayit*) or small patrilineage (*beit 'ab*), literally "house of one's father." Several related lineages made up the *mishpakhah*—the much larger "family," or clan. A group of clans or *mishpakhot* composed a tribe (*shevet* or *matteh*).

The most inclusive grouping was the *'am* (people), more appropriately translated "kindred," which in the case of earliest Israel was known as the *'am Yhwh*, the "kindred of Yahweh" (Judges 5), and as the "tribes of Israel" (*shivtei Yisrael*) or "sons of Israel" (*benei Yisrael*). The "sons of Israel" was simply the family writ large. In other words, Israelites considered themselves one very big family or kin group, whether they were related by actual blood ties or not. At the head of this "family" was God the father.

Kinship language provides the key to most major concepts not only in the Hebrew Bible, but also in the New Testament. In one of the most often cited, but seldom understood, passages from the Gospel of John (14:2), Jesus says: "In my father's house are many mansions," by which he means that in God the father's household (the multiple family compound; *oikia* = *beit 'ab/'abba*) are many houses (single family dwellings). The heavenly household is patterned after the earthly one.

In the Israelite conquest described in the Bible, when the Israelites were unsuccessful in their initial assault on Ai (after their victory at Jericho), they tried to identify—apparently by lot—the sinner responsible for their defeat. The lot ultimately fell to an individual, Achan, who was found to have violated the proscription against taking booty after the destruction of Jericho. To identify Achan, first the "tribe" (*shevet* or *matteh*) was chosen—Judah. Then the "clan" (*mishpakhah*)—Zerah. Then the "house" or lineage (*bayit*)—Zabdi. Finally, the "individual" (*geber*)—Achan (Joshua 7).

The small Israelite village was no doubt organized along kinship lines. Compound names of early Israelite villages, such as the "Hill of Saul" (*gib'at shaul*), the "Diadem of the House of Joab" (*'atrot beit yo'ab*), or the "Enclosure

Iron Age Pillared House

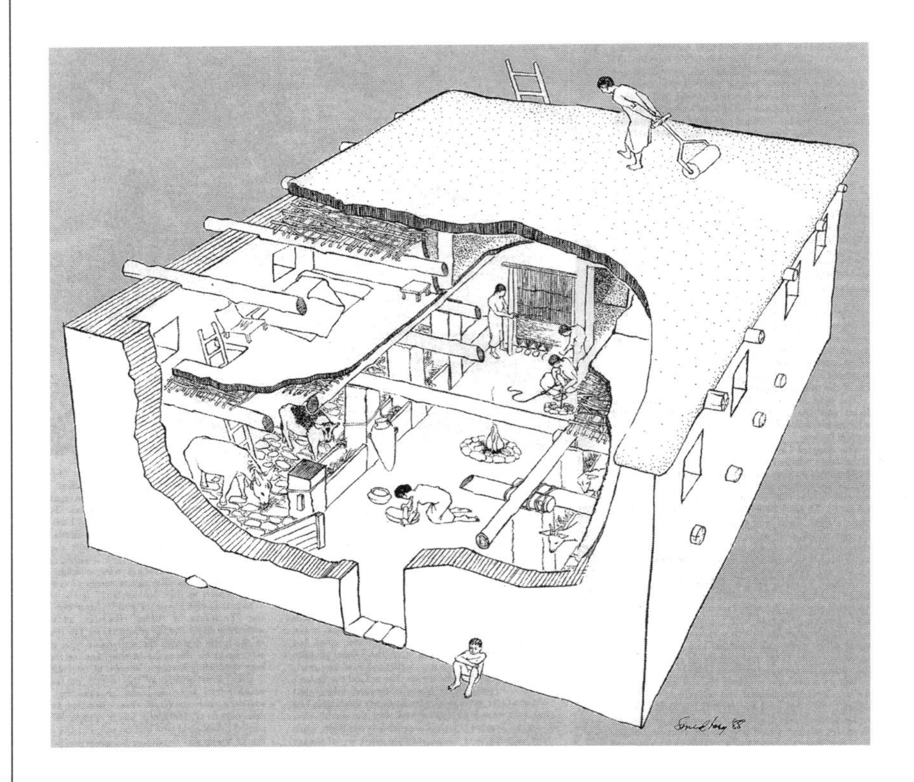

of Addar" (*khatzar 'addar*), reveal something about the kin groups there. The first element in the name describes the settlement type; the second element yields the name of the founding families and later the leading lineage or lineages in the village.

Even more telling in this regard are genealogies, which often serve as social charters for kin-based societies such as Israel. For example, among the descendants of Manasseh was a great-great-grandson named Zelophehad who had no sons but five daughters, one of whom was Tirzah (see Numbers 26:29-34; Joshua 17:3). Tirzah is not just the name of a person but also a place name—in fact, the name of a one-time capital of the northern kingdom of Israel, now securely identified with Tell el-Farah (north) and excavated by Roland de Vaux.

Similarly with Birzaith, a name that appears among the "sons" of Asher in the genealogical list in 1 Chronicles 7:31. This person-lineage-place name can

The typical Israelite house in the Iron I period (c.1200-1000 B.C.E.), and in later biblical times as well, was home to both people and animals. Averaging about 50 feet long and 30 feet wide, the house was small but efficient. The flat roof, made of earth and chalk, could be tamped down with a roller after the rain.

In the main central room, food was prepared, often using ingredients stored in the pantry, or broadroom, at the back of the house. Here, a woman grinds grain, using upper and lower rubbing stones, after having readied a fire on the hearth in the middle of the room. Water could be drawn from the cistern hewn into the bedrock below the tamped-earth floor. To the left of the entrance to the broadroom, another domestic chore, weaving, is performed on a vertical loom.

The ground-floor side rooms provided plenty of stable space for the family livestock, which was probably brought into the house at night. In winter, warmth radiating from the animals up to the second floor, where the family ate and slept, would have provided an effective, if malodorous, heating system. Upstairs, a bedroll for sleeping has been prepared.

Paving stones in the side rooms allowed secure footing as urine seeped between the stones into the earth below. On the left, between the front wall and the first stone pillar, the artist has drawn a wooden gate. Between the other stone pillars, which separated the central room from the side stables, low curtain walls kept the animals out. Some of these curtain walls had built-in mangers. With the discovery of these ground-floor stables and curtain-wall mangers, we have a new understanding of the biblical references to the "fatted" or "stall-fed" calf.

In fact, Luke must have had these mangers in mind when he said that Mary "brought forth her firstborn son, and wrapped him in swaddling clothes, and laid him in a manger because there was no room for them in the inn" (Luke 2:7). The first Christmas probably did not take place in a barn or cave, as creche scenes usually depict, but in a farmhouse in Bethlehem that may have looked a lot like this house.

be none other than the Iron Age settlement located beneath modern Bir ez-Zeit, about 15 miles north of Jerusalem. At some point, clans from the tribe of Asher, from their territory near Acco, migrated south into the central hill country and established themselves there, much as some of the Danites migrated to the north.

Shechem was a descendant of Manasseh, who lent his name to a town and district. In fact, the famous Samaria ostraca (singular, ostracon), inscribed potsherds dated to the reign of Jeroboam II (786-746 B.C.E.), indicate that many of the "sons" and "daughters" (lineages and clans) of Manasseh still inhabited the districts around Samaria in the eighth century B.C.E.

Each village probably had a council of elders (*zeqeniym*). In 1 Samuel 16:4, for example, the "elders of Bethlehem" go out to meet Samuel. (See also 1 Samuel 11:3 and 30:26-31.) The council of elders was probably chosen from the heads of households of the more prominent lineages of the village. From these village councils of elders, the most prominent members, no doubt were co-opted to serve on regional or clan councils, and so on up the segmentary ladder of representation.

As we have noted, livestock in the villages consisted primarily of sheep and goats. The agricultural products were largely cereals—wheat and barley, although a few settlements cultivated vines and olive trees. The latter produced "cash crops"—wine and olive oil—which tended to propel the economy toward trade links with the outside world and dependency on interregional, or even international, exchange networks. But vine and olive tree cultivation was relatively rare in Iron I villages.

The circumstances of the Israelite mountain habitat and continued hostilities with the peoples of the plains, whether Canaanites, Egyptians or Sea Peoples (including the Philistines), fostered what has been called an *économie locale*, or local small-scale economy. Moreover, the investment in permanent quarters and pioneered land in the hills promoted independence and isolation from surrounding complementary regions, especially the "bread baskets" of the coastal plains and broad valleys.

A description of the independent villagers of Mount Lebanon by a modern anthropologist, William R. Polk, is probably applicable to their ancient counterparts among the Israelite settlers in the hill country:

> Throughout history, the natural barrier of the mountains defended the inhabitants. [Mount] Lebanon became a refuge for such religious and ethnic minorities as the Druze and Maronites. The independent mountaineers stand in stark contrast to the humbled peasants of the Biqa Valley or the Nile Delta. The mountains provided men with the opportunity for freedom, and they realized it during much of their history. The cult of the warrior, the notion of independence of the clan, the village, and the district became integral parts of the culture of the people. Villagers marched to war under their village flags. Villagers as groups drove away tax collectors during extended periods of modern history. And perhaps most important, they were able to develop a permanence in habitation and mores which was impossible for the more exposed lowland peasant.[18]

The mountain areas are traditionally "the country of small peasant proprietors, poor but free, devoting their lives to producing all their needs from their land."[19]

The striking contrasts between the hills and the plains are highlighted continually by the archaeology of Palestine in the Iron I period, as the wealth of Canaanite and Sea Peoples material culture is compared with the poverty of the highland settlements of the Israelites. Despite their independence and economic self-sufficiency (a condition scholars refer to as autarky), these highland villages forged significant bonds with one another, thereby creating larger and larger sociopolitical orders. The Song of Deborah requires us to assume tribal, and even supra-tribal, orders that extended not only to the highlands, but even to their kin in the valleys and plains.

The most inclusive tribal grouping in premonarchic Israel was the confederation, a loosely structured alliance of tribes reinforced by religion and activated for mutual defense. In the Song of Deborah, a ten-tribe confederation—the "kindred (or people) of Yahweh"—is described, of which only six tribes participated in the battle against the Canaanites. The tribes that failed to respond were scorned by those who rallied to the battle, but they could not be coerced into joining the fight. There were times when "ethnic" bonding did not prevail over more compelling realities, such as the nontribal economic and political alignments that caused Dan, Asher, Reuben and Gilead/Gad to sit out the battle.

In short, I believe we can understand the responses to Deborah's muster in economic terms—the tribes that answered the call (Ephraim, Benjamin, Machir [Manasseh], Zebulun, Naphtali and Issachar)—had far fewer economic entanglements with non-Israelites than the tribes whose livelihoods depended to a large extent on maritime trade (Dan and Asher) or on specialized pastoralism (Reuben and probably Gilead). The six tribes that answered the call were economically independent, isolated and self-reliant. The areas where these tribes lived are the areas in which archaeological surveys and, to some extent, excavations have revealed a concentration of Iron I villages. Ephraim, Benjamin and Machir (Manasseh) inhabited the hill country of central Palestine, Zebulun and Naphtali, the hilly Galilee.

The location of the tribal territory of Issachar during the Iron I period is uncertain. The traditional territory of Issachar, in Lower Galilee between Mount Tabor and the Sea of Galilee, was not densely occupied until about 1000 B.C.E., according to the survey of Zvi Gal.[20] Gal suggests that in the 12th to 11th centuries B.C.E. Issachar may also have been part of the central hill-country population. This would accord well with the Song of Deborah:[21]

> Issachar's chiefs were with Deborah;
> As Barak, so was Issachar—
> Rushing after him into the valley.
>
> Judges 5:15 (NJV)

A closer examination of the economic circumstances of the tribes of Reuben and Gilead/Gad will explain why they did not follow Barak. In contrast to the tribes that answered the call, which were for the most part small-village agriculturists, Reuben and Gilead/Gad, which sat out the battle, were pastoralists—large herders specializing in sheep and goats. Both Reuben and Gilead/Gad were well known for their large herds, as Numbers 32:1 reflects:

> Now the Reubenites and the Gadites had a very large number of livestock, and they saw the land of Jazer and the land of Gilead, and behold, the place was cattle country [that is, a grazing range].

The pastoralist vocation of Reuben and Gilead/Gad is also reflected in the Song of Deborah:

In the divisions of Reuben
great were the searchings of heart.
Why did you sit beside the hearths [or sheepfolds],
listening to pipings for the flocks?
In the divisions of Reuben
great were the searchings of heart.
Gilead remained camped beyond the Jordan.

Judges 5:15-17

What difference does it make if the tribes that answered the call were village agriculturists, while Reuben and Gilead/Gad were herders? We have already analyzed the economic independence and self-reliance of the hill-country farmers. Can't the same be said of seminomadic pastoralists? The answer is no, as modern scholars have discovered (or perhaps I should say rediscovered).

The image of nomads and seminomads as self-sufficient, independent and solitary denizens of the desert or steppes is a mirage of 19th- and early 20th-century scholars that has now been thoroughly refuted. Nomads and pastoralists are not autarkic, that is, they are not economically self-sufficient. As Anatoly M. Khazanov noted in his magisterial synthesis *Nomads and the Outside World*, a "specialized pastoral economy, in contrast to the economy of many comparable forms of agriculture, itself cannot provide even all of the immediate requirements of nomads."[22] The limited division of labor within the pastoralist economy makes herders dependent on farmers and townspeople not only for many food products, but also for handicrafts and other items of material culture. Trade with an agriculture-based economy is essential for any type of nomadism, and pastoralists are in much greater need of it than agriculturists.[23]

Late 20th-century scholars are rediscovering what the great 14th-century Arab historian and sociologist Ibn Khaldûn understood very well. In his classic *Muqaddimah: An Introduction to History*, he observed:

> ...desert civilization is inferior to urban civilization, because not all the necessities of civilization are to be found among the people of the desert. They do have some agriculture at home but do not possess the materials that belong to it, most of which [depend on] crafts. They have ...milk, wool, [camel's] hair, and hides, which the urban population needs and pays the Bedouins money for. However, while [the Bedouins] need the cities for their necessities of life, the urban population needs [the Bedouins] for conveniences and luxuries.[24]

Accordingly, the pastoralist economy of Reuben and Gilead/Gad was inextricably intertwined with the economies of sedentary populations, leaving these two tribes far less independent than their fellow tribesmen in the hills, whose mixed economy of farming and herding made them more economically independent. The hill-country farmers had less to lose by going to battle than their pastoralist cousins.

Dan and Asher, which also failed to respond to the muster, did so for different reasons. According to the Song of Deborah, they were seafaring tribes. The verse about the Asherites, as we shall see, is clear cut and presents few problems. Not so the verse about the Danites. Traditionally, this verse has been translated: "And Dan, why did he abide [*yagur*] with the ships?" The word *yagur*, translated "abide," is related to the word *ger*, commonly translated "sojourner," "stranger," "resident alien" or the like. As W. Robertson Smith pointed out almost a century ago, *ger* has its origin in kinship terminology: "The *ger* was a man of another tribe or district who, coming to sojourn in a place where he was not strengthened by the presence of his own kin, put himself under the protection of a clan or a powerful chief."[25]

All scholars agree that the Danites never controlled the territory assigned to them in Joshua 19:40-48, which extended as far as Joppa on the Mediterranean coast. Ultimately, the Danites moved to the north, inland, where they conquered the Canaanite city of Laish and renamed it Dan.[26] But before they moved, the "Amorites pressed the Danites back into the hill country" (Judges 1:34, RSV). In this period, the Danites were *gerim*, a client tribe with no landed patrimony (*nakhalah*) of their own under the patronage of the possessors of the land. As we read in Judges 18:1: "In those days the tribe of Danites were seeking *nakhalah* [landed inheritance, tribal territory, patrimony] in which to settle, for to that day no *nakhalah* had fallen to them among the tribes of Israel."

In light of this background, I would translate the verse about Dan in the Song of Deborah as follows: "And Dan, why did he serve as a client on ships?" In this translation, *yagur* means "to serve as a client," as a *ger*, rather than the traditional meaning of *yagur*, "abide." By "client," I mean an economic dependent attached to a patron, a kind of economic ward.

If this translation is correct, then we may conclude that at least enough Danites had been hired or pressed into service by the shipowners or shipping companies on the coast in the Jaffa region to inspire this saying about them. We cannot be sure who their patrons were. If the saying dates to the period before the Sea Peoples settled on the coast, then the shipowners were probably Canaanites. If this description applies to some time after 1175 B.C.E., then the Danite patrons were one of the Sea Peoples, probably the Philistines. Whatever the exact date, however, there would seem to be little doubt that the Danites were "clients on ships," presumably while they still lived in the south.

As we know from Judges 1:31-32, Asher "dwelt among the Canaanites" in the Acco region on the Mediterranean coast. Nestled in the hills of western Galilee, in territory traditionally ascribed to Asher (Joshua 19:24-31), Rafi Frankel has recently located a number of small Iron I villages or hamlets, which he plausibly associates with the Asherites.[27] These villages in the hills overlook, and have easy access to, the rich maritime plain of Acco. From their territorial homeland, tribesmen from Asher may have commuted to work as agricultural laborers on Canaanite estates in the plain or as seamen and dock-workers at the port of Acco. Whatever the case, these new discoveries give vivid meaning to the saying in the Song of Deborah: "Asher remained at the seacoast and over its inlets dwelt" (Judges 5:17).

The reluctance of Dan and Asher to join the highlanders in the war against the Canaanites seems understandable in light of their economic dependence on non-Israelite groups in the maritime trade. Like Reuben and Gilead/Gad, Dan and Asher had ties to non-Israelites that proved stronger than those that bound them to the tribal confederation.

It is a tribute to the poet who composed the victory ode we call the Song of Deborah that he or she did not conceal the realities of the situation by portraying a united front against the enemy; still, the four tribes that did not answer the call were chided. Meroz, an enigmatic and otherwise unknown group, on the other hand, is cursed for failing to join the Israelites in battle:

> "Curse Meroz!" said the messenger of Yahweh,
> "Bitterly curse its inhabitants,
> Because they came not to the aid of Yahweh,
> To the aid of Yahweh against the warriors."
>
> Judges 5:23

Perhaps the poet recognized the economic predicament of the Israelite tribes that sat out the battle.[28]

Afterword

Seth Landa, of the Bronx, New York, offers alternatives to some parts of Stager's analysis and additional support for others:

Stager states that in the prose account (Judges 4) Barak musters his troops from the tribes of Naphtali and Zebulun only and that the other tribes mentioned in Judges 5 are omitted. Actually, the prose account only informs us which tribes Barak called to battle, not who actually participated. The text reads: "And Barak called Zebulun and Naphtali to Kadesh" (Judges 4:10). The Kingdom of Hazor was located in the midst of these two tribes. We know from Judges 1 that after the death of Joshua each tribe was responsible for conquering their own territory. Thus, Barak could not put out a general call to arms. He could only demand the participation of Naphtali and Zebulun, though he may have hoped for outside support. Perhaps this is why Deborah's poem merely chides the tribes who did not join the battle, rather than cursing them. Only two tribes were required to go to war. The others that volunteered were praised, but the ones that did not could not be too vigorously condemned.

Commenting upon the absence of Judah and Simeon from either account, Stager feels that these tribes were not yet a vital part of the tribal confederation. Yet they were allocated land by Joshua and appear on tribal lists before and after the time of Deborah. A more plausible explanation may be that these tribes bordered on another security threat, namely the Philistines, who already were involved in skirmishes with the Israelites (Judges 3:31). These two tribes could not send armies to the north without leaving their own populations at risk.

Gilead, which did not join in, may be identical with Gad because the land of Gilead was divided between Gad, Reuben and Manasseh. But Gad may, instead, refer to Gilead the son of Machir, both descendants of Manasseh. This would fit nicely with professor Stager's description of the social order of the Israelites being based along kinship lines. The tribe of Manasseh was divided, the clan of Machir joined in the battle, while the "sub-clan" of Gilead, the son of Machir, stayed behind.

Professor Stager interprets the verb *yaqur* (Judges 5:17) as a reference to the tribe of Dan serving as "clients on ships." He suggests that they served on the Mediterranean coast under the Canaanites or Philistines. An alternate explanation offered by the first-century B.C.E. biblical translator Jonathan ben Uzziel is that this verse refers to the part of the tribe of Dan that moved to the north and conquered the city of Laish. This would place them in the vicinity of the Jordan River, as well as near the kingdom of Hazor. Perhaps they were employed on ships operated by the Canaanite enemy sailing the Jordan and the Sea of Galilee. This would certainly explain Dan's reluctance to do battle with the Canaanites. ***BAR*** *15:3 (1989), p. 19*

PART III

Archaeology and the Bible

Archaeology and the Bible Introduction

As we have just seen, the historical conclusions of source critics often contradict traditional ideas about the sacred history of the Bible. Many people share the view of G. E. Wright in *God Who Acts* that "in biblical faith everything depends on whether the central events actually occurred."[1]

The first biblical archaeologists were motivated by the desire to validate the Bible through science; perhaps they hoped to counteract negative influences from other sources. Archaeologists also hoped unearthing material evidence would bring the Bible to life, much the way trips to the Holy Land had for generations of pilgrims and tourists. But they soon discovered that the road from artifact to biblical insight is not direct. Problems arose at every turn—disagreements about identifying sites, dating artifacts, interpreting finds.

First of all, correlating specific sites with specific biblical narratives depended on knowing the location of ancient cities. But in most cases, reliable information was scarce. Jerusalem and Hebron, Nazareth and Bethlehem, and geographic features like the Sea of Galilee and the Dead Sea were known to everyone. But after the failed Jewish uprising of the second century C.E., the Romans changed the names of many sites. Jerusalem became Aelia Capitolina; Shechem became Neapolis; even Judea was renamed Palaestina. Identifying biblical sites suddenly became difficult. Archaeologists had to begin at the beginning—by piecing together maps.

A few important sites, like the Church of the Nativity in Bethlehem and the Church of the Ascension in Jerusalem, were marked by shrines, but the locations of hundreds of other places mentioned in the Bible were lost. In 1838, when Edward Robinson, a New England Puritan, visited the Holy Land, biblical geography was in a sorry state. He believed many of the sites venerated by pilgrims at the time were tourist traps created by enterprising monks and merchants and that the true identities of ancient sites were probably preserved in the place names used by local peasants. Robinson theorized that even though the Romans had substituted Latin names for the ancient Hebrew ones the common people who spoke Aramaic or Arabic may have continued to use the familiar Semitic names. Thus, biblical Beth-Guvrin, which had been officially renamed Eleutheropolis, was identified with the place called Bet Jibrin in Arabic; Lod, renamed Diospolis, was preserved in the Arabic name Lydda; and Acco, called Ptolemais, was Acre. It is no exaggeration to say that Robinson's book *Biblical Researches in Palestine,*[2] published in 1841, filled in the map for generations of archaeologists, although, as Ziony Zevit notes, scholars are still arguing about the location of Ai and some other places mentioned in the Bible.

When scientists arrived to explore biblical sites, they often found that treasure hunters had gotten there first. When Napoleon invaded Egypt in 1798, he collected more than 100 statues and other artifacts—including the Rosetta Stone, the key to deciphering Egyptian hieroglyphics. When the British defeated Napoleon, the victors co-opted his collection for the British Museum in London. Ancient sites in Italy, Greece and the Near East were routinely dug up and dismantled by treasure hunters searching for exhibition-quality artifacts. By modern standards, we would say that important archaeological sites were looted, as William Flinders Petrie, the acknowledged founder of scientific archaeology in Palestine, argued. But Petrie was shocked that common objects like tools, pottery and weapons had been discarded by the looters as worthless; these were the very objects he considered the "key[s] to digging...the alphabet of work."

A common archaeological feature in the Near East is the tell, or mound, which rises above the surrounding plain. Tells are distinguishable from natural hills by flat summits—the sites of settlements—and smooth, even slopes that cover walls and other fortifications. Petrie theorized that when walls made of baked mudbrick, the main building material in this area, were destroyed by war, fire or earthquake, the bricks crumbled and, in a sense, returned to the earth. Over a long period of time, blowing soil and dust raised mounds that buried the remains of stone walls and buildings under thick layers of soil, on which new structures were built years later. Petrie tested his theory in 1890 when he was sent by the Palestine Exploration Fund to examine Umm Lakis, which was thought to be the biblical city of Lachish. Petrie soon realized that the site was a late Roman settlement and began looking in the same area for a more promising site. Several miles away he found Tel el-Hesi, which abuts the Wadi Hesi, a dry riverbed that is transformed into a torrential river by winter rains. Over the years, Wadi Hesi had washed away a sixty-foot-thick section on the east side of the mound. There, visible to the naked eye, from top to bottom, was the stratification Petrie had been looking for—city piled upon city.

Petrie's second insight was that he could date each stratum by the pottery. Because pottery was common and inexpensive, yet indispensable, it was constantly being produced and, therefore, reflected changes in style. The shapes of dishes, bowls, cups, jugs and lamps are remarkably similar in a given area at a given time. When fashions change, especially the shape of the rim or base, and the shape or placement of handles, the new style permeates the area as long as it is fashionable. Thus, it is possible to develop a typology of pottery—a systematic history of styles and shapes. Petrie believed that, by associating certain styles of pottery with certain strata at Tel el-Hesi, he could construct a sequence that he could apply to finds at other sites. Following his lead, archaeologists have done just that.

Some have even tried to correlate biblical history with pottery styles. For example, in the 12th and 11th centuries B.C.E. there was a decline in the quality of pottery. The clay contains large grits, shapes are not carefully finished, surfaces are duller and rougher. All of this suggests social upheaval. Painted vessels from 12th-century Ashdod show Mycenaean derivation, reinforcing the theory that the Philistines originated in the Aegean among the so-called Sea Peoples who invaded the Egyptian territories in the eastern Mediterranean. Blown glass tableware and jewelry show Roman influence in Judea and Galilee after the first century B.C.E.

The initial impetus of men like Edward Robinson and organizations like the Palestine Exploration Fund was to corroborate the biblical narrative scientifically. Because cities were destroyed every 50 years, on the average, it was fairly easy—and seductive—to associate the destruction levels at any number of sites with biblical events like the Israelite conquest of Canaan, and to date the Exodus accordingly. Later findings, however, frequently undercut these correlations, as happened at Ai.

Using new techniques in physics and chemistry, scientists can now establish the absolute age of artifacts and associated strata. Radiocarbon dating tracks the decay of radioactive carbon 14 in organic matter—wood, bone, leather, charcoal and plant derivatives like cloth, rope and ink. Carbon 14 is a minute component of the carbon dioxide absorbed by all living things, so measuring the amount of carbon 14 in a sample can establish to within 40 years the date a person died, an animal was slaughtered, a tree was felled or cotton was picked. Another process, thermoluminescence, although much less accurate than carbon 14 dating, can determine when pottery was fired. The alpha, beta and gamma particles that minerals absorb from the environment are destroyed by the high temperature of a pottery kiln; thermoluminescence in pottery, therefore, must have been absorbed from radiation in the environment after the piece was fired.

Using methods like these, archaeologists have become fairly confident in dating ancient finds. And many believe that the destruction levels at some sites, Jericho and Ai, for example, do not correspond to the likely dates of the Israelite entry into Canaan. In fact, little has been found that correlates directly with biblical events. The initial goal of corroborating the historical accuracy of the Bible has evolved into fleshing out the background of the Bible—the lifestyle, art, flora and fauna that shaped language and thought in the biblical world. Instead of looking for direct connections, scholars now debate how archaeology can help us understand poetic metaphors and obscure words.

An incense stand from 10th-century B.C.E. Ashdod is decorated with the images of musical instruments like the *nebel* and *kinnor* of the psalms. Carved ivory from Ahab's palace in Samaria shows that the *kerub*, or cherub, that spread its wings over the Holy Ark in Exodus 25:20 was very different from the chubby-baby angels of Italian Renaissance paintings. And archaeologists have also found clues to the identity of the *marzeaḥ* that Amos denounces.

More and more, biblical archaeologists have become intrigued with the details omitted from the Bible. Lachish, for example, is barely mentioned in the Bible but has become a major archaeological site. Despite his genius, Petrie was mistaken in identifying Tel el-Hesi as Lachish. The correct location was established as Tel el-Duweir, where letters sent to the military commander of Lachish were discovered in a room in the gate-tower. These letters describe the intrigue and low morale among the soldiers who were awaiting the attack of Nebuchadnezzar in 587 B.C.E.; they even describe a prophet who was "weakening the hands" of the people—similar to the accusations leveled against the prophet Jeremiah. These "letters from the front" add flesh and blood to the brief mention in Jeremiah 34 that "Lachish and Azekah alone remained of the fortified cities of Judah."

The same kind of thing happens with the stele of the Moabite king Mesha. Erected soon after the start of Mesha's revolt against his Israelite overlord, the stele glorifies Mesha's victories, which merit only one verse in 2 Kings: "When Ahab died, the king of Moab rebelled against the king of Israel." The remaining 22 verses of the biblical account describe the subsequent Israelite suppression of the revolt. The Moabite defeat does not appear on the Mesha Stele. Archaeologists have also developed in-depth pictures of cardboard villains in the Bible—the Philistines, the Edomites, even the Egyptians. We now know enough about the latter, in fact, to compare their religion and literature to those of the Hebrews.

The ability of archaeologists to fill in the blanks in the Bible means they must pay more attention to anthropology and sociology and less to theology and politics. Instead of pursuing an agenda determined by priests and kings and focusing on temples and palaces, biblical archaeologists have turned their attention to the aspects of daily life omitted in the Bible—what average people did day by day, what they wore, what they ate, how they worked, how they amused themselves. In fact, as Richard A. Batey shows, studies of this type at Sepphoris, in the Galilee near Nazareth, have changed our understanding of the milieu and ministry of Jesus.

Rather than trying to corroborate the Bible, archaeologists now argue that information about people, places and even ideas that may or may not have interested the writers of the Bible are valuable in and of themselves. If it is true that the winners get to write history and the Bible was written by winners, then archaeologists may uncover the secrets of the losers, people who have been silent for thousands of years, expanding our knowledge of the Bible in ways we have yet to imagine.

CHAPTER 5

Amos' Denunciation of the Marzeaḥ

Philip J. King

Biblical archaeology, says King, is "a biblical, not an archaeological, discipline. It is the responsibility of biblical scholars, not archaeologists, to ferret out pertinent material evidence and apply it to the Bible." This is precisely what King does by giving us a deeper understanding of the ritual known as marzeaḥ. *Since archaeologists, as well as historians, are no longer preoccupied with kings and battles, a fuller picture of the ancient world has emerged, one that includes economics, living standards and social structure–the very things that concerned prophets of morality like Amos. Thus, "few social institutions in antiquity have been so illuminated by archaeology as the* marzeaḥ."

Troubled by social injustice and the abuse of wealth, Amos denounced the excesses of the ruling class, including the revelry of the marzeaḥ, *which included five elements: relaxing, eating, singing, drinking and anointing with oil. We have a better idea of all of these from finds in Samaria, where Amos preached, and the surrounding countries, dating from before and after that time. Elaborate ivory carvings illustrate the "beds of ivory" that epitomize ostentatiousness of the wealthy and exploitation of the poor–"not only self-indulgence, but also pagan immorality and flagrant injustice." Fatted calves, which appear also in the stories of the prodigal son (Luke 15:23-27) and the witch of Endor (1 Samuel 28:24), exemplified profligate feasting. Wine bowls instead of cups indicated inordinate drinking and, perhaps, the sacrilegious use of sacred vessels. The Bible, King concludes, "gives only sketchy descriptions of articles of everyday life." This is one area where archaeologists can fill in the details.–Ed.*

Archaeologists often accuse biblical scholars of ignoring archaeological evidence that could significantly illuminate biblical texts. As one archaeologist recently said, "Most [biblical] commentators do not even make use of archaeology where it can contribute best, namely in illustrating the material

THE SPHINX on this fragment of an openwork ivory plaque strides through a thicket of lotus blossoms. A mythological creature with a human head on a lion's body, the sphinx is an Egyptian motif adopted by the Phoenicians. Sometimes the sphinx has wings, as in this example dated to the ninth or eighth century B.C.E. This sphinx also wears a flattened double crown of Egypt, a curled wig, and a "Phoenician apron." The animal's rib cage and musculature appear in detail despite the diminutive size of the ivory—just over 3 inches high. Although this fragment was found in Samaria, the sphinx resembles several pieces from Nimrud. Ivory, a luxury in the ancient Near East, is condemned by the prophet Amos in his indictment of the *marzeaḥ* (Amos 6:4-7). *Photo: Israel Museum*

culture of a given period, either in general or in terms of a specific reference in the [biblical] text."[1] For the most part, archaeology remains the great untapped resource in biblical studies, despite the fact that the Bible and archaeology are closely related.

As readers of *Biblical Archaeology Review* know, there is a great deal of disagreement concerning the term "biblical archaeology."[2] I still find Albright's[3] definition satisfactory. Biblical archaeology, he said, "is the systematic analysis or synthesis of any phase of biblical scholarship which can be clarified by archaeological discovery."[4] Biblical archaeology is, therefore, a biblical, not an archaeological, discipline. It is the responsibility of biblical scholars, not archaeologists, to ferret out pertinent material evidence and apply it to the Bible. There is a crying need for synthesizing works that bring archaeological data to bear on the biblical text.

Correlating archaeological data with the biblical record is not as easy as it sounds, however. The process is complicated because artifacts may be mute and ambiguous, and the biblical text may be tendentious or even unintelligible. Nevertheless, archaeological evidence can enhance understanding of the biblical text by confirming, correcting or supplementing it. The biblical text itself, of course, must be analyzed by literary criticism, form criticism and tradition criticism.

In recent years, archaeologists have adopted increasingly sophisticated research methods, often borrowed from the natural and social sciences (anthropology in particular), making it possible to go far beyond their preoccupation with political history. No longer are archaeologists concerned exclusively with kings, wars and conquests; they have turned their attention to social history as well. They have become absorbed with daily life in ancient Israel, including religion, politics, economics, trade, living standards and social structures.

I would like to illustrate how developments in archaeology can help us understand a biblical text by taking an example from the book of Amos, an eighth-century B.C.E. prophet who was a herdsman and a dresser of sycamore trees. Although he came from the village of Tekoa, south of Jerusalem, he preached in the northern kingdom of Israel, where he was associated with the capital city of Samaria and the royal sanctuary at Bethel. Acknowledging the universal sovereignty of Israel's God, Amos was vitally aware of political events in bordering nations, as well as in Israel. Active during the peaceful and prosperous reigns of King Uzziah of Judah (783-742 B.C.E.) and King Jeroboam II of Israel (786-746 B.C.E.), Amos' prophetic ministry lasted only a short time. He was a rugged outdoorsman who preached the severity of divine judgment. Influenced by the Mosaic covenant that was based on responsibility rather than privilege, Amos was deeply disturbed by the rampant social injustices of his time, especially among the venal upper classes. Wealth had created a social imbalance resulting in two distinct classes, the rich and the poor.[5]

> Woe to those who lie upon *beds of ivory*, and stretch themselves upon their couches, and eat lambs from the flock, and *calves from the midst of the stall*; who sing idle songs to the sound of the harp, and like David invent for themselves instruments of music;[6] *who drink wine in bowls*, and anoint themselves with *the finest oils*, but are not grieved over the ruin of Joseph! Therefore they shall now be the first of those to go into exile, and the revelry [*marzeaḥ*] of those who stretch themselves shall pass away.
>
> Amos 6:4-7, RSV

This passage foretelling the doom of the northern kingdom of Israel and its luxury-loving society in the eighth century B.C.E. is one of Amos' most famous sermons. The object of his indictment is the *marzeaḥ* (pronounced mar-zay-ach), often translated as "revelry" (as here) or "banquet."

Not many social institutions in antiquity have been as well documented by archaeologists as the *marzeaḥ*, although many aspects of it are still obscure and are the subject of scholarly debate.[7] One thing, however, we know for sure. The *marzeaḥ* had a long history, extending at least from the 14th century B.C.E. through the Roman period. In the 14th century B.C.E., it was prominently associated with the ancient Canaanite city of Ugarit (modern Ras Shamra), on the coast of Syria, as we know from cuneiform tablets found there. It was also popular at Palmyra, on the northern edge of the Syrian Desert, about 120 miles northeast of Damascus, in the Roman period (the first to the third centuries C.E.).

The *marzeaḥ* was a pagan ritual that took the form of a social and religious association. The term may denote the group of people who participated in the rite or the building where the rite took place. The occasion for the meeting could be joyful or sorrowful; sometimes the *marzeaḥ* was the setting for mourning rites that included eating and drinking. Whether ritual banquets or memorial meals, these feasts lasted for several days and were accompanied by excessive drinking. Wealth and affluence were apparently prerequisites for participation in the *marzeaḥ*. At Palmyra the *marzeaḥ* took the form of a funerary cult that fits Amos' description.

The purpose of the funerary aspect of the *marzeaḥ* was to console mourners. By sharing food and drink with them, the participants in the *marzeaḥ* provided solace and comfort. Some scholars regard the funerary *marzeaḥ* as a feast for–and with–deceased ancestors (or *Rephaim*, a proper name in the Bible for the inhabitants of Sheol, the underworld.)

The passage from Amos that I have quoted is clearly a description of a *marzeaḥ*, although many commentators have failed to identify it. Whether or not it is a funerary *marzeaḥ*, overindulgence is clearly indicated. The only other biblical reference to a *marzeaḥ* occurs in the Book of Jeremiah, where the prophet clearly describes a funerary *marzeaḥ*:

> For thus says the Lord: "Do not enter the house of mourning [*beth marzeaḥ*], or go to lament, or bemoan them....No one shall break bread for the mourner, to comfort him for the dead; nor shall anyone give him the cup of consolation to drink for his father or his mother. You shall not go into the house of feasting to sit with them, to eat and drink."
>
> Jeremiah 16:5,7-8

Although the term *marzeaḥ* is not used in Numbers 25, we learn that the Israelites had gone whoring with Moabite women and offered sacrifices to their god Baal of Peor. The Israelites ate of the sacrifices and worshiped Baal. Other goings-on in this pagan ritual, which could very well be a *marzeaḥ*, are suggested by the rage of the priest Phinehas:

> When Phinehas the son of Eleazar, son of Aaron the priest, saw it, he rose and left the congregation, and took a spear in his hand and went after the man of Israel *into the inner room*, and pierced both of them, the man of Israel and the woman, through her body.
>
> Numbers 25:7-8

In denouncing participants in the *marzeaḥ*, Amos lists five components of this revelry following the traditional order of ancient banquets, known from other sources, such as those at Palmyra referred to earlier. The five elements are: (1) reclining or relaxing; (2) eating a meat meal; (3) singing or other musical accompaniment; (4) drinking wine; and (5) anointing oneself with oil.

The first element of the *marzeaḥ* that Amos refers to is "beds of ivory." Before that, he mentioned ivory in his description of the ostentation of the residents of Samaria, who lived in "ivory houses" (Amos 3:15), that is, homes decorated with costly ivory inlays. To the prophets, Samaria, the capital of the northern kingdom of Israel in the eighth century B.C.E., with its "ivory houses," symbolized not only self-indulgence, but also pagan immorality and flagrant injustice. Amos contends that exploitation of the poor made such luxury possible.

As a luxury item, ivory has a long and fascinating history in the Near East.[8] The principal source of commercial ivory was the elephant, the two main species being the African and the Asian (sometimes incorrectly identified as the Indian) elephant. Weighing as much as six tons, the African elephant is the larger of the two, with tusks averaging six feet in length; a pair of tusks may weigh as much as 100 pounds. The Asian elephant is smaller, and only the males have tusks, which average five feet in length, with a pair weighing about ten pounds. A subspecies of the Asian elephant is the Syrian elephant, which became extinct after the eighth century B.C.E. However, the Syrian elephant may have been the principal source of ivory for the Phoenicians and Syrians, who supplied the Canaanites and Israelites.

There are many references to elephants in ancient texts but none in the Bible. Assyrian and Egyptian sources of the 15th century B.C.E. mention elephant hunts in North Syria. Pharaoh Thutmose III (1490-1436 B.C.E.) described a hunt in which 120 elephants were killed for their ivory. The famous Black Obelisk of the Assyrian monarch Shalmaneser III (859-825 B.C.E.) bears a classic depiction of an Asiatic elephant.

According to an Assyrian record, King Hezekiah of Judah (715-687 B.C.E.) sent ivory as tribute to Sennacherib of Assyria when Sennacherib invaded Judah and besieged Jerusalem in 701 B.C.E. Listed among Hezekiah's items of tribute are inlaid ivory couches, ivory armchairs and elephant hides and tusks. The gradual disappearance of elephants in the ancient Near East was the result of extensive cultivation of elephant habitats and the slaughter of elephants to satisfy the growing demand for ivory.

There were at least two, perhaps three, schools of ivory carving in biblical times. One was in North Syria, another was in Phoenicia and a third, perhaps,

THIS IVORY BED, which was found in a royal tomb at Salamis, Cyprus, dates to Amos' lifetime, the eighth century B.C.E. Beds or couches decorated with ivory inlays were used by participants in the *marzeaḥ*. *Photo: Cyprus Department of Antiquities*

was in South Syria. Thousands of ivories have been found at Nimrud in northern Assyria (present day Iraq). These ivories were carved in North Syrian style, which reflects a Canaanite-Mycenaean tradition. Scholars speculate that either they were brought to Nimrud as booty or the artisans who made them were taken to Assyria as part of the transfer of populations.

Unlike the ivories found at Nimrud, the motifs decorating Phoenician ivories are clearly of Egyptian inspiration. Here, Egyptian traditions of art and mythological symbolism have been adapted to Canaanite-Phoenician themes. The ivories found in ancient Israel were crafted by Phoenicians. The distinctions between the Syrian and Phoenician styles have been summarized as follows:

> Syrian-style ivories may be characterized by a greater sense of action, by squatter, more powerful proportions, and by more highly charged compositions, compared with the more quiescent, elegant, and slender figures harmoniously disposed in space, of the contemporary Phoenician style.[9]

In ancient Israel, the most significant collections of ivories have been recovered at Megiddo and Samaria. At Megiddo, more than 300 ivory fragments, dating from the beginning of the Iron Age (12th century B.C.E.), were found in the palace treasury room. Samaria yielded more than 500 ivory fragments, which are more pertinent to the passage from Amos because they date to the ninth or eighth century B.C.E. (probably the latter). From the Egyptian motifs decorating these ivories, which suggest that the style originated in Phoenicia, we can infer that they came from Phoenicia. Egyptian symbolism on the Samaria ivories includes various deities, such as Horus, Ra, Heh, Isis, Nephthys and Osiris. Many Egyptian motifs were adapted by the Phoenicians, who were the conduits of most things Egyptian in the region.

The pagan symbolism adorning the Samaria ivories may have angered Amos as much as the luxury and affluence the ivories reflected. In his description of the *marzeaḥ*, he gives prominence to beds of ivory, couches decorated with ivory inlays on which guests sprawled during the festivities. In fact, an ivory bed from the eighth century B.C.E. was uncovered in the cemetery at Salamis in Cyprus,[10] a vivid illustration of the "beds of ivory" Amos abhorred.

ON THIS FRAGMENT OF A PHOENICIAN IVORY from Samaria, a line of stylized palm trees with alternating pairs of lotus blossoms and buds beside each tree is carved in high relief. Although this piece dates to the ninth or eighth century B.C.E., the sacred tree was a mythological motif as far back as the third millennium B.C.E. ***Photo: Erich Lessing/Courtesy of the Israel Antiquities Authority***

The next element in the *marzeaḥ* passage is "calves from the midst of the stall," which were slaughtered for their choice meat. This phrase refers to stall-fattened, tender calves. The Hebrew word for "stall" (*marbeq*) designates an enclosure where animals were fattened. A recent study of tripartite public buildings at Megiddo, Beer-Sheva, Hazor and elsewhere has shown that they were constructed as stables, specifically for housing and conditioning war horses.[11] John S. Holladay, the author of the study, believes horses were kept in stables rather than open enclosures in the ancient Near East. Building on Holladay's study of public stables, Lawrence E. Stager has convincingly argued that domestic stables were also located within, not separate from, domestic dwellings,[12] which had central rooms and side rooms with ceilings supported by pillars. Troughs for feeding the animals were constructed between the pillars. In short, the ground-floor side rooms were used as domestic stables.

This background is helpful for understanding several biblical references to "calves from the midst of the stall," or fatted calves. When King Saul consulted the witch of Endor, for example, she served him a meal consisting of a stall-fed calf that she had "in the house" (1 Samuel 28:24). The "prodigal son" was served the same delicacy when he returned to his father's house (Luke 15:23-27). To Amos, eating

MAᶜADANAH'S SEAL. This seventh-century B.C.E. seal made of brown jasper, called Maᶜadanah's seal, measures only one-half by three-eighths by one-quarter inch and is engraved with a lyre and a two-line inscription in ancient Hebrew script written as a mirror-image so that the impression in clay could be read correctly. The inscription reads: "(Belonging) to Maᶜadanah, the king's daughter." The previously unknown name derives from a Hebrew root meaning "delight." The lyre in this engraving is the asymmetrical type, the *kinnor*, which is characterized by vertical arms of unequal length. Twelve strings attach to the crossbar. The sound box at the bottom is decorated with a string of pearls along the outer edge and a rosette in the center.
Photo: Israel Museum

"calves from the midst of the stall" was an example of profligate feasting by affluent residents of Samaria.

Turning to Amos' reference to "the sound of the harp," we know that music played a vital role in the lives of ancient peoples. Archaeological finds have taught us a great deal about the instruments they used.[13] Only two stringed instruments, the *nebel* and the *kinnor*, are mentioned in the Bible. Frequently they are named together. Both are lyres. The *nebel* was a larger and, perhaps, more solemn instrument, intended for liturgical use. The *kinnor*, unlike the *nebel*, was asymmetrical. Both had a body, two arms and a yoke (or crossbar), but the arms of a *kinnor* were of unequal length. Used for both sacred and secular purposes, the *kinnor* was the instrument used by David and the Levites.

In his description of the *marzeaḥ* Amos uses the word *nebel*, the larger of the two instruments, which was ordinarily reserved for religious functions. In the Revised Standard Version, which I have quoted above, *nebel* is translated as "harp," but this is probably inaccurate. The basic distinction between a lyre and a harp is that a harp has no yoke (crossbar). To date, not a single harp has been recovered from Syria-Palestine, so "lyre" is a preferable translation.

A beautifully crafted seal, dating from the seventh century B.C.E., bears the tantalizing Hebrew inscription: "[Belonging] to Maʿadanah, the king's daughter." This is the first occurrence in the history of Israel of the name Maʿadanah, which is derived from a Hebrew root meaning "delight"; she is not further identified, nor is her father, the king. What makes this tiny scaraboid (beetle-shaped) seal of brown jasper especially memorable is the delicate *kinnor* that decorates it. The lyre is asymmetrical, consisting of a sound box, two unequal arms and 12 strings attached to a yoke. A string of pearls adorns the outer edge of the sound box, which has a rosette in the center. The king's daughter may have chosen the lyre as her emblem because she played this instrument.

A poignant representation of three lyre players also appears on an Assyrian relief from Nineveh commemorating Sennacherib's conquest of the Judahite city of Lachish in 701 B.C.E. The Judahite prisoners of war are depicted playing lyres on their way to Assyrian captivity under the watchful eye of an Assyrian soldier armed with a club and a bow.

With this background information, we can imagine the celebrants at the *marzeaḥ*, whom Amos describes as singing with lyre (*nebel*) accompaniment, the lyre normally used for religious functions.

Excessive consumption of wine is the fourth element of the *marzeaḥ*. The celebrants drink "wine in bowls." The Hebrew word *mizraq*, used here for a wine bowl, is unusual. The root, *zrq*, means "to throw" or "to sprinkle" (dust, ashes, water or blood). In the ceremony of covenant ratification at Sinai, "Moses took half of the blood and put it in basins, and half of the blood he threw [*zrq*] against the altar" (Exodus 24:6). A *mizraq* is a dish or basin used for sprinkling (so it must have had a wide mouth), which is frequently mentioned in the Bible in cultic contexts. For example, in the description of the altar used for burnt offerings, we are told: "You shall make pots for it [the altar of burnt offering] to receive its ashes, and shovels and basins [*mizraq*] and forks and firepans; all its utensils you shall make of bronze" (Exodus 27:3).

Amos may have referred to sacred vessels used at the *marzeaḥ* to underscore the sacrilegious nature of the event. At the same time, he may have wanted to emphasize the unusually large capacity of these bowls as a way of condemning the inordinate drinking, which was an integral part of the *marzeaḥ*. Bowls that archaeologists classify as *mizraq* are sometimes as much as 18 inches in diameter.

A fluted bronze bowl (*phiale*) with a Phoenician dedicatory inscription may cast light on the drinking containers used in the *marzeaḥ*. This bronze bowl was found in modern Lebanon, according to the dealer through whom it was purchased. Stylistic elements suggest it dates from the fourth century

B.C.E. The bowl measures seven inches in diameter and is typical of the shallow, handle-less bowls depicted in libation scenes. Assyrian prototypes of this bowl are known from Amos' time, when Israel was under Assyrian rule. The most important feature of this bronze *phiale* is the inscription, which reads: "We offer two cups to the *marzeaḥ* of Shamash," the sun god of the Semitic pantheon, another clue to the nature of the *marzeaḥ* as well as to the kind of drinking vessels used in the ritual.[14]

The final element we shall examine in the quotation from Amos is the reference to anointing with "the finest oils." Mentioned more than 200 times in the Bible, olive oil was both a necessity of life and a gift from God. Second in importance only to wine, oil production was a major industry in ancient Israel, and olive oil was exported to Egypt and Mesopotamia, where olives were not cultivated. Alluding to the prosperity of the oil merchants, Hosea tells us: "They make a bargain with Assyria, and oil is carried to Egypt" (Hosea 12:1).

The many stone olive presses found recently in surveys and excavations in modern Israel, at such sites as Tel Miqne (Ekron), Tel Batash (Timnah) and Tel Dan (Dan), add substantially to the large number of olive presses previously known. In biblical times, olive oil was used to prepare food, to soften the skin, to fuel lamps, to treat illnesses and to prepare cosmetics. Olive oil was also used in sacrificial rites.

Olive trees, which are still plentiful in the Mediterranean region, can survive for a thousand years. The principal predator of the olive tree is the locust. "The locust devoured your fig trees and your olive trees" (Amos 4:9).

Two separate processes are involved in the extraction of olive oil—crushing and pressing. Crushing consists of grinding the olives into a soft paste by rolling a large stone (the crushing stone, or *memel*) over the olives spread on a flat surface of rock or on the floor of a shallow basin (*yam*). Alternatively, olives can be crushed by treading or trampling, as mentioned in Micah 6:15.

To extract the oil, the pulp must then be pressed; this is done by placing the crushed olives in woven baskets (*aqalim*) with holes in the bottom. The baskets are placed on the pressing surface, and pressure is exerted on the olives by a long beam weighted with stones and secured in a wall-niche behind the press. The olive oil flows through the basket openings into a rock groove leading to a central vat or bowl. Presses like these were used throughout Iron Age II (1000-586 B.C.E.).

More than 100 oil presses were recently found at Tel Miqne, identified with the Philistine city of Ekron, near the Mediterranean coast of Israel, which must have been an important olive oil production center in the seventh century B.C.E. Most of the presses recovered at Tel Miqne were equipped with larger-than-usual pressing surfaces and central collecting basins and could produce more than twice as much oil as simpler, smaller presses.

The initial crushing, which is done in a vat prior to the pressing process, yields the finest quality oil, called pre-pressed or virgin oil. As Lawrence E. Stager explains, the "finest oil" was used in the *marzeaḥ*.[15] Inscribed potsherds called ostraca, which were found in Samaria and which date to the eighth century B.C.E., often mention *shemen raḥuṣ*, literally "washed oil," which refers to a technique for extracting the finest oil by pouring water over the crushed olives to "wash" off the oil. When the mixture of oil and water was stirred, the oil floated to the surface and was skimmed off by hand. This virgin oil, or in the words of Amos, "the finest oil," was the oil with which the dissolute celebrants at the *marzeaḥ* anointed themselves.

Amos, the great prophet of social justice, targeted three aspects of daily life as egregious violations of covenant responsibility–injustice in the courts, excessive luxury among the upper classes and insincere worship in the sanctuary. The poor were denied their rights in court, and the affluence of the rich was the direct result of exploitation of the poor. Worship had become more form than substance, and consequently, conduct in the marketplace was unaffected by worship. Amos spoke from the conviction that social justice is an integral part of the Mosaic covenant, which regulates relations not only between God and man, but also between man and man. Amos went so far as to say that the "day of the Lord," a day of reward and vindication, would be, instead, a day of destruction. Although the hour was late, Amos preached, there was still time for repentance, *teshubah*.

In the biblical text, everyday life is described sketchily, if at all. Archaeological evidence can fill in some of the gaps and provide insights into the religious, social and economic life of the biblical world. We have focused here on a few details, but a more comprehensive study would yield information about the development of agricultural practices and trade and industry related to pottery, wine and metalworking, as well as oil production, all of which contributed to the creation of the pyramidal social structure in Israel the prophets inveighed against so vehemently.

CHAPTER 6

Sepphoris
An Urban Portrait of Jesus

Richard A. Batey

The traditional image of Jesus is of a rural preacher from an isolated village in the outback. But archaeological evidence now shows that Jesus lived only an hour's walk from Sepphoris, a major Greco-Roman metropolis of 30,000 inhabitants with a cosmopolitan culture and government installations. A radical revision of Jesus is necessary.

According to Batey, "Sepphoris must occupy a central position in the scholarly effort to recover the world of Jesus." Galilean culture was more urban and sophisticated than we previously imagined, and because Jesus lived close to the capital of the Galilee, he would have known firsthand about the administration of the government and the life-style of the rich and powerful. Gospel accounts of his dealings with tax collectors, bureaucrats and soldiers must be reinterpreted in this light. So too, the metaphors and imagery in Jesus' speeches must be reevaluated, especially the parables that feature kings.

Jesus may also have attended the theater in Sepphoris or seen actors performing in the streets. If so, his frequent use of the word hypocrite *may have been meant literally, in the original Greek sense of "actor." And Jesus may have spoken Greek as well as Aramaic and had a surprisingly extensive education.–Ed.*

"A city set on a hill cannot be hid" (Matthew 5:14). Words spoken by Jesus almost 2,000 years ago sprang to mind as I stood on a ridge at the edge of modern Nazareth. The hill, three miles north and seven hundred feet below me, was the site of ancient Sepphoris, a beautiful Greco-Roman metropolis, adorned with colonnaded streets, a forum, an imposing theater, a palace and resplendent villas of white limestone and colored marble, set amid the forested hills and fertile valleys of northern Israel. In the decades following the birth of Jesus, Sepphoris was the chief city and capital of Galilee.

My view from Nazareth, one that Jesus could have seen, was described by Professor Leroy Waterman of the University of Michigan, who excavated at Sepphoris in 1931:

> Across the rolling uplands to the north the peak of snowy Hermon hangs like a fleecy cloud above the horizon; to the west, the blue Mediterranean shimmers under the afternoon sun like a vast molten mirror, while halfway between, in full view and only an hour's walk from Nazareth, lies the site of the city that at the beginning of the first Christian century reared its brilliant acropolis, Sepphoris, "the ornament of all Galilee," its capital and its largest and most ornate city, and at that time second only to Jerusalem in importance in all Palestine.[1]

Archaeological excavations at Sepphoris continue to yield evidence of a sophisticated urban culture that places Jesus in a radically different environment from the one we supposed, an environment that challenges traditional assumptions about Jesus' life and ministry. The popular picture of Jesus as a rustic who grew up in the relative isolation of a small village of 400 people in the remote hills of Galilee must be integrated with the newly revealed setting of a burgeoning Greco-Roman metropolis boasting upwards of 30,000 inhabitants–Jews, Arabs, Greeks and Romans. Sepphoris–powerful, prosperous, peace-loving–was linked with other Greco-Roman centers on the trade routes of the Greek-speaking East.

Herod Antipas, son of Herod the Great and the ruler who beheaded John the Baptist (Matthew 14:10; Mark 6:16; Luke 9:9), rebuilt Sepphoris in 4 B.C.E. after the death of his father. For almost three decades after Jesus' birth, Sepphoris was the capital of Galilee and Perea, a large territory east of the Jordan River. The proximity of Sepphoris to its satellite village, Nazareth, made contact between Nazareth and this influential urban center convenient and natural.

After the death of Herod the Great, riots and rebellions flared up in several places throughout his kingdom. Sepphoris was the center of uprisings in Galilee. There, a rebel leader named Judas the son of Ezekias attacked Herod's arsenal and armed his men with the weapons stored there. The people of Sepphoris were unwilling–or perhaps unable–to stop him. Judas' rash action prompted the Roman legate of Syria, Quintilius Varus, to order his legions to crush the rebels in Galilee. The Roman army, commanded by Varus' son and Gaius, a friend of Varus, was supported by infantry and cavalry sent by Aretas, the Nabatean king of Arabia. This combined force attacked Sepphoris, captured and burned the city and sold the inhabitants into slavery.[2]

When Antipas returned to Galilee from Rome in the spring of 3 B.C.E., he selected the smoldering ruins of Sepphoris for the location of his new capital. Centrally situated in Galilee, Sepphoris already had a long and impressive history as a seat of government. Antipas launched a vast construction project that lasted throughout the lifetime of Jesus, who was born about 6 B.C.E. Sepphoris became the nerve center for government control of Galilee and

Perea. Political policy, military strategy, economic regulations and cultural affairs were administered from this seat of power, and influences from Sepphoris affected the people living in Nazareth as well as other satellite villages. Josephus tells us that Sepphoris was the largest and most beautiful city in the region.[3]

We may envision Antipas riding up to the crest of the Sepphoris hill escorted by his elite horse guard. Accompanying him are architects, engineers and city planners like the ones who had recently built Caesarea Maritima, Sebaste, the Jerusalem Temple and Herod's palaces in Jerusalem and Jericho. They pause among the ashes and broken walls on the summit to survey the landscape. To the north, the broad, rich Bet Netofa Valley is green from the spring rains. The valley stretches from the Mediterranean Sea east toward the Jordan Rift and the Sea of Galilee. Verdant forests cover the surrounding hills. Mount Carmel, 18 miles to the west, juts into the Mediterranean. A high ridge three miles to the south hides the village of Nazareth nestled around its pleasant spring from view.

The city plan, laid out on the Roman grid pattern adjusted to the contours of the land, has all the elements of a splendid Roman provincial capital—a main east-west street (the Cardo) leading to the forum, Antipas' royal residence with an imposing tower and a breathtaking panoramic view, a 4,000-seat theater, baths, archives, a gymnasium, a basilica, waterworks and other buildings. The new capital was named Autocratoris, the Greek translation of the Latin *imperator*, a title given to Augustus meaning "commander-in-chief."[4]

In 1989, I made an inspection tour of the Sepphoris acropolis with James F. Strange, the veteran archaeologist with whom I have worked since 1980 to initiate and carry out the excavation of the ancient city. All around us rose the purposeful sounds of archaeologists in action. What a contrast to the silent, abandoned acropolis overgrown with thistles and cacti that my wife, Carolyn, and I had first scouted in the summer of 1979. At that time, the trenches left by Waterman's 1931 excavation had eroded, and the walls had collapsed. Around the summit, young pine trees planted by the Jewish National Fund were taking root among the scattered stones of the Arab village, Saffuriyye, which was bulldozed in the aftermath of the 1948 war. The lone structure left standing was the Roman-Crusader fortified tower, which had been used as the village schoolhouse.

In 1983 Jim Strange directed the first University of South Florida Excavations at Sepphoris, while I worked as the administrative director. Since then, we have returned year after year, digging squares down through the Arab remains, through the Byzantine occupation layers, down to the neatly cut Herodian-style ashlars of the Roman city and even older levels below. The team has always kept scrupulous records of the stratigraphy as we sliced down through the layer cake of history, recording every coin and style of potsherd for computer analysis of density, distribution and dating. No shortcuts. No treasure hunting. A solid, unassailable scientific record.

Aerial cameras revealed walls and aqueducts; ground-penetrating radar scanned a labyrinth of tunnels, cisterns, grain silos, wine cellars and storage chambers carved into solid rock far below the debris of centuries. Special studies brought to light the formidable water supply system, the source of clay for Sepphoris pottery and the diet of the ancient population.

"Here was the east gate, leading toward Tiberias and Nazareth," Jim said. He was wearing his old sweat-stained leather hat and his flip-down sunglasses that protected his kind gaze from the harsh glare of the sun. His full beard, streaked with gray, could not hide the warm, disarming smile that had encouraged many volunteers to work happily to the point of near exhaustion. "The wall surrounding the acropolis ran in this direction," he added, gesturing with an outstretched arm.

Walking in the direction of the afternoon sun, he pointed out the main features of the city. "The colonnaded main street, bordered by shops and public buildings, ran west to intersect the major north-south thoroughfare." On the north face of the acropolis, beyond the forum, stood the excavated remains of the magnificent 4,000-seat theater built by Herod Antipas early in the first century.

Jim continued to map out the ancient *polis* with its markets, pools, fountains, public baths, ritual baths (*mikva'ot*), residential district and even the probable location of the royal palace of Antipas, which surely was modeled after his father's grandiose winter palace near Jericho.[5] The fragmentary remains of mosaics, wide plaster ceiling moldings, frescoed walls, several varieties of imported marble, as well as artistically crafted white building stones all attest to the opulence of this once thriving city.

Sepphoris must occupy a central position in the scholarly effort to recover the world of Jesus in Galilee. That is why it has captured the attention of leading New Testament scholars. In 1983, I was invited to present a slide lecture on Sepphoris at a plenary session of the annual meeting of the Studiorum Novi Testamenti Societas, the prestigious international society. The lecture was warmly received, and a number of enthusiastic colleagues encouraged me to continue the excavations.

In 1985, the National Geographic Society loaned us a ground-penetrating radar to facilitate our excavations. The radar proved to be reliable for predicting subsurface features prior to excavation. At one time, Sepphoris occupied approximately 500 acres, and the radar helped to focus our digging on promising areas.[6]

Another team, the Joint Sepphoris Project directed by Ehud Netzer of Hebrew University and Eric and Carol Meyers of Duke University, also began to excavate at the site in 1985. Since then, the two teams have worked side by side, accelerating the recovery of this historical city. The significance of Sepphoris–a city vitally important to both Jews and Christians–is becoming increasingly evident with every spade of dirt.

In short, Jesus lived in a Galilean culture much more urban and sophisticated than we had previously believed. To acknowledge this is to see the man and his ministry from a radically different point of view. Jesus in the Gospels was acquainted with the policies of kings, government, tax collectors, wealthy landlords and poor peasants, as well as with actors from the theater. All these characters assume significant new roles on the stage of an urban and cosmopolitan Galilee.

A ten-minute walk from the Nazareth spring to the top of the ridge north of the village provides a magnificent vista of the broad, fertile Bet Netofa Valley 1,000 feet below. The hill of Sepphoris, three miles north, rises almost 400 feet from the valley floor. The construction of an influential Roman capital city so near Jesus' home in Nazareth redefines the carpenter's occupation in central Galilee. To erect Herod Antipas' new capital, many skilled workers from surrounding towns and villages came to Sepphoris. Artisans from Nazareth would surely have been among them.

Joseph and Jesus must have known about the construction of the new capital and been acquainted with artisans and other workers employed on the site. Several years ago, Shirley Jackson Case, professor of New Testament at the University of Chicago, made a fascinating observation based on her reading of Josephus:

> Very likely "carpenter" as applied to Jesus meant not simply a worker in wood but one who labored at the building trade in general, and it requires no very daring flight of the imagination to picture the youthful Jesus seeking and finding employment in the neighboring city of Sepphoris. But whether or not he actually labored there, his presence in the city on various occasions can scarcely be doubted; and the fact of such contacts during the formative years of his young manhood may account for attitudes and opinions that show themselves conspicuously during his public ministry.[7]

Sepphoris provides a significant new perspective for understanding the world in which Jesus lived and worked, both as a carpenter and as a religious teacher. The construction of Herod Antipas' Sepphoris, viewed from the ridge above Nazareth, is reminiscent of a scene from Virgil's epic poem, the *Aeneid*—a passage that Antipas had probably read during his studies in Rome. In that passage, Aeneas, the legendary founder of Rome, and his companion climb to the brow of a hill overlooking the building of the city of Carthage. Located on the North African coast near present-day Tunis, Carthage had rivaled Rome's expansion in the Mediterranean. It is interesting that the Phoenician city of Tyre, less than 40 miles north of Sepphoris, had founded Carthage as an important colony for their trading empire. Virgil compares the scene of Carthage under construction to a beehive. "Even as bees in early summer, amid flowery fields, ply their task in sunshine." Virgil describes the vast building project at Carthage and points out the major urban installations and facilities:

> And now they were climbing the hill that looms large over the city and looks down on the confronting towers. Aeneas marvels at the massive buildings, mere huts once; marvels at the gates, the din and paved high-roads. Eagerly the Tyrians press on, some to build walls, to rear the citadel, and roll up stones by hand; some to choose the site for a dwelling and enclose it with a furrow. Laws and magistrates they ordain, and a holy senate. Here some are digging harbours, here others lay the deep foundations of their theatre and hew out of the cliffs vast columns, lofty adornments for the stage to be![8]

There is no record of Jesus visiting Sepphoris in the Gospels, which give only fragmentary accounts of Jesus' life and ministry. After Jesus became widely recognized as a religious leader and Antipas tried to kill him (Luke 13:31), Sepphoris was no longer a safe place for Jesus to proclaim the coming kingdom of God. However, the Gospels do tell of Jesus' travels throughout the cities and villages of Galilee and into Phoenicia, through the regions of Caesarea Philippi and the Greek cities of the Decapolis, as well as journeys through Samaria to Jerusalem in Judea. It is difficult to believe that Jesus grew up in sight of Sepphoris and never visited the capital or met people who lived and worked there. Even casual contact with the capital would have given Jesus firsthand knowledge of Greco-Roman city planning, architectural design and sophisticated engineering technology—as well as a cosmopolitan life-style.

The image of king occurs in a number of parables and sayings attributed to Jesus in the Gospels. Was Jesus' understanding of kingship influenced by his knowledge of Antipas' policies and rule at nearby Sepphoris? From prison, John the Baptist sends two of his disciples to ask Jesus if he is the one anticipated by John's ministry or if they should look for someone else. Jesus tells them to report to John the healings Jesus performed (Matthew 11:2-6). After they depart, Jesus asks the crowds if they had gone to see in the wilderness "a man dressed in soft raiment?" Then he alludes to the ease and luxury characteristic of Antipas' court. "Behold, those who wear soft raiment are in kings' houses" (Matthew 11:8). Or as Luke phrases it, "Behold, those who are gorgeously appareled and live in luxury are in kings' courts" (Luke 7:25). Herod the Great built palaces in Jerusalem and Jericho, as well as in the fortresses at Masada, Herodium, Alexandrium and Machaerus. Antipas erected royal palaces at both Sepphoris and Tiberias. The luxury and ostentation of the Herodian court was legendary, and no expense was spared to create an atmosphere of conspicuous affluence.

One of Jesus' followers was Joanna, the wife of Antipas' finance minister, Chuza. She followed Jesus about Galilee in the company of several other women, who underwrote the expenses of his itinerant ministry (Luke 8:3). Joanna was certainly one person who could have told Jesus about the splendor in which Antipas and his court officials lived. The excesses and extravagances of the royal family contrasted sharply with the conditions of the poor peasants dwelling on the land. Jesus alludes to his own homelessness, "Foxes have holes, and birds of the air have nests; but the Son of Man has nowhere to lay his head" (Matthew 8:20; Luke 9:58).

Jesus appears to have been acquainted with Antipas' banking policies carried out at the central bank at Sepphoris. Once Peter asks Jesus, "Lord, how often shall my brother sin against me, and I forgive him? As many as seven times?" Jesus answers, "No, seventy times seven!" (Matthew 18:21,22). Then Jesus relates a parable about a king to illustrate the nature of forgiveness (Matthew 18:23-35).

The king wanted to settle accounts with his debtors. One man brought before him owed the staggering sum of 10,000 talents, which in today's currency would run into tens of millions of dollars.[9] Antipas' annual revenue from both Galilee and Perea was only 200 talents.[10] So the man's debt was astronomical, and there was no possibility of repaying it. The king commanded that the man, along with his wife and children and all his possessions, be sold as partial payment of the debt. This judgment was consistent with the legal practice stipulated in Exodus 22:3 (compare Amos 2:6, 8:6; Nehemiah 5:4-5).[11] Confronted with the horror of this prospect, the debtor broke down and begged, "Lord, have patience with me, and I will pay you everything."

Touched by the man's condition, the king ignored the incredible promise and ordered that the huge debt be canceled. But, no sooner had the forgiven man left the king's presence than he ran into a fellow servant who owed him a small sum, a mere 100 denarii, about $50. He throttled the poor fellow and demanded immediate payment in full. His fellow servant's plea echoed his own words, "Have patience with me, and I will pay you." But the forgiven man refused and put his debtor in prison until he had paid his small debt.[12]

When word reached the king of the heartlessness of the servant he had so graciously forgiven, he summoned the ungrateful servant and angrily rebuked him, "You wicked servant!" he said, "I forgave you all that debt because you besought me; and should not you have had mercy on your fellow servant, as I had mercy on you?" Then the king condemned the man to the torturers until he paid his debt or until death freed him. The parable concludes with the admonition, "So also my heavenly Father will do to every one of you, if you do not forgive your brother from your heart."[13]

In another episode, Jesus says that any king contemplating a war against another king would first seek advice from his military strategists to determine if he could repel an attack with 10,000 soldiers, although outnumbered two to one. If his army is judged inadequate and defeat is likely, the king would surely commission an embassy to negotiate a peace treaty (Luke 14:3 1-32).[14]

The reference to planning a military campaign is significant. Given the strategic location of Galilee and Perea, which served as a buffer between Rome and both the Parthian empire and the Nabatean kingdom, Antipas was

Theater at Sepphoris

Jesus apparently did not think well of the theater, for he was fond of using the term "hypocrite," originally denoting an actor, as an analogy for religious pretense. He uses some form of the word "hypocrite" 17 times; by contrast, the word never appears in Paul's letters. In the Sermon on the Mount, for example, Jesus warns, "Beware of practicing your piety before men in order to be seen by them...you must not be like the hypocrites." (Matthew 6:1,5). Jesus' analogy suggests familiarity with the theater. And what better place for him to have become familiar with the theater than in Sepphoris, just three miles from his home in Nazareth?

The theater at Sepphoris was probably a part of the decades-long rebuilding program that Herod Antipas, tetrarch of Galilee and Perea (4 B.C.E.-39 C.E.), launched in 3 B.C.E. The previous city on the site had been destroyed by the Romans when they put down rebellions following Herod the Great's death in 4 B.C.E. Building on the foundations of the old city, Antipas turned Sepphoris into his capital. According to the first-century Jewish historian Josephus, Antipas made Sepphoris the largest and most beautiful city in the region. At some point during the reconstruction, Antipas probably installed the theater. Construction of the theater at that time would be consistent with a wave of first-century theater building in the Roman world as the provinces tried to imitate the urban sophistication of Rome.

Appropriate for a capital, the large theater at Sepphoris had a stage 156 feet wide and 27 feet deep and seating for 4,000, the same capacity as the theater in the great port city of Caesarea. Archaeologists have uncovered the front and back walls of the stage, but not the floor, which was probably made of wood that decayed long ago. This raises the interesting possibility that Jesus and his father, being carpenters, may even have helped build the stage.

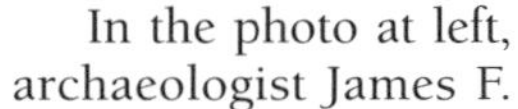

In the photo at left, archaeologist James F. Strange, director of the University of South Florida excavation at Sepphoris, addresses volunteers from an unexcavated portion of the stage area. The steps, carved out of the bedrock, originally supported smoothly polished limestone seats. Behind the top row of seats, excavators found remains of a colonnade that once supported a roof to shelter the audience.

The theater has been dated to the early first century by pottery found beneath the walls and in underground cisterns beneath the seats. This pottery consists of storage vessels, bowls and juglets that probably held water and wine for workmen building the theater. Characterized by the red color, thin walls and general style, such pottery is typical of early first-century Roman pottery. However, Eric Meyers, co-director of the Duke University/Hebrew University team, which is also digging at Sepphoris, believes he has seen identical pottery in a second-century context at another site; if so, the pottery at Sepphoris would no longer necessarily indicate a first-century construction date. Thermoluminescence dating, a technique that tells when an object was last subjected to fire, cannot be used to date the pottery in this case because there is some doubt about its reliability and the range of dates would be too large to resolve the dispute.

Only two coins found in the theater date to before the time the theater was last used, about 450 C.E., when the site was deliberately covered over with earth. (Earlier coins were probably picked up by other theater patrons.) Two first-century coins found under the northwest corner of the back wall cannot be used to support the first-century date because they were found in an unsealed context and may have been left there at a later time.

preoccupied with his military strength. In typical Herodian fashion and with considerable success, he attempted to stabilize his realm with a strong and efficient army. Aretas, the Nabatean king, routed Antipas' army in the autumn of 36 C.E., but the defeat was facilitated by treachery rather than weakness. So impressive was Antipas' huge military buildup that Agrippa, his brother-in-law, successfully accused him before the Roman emperor of plotting sedition. When Antipas admitted that he had stockpiled a large store of weapons, he was sent into exile.[15]

Jesus' saying reflects an awareness of the kind of military planning and preparations kings continually make to secure themselves against aggression. Jesus encourages his followers to be circumspect, to count the costs and be willing to pay the price that maintaining the security of God's kingdom will require. "So therefore, whoever of you does not renounce all that he has cannot be my disciple" (Luke 14:33).

The references to kings in the parables and sayings attributed to Jesus in the Gospels are evidence that Jesus' cultural horizons were much broader than those of a remote Galilean villager. The image of the king consistently focuses on the concept of sovereignty over his subjects. The king determines their economic fortunes, whether they are free men or slaves, in fact, if they shall live or die (Matthew 18:23-35, 22:1-14, 25:31-46). The king's judgments are sometimes harsh and exacting, sometimes tempered with mercy, but his authority is never successfully challenged. Jesus' understanding of kingship may well reflect his awareness of Antipas' rule from Sepphoris and Tiberias. Antipas' appointment as king, or tetrarch, came directly from Rome, and he thus represented the power of the vast empire over his territories. Jesus skillfully employs the figure of the king as an unquestioned authority as a parallel of God's sovereignty over creation, and he uses the king as a challenge to his disciples to appreciate the seriousness of life in the dawning kingdom of God.[16]

Was Jesus acquainted with stage actors? The classical Greek word *hypocrites*, translated into English as "hypocrite," primarily means stage actor, that is, one who plays a part or pretends. The word *hypocrites* can also describe a deceitful person.[17] The word appears 17 times in the New Testament, all in the sayings of Jesus in the Synoptic Gospels–Matthew, Mark and Luke. Jesus uses the image of an actor to criticize people whose religion is external form rather than inner fidelity to God. As one commentator has written, "The word [*hypocrites*], derived from the theater, denoted an actor, the one who played a part or acted a false role in public life; here [Matthew 6:2] used of people who want to be known as pious and so help the needy not in a generous sympathy but in a selfish effort to win praise from men."[18]

Jesus challenges his disciples to acknowledge God, who looks into the secret heart, and to turn away from a religion of pretense and sham. As another commentator has written, "Such people are 'hypocrites' [literally "stage actors"]. Out of a good deed, which should be done in private, they create a public spectacle, with themselves as director, producer and star, bowing to the audience's applause. Hypocrisy is the split in a religious person between outward show and inner reality."[19]

The beautiful theater constructed by Antipas at Sepphoris was the closest one to Nazareth. However, there were other theaters in the areas where Jesus traveled. Almost a decade before Antipas was born, his father, Herod the Great, had built a lavish theater at Jerusalem as part of his preparation for celebrating the Actium games in 28 B.C.E. This celebration was in honor of Octavius' victory over Antony and Cleopatra.[20] According to Luke 2:41-42, when Jesus was 12 years old he accompanied his parents "as usual" on their annual pilgrimage to Jerusalem at Passover. On these trips, it is probable that he became acquainted with the theater in Jerusalem.

Herod the Great acquired a reputation as a theater builder. He erected a theater at his winter palace in Jericho and another in the fortified city of Samaria, which he renamed Sebaste, the Greek translation of Augustus. According to the Gospels, during his brief public ministry, Jesus traveled in the vicinity of both Jericho and Samaria (Mark 10:46; John 4:3-6), which were on the two main pilgrimage routes between Galilee and Jerusalem. Herod built a theater in his port city of Caesarea Maritima and even constructed one in Sidon, just north of his kingdom, as a sign of friendship toward the neighboring peoples. Jesus also traveled in the district of Tyre and Sidon, that is, Phoenicia (Mark 7:24,31; Matthew 15:21).

According to the Gospel of Mark, Jesus also went through the region of the Decapolis, east of the Sea of Galilee (Mark 7:31). Matthew adds that a significant number of people from the Decapolis were in the crowds that followed Jesus and heard the Sermon on the Mount (Matthew 4:25). The people in these ten Greek cities spoke primarily Greek. Theaters were standard features of city architecture and exerted a strong and pervasive influence on urban culture.

In the Sermon on the Mount, the "hypocrite," or "stage actor," is a recurring image. Jesus draws on urban images that reflect a shared awareness of the actor's art, and he calls upon his disciples to make a genuine commitment to God's sovereignty over all of life. "And when you pray," he says, "you must not be like the hypocrites, for they love to stand and pray in the synagogues and at the street corners, that they may be seen by men" (Matthew 6:5).[21] The public display of piety by some of his fellow Jews is calculated to impress observers. Like actors repeating their lines with studied gestures and inflections, they recited their prayers just to be seen.

Jesus instructs his disciples that when they bestow alms or make charitable donations they must not seek honor and public acclaim by, figuratively speaking, sounding a trumpet in the synagogue or streets–like an actor whose dramatic entrance on stage is announced with a trumpet fanfare. "To sound the trumpet, a metaphorical expression comparable to 'toot your own horn,' is likely drawn from the fact that rams' horns were blown and alms were given at the autumn public fasts for rain."[22] Charitable gifts should be made privately so that the left hand does not know "what the right hand is doing...and your Father who sees in secret will reward you" (Matthew 6:3-4).

"When you fast," Jesus instructs his listeners, "do not look dismal, like the hypocrites, for they disfigure their faces that their fasting may be seen by men" (Matthew 6:16). It was customary during religious fasts, as an expression of grief or sorrow for sins, to dress in sackcloth, tear one's clothes and place ashes on one's head. This appearance, accompanied by a long and somber face, was an open display. The comparison appears to be with tragic actors who make up their faces to portray dramatically the agony of their characters. In the theaters of the Roman provinces, actors or mimes frequently preferred makeup to masks because makeup allowed them greater flexibility of facial expression.[23] Subtle nuances could be communicated by distorting the mouth or casting a sidelong glance.

Josephus accurately reported that after the destruction of Sepphoris in 4 B.C.E. Antipas rebuilt the city on the grand scale of a splendid Roman capital. Thousands upon thousands of pieces of datable pottery, a dozen colors of imported marble, fragments of bright frescoes, artistically molded plaster, smooth limestone columns, ornately cut capitals, hundreds of coins, scores of whole ceramic vessels, beautiful mosaics, bronze figures, gold chain, carved ivory and other artifacts all attest that Sepphoris, in the early and middle Roman periods, was indeed a thriving metropolis.

Continuing excavations at Sepphoris have raised the curtain on a new act in the ongoing drama of Jesus and the movement that cast him in the leading role. The stage on which he acted out his ministry was cosmopolitan and sophisticated, and his understanding of urban life was more extensive than was previously imagined. The realization that Jesus grew up in the shadow of Sepphoris, a burgeoning Roman capital city, casts new light on the man and his message–light that changes our perception of Jesus as a rustic from the remote hills of Galilee. The people to whom Jesus proclaimed his message of hope and salvation–whether Jews, Greeks, Romans or other gentiles–were struggling to find meaning in a culture where Jewish traditions and Greco-Roman urban values collided. Jesus' teachings reflect an awareness of city life, which was shared with his cosmopolitan audience, and he addresses issues that are curiously contemporary.[24]

This article is adapted from Jesus and the Forgotten City *(Grand Rapids, MI: Baker Book House, 1991).*

Afterword

Many scholars have pondered the valuable, but sometimes uncomfortable, relationship between archaeology and Bible study. In Recent Archaeological Discoveries and Biblical Research,[1] *William G. Dever argues that the field of "biblical archaeology" is inherently problematic because it implies not pure science but using scientific methods for other purposes. In a review of Dever's book, Michael David Coogan of Stonehill College takes up this issue:*

In this provocative, often insightful volume, originally the Stroum Lectures in Jewish Studies at the University of Washington, William Dever gives his latest, but still "preliminary," thoughts on the relationship between archaeological and biblical evidence. In the central chapters of the book, Dever describes in illuminating detail how the results of recent (and occasionally not so recent) excavations have affected our understanding of three major issues and periods in the history of Israel.

In chapter 2, he discusses the early Iron Age (1200-1000 B.C.E.), the period of Israel's emergence in Canaan, and by means of tables conveniently correlates archaeological data and the biblical record. Dever argues forcefully for a version of the "peasant revolt" hypothesis, which was first proposed by George Mendenhall in 1962 and elaborated by Norman Gottwald in his magnum opus, *The Tribes of Yahweh.*[2] This hypothesis is certainly defensible, and, I think, partly correct, but Dever overstates his case and takes insufficient account of alternate interpretations. Thus, his assertion that "recent archaeological discoveries...cannot any longer be construed as supporting nomadic infiltration, much less conquest models, as previous scholars had maintained" is one-sided; some of the evidence he adduces comes from the investigations of Israel Finkelstein, who reaches the opposite conclusion, that the Israelite settlers of the hill country came from a pastoral background.[3]

Chapter 3 is devoted to monumental art and architecture in the period of the United Monarchy, the reigns of David and Solomon, and is a careful, enlightening correlation of biblical and excavated evidence, some of which has been uncovered by Dever himself.

In chapter 4, he discusses in detail the contributions of archaeology to understanding the religion of ancient Israel. Dever correctly recognizes that the biblical evidence is selective and skewed—his earlier metaphor for the Bible as a "curated artifact" is brilliantly apt—and that archaeological data enable us to construct a much more complex picture of Israelite cultic practices. Especially important here are recent discoveries such as Kuntillet 'Ajrud, the "Bull Site" near Dothan and the controversial ruins on Mount Ebal.

But throughout the volume, particularly in the introduction and conclusion, runs a familiar subtext, that is, Dever's polemic against "biblical archaeology," by which he seems to mean the tendentious use of excavated evidence to prove the truth of the Bible, especially by such scholars as William F. Albright and G. Ernest Wright. I have a number of problems with this argument. It is unfair to criticize scholars of an earlier period for not using current methods; their approach was the one used at the time. Furthermore, the recent shift in emphasis from issues of chronology and the grand tradition, represented by classic texts and monumental remains, to the lives of ordinary people has changed not only biblical archaeology, but also archaeology in the rest of the ancient literate world, especially Egypt, Mesopotamia, Greece and Rome. Some methods recently used to recover this elusive perspective have been borrowed from archaeologists who investigate the remains of prehistoric and nonliterate cultures; the data at their disposal are less abundant, and so every scrap has been saved and analyzed—something no excavator of a tell could possibly do. The shift in emphasis is part of a larger pattern. The study of history has changed in the last generation, and the development of the social sciences, especially anthropology and sociology, is a manifestation of the same phenomenon. Dever ignores this broader intellectual context; it is at least naive, if not tendentious, to describe changes in archaeology of the Levant as the result of the supposed demise of "biblical theology."

There have also been changes in biblical studies, although at times Dever seems unaware of them. Few scholars today would argue for the unity of the Hexateuch and fewer still would include Judges under that term. The "court history of David" (2 Samuel 9-20; 1 Kings 1-2) can only superficially be described as a "reasonably reliable historical source"; it is a carefully composed, literary document, the primary purpose of which seems to have been propagandistic. The inadequacy of the "God who acts" model as an explication of biblical religion has long been apparent. According to Wright's classic formulation of this model, the Bible is the "recital" of what God has done in history, for history is the arena of divine action.[4] Even scholars who might be considered Albrightians have recognized that this formulation does not account for many of the sapiential (wisdom literature), hymnic, cultic and legal traditions preserved in the Bible. (Curiously, having rejected the "mighty acts of God" concept as insufficient in the first chapter, Dever uses it in later summaries of the "central claim" of the Bible.)

The application of new models to biblical traditions, prompted in part by the discovery of new evidence, has been going on for a long time in biblical studies, as is evident, for example, in the works of Mendenhall and Gottwald. Both are biblical scholars, and neither is a professional archaeologist, yet both are cited approvingly by Dever (and incidentally, both are also "Protestant churchmen," a biographical detail Dever does not mention but often provides for those with whom he disagrees). Moreover, attention to more general patterns, rather than elite patterns, was evident more than 30 years ago in such works as *Ancient Israel: Its Life and Institutions* by Roland de Vaux,[5] a biblical scholar and archaeologist who anticipated many of Dever's arguments in his essay "On Right and Wrong Uses of Archaeology."[6] The maturation of "biblical archaeology" as a discipline has been influenced by a variety of factors and individuals, of whom Professor Dever is one. ***BAR*** *16:3 (1990), p. 6*

Finally, in a review of Raymond E. Brown's Recent Discoveries and the Biblical World,[7] *Keith Schoville of the University of Wisconsin argues that archaeologists and biblical conservatives should try harder to understand each other:*

Covering mostly 20th-century excavations, *Recent Discoveries* is divided into two parts. The first is devoted to "Discoveries of Tablets and Scrolls" ranging from the cuneiform of Ebla to the hieroglyphic of Tell el-Amarna to the alphabetic of Qumran. In part 2, "Archaeological Discoveries and History," Brown describes artifacts from major sites like Jericho, Hazor and Megiddo and explores how prevailing interpretations of these finds affect our understanding of the Bible.

In the second section, Brown purposefully illustrates how archaeology both clarifies and confuses information from the Bible. For example, he points out that "if the walls of Jericho came tumbling down, they did so centuries before [the supposed time of Joshua in the 13th or 12th century B.C.E.]." Brown reminds us that excavations at Megiddo, and at Hazor, "confirm part of the biblical report about Solomon's building activity, but also challenge the Bible's neglect of Omri and Ahab."

Brown's examination of sites and discoveries is useful. His stated goal, however, of squelching the tendency toward a fundamentalistic attitude toward the Bible is unwarranted and inappropriate. He defines fundamentalism as "a mind-set wherein the expression of divine revelation is thought not to be time-conditioned." The idea that the Bible is time-conditioned is one way of reconciling biblical narrative with modern science. Time-conditioning refers to the idea that the way biblical writers understood how God acts was influenced by the time in which they lived. Brown claims that the fundamentalist rejection of this notion causes a "religious tragedy." Thus, for example, sciences based on evolution are rejected in favor of what fundamentalists believe is the higher truth of the Bible. According to Brown, they either reject the testimony of science in favor of literal biblical testimony, or they glibly harmonize the contradictions between them.

I wonder if fundamentalism can be so narrowly defined. I venture to think Brown applies the label to individuals who hold a high view of the Bible as the word of God and who do not quickly accept the "assured results of scientific research," a euphemism for "the current consensus." Fundamentalists who read the Bible as revelation can also be open-minded about how God reveals himself in history. And conservative Bible readers have every right to be as skeptical of the current "assured results" as scholars have to be skeptical of Bible readers who reject time-conditioning in revelation. Archaeology is a science that deals with the fragments of history, and conclusions may be modified by new material evidence.

Although some scholars call fundamentalists "fanatics," there is certainly some merit in the fundamentalist reluctance to accept every new interpretation of archaeological data. Scientists and fundamentalists are members of the same species–human–and ought, therefore, to treat one another more kindly. Both are subject to error. At the least, we can say that Dr. Brown is both erudite and honest, and he makes no secret of his bias against fundamentalists. If one overlooks the bias, one can still benefit from his erudition. ***BAR*** *12:1 (1986), p. 17*

PART IV

Sociology and the Bible

Sociology and the Bible
Introduction

The "new" archaeologists have refocused attention away from kings and palaces and toward ordinary people and their everyday lives. Using new statistical and quantitative models, they can now study population density, rates of growth and economic activity (the so-called "ecology of socioeconomic change"). Scientists can then apply these models to regional studies of urban centers and food sources, settlement patterns and land use, the evolution of farming and the growth and decay of cities. Petrie started a revolution when he argued that archaeologists should study broken pottery instead of throwing it away. But scientists today have gone much further, scouring sites for ancient seeds, pollen, animal bones and even feces, trying to understand the health and dietary habits of ancient peoples.

As data accumulate, scholars are learning how the location of a cemetery reflects social structure, how the pattern of agricultural settlements and urban centers is related to the growth of the state, how changes in burial rites reflect changes in the belief in an afterlife. In the area of biblical studies, scientists are developing the field of paleo-anthropology and applying sociological methods to reveal patterns of human behavior and organization, models of family structure, social dynamics and economic interaction. But because data must be extracted directly from the Bible, which is a literary composition, not a census report, scientists have developed a socio-literary approach to distinguish the data from the interpretation of biblical writers, as well as, in the words of Norman Gottwald, "the extent of consonance and dissonance between biblical meanings in their original context and biblical meanings construed as authoritative" by later generations. In "Coarse Language in the Bible? It's Culture Shocking!"[1] Harvey Minkoff describes what happens when rough and tumble stories become sacred literature and strong language suddenly turns up in church.

Sociologists touch upon basic assumptions by biblical authors about Israel and by readers about the Bible. Biblical writers are emphatic about the origins of Israel—Abraham begat Isaac, Isaac begat Jacob, known as Israel, who had 12 sons. After being enslaved in Egypt, the children of Israel—that is, Jacob's descendants or extended family—invaded Canaan and settled there, thus fulfilling God's promise to Abraham, Isaac and Jacob. This promise and fulfillment represent the special relationship between Israel and God, which confers on Israel the status of a chosen people, a nation of priests, a holy community.

Sociologists studying the Bible acknowledge this self-definition but point out that Israel was also a typical Near Eastern monarchy with the same material culture as surrounding peoples—the same architecture, pottery, husbandry. Even Israelite religion had many local trappings—a temple, a priesthood and sacrifices. Although history has shown that something about Israel was—and is—unique, that mysterious "something" is not apparent in a superficial reading of the Bible.

One of the first victims of the historical method was the tradition that Israel invaded and conquered Canaan as described in the Book of Joshua. Modern scholars maintain that the Israelites gradually infiltrated and settled the land. And the idea of Israel as a single family has been replaced by the theory that separate clans united little by little and later created a national mythology of family relationship. Historian George Mendenhall even argues that Israel arose from a "peasant revolt" of the Canaanite underclass and not from tribes that entered Canaan from the outside. Norman Gottwald adds to Mendenhall's argument that Israel's distinctive religion—Yahwism—was made possible by this egalitarian revolution. Gottwald's theory is explored in P. Kyle McCarter's article, "Gottwald's Socio-literary Approach to the Bible," and the entire Mendenhall-Gottwald hypothesis is reevaluated by Israel Finkelstein in "Searching for Israelite Origins."

Not all socio-literary studies are focused on the big picture. In "The Question of Israelite Literacy," Alan Millard, for example, lays out the evidence of literacy in ancient Israel. Literacy, he points out, is taken for granted in the Bible—the Ten Commandments is a written covenant between God and Israel and bills of divorce had to be executed in writing. Nevertheless, scholars have traditionally assumed that these were anachronisms.

CHAPTER 7

Gottwald's Socio-literary Approach to the Bible

P. Kyle McCarter, Jr.

"Jewish colonialism" is an unusual way to characterize the Babylonian Exile, but Gottwald feels that it describes the experience of most Jews after they lost their independence in 587/6 B.C.E. Many survivors of the destruction were forcibly resettled as colonists in foreign lands, and those who remained in their homeland became unwilling colonials under a foreign ruler. Gottwald's innovative interpretation of the Exile is an example of the revolutionary applications of socio-literary analysis to the Bible.

Biblical sociologists begin with the premise that texts do not exist in isolation. Every text reflects the social conditions out of which it emerged, and its incorporation into a culture reflects its continued value to a community. By social context Gottwald means not only the leaders and established traditions of a community, but also the whole range of social and economic classes and value systems. In his "socio-literary" study of the Bible, Gottwald combines the concerns of social science with literary concerns, such as genre, form and the process of canonization.

Gottwald agrees with Karl Marx that the driving force in history is "the way people interact...to produce the means of subsistence." The distinctive religion of Israel, therefore, developed from the class struggle between dispossessed Canaanites and the established order, which was supported by the established religion; the "egalitarian" revolution of the proto-Israelites created the conditions conducive to Yahwism. Once in power, however, Yahwism was used to maintain the new power structure.

As McCarter observes, Gottwald's overall picture of the emergence of Israel has been favorably received, even though many scholars reject his Marxian definition of heroes and villains and even question the existence of the egalitarian society Gottwald describes. McCarter concludes that the value of the socio-literary approach transcends its Marxist limitations.–Ed.

Norman Gottwald, a leading North American biblical scholar, has just published a comprehensive introduction to the Hebrew Bible that will surely make his name known to a very wide audience. The book is *The Hebrew Bible–A Socio-Literary Introduction.*[1]

Gottwald's approach to the study of ancient Israel is sociological. He works from the conviction that institutions and beliefs can only be understood as part of a larger social context. The ideas expressed in the Hebrew Bible, therefore, must be studied in light of the social conditions out of which they emerged.

At first glance, this premise may seem commonplace. Modern critical scholarship is based on the assumption that biblical writings must be understood in their original historical context. But Gottwald, and others like him, mean more by the term social context than is conventionally meant by historical context. Social context includes not only the political situation of the time, but also the full range of factors that affect the life of a people. "A people," moreover, is understood to include not only the leading figures of the day–the ones whose names appear in the history books–but also aristocrats, commoners and slaves, the full range of the population.

Anyone aware of recent trends in archaeology will recognize a parallel between Gottwald's approach to the history of ancient Israel and one aspect of the so-called "new archaeology." Archaeologists have begun to move beyond the boundaries of their old alliance with historians to explore new relationships with anthropologists. As a result, archaeological study has become more generalized, an attempt to reconstruct an excavated culture in its entirety. Artifacts that relate a site to the events of recorded history are still considered important, but they are not sought or studied to the exclusion of artifacts that shed light on the daily lives of ordinary people. In the same spirit, Gottwald and those who share his approach are striving for a comprehensive social analysis of ancient Israel, an analysis not restricted to groups or individuals whose names tend to appear in the history books.

An instructive example of how this approach influences Gottwald's presentation is the way he treats what we traditionally call the Exilic (586-538 B.C.E.) and post-Exilic periods, referring to the time of the Babylonian captivity and the subsequent return. Gottwald rejects the familiar terms "Exilic" and "post-Exilic" because they focus attention "on the deportation of upper-class Judahites to Babylon and their extended captivity there." For the majority of Jews, Gottwald says, exile–which "suggests a temporary compulsory removal from the land that was completely reversed at the earliest opportunity"–does not fully describe the process of dispersion and restoration that most of the population experienced. Gottwald prefers to speak of "Jewish colonialism," by which he means both "the settlement or colonization of Jews in foreign lands" and the "subservience of all Jews"–inside and outside their homeland–"to the political dominion of great empires." Thus, the sections of the book dealing with what we are used to thinking of as the Exilic and post-Exilic periods are collectively titled "Home Rule under Great Empires: Israel's Colonial Recovery." And the designation of the community under discussion is "Colonial Israel."

Before turning to other sections of Gottwald's new book, we ought to look back to an earlier book, for which Gottwald is best known in the scholarly community. *The Tribes of Yahweh*,[2] a comprehensive study of Israel's history and a clear exposition of Gottwald's distinctive approach, is an account of what he takes to have been the formative period in the history of Israel, the period after the Israelites had taken control of the land of Canaan but before they had established the monarchy. The book is subtitled *A Sociology of the Religion of Liberated Israel, 1250-1050* B.C.E. Gottwald's thesis is that Israel emerged as a revolutionary social movement from the matrix of Canaanite culture at the end of the Late Bronze Age.

Gottwald describes early Israel as an alliance of several components of Canaanite society, including peasants, farmers, pastoralists, outlaws, mercenaries and adventurers–in short, all those who were disenfranchised by or disaffected from the feudalism and imperialism of the day. In a process Gottwald calls "retribalization," long-suppressed rural and village networks of mutual cooperation were revived and expanded beyond the level of family and clan. For about two centuries, Israel existed as a decentralized "anti-state," a radically egalitarian society resistant to the statism and hierarchical class structure of Canaan. With the rise of their own monarchy at the end of the 11th century B.C.E., however, the Israelites reverted to the very practices they had once opposed, and the result was restoration of the oppressive hierarchical social system of the earlier period.

This description may sound vaguely (or perhaps not so vaguely!) like modern revolutionary rhetoric, and Gottwald freely admits his fascination with possible parallels between ancient Israel and the revolutionary movements of our own time. *The Tribes of Yahweh* is dedicated to "the memory and to the honor of the first Israelites," whom Gottwald describes in his dedication, in the words of "an anonymous tribute to the people of Vietnam." In another book, *The Bible and Liberation*,[3] a collection of essays, Gottwald stated two goals: (1) to bring to light the actual social struggles of our biblical ancestors and to locate the human and religious resources they drew upon in the midst of those struggles; and (2) to tap biblical social struggles and religious understandings as important resources for directing us in the social struggles we are presently engaged in.

These principles inform all of Gottwald's work. He believes the most useful method of achieving them is the historical cultural-materialism of Karl Marx, a comprehensive approach to all human phenomena deriving from "the way people interact in mutual and reciprocal association to produce the means of subsistence." Once we understand how the ancient Israelites organized themselves to satisfy their material needs, Gottwald believes, we can then understand various other aspects of their society–including government structures, literature and even religion–as an integrated system.

Thus, the Marxian historical cultural-material approach provides "the most coherent and promising understanding for developing research strategies in the social sciences."

Some of Gottwald's readers (including the present reviewer) do not agree that culture is always a function of economy. Systems of thought and belief, rather than material needs, can also determine the ways people satisfy their material needs. Thus, to the extent that Gottwald follows Marx in arguing that the material always has priority, his work is controversial (especially in the area of religion) and will surely be debated for a long time.

There is a tendency to associate Gottwald with George Mendenhall, who pioneered the application of sociological analysis to the history of ancient Israel.[4] Both Mendenhall and Gottwald reject the idea that the Israelites entered Palestine at the end of the Late Bronze Age from outside Canaanite society. They agree that Israel arose as a revolutionary social movement from within. Mendenhall believes, however, that this movement was promoted, facilitated and to some extent created by the new Yahwistic religion. Gottwald argues the opposite. Yahwism, he says, although it eventually became a factor that supported the social ideals of the early Israelites, was a function of the revolution. In other words, the egalitarian social relations of the revolutionary proto-Israelites created the conditions under which Yahwism emerged from the matrix of Canaanite El-worship. Once established, Gottwald argues, Yahwism became a powerful force for sustaining the social system that produced it. Gottwald calls this "the Yahwistic feedback loop in Israelite egalitarianism," arguing that it was "the single most significant servomechanism for the society."

To a certain extent, therefore, Gottwald's understanding of early Yahwism is faithful to Marx's understanding of religion. Marx (if I understand him correctly) defined religion as a function of class relations used by the powerful to justify their superior position and by the powerless to validate their class struggle.[5] Gottwald's interpretation of early Israelite religion is generally consistent with this definition.

Nevertheless, Gottwald does not seem entirely satisfied with Marx's view of religion. He agrees that religion is a function of the social system, but he also stresses the reciprocal relationship that developed between early Yahwism and early Israelite sociopolitical egalitarianism. He also suggests that there may be some form of religious consciousness that is not an expression of the class struggle, although the source of this consciousness and the ways in which it manifests itself are not clear.

Controversial as they are, Gottwald's views have been favorably received in the scholarly community. The publication of *The Tribes of Yahweh* was met with keen and widespread interest, and reviewers anticipated it would have a great impact on the field of biblical history. Some compared it to Albright's *From the Stone Age to Christianity*[6] and even Wellhausen's *Prolegomena to the History of Israel*[7] and Weber's *Ancient Judaism*.[8] Now that the sensation has subsided,

The Tribes of Yahweh continues to be studied, and Gottwald is acknowledged as the leading figure in the sociological study of ancient Israel, a collective enterprise that has won the endorsement of some of our most talented biblical scholars.

At the same time, doubts about *The Tribes of Yahweh* and Gottwald's program in general have persisted. In the first place, Gottwald populates the ancient world with good guys and bad guys, heroes and villains. To be sure, this scenario is consistent with the Bible itself, where the Israelites wear the white hats and the Canaanites the black. To Gottwald, however, the divide is along class boundaries, not ethnic differences. The Israelites are heroes when they are the oppressed component of Canaanite society, when they rebel, and when they establish an egalitarian anti-state; but they become villains when they erect a hierarchical government of their own. Many readers of *The Tribes of Yahweh*, however, question whether right and wrong are this simple and apparent, and critics have called on Gottwald to relax his ideological zeal.

Second, many scholars doubt that the egalitarian society Gottwald reconstructs in premonarchical Israel ever existed. It is fairly easy to demonstrate a potential for revolution within the city-state system of Late Bronze Age Canaan, and Gottwald does this impressively. It is also easy to expose the weaknesses of the conquest and immigration models of Israel's formation preferred by other scholars, and again Gottwald proves more than worthy of the undertaking. It is much more difficult, however, to demonstrate convincingly that a revolution actually took place, and most difficult of all to demonstrate that the result was a prolonged experiment in social equality and economic cooperation.

Although Gottwald is energetic, resourceful and often brilliant, he is handicapped by the same difficulty faced by all scholars who have attempted to shed light on premonarchical Israel–an almost total absence of reliable and useful evidence. In short, Gottwald succeeds in persuading us that an egalitarian Israel *could* have existed, but leaves us wondering if it *did* exist. Finally, many scholars continue to suspect that ideas produce culture, rather than the reverse. After careful reflection, therefore, they remain intellectually uncomfortable with materialism, either in its Marxist formulation or in more recent adaptations by contemporary social scientists like Marvin Harris.[9]

The Tribes of Yahweh, however, is not under review here. I have dwelt on the strengths and weaknesses of that book only for the purpose of alerting prospective readers of *The Hebrew Bible–A Socio-Literary Introduction* to some of the issues raised in Gottwald's most recent work, which will now be easier to explain.

Let us begin with the subtitle. What is a "socio-literary introduction"? "Socio-" indicates that the author pays significant attention to the kinds of issues that are best approached by methods drawn from the social sciences, which is what we would expect from Gottwald. "Literary" (in this case) refers to various new approaches to the Bible that stress its status as literature, often without regard to questions of compositional history. "Socio-literary," therefore, leads us to believe that this introduction is based on recently developed and sometimes experimental methods. And it is.

Nevertheless, the subtitle is somewhat misleading. Newer approaches are certainly in evidence here, but not to the exclusion of the traditional approaches. Source criticism, form criticism, redaction criticism–all of these are also explained and applied. Archaeology is drawn upon where appropriate, as is philology, at least to a limited extent. Indeed, methodological breadth is one of the great merits of Gottwald's book. Students can be confident that, despite Gottwald's avowedly avant-garde tendencies, they will be introduced to the central questions that have exercised the imaginations of scholars for the past two centuries.

Gottwald discusses methodological issues systematically in his treatment of each historical period. Typically, he begins with a review of the pertinent part of the biblical record, noting literary characteristics of the material. Next he reviews modern scholarship on the traditional issues of compositional history—what scholars think about the composition, authorship, date and redaction (editing) of this part of the Bible. Then he turns to newer literary approaches and discusses insights into the text afforded by these studies. Finally he discusses what he calls the "sociohistoric horizons" of the material. From what community or communities did this part of the biblical corpus emerge? What is the relationship between text and social context?

This is a good scheme, but not faultless. Because they are treated in a separate section, the new literary approaches are sometimes emphasized out of proportion to their contributions to our understanding of a given part of the Bible. Moreover, the final position of the sociohistorical discussion inevitably lends it a certain authority. The reader gets the impression that this part of the analysis is the "last word," or, at least, the "latest word" on the subject. And for Gottwald, perhaps, it is.

Despite these problems, the advantages of Gottwald's approach are at least as numerous as the faults. He is particularly good about maintaining the distinction between text and criticism. The reader always knows whether he is describing the Bible or expounding an analysis of background or interpretation of meaning. This is a major virtue of this book, which contrasts sharply with a major weakness of recent American scholarship, where the tendency has been to confuse exposition of the biblical world with the Bible itself.

We must grant, then, that Gottwald provides a broad view of the Bible in contemporary scholarship. And his introduction is not slanted. He makes no attempt to instill a set of idiosyncratic opinions in the minds of impressionable beginning students. Nevertheless, opinions as distinctive and zealously held as Gottwald's are bound to affect his presentation. How does Gottwald's "historical cultural-materialist" interpretation of Israelite history, as developed in *The Tribes of Yahweh* and other studies, affect his treatment of the various segments of the biblical story in *The Hebrew Bible–A Socio-Literary Introduction*? The following is a preliminary answer to this question.

The Patriarchal Age

In Gottwald's treatment of this period, "Traditions about the Fathers and Mothers of Israel," he notes the scholarly preoccupation with dating the patriarchal period and reviews the various arguments–historical, archaeological and philological–in support of one date or another. Then he rejects them all. Following a position already staked out in *The Tribes of Yahweh*, Gottwald argues that the ancestor stories are reflections of the social organization of the tribal period (i.e., the period he calls "retribalization," c.1250-1050 B.C.E.) and the historical circumstances from which the tribes emerged. "Their clearest sociohistoric horizon," he says, "lies in the effort of united Israel in Canaan to develop a synthesized account of its origins."

Gottwald criticizes the tendency of modern American scholars to reconstruct a historical patriarchal age. Instead, he favors the theory that Genesis 12-50 is a retrojection of the ideals of a later age on the remote past. Thus, he aligns himself with the conventional position of the older literary critics (source critics) with one important exception. Gottwald believes the patriarchal stories reflect the ideals of the immediate premonarchical period rather than the monarchy.[10]

Exodus and Sinai

Gottwald shares the majority view that most of the legal material in Exodus, Leviticus and Numbers was added by a Priestly writer of the late Exilic or early restoration period (c.550-450 B.C.E.). His opinion of the narrative material in these books, however, is distinctive. As in his treatment of the patriarchal age, he does not stress the historical background; instead, he emphasizes their status as ideological retrojections from the tribal period. In this case, however, he does find a historical, 13th-century B.C.E. element in the traditions. In general, this has to do with the introduction of Yahwism, which Gottwald dates to this period, and the experiences of the Moses group, a band of former slaves sharing a common ideology. Following a line of reasoning accepted by many scholars, Gottwald argues that the captivity in Egypt and the Exodus were the experiences of a Mosaic-Levitical group that were later generalized as the common history of all Israel. In accordance with the position he adopted in *The Tribes of Yahweh,* he explains the centrality of the private history of this group in the larger tradition as a consequence of their leadership in the formative period.

The Conquest and the Period of the Judges

Gottwald agrees with most modern scholars that Joshua and Judges are part of the Deuteronomistic History, an account of Israel's experiences in the Promised Land that extends from Deuteronomy through 2 Kings. Although the

Deuteronomistic History has a pronounced theological outlook based on the teachings of Moses as set forth in Deuteronomy, Gottwald's emphasis is very much on the historical period corresponding to Joshua and Judges, which is, after all, the crucial era in his program. He provides the reader with a careful analysis of the three leading explanations of Israel's claim to the land—the conquest model, the migration model and the revolution model. After carefully analyzing the weaknesses of the first two models, not surprisingly, he presents the third as solving most of the problems.

The United Monarchy

It comes as no surprise that Gottwald understands the establishment of the Israelite monarchy as a counterrevolution that led to social disaster. He describes a rapid evolution from the "chieftainship" of Saul to the "hierarchic kingship" contrived by the combined efforts of David and Solomon. In his description of the impact of this development, he abandons the precise, restrained prose that characterizes most of the book in favor of the impassioned rhetoric of a political tract.

Solomon's economic successes, he says, secured "a luxuried and privileged life for a small upper class," but they offered no advantage to the common people because "whatever improvements in productivity occurred were vulnerable to siphoning off for the benefit of the already-bloated rich." The policy of the state consisted of "transferring wealth from the mass of productive people to a parasitic nonproductive class." "An entrepreneurial wealth accumulated" as members of the upper class used taxation and exploitative lending policies to force the common people into tenancy and serfdom. Trade, diplomacy and war meant glory for the upper classes but suffering for "ordinary Israelites who bore the brunt of their leaders' vaunting ambitions."

This situation is contrasted with the egalitarianism of the preceding age when political decisions were made not "by a small minority in the royal court" but "by tribal elders sifting the mind of the people for a consensus," when "land [was] held in perpetuity by extended families and...protective associations of families guarded the patrimony of each household" and when "the old restraints on self-aggrandizement" had not yet been "worn down by legal loopholes and circumventions of custom."

The Divided Monarchy

Apart from special emphasis on the prophets as spokesmen for social reform, Gottwald's treatment of the independent histories of Israel and Judah can not be described as peculiar to his sociohistorical approach.

Exilic and Post-Exilic Judaism

We have already noted Gottwald's dislike for the terms "Exilic" and "post-Exilic." He uses them elsewhere in the book (perhaps as a concession to their familiarity), but in the chapters concerned with the historical situation they conventionally describe, he prefers the term "Colonial Israel." The cultural and religious tenor of the age are described in terms of responses to the dominion of a series of foreign empires–Babylonian, Persian, Macedonian-Ptolemaic and Seleucid.

How, then, will *The Hebrew Bible–A Socio-Literary Introduction* be received? Will it acquire a wide readership? Will it capture a major share of the textbook market, as Gottwald and Fortress Press hope? Or will Gottwald's commitment to Marxian categories of analysis be detrimental?

The last possibility is, I think, unlikely. Gottwald has done a good job of keeping explicit references to Marx and Marxian ideas out of the book. The most negative estimate, I think, is that the book will cause a stir for a year or two and then fall into a state of partial neglect. Because Fortress Press has earned the respect of American scholars working and teaching in the field of biblical studies, and with this respect credibility and a formidable marketing capacity, at the very least we can expect Gottwald's book to be widely tested in classrooms for a season or two. It is possible, however, that it will eventually be rejected by those who are not sympathetic to Gottwald's approach. In that case, the book would enjoy a fairly small market share after a trial period of a few years.

In my opinion, however, the book has a bright future. As I have already indicated, this is not an idiosyncratic introduction, and Gottwald's distinctive views rarely interfere with his presentation of essential materials. Moreover, reception of the book, I think, will have less to do with sentiment for or against Gottwald's views than appreciation of the conspicuous merits of the book as a whole. The most important of these is the way the author's obvious gifts as a teacher are incorporated into the substance of the book. Or, to put it simply, Gottwald communicates his material very well. He writes clear, straightforward prose, and his exposition reflects extensive teaching experience as well as considerable pedagogical skill. He takes nothing for granted, explains everything and takes care not to skip over parts of explanations (a rare quality in scholarly writing). The text is generously supported by charts, diagrams and tabulations that reinforce and further clarify the larger issues. All of these make the book wonderfully useful for teaching.

A second merit is the comprehensiveness of the presentation. Breaking with an unfortunate pattern in other introductions, Gottwald includes "late" materials and "legal" materials. He introduces everything, and his thorough treatment of each section displays a keen sense of what is important and what is not, a virtue only slightly vitiated by his penchant for recent or contemporary opinion.

Individuals searching for a private avenue into the world of modern biblical scholarship will find the way fully mapped out in these pages. And students enrolled in introductory Bible courses will receive more complete training if their instructors adopt this book as a text. With the exception of a few (who may find the book too comprehensive for their particular classroom needs), teachers will welcome the thoroughness of Gottwald's treatment.

Personally, I am grateful to Norman Gottwald for this book, and I plan to use it in my introductory courses. I also intend to keep a number of copies on hand for friends and students, and I expect to turn to it frequently for my own instruction.[11]

CHAPTER 8

Mendenhall Disavows Paternity of Gottwald's Marxist Theory

Bernhard W. Anderson

Three models have been proposed to explain Israel's emergence in Canaan: conquest (the explanation in the Bible); peaceful immigration; and a peasant revolt. The latter model was first proposed by George E. Mendenhall and was later given a Marxist incarnation by Norman Gottwald, as described in the previous chapter. Although Mendenhall and Gottwald both support the peasant revolt model, they disagree on crucial aspects of it. Perhaps their most significant disagreement is about whether Israel's special religion predated and motivated Israel's emergence or developed from the social, political and economic conditions of the emerging nation.–Ed.

Israel emerged as a people just before the period of the Judges, at the end of what archaeologists call the Late Bronze Age (1550-1200 B.C.E.) and the beginning of Iron Age I (1200-1000 B.C.E.)–the time when the Israelite tribes settled in the land of Canaan. Scholars have explained Israel's emergence in Canaan according to three different models, the immigration model, the conquest model and the peasant revolt model.[1]

According to the immigration model, this period should be called the time of the settlement in Canaan, which took place over several generations and was not completed until the time of David (c.1000 B.C.E.). There was no initial military assault on Canaanite cities, but only a gradual, nomadic infiltration. Pastoral nomads–Israelite tribes–from the desert to the east and south of Canaan moved into the sparsely settled hill country in search of pastures for their flocks and cattle. As a rule, they lived on good terms with the Canaanites and even intermarried with them. There were occasional clashes but no serious conflicts until the 11th century B.C.E., when the expanding Israelites moved beyond the hills into the fertile plains where strong Canaanite cities were located.

According to the conquest model, this period should be designated the conquest of Canaan. Scholars who subscribe to this position generally concede that the account of a military conquest in Joshua 1-12 is somewhat glorified. The biblical writer may have telescoped events by attributing military feats to Joshua that were actually carried out by others, or he may have magnified the story by reporting modest gains as whopping victories, as is sometimes done in modern war summaries. Nevertheless, in spite of signs of telescoping and exaggeration, there is good evidence for the central claim of the Book of Joshua that in the 13th century B.C.E. warlike Israelites, probably spearheaded by the tribes of Joseph (Ephraim and Manasseh) and the tribe of Benjamin, were victorious in wresting a good part of the central hill country from the Canaanites.

According to the peasant revolt model, Israel's emergence is accounted for not by invasion from outside but by an uprising inside the land of Canaan, a so-called peasant revolt. The peasant revolt model originated in a seminal essay, "The Hebrew Conquest of Palestine,"[2] which was written more than two decades ago by George E. Mendenhall of the University of Michigan. In this essay, Mendenhall argued that in the late 13th century B.C.E.—in archaeological terms the period of transition from the Late Bronze Age to Iron Age I—"there was no real conquest of Palestine at all" as described in the Book of Joshua. The so-called "conquest" was really an internal uprising ignited by Hebrews who advocated commitment to, and covenant solidarity with, Yahweh, the liberating God of the Exodus. This socioeconomic revolution began in Transjordan, where Yahweh-worshiping fugitives from Egypt joined with discontented elements of the population to overthrow the Amorite kingdoms of Sihon and Og. The revolutionary ferment spread across the Jordan to the west bank, where the rural population, restive under the yoke of the Canaanite city-state system, "rejected the old political ideologies in favor of the covenant community of Yahweh."

Influenced by Mendenhall's thesis, John Bright, the eminent biblical historian, modified his own views in the second edition of his standard *History of Israel*.[3] Bright still supported William F. Albright's view of a military invasion from without, but he recognized that the Israelite occupation of Canaan was facilitated by dynamic elements within the Canaanite political and social situation and that, to some degree, the conquest was "an inside job."

Discussion of the "internal revolt" theory took a new turn in 1979 with the appearance of Norman Gottwald's massive work, *The Tribes of Yahweh: A Sociology of the Religion of Liberated Israel, 1250-1050 B.C.E.*[4] Gottwald is a younger scholar who now teaches at the New York Theological Seminary in New York City. His book is monumental in the history of biblical studies because it advocates, with impressive erudition and radical consistency, a sociological methodology for interpreting the data pertaining to the origins of the people Israel. Gottwald accepted and built upon Mendenhall's hypothesis of a peasant revolution.

Today, Mendenhall and Gottwald are linked as advocates of the hypothesis of an internal or peasant revolt, and they stand together in opposing the alternative views of peaceful nomadic (or "semi-nomadic") infiltration (advocated by Albrecht Alt, Martin Noth, Manfred Weippert and others) and a decisive military invasion from outside Canaan proper (as advocated by W. F. Albright, G. Ernest Wright, Paul Lapp, Yigael Yadin and others).

Both Mendenhall and Gottwald are modern historians who appraise the biblical record critically. At the outset of his 1962 essay on the Hebrew conquest, Mendenhall put the matter clearly. The biblical record is confessional, that is, it is intended to glorify Israel's God, who was believed to be actively present in the unfolding story of Israel. "This biblical emphasis upon the 'acts of God,'" he wrote, is difficult for us today; it seems to be "the very antithesis of history, for it is only within the framework of economic, sociological and political organization that we of today seek understanding of ourselves and consequently of ancient man."

Gottwald's book, *The Tribes of Yahweh*, is a massive commentary on that statement. Both Mendenhall and Gottwald reject appeals to "supernatural" causation and, therefore, agree that the biblical account cannot be taken at face value. According to Mendenhall, "From the point of view of the secular historian interested only in sociopolitical processes," something quite different actually happened than what the Bible describes.

Both Mendenhall and Gottwald also oppose the entrenched view that the ancient Israelites were pastoral nomads who emanated from the desert south and east of Canaan. Gottwald has been particularly effective in using a sociological method to lay this view to rest and to show that ancient Israelites were agriculturalists, like the Canaanites. The difference between "Israelites" and the indigenous population should not be seen in terms of a tent-dwelling nomadic population and a sedentary population.

Mendenhall delivered the initial salvo against the romantic assumption of a "sharp contrast between nomad and sedentary villager." Urbanization, in his judgment, invariably "creates a deep schism between city and village," and this contrast—between urban and rural social life—characterized ancient Canaan, "not [the contrast] between the village farmer and the shepherd who may typically be bloodbrothers." The appearance of Israelites on the scene, in the view of both Mendenhall and Gottwald, had the effect of raising the internal tension between the city and the village within Canaanite society to the boiling point of social revolution.

Finally, both scholars are social idealists with regard to the period of the tribal confederacy, roughly the two centuries before the rise of the Israelite monarchy under Saul, David and Solomon. In Mendenhall's view, Israelites took the lead in "withdrawing" from the "power-centered, status-centered" Canaanite society, dominated by petty city-state kings with their monopoly of power, and constructing a society governed by the ethical obligations of the covenant.

But Gottwald argues that the Israelites fomented a social revolution, essentially a class struggle, which brought into being an egalitarian society in which all members shared power and reaped the harvest of their work. But both scholars consider the period of tribal confederacy a kind of golden age that was too soon eclipsed by the oppressive social organization (monarchy) introduced by David and expanded by Solomon.

One might suppose that in light of their common positions Mendenhall and Gottwald would be supportive of each other. In scholarship, however, as in American political campaigns, party representatives often fall to battling one another rather than their political opponents. That is what has happened here—at least on the part of Mendenhall.

In a recent essay, Mendenhall disowns Gottwald as his intellectual progeny, condemning Gottwald in tartly polemical terms:

> What Gottwald has actually produced [in *The Tribes of Yahweh*] is a modern version of the ancient myth-making mentality....Gottwald's "scientific" account of the "liberated" tribes of Yahweh consists largely of an endless series of hyphenated pseudo-social science terms (on one page by actual count there were 14 hyphens and 14 periods) foisted with limitless faith upon the hapless ancient tribesmen who unfortunately were too benighted to know that they were conforming to the canons of a nineteenth-century ideology. Gottwald's work should have been dedicated to George Orwell, whose picture of political bureaucrats rewriting history to make it fit a political party line is remarkably apt in 1983.[5]

The Tribes of Yahweh, says Mendenhall, suffers from a "total lack of historical perspective." The concepts Gottwald uses to describe the process of the peasant revolt, like "retribalization" and "egalitarian" are, says Mendenhall, "absurdit[ies]."

Gottwald's "system," according to Mendenhall, "is a straitjacket that ignores what doesn't fit, because his myth demands that 'it must be so.'" In short, Gottwald makes "a parody of biblical studies" and produces "pseudo-historical propaganda....Gottwald's class-struggle elaboration is almost totally irrelevant to the historical processes involved in the events that ranged from about 1250 to 1100 B.C.E." Worse, his work has had "deleterious effects. Its attempts to present us with a historical account of the beginnings of biblical history is truly a tragic comedy of errors. He has not really succeeded in projecting himself back in time beyond the late 1930s."

Why should scholars who agree so fundamentally differ so radically? Mendenhall and Gottwald disagree vehemently over the "ideal model" (to use Mendenhall's term) to be used to make sense of the fragmentary and ambiguous evidence—literary and archaeological—that bears upon the origins of Israel. The disagreement is sharpest over the issue of power. Mendenhall believes that the Israelites offered a "covenant of peace," which, unlike the effete Canaanite city-state system, abjured the use of power to determine legitimacy or to gain security. In his famous 1962 essay Mendenhall wrote: "Land tenure, military leadership, 'glory,' the right to command, power, are all denied to human beings and attributed to God alone [in emerging Israel]."

Gottwald regards this as historically unrealistic. His "ideal model" is a proletarian society where power is not surrendered but is redistributed on an egalitarian basis, with the result that the people, "liberated Israel," share the fruits of their work and live together as fellow human beings.

The two scholars also disagree about the role of religion in the social process. Mendenhall regards the Israelite religion, with its cohesive network of ethical obligations, as the major catalyst in the revolution that destroyed the corrupt Canaanite city-state system and created a tribal confederacy based on a covenant with God. Mendenhall draws a sharp distinction between Israel as a religious community, a kind of "transpolitical" church, and Israel as a nation-state, which existed in a sociopolitical context. Indeed, the "faith of Israel" infused the sociopolitical context of ancient Canaan with a perspective, a motivation and an initiative that elude sociological or historical understanding.

Gottwald, however, insists that Israelite "religion" can not be isolated from the social, political and economic context; indeed, he says, the Yahweh faith was "the function of sociopolitical egalitarianism in premonarchic Israel." In other words, Gottwald says, religion and politics were intimately related in ancient Israelite society, acting on each other to produce revolutionary ferment.

What is the relation between faith and ideology? We now find ourselves on sensitive ground where even academic angels—if there be such!—fear to tread. In the view of both Mendenhall and Gottwald, Canaanite religion—so-called Baal worship—was an ideology designed to legitimate the city-state system of Canaan and, at the same time, to pacify village farmers in the countryside who lived close to the soil. The tension between "Yahweh" and "Baal," then, was rooted in "the contrast between urban and village culture," says Mendenhall. The question, however, is whether this critical knife cuts both ways. Did the religion of Yahweh, like the contrasting religion of Baal, also have an ideological basis? For Gottwald the answer is clearly "yes."

To put the question directly, is "God" (Yahweh), like Baal, only a symbol derived from, and at the same time expressive of, the dynamics of the social history of a people? Is Yahweh something like "Uncle Sam" in the political history of the United States?

That is where Gottwald seems to come out. And, aggravated by his frank preference for Marxist sociology, this is what nettles Mendenhall, who is shocked by Gottwald's bold statement in *The Tribes of Yahweh*, "Since the primary manifestation of Yahweh is Israel itself, any misconstruction of Israel entails a misconstruction of Yahweh." This statement amounts to what is known as "reductionism." It implies that Gottwald's socialized interpretation of ancient Israel reduces its God, Yahweh, to a force within the social process.

This is the crux of the argument. The manifestation of Yahweh in history—if truly a historical manifestation (as opposed to ideas or ideals that transcend history)—is inseparable from the historical experience of the people who worship Yahweh. Saying this enables one to take seriously the real presence of God in the concrete, earthly places where people live, suffer and die. The question is whether this assertion also pushes one to a conclusion that divests Yahweh of transcendence, except in the watered-down sociological sense that the people bound in covenant with Yahweh have a social solidarity and historical vocation that differentiates them from other peoples.

It is difficult to square this limited view of divine transcendence with the biblical witness, where Yahweh, the Holy One, is beyond all categories and experiences of the human world and, at the same time, the one who enters into the limitations and relativities of human history offering saving power and making ethical demands. Viewed from this perspective, the cardinal sin is worship of the golden calf, that is, attempting to identify the liberating and commanding God with anything in the realm of human culture.

Here we seem to have a theological/philosophical monster by the tail! The intraparty dispute between Mendenhall and Gottwald yields implications and reverberations that will be sensed for a long time to come, especially as the discussion is drawn into the arena of biblical theology and systematic theology.

The increasing attention being paid to the peasant revolt model of the Israelite occupation of Canaan is the result, in large measure, of the rising influence of sociology on biblical studies in the last decade. Clearly, sociology seems indispensable to our "understanding of ourselves today, and consequently of ancient [peoples]," to echo Mendenhall again. But what are the limitations of the sociological method? Is the peasant revolt model "a modern construct superimposed on the biblical traditions," as one historian has recently asked?[6]

Before this question can be answered by advocates of the peasant revolt hypothesis, advocates of other theories of Israel's emergence demand to be heard. The issues in this debate are far from settled. It may well be that in the final analysis the explanation will be a combination of elements from all three major models—infiltration, conquest and internal revolt—if we are to understand fully the complexities of Israel's emergence in Canaan.

Afterword

Norman K. Gottwald concisely explains an important element of his revisionist history in "Were the Early Israelites Pastoral Nomads?":

The Bible relates that early Israel entered Canaan twice–once in the patriarchal age and a second time after the Exodus from Egypt. Prior to 1960, virtually all commentators on Israelite origins pictured early Israel as a pastoral nomadic people who penetrated Canaan from the desert, and who, in the course of settling down on the land, underwent a massive transition to an agricultural economy. Then, slowly and unevenly, the social structure developed into village organization, and finally, as Israel began to take over the major cities of Canaan, moved toward urbanization.

Those who accepted the conquest model of settlement and those who preferred the immigration model of settlement were alike in positing for Israel an original socioeconomic base of pastoral nomadism and an original or transitional territorial base in the desert steppes to the south and east of Canaan....

In the last few decades ethnological and ecological studies have greatly refined our understanding of pastoral nomadism. This new material makes it utterly impossible to retain, in anything like the form it has enjoyed for more than a century, the model of early Israel as pastoral nomads who inhabited the desert and the steppe prior to their entry into Canaan.

To understand why this model can no longer be defended, we must understand pastoral nomadism as a socioeconomic form of social organization, especially as it relates to other forms of social organization such as village farming and urbanization.

Most biblical scholars do not have a comprehensive understanding of pastoral nomadism, either generally or as it existed in the ancient Near East. As a result, they have been at the mercy of the old uncritical models of pastoral nomadism, which were based on faulty perceptions about the relations between pastoral nomads and settled peoples. For example, we know that camel or horse nomadism (typical of large parts of the Middle East today) was not developed until after 1200 B.C.E.[1] when domestication of the camel made deep penetration of the desert possible. This was initially thought to be a blow to the pastoral nomadic dogma. Advocates of Israelite pastoral nomadism, however, soon adjusted their schema and described the pre-camel nomads as "ass nomads" or "semi-nomads" or "half-nomads." But they did not change their basic model.

To better understand the nature of pastoral nomadism, we must first free ourselves of some outmoded 19th-century models of how civilization developed and the role of pastoral nomadism in this development. Unfortunately, it is still widely taken for granted that the domestication of animals preceded the domestication of plants and that early men in the ancient Near East were pastoral nomads who later evolved into farmers. Thus, Israel is pictured as emerging out of a "primitive" nomadic womb in the desert and reaching "civilized" agricultural maturity in Canaan.

An overwhelming number of pre-historians and ethnologists now agree that this schema is grossly mistaken. Neolithic plant domestication and agricultural village life first developed in the grassy uplands along the foothills rimming the outer edge of the Tigris-Euphrates basin and then spread into the river valleys as the complexities of irrigation and transport were mastered.[2] Neolithic communities moved from general food collecting to incipient cultivation and domestication of plants, then to primary village farming, and finally to towns and cities—with no evidence of a transitional pastoral nomadic stage.[3] C. A. Reed finds that goats were domesticated in the agricultural village setting before 6000 B.C.E. and sheep by about 5000 B.C.E.[4]

The upshot of this drastically altered developmental perspective is that pastoral nomadism must now be understood as a culturally and socioeconomically marginal, late development, a specialized offshoot and adaptation of the agricultural-pastoral village community. J. A. Luke succinctly states the diametrical opposition between the new understanding and the earlier view:

> Early Mesopotamian culture evolved *toward* the steppe and desert, not out of the desert to the sown [land]. As a relatively late rather than an early phase of this process, pastoralism based on sheep and goats—the animals which remain primary for the Near Eastern village today—developed from the agricultural village.[5]

This historical background should enable us to arrive at a more realistic understanding of the true nature of pastoral nomadism—a new understanding which, as we shall see, is fully reflected in the Bible.

Pastoral nomadism is a socioeconomic mode of life based on the intensive domestication of livestock, which requires seasonal movements dictated by the need for pasturage and water. Pastoral nomadism is distinguishable, on the one hand, from other forms of nomadism such as hunting and gathering nomadism,[6] and, on the other hand, from *migration*, which is the irregular or occasional movement of a group impelled by natural or historical factors external to occupational pursuits. Pastoral nomads, in effect, operate what one commentator has called "living farms, or factories on the hoof."[7]

It is easy to misconstrue the distinctiveness of the pastoral nomadic mode of life as though it were a totally independent, self-contained whole. In fact, given the primary need for pasturage and water, pastoral nomads are linked to settled zones. The prevailing pattern in the Near East is that winter rains allow herdsmen to move out into the steppes to graze their flocks and herds, whereas in the summery dry season they must move back into close proximity with the settled zone to find pasturage and water. Nomads must, therefore, reach agreements with settled people regarding grazing and water rights....

Pastoral nomads are frequently so integrated into the settled zone that the two groups are indistinguishable from each other in most regards. Even where entire groups are solely involved in pastoral nomadism, they must arrange with settled peoples for water and pasture rights in the dry season and for securing certain foods and other supplies.

This new understanding of pastoral nomadism sharply challenges the idea of "pan-nomadic" mentality in ancient Near Eastern and biblical studies. The Arabian Desert can no longer be conveniently considered an inexhaustible source of population influxes, military conquests, dynastic changes, cultural departures and religious mutations in the Fertile Crescent.[8] Instead, attention must now be focused on the dynamics of social and cultural conflict and change *within* the arable zones. In this readjusted framework, pastoral nomadism is no longer a blanket explanation for disturbed social and cultural conditions and is, instead, one limited expression of the total social complex with far less change-promoting significance than was formerly thought.

The representation of "land-hungry" nomads lurking in large numbers on the fringes of the sown land, waiting for a chance to break in and dispossess the agriculturalists, is a parody on a minor motif of nomadism torn out of context and invalidly used as a general formula to explain historic shifts of power in the ancient Near East.[9]

Indeed, what we know of the origins of pastoral nomadism and its operations in historic times leads us to conclude that the movement of pastoral nomads to settled life was more a return than an advance, and that attacks of pastoral nomads on settled peoples were more a matter of internecine strife in an agricultural-pastoral mix, or a resistance struggle against central authority, than attempts at annihilation or conquest by cultural outsiders.

When biblical narratives are carefully reexamined in this context, it is clear that pastoral nomadism was a minor component in ancient Israelite socioeconomics. The patriarchal stories of early Israel tell of many movements of Abraham and Lot, of Isaac, of Jacob and Esau, and of Joseph and his brothers. These movements are pictured as originating in upper Mesopotamia, ranging back and forth across Canaan and Transjordan, and ending in a descent into Egypt. The accounts are edited in such a way as to give the appearance of a continuum of action involving one group over several generations.

Some of the data suggest circumstances typical of transhumant seasonal treks. But most of the movements are described with reference to circumstances of famine, intermarriage, pilgrimage, or intergroup conflicts, factors that are better understood as evidence of migration than of pastoral nomadism.

Moreover, a close analysis of the modes of production mentioned in the biblical stories helps us to determine the socioeconomic realities behind the motif of migration-as-preparation-for-a-religious-destiny. The socioeconomic data, which have been generally understood to indicate pastoral nomadism, turn out to be far from lucid or compelling. There are traits, such as the sizable flocks and herds, which accord with pastoral nomadism. It is not clear, however, that these are evidence of a form of pastoral nomadism that would distinguish the proto-Israelites from other groups living in the same region.

The basic "at-homeness" of the patriarchal communities in rural Canaan is emphasized by the prominent agricultural component in the socioeconomic descriptions. Abraham and Lot (Genesis 12:16, 13:5, 20:14, 21:27, 24:35), Isaac (Genesis 26:14) and Jacob (Genesis 32:5,7,15) all have oxen or cattle, bovines, which in the Near East were bred only in the settled zone. Abraham buys part of a field near Hebron to bury his dead (Genesis 23). He sacrifices a heifer, a turtledove and a pigeon (Genesis 15:8), and he offers his guests bread, cakes made from meal and a calf (Genesis 18:1-8). Isaac sows and reaps plentifully in the vicinity of Gerar (Genesis 26:12-14), and, as he drinks wine with his meat, Isaac blesses Jacob with promises of abundant grain and wine (Genesis 27:25-29). Jacob boils pottage of lentils (Genesis 26:29-34), and he gives 40 cows and 10 bulls to Esau (Genesis 32:15). Reuben gathers mandrakes "in the days of wheat harvest" (Genesis 37:5-8), and Jacob sends balm, honey, gum, myrrh, pistachio nuts and almonds to Joseph in Egypt (Genesis 43:11).

These biblical passages referring to agricultural practices and products are considerable evidence that the patriarchal communities engaged in diversified and intensive agriculture. I am well aware that some or all of these features might be dismissed as anachronisms from a later agricultural stage of Israelite life. If we strip them away, however, we are not left with an undisputed primitive pastoral nomadic core. As a matter of fact, it is just as logical, perhaps even more logical, to assume that pastoral nomadic traits in the patriarchal stories are anachronisms that embroider the motif of migration as a preparation for religious destiny....

Our understanding of the socioeconomic circumstances of the Israelites during the Exodus from Egypt is similar to the understanding we have presented of the patriarchal period. Traditionally, the Israelites have been pictured as wanderers in the wilderness en route from Egypt to Canaan. Virtually all scholars have assumed that this is bona fide proof of the pastoral nomadism of early Israel. Although the socioeconomic data on the Exodus Israelites are sketchy and uncoordinated, this much is clear. The wandering in the wilderness is presented not as a regular seasonal movement but as a major displacement from one place of settlement to another–in short, a migration rather than pastoral nomadism. The Exodus Israelites are described as stock-breeders in Goshen. At the crossing of the sea, the fleeing people take with them flocks of sheep and goats and herds of large cattle (Exodus 12:32, 38), which are again alluded to in the wilderness (Numbers 11:22, 20:4,8,11). As we have noted, cattle and oxen were bred only in settled areas of the Near East.

The complaining Israelites recall a diet in Egypt that includes fish, cucumbers, melons, leeks, onions and garlic, which suggests that they had been fishermen and small gardeners (Numbers 11:5). The Israelites also take eagerly to eating the manna, which is described as a bread substitute, "like coriander seed" (Numbers 11:7-9). The impression is of an eclectic community, which, on the whole, was unfamiliar with the wilderness and unaccustomed to living there. Although we should like much fuller information, we can at least say that the socioeconomic data on the Exodus Israelites are in no way specifically pastoral nomadic and, in fact, tell against an exclusively pastoral nomadic reconstruction of the community....

As for the social process by which Israel became established in Canaan, there are simply too many indications of continuity between the people of Canaan and the people of Israel to make it plausible that Israel was both an entirely new populace that replaced the Canaanites and a populace with an entirely different socioeconomic mode of production.

Certainly Israel brought major changes to Canaan, but the changes do not suggest a new populace of pastoral nomads. The Israelite mutations in Canaan are more accurately described as new forms of social organization that took power from old urban powerholders and brought to the fore political forces of the agricultural hinterland.

The basic division and tension in the ancient Near East at the time of Israel's emergence was not between sedentariness and semi-nomadism, between settled zone and desert or steppe. The crucial conflict in the ancient Near East during Israel's emergence was between city and countryside. At the time, centralized authority was more or less solidly based in the most prosperous regions of the Fertile Crescent and operated out of urban centers extending control into the countryside through taxation in kind and forced military service and draft labor.

The city stands over against the countryside; centralizing and stratified monarchic and aristocratic classes stand over against peasant and pastoral populations. Whether the rural populations were primarily farmers, stockbreeders or a combination of the two, they had much more in common with each other than they did with urban elites. The shift from Canaan to Israel was primarily a shift in social and political forms—a shift in who exercised power by what means and for what ends. It was a shift from hierarchic urban government to tribal self-management, with a corresponding transformation in religious forms from many gods supporting the hierarchic state to one God bringing tribal peoples to birth and defending the new social system....
BAR *4:2 (1978), p. 6*

CHAPTER 9

Searching for Israelite Origins

Israel Finkelstein

Finkelstein rejects Gottwald's argument that the Israelites emerged directly *from Canaanite urban centers. But he accepts the notion that nomads and city dwellers were two components of a single society "characterized by symbiosis rather than by confrontation." He is also wary of the "literary" evidence: "...attempts to reconstruct the course of Israelite settlement on the basis of the biblical accounts have not been successful....[W]hat they really reflect is the version of history that was current in Jerusalem at about the end of the period of the monarchy."*

Finkelstein believes that the settlements scholars associate with the early Israelites "suggest that the people settling in the hill country...came from a pastoralist background." Recent evidence, however, shows a connection between Canaanite and so-called Israelite material culture and lends support to the theory that Israel emerged from within Canaan. Finkelstein argues, however, that these similarities probably reflect the common influence of prevailing models, socioeconomic conditions and the environment on different peoples living in close proximity.

He believes that "stresses and strains within the Canaanite sociopolitical system" in the 17th and 16th centuries B.C.E. *caused the abandonment of many sites and the contraction of others. The population, although not decimated by war or disease, became nomads, who "suppl[ied] the sedentary dwellers with animal products in exchange for surplus grain." When the urban sites fell victim to Egyptian military campaigns and invasion by the Sea Peoples, the nomads were forced to take up dry farming on vacant land. By the tenth century* B.C.E.*, a majority of the nomads had become sedentary. Thus, "the vast majority of the people who settled in the hill country...must have been indigenous; they were not, however, as suggested by...the Mendenhall-Gottwald model...*direct *dropouts from the Canaanite cities." In other words, Israel did not emerge as the result of a "peasant revolt."–Ed.*

The emergence of Israel in the hill country of Canaan poses intriguing questions for archaeologists as well as biblical scholars. The archaeological evidence of the "Israelite settlement"[1] consists of dozens of hill-country sites dated to the period archaeologists call Iron Age I (c.1200-1000 B.C.E.). At the heart of research on the emergence of Israel lies the question of the origin of the people who settled these hill-country sites. Until we answer this question, we cannot solve the riddle of Israelite settlement.

Until the early 1960s, scholars were virtually unanimous in concluding that the newcomers came from the desert, or the desert fringe, to the east. The differences among scholars concerned the way they appeared on the scene, by military conquest (Albright and others)[2] or by peaceful infiltration (Alt and his followers).[3]

In the last two decades, a new, revolutionary theory promulgated by George Mendenhall and Norman Gottwald has taken center stage. These two scholars have rejected the theory that the settlers originated in the eastern desert. Instead, Mendenhall and Gottwald believe the settlers were refugees from the lowest, exploited classes of urban Canaanite society in the Late Bronze Age (c.1550-1200 B.C.E.).[4] According to a slightly different version of this theory, the roots of Israel can be found in an early rural framework in the hilly areas of the country. This "sociological" point of view has influenced discussions of other archaeological periods as well and has stimulated scholars to look for solutions to archaeological-historical problems *within* the social structure of a given country, rather than speculating about migrations or incursions from outside.[5]

Although I reject many of the central tenets of the Mendenhall-Gottwald approach (especially the notion that the Iron I hill-country settlers came *directly* from urban centers in the lowlands), I do accept two of the premises. Before the camel was domesticated as a herd animal, which apparently occurred only toward the end of the second millennium B.C.E., no sizable group of people could live deep in the deserts of the ancient Near East. Accordingly, the nomads (that is, pastoralists who herded flocks, not camels, and who therefore did not live deep in the desert) and the sedentary dwellers were probably specialized components of a single dimorphic society. These two groups lived in proximity and established mutual economic and social relations. The sedentary dwellers supplied the nomads/pastoralists with grain and other agricultural products, and the pastoralists supplied the farmers with meat and other animal products. Their relationship was characterized by symbiosis rather than confrontation.

Tracing the roots of a specific group like the Israelites–regardless of time or geographic location–requires that three avenues of inquiry be pursued: (1) all extant historical sources; (2) the material culture of the group, including socioeconomic characteristics and relationship to the material culture of the preceding period; and (3) the settlement pattern of the period in question compared to the previous period (and sometimes the succeeding period). Let us see what such an inquiry can tell us about the origins of the Israelites.

The principal historical source concerning the period of the Israelite settlement is, of course, the Bible. Without denigrating its overwhelming importance for reconstructing the history of Israel, the fact remains that attempts to reconstruct the course of Israelite settlement on the basis of biblical accounts have been unsuccessful. The main reason is that the biblical narratives were redacted (that is, edited) centuries after the events. As a result, they reflect the version of history that was current in Jerusalem around the end of the period of the monarchy (seventh century B.C.E.).

Let us turn then to the other two categories–material culture and settlement patterns. Evidence in both of these areas strongly suggests that the people who settled in the hill country in Iron I, at least most of them, came from a pastoralist background. The only conclusive evidence about the nature of the material culture is the layout of the Iron I sites, elliptical site plans with a series of broadrooms encompassing a large central courtyard, an arrangement adapted from nomadic tent camps (see box on pp. 134-135). The proliferation of storage silos dug into the ground at Israelite settlement sites may also be characteristic of a nomadic society in the process of sedentarization. This phenomenon can be observed today in the settlements of newly sedentarized Bedouin in the Negev and the Judean Desert, where the first structures erected are for storage of grain and straw. Storing silage is the first problem for which such societies must find a permanent architectural solution.[6]

The settlement pattern clearly shows that Israelite settlement was densest in areas suitable for raising cereal crops and pasturing animals and relatively sparse in areas suitable for horticulture (such as raising grapes or olives, which take longer to mature) and mixed agriculture.

Let us now turn our attention to how the material culture of the Israelite settlements relates to Canaanite material culture of the Late Bronze Age. Scholarly opinion on this matter is divided. According to the most widely accepted view, there was a sharp contrast or break between Late Bronze Canaanite material culture and Iron I Israelite material culture. More recently, however, points of contact and continuity have been highlighted, especially with respect to pottery.[7] Naturally, this continuity adds considerable weight to the argument of the Mendenhall-Gottwald school.

Despite this continuity, which might suggest that the Israelites emerged from within Canaan, there are a number of counterbalancing factors that must not be overlooked. Even if new groups of people entered the area, we might not find a total cultural break. The material culture of the new group would certainly be influenced by the prevailing material culture in the area, thus creating a seeming link to the previous period.

Equally important, material culture is influenced primarily by socio-economic and environmental conditions. It is possible, therefore, that the material cultures of two contemporaneous peoples living in close proximity will be dissimilar–for example, Israelite material culture in the hill country differs greatly from the contemporaneous Philistine culture in the southern coastal plain and the Shephelah. Similarly, if we compare Late Bronze Age Canaanite material culture, which was primarily urban and commercially interconnected, with the material culture of the Iron I inhabitants of the hill country who lived in isolated villages and were preoccupied with daily subsistence, we would expect the material culture of the two groups to be dissimilar. In places where Israelites and Canaanites lived in physical proximity and shared a common environment, however, we would expect to find similarities in pottery, despite differences in socioeconomic conditions.[8]

A comparison of the archaeological finds of hill-country Iron I sites with finds of Late Bronze Age urban centers, especially with respect to the layout of the hill-country sites, leads us to conclude that most of the people who settled in the hill country in Iron I came from a background of pastoralism and not *directly* from the urban lowland Canaanite polity of the Late Bronze period. The people who tended flocks did not originate deep in the desert—they apparently did not herd camels. Previously, they probably lived on the fringes of the settled areas, or perhaps even in the midst of the sedentary dwellers.

The material culture of sites known to be Israelite, that is, sites in the central hill country, is completely different from the material culture of the Canaanite centers. The contrasting socioeconomic character of the two cultures, the disparate environmental settings and the changes occurring all over the area at the end of the 13th and beginning of the 12th centuries B.C.E. underlie these differences. Points of contact between the two cultures, notably in pottery types, attest to relations between the settlers and the nearby Canaanite centers, some of which continued to exist until at least the mid-12th century B.C.E. and probably even later.

From the human-ecology point of view, the land of Israel can be divided into two zones of occupation: (1) regions where permanent settlement was continuous over a long period of time, with a few relatively short gaps. These are the fertile areas of the coastal plain, the Shephelah and the northern valleys; (2) marginal regions, where sedentary activities waxed and waned depending on conditions. Marginal areas include the semi-arid areas of the Negev Highlands, the Beer-Sheva Valley, the Judean Desert and considerable areas of the hilly regions of Upper Galilee, Ephraim and the Judean Hills. These mountainous areas can be described as ecological "frontier zones," with difficult rock formations and dense copses that were obstacles to settlement. A limited area was available for agriculture, travel from one place to another required great effort, and hewing out cisterns was difficult.

Prior to the Iron Age, before the hilly regions were rendered arable by generations of labor, settlers chose to live on the coastal plain and in the northern valleys. Penetration into the "frontier zones" of the hill country took place only when more favorable areas became overcrowded. Conversely, when there was a decline in occupation, the marginal areas of the hill country became depopulated first. Because discontinuity of occupation was more acute in the "frontier zones" than in the northern valleys and the coastal plain, these areas were sensitive barometers of historical change. Even when permanent habitations were sparse, however, the "frontier zones" of the hill country were well suited to the needs of pastoralists, who exploited them primarily for summer pasturage.

Before drawing conclusions from these general observations, let us examine the third factor I mentioned at the outset–settlement patterns. As we shall see, understanding the patterns of settlement in the central hill country during the interval from Middle Bronze II to Iron I is crucial to clarifying the course of Israelite settlement and also sheds light on the origins of the Israelite population.

In Middle Bronze IIB (c.1750-1650 B.C.E.), the entire country flourished.[9] Unlike earlier periods of prosperity, however, an unprecedented number of people settled in the central hill country as well. Hundreds of sites of every size–fortified cities, villages and individual farms–were founded throughout the hill country, especially along the fertile intermontane valleys, but also in more remote and inhospitable areas.

One investigator, Adam Zertal, has found 116 MB II sites in his survey of the hill country of Manasseh.[10] I have examined another 60 sites in Ephraim. Although comprehensive archaeological information from Benjamin and Judah is lacking, many more sites were founded there in MB II than in the preceding periods (although far fewer than in the northern hill country referred to above). Altogether, some 200 MB II sites have been found in the central hill country. As exploration continues, many more will no doubt be discovered.

Study of the pottery from these sites is just getting underway, so the chronological subdivisions of the period have yet to be nailed down. But preliminary examination of the finds from the Middle Bronze sites encountered in the survey of Ephraim and the finds from my excavations at Shiloh[11]–an urban center in the heart of the region–produced the following tentative results. The wave of settlement crested in MB IIB (c.1750-1650 B.C.E.). At that time, the small village was the primary unit of settlement (but some of the sites may represent pastoralist groups). In MB IIC (1650-1550 B.C.E.), activity in the region changed somewhat. A number of unfortified sites were abandoned, while a few impressive fortified centers arose.[12] At the end of the MB II (c.1550 B.C.E.), the fortified centers of the hill country, as well as many of the major cities of the lowlands, were destroyed.

In contrast to the extraordinary prosperity of MB II, the Late Bronze period was characterized by a severe crisis in settlement throughout the country. Ironically, the Late Bronze period was, until recently, thought by some scholars to mark the apex of development in the land of Israel in the second millennium B.C.E. The relative abundance of historical records (such as the Amarna letters) and the richness of the material culture artifacts (pottery, ivories and other objects) unearthed in excavations at the large tells created this false impression. Now, thanks to the extensive surveys, a more realistic assessment of the state of Late Bronze settlement can be made. Despite certain achievements in the realm of material culture, and despite close commercial links with other Mediterranean shores, the land of Israel in the Late Bronze Age had fallen far from its former glory.[13]

The most serious crisis was in the hill country, where the number of settlements fell drastically. Only 21 Late Bronze sites have been found in Manasseh, a mere 5 sites in Ephraim and just 2 or 3 in Benjamin and Judah. Altogether only 25 to 30 sites were occupied in the Late Bronze II (c.1400-1200 B.C.E.) between the Jezreel and Beer-Sheva Valleys. Human activity was confined mainly to the large central tells, the majority of which have long been known. It is unlikely, therefore, that many Late Bronze sites will be discovered in the future, because it is difficult to overlook major settlements. Other regions were also practically deserted during the Late Bronze period. Only two or three sites were found in Upper Galilee, five in Lower Galilee, none in the Beer-Sheva Valley and a few on the Transjordanian plateau.[14]

Moreover, many of the occupied sites shrank in size. For example, the fortified Middle Bronze settlement at Shiloh was abandoned and replaced by small-scale cultic activity in the Late Bronze Age.[15] The survey shows that the contraction was pronounced at other sites as well. Only in the southern coastal plain, the Shephelah and the northern valleys was there lively human activity during this period.

The decline of occupation during the transition from the MB II to Late Bronze has also been noted in recent studies on the size of the sedentary population. The number of inhabitants west of the Jordan has been estimated at 140,000 in MB II. The Late Bronze population, however, is estimated at less than half that–about 60,000 to 70,000.[16]

In Iron I there was a dramatic resurgence in the hill country. About 240 sites of the period are known in the area between the Jezreel and Beer-Sheva Valleys–96 in Manasseh,[17] 122 in Ephraim (including the vicinity of 'Izbet Sartah to the west) and 22 in Benjamin and Judah. In addition, 68 sites have been identified in Galilee, 18 in the Jordan Valley and dozens more on the Transjordanian plateau. Because sites proliferated all over the region in Iron I, no doubt more will be discovered in the future.

The three patterns of settlement of MB II, Late Bronze and Iron I settlements illuminate the problem of determining the origins of the early Israelites. There are two critical questions that must be answered. Where did more than half of the population of the country as a whole (and almost the entire hill-country population) "vanish" to at the end of the Middle Bronze Age? And where did the people who settled the hundreds of sites in Iron I come from?

Our survey of Ephraim suggests that the decline in MB II settlements began before the end of the Middle Bronze period. The process was apparently gradual and took place mainly during the 16th century B.C.E. The reasons for the disintegration of permanent settlements at the end of MB II are not entirely clear. At first glance, we might be inclined to blame Egyptian military conquests at the beginning of the New Kingdom, which would have dealt a massive blow to Canaan. No archaeological (or even historical) evidence has been found, however, indicating that sites across the country were destroyed at that time. Moreover, even an Egyptian campaign into Canaan does not explain the wholesale abandonment of hundreds of small unfortified settlements.

The more likely explanation lies in stresses and strains within the Canaanite sociopolitical system.[18] These internal problems initially led to the disbanding of some unwalled settlements throughout the hill country and to the strengthening of central sites. Subsequently, these stresses and strains brought about the total abandonment of small sites and the contraction of fortified centers. It is possible that Hurrians and other northern peoples entered the land of Israel at the end of the 17th century B.C.E. and were also implicated in these changes.[19] The frequent destructions of Shechem, the most important site in the central hill country, might reflect turbulence and unrest during this period.[20]

Nevertheless, for whatever reasons, the settlements declined and disappeared. That much is clear. What happened to the sizeable population if it was not decimated by war or pestilence? There is plenty of documentary evidence about nomads in the Near East settling down in recent generations, as they did in antiquity. But there is little literature about the reverse trend–the nomadization of sedentary peoples–although this trend is also known in modern times.[21]

Reversion to nomadism can be caused by increasing population pressure on finite natural resources, natural disasters, confiscations by the authorities, heavy taxation, insecurity, etc. An excellent example comes from recent history. Heavy Ottoman taxation and misrule in the 18th and 19th centuries brought about the destruction of the rural framework in Palestine and southern Syria, and, apparently, a large part of the sedentary population reverted to nomadism.[22]

It seems probable that this is what happened in the "frontier zones," including the hill country, toward the end of the Middle Bronze Age. The network of permanent settlements fell apart, and many of the inhabitants adopted a nomadic existence. This would explain their archaeological "disappearance," for we have yet to find a way to detect and identify the activities of nonsedentary pastoral groups, especially in nondesert regions.

This reconstruction of events brings us back to population estimates. During the transition from the Middle Bronze to Late Bronze periods, the number of people in the country did not actually shrink in half. But there was a change in the proportion of sedentary dwellers to pastoralists, although only the reduced ranks of the former are reflected in archaeological finds and, consequently, in population estimates. The new pastoralists of the Late Bronze Age were simply not counted.

At the beginning of the 20th century, the Bedouin in the land of Israel constituted about 15 percent of the population.[23] In other periods, the percentage may have been far different. In Iron II (1000-586 B.C.E.) and the Roman-Byzantine period (37 B.C.E.-640 C.E.), when the polity was well organized, there was a sedentary majority. In the Intermediate Bronze Age (c. 2350-2000 B.C.E.) and perhaps in the Late Bronze and early Iron I periods as well, there was a preponderance of nonsedentary inhabitants.

But can we produce any archaeological evidence whatsoever–or even the slightest hint from historical sources–to prove the existence of a large population of pastoralists in the land of Israel in the Late Bronze Age? Archaeologically, there are two intriguing clues. The first is the phenomenon of isolated sanctuaries, some unrelated to permanent settlements, some located near permanent sites but outside the built-up areas. The first type–unrelated to any settlement–includes the sanctuary at Tell Deir 'Alla, which the excavator describes as a "shrine of wandering Bedouin." Other examples are the Late Bronze cult place at Shiloh, where no permanent settlement has been found; perhaps the Late Bronze shrine at Tel Mevorakh, described by the excavator as a roadside sanctuary, and perhaps the Amman airport structure. The second type–sanctuaries located close to, but not within, permanent settlements–includes the building discovered near Tell Balatah at Shechem, which is generally identified as a shrine, and the Fosse Temple at Lachish.[24]

These sanctuaries should be regarded as archaeological evidence of nonsedentary groups in the Late Bronze Age for the following reasons: (1) isolated sanctuaries are unknown in those periods of antiquity characterized by urban activity; (2) faunal analysis of remains from Shiloh suggests that the Late Bronze cult place served a population of pastoralists;[25] (3) at both Shechem and Lachish, there were also temples within the bounds of the city.[26] The need for extramural shrines is difficult to explain unless they served the needs of nonsedentary groups outside the settlement; and (4) most of these shrines were situated in typical "frontier zones"–the central hill country, the Jordan Valley and the Transjordanian plateau.

Another archaeological indication of the existence of a significant population of pastoralists in the Late Bronze Age is the relatively large number of cemeteries that were not adjacent to permanent settlements. These have been found in various places, especially in the hilly regions and on the Transjordanian plateau–once again, unequivocally marginal areas–what I have been calling "frontier zones."[27] These cemeteries apparently served a nonsedentary population. Scattered cemeteries were not as widespread during times of intense permanent settlement; they are found in periods, such as the Intermediate Bronze Age, when a large proportion of the population was nomadic.

We must ask, however, if groups of pastoralists could have achieved a level of material culture as highly developed as the culture reflected in the Late Bronze finds at the Amman airport structure and the Lachish temple and in the debris of the cult place at Shiloh? The answer appears to be yes. The finds from these sites and from the cemeteries are almost all cultic, and, therefore, need not be representative of ordinary, everyday material culture, which was probably much simpler.

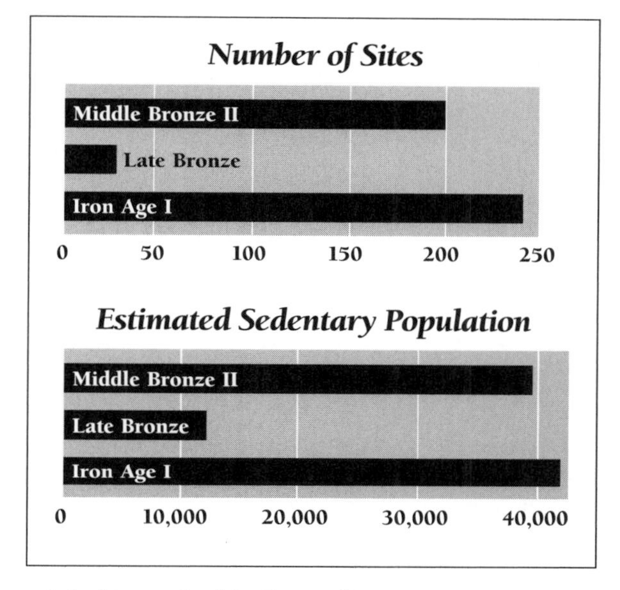

Because similar highly developed ritual objects were common at contemporaneous Late Bronze urban centers in Canaan, it is likely that these artifacts came into the possession of nomadic pastoralists as a result of close ties with the sedentary inhabitants in this dimorphic society. Nor can we preclude the possibility that certain cult sites (Shechem and Lachish, for example) were used by some residents of nearby cities as well. Furthermore, some members of the shepherd and nomadic groups might have established close relations with urban dwellers, and may even have sojourned in physical proximity to, even within, cities.[28] If so, they would have adopted some aspects of urban material culture.

There is even some historical evidence for the existence of significant nonsedentary groups in the Late Bronze Age. New Kingdom Egyptian sources such as the Amarna letters refer to certain population elements operating outside of, but alongside, urban Canaanite society. The most important of these may be the Shosu=Sutu groups.[29] Indeed, many scholars have suggested that the early Israelites may have originated from these groups, or, at least, been associated with them.[30] Interestingly enough, these elements are generally mentioned in conjunction with the "frontier" regions of the country—Transjordan, the hill country and the south.

Now let us turn to the transition from the Late Bronze Age to Iron Age I, when the process we have just described was reversed. At the end of the 13th century B.C.E., the socioeconomic and political tides turned, and conditions became favorable for groups of pastoralists to settle down. It is difficult to analyze the historical causes for this change, simply because our ignorance about the period exceeds our knowledge.

The most important and useful method of analysis involves the comparative study of similar processes in modern cultures. Various studies in the last generation in the Middle East—as well as in more distant lands—have identified

Oval Settlement Sites

A striking characteristic of the material culture of early Israelite sites is the layout of settlements. Architectural styles are conservative and reflect deep-rooted traditions over long periods of time, and the layout of some sites suggests the inhabitants were originally pastoral nomads.

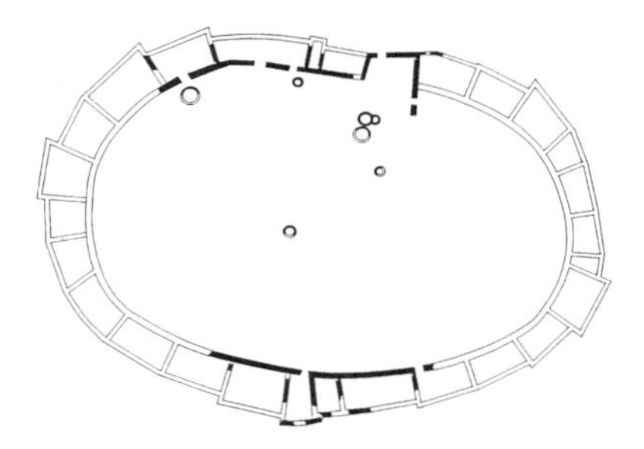

'Izbet Sartah

Let us look first at the layout of 'Izbet Sartah, level III, one of the earliest known Israelite settlement sites.[31] The layout is oval shaped, with a row of broadrooms surrounding a large central courtyard (top plan).

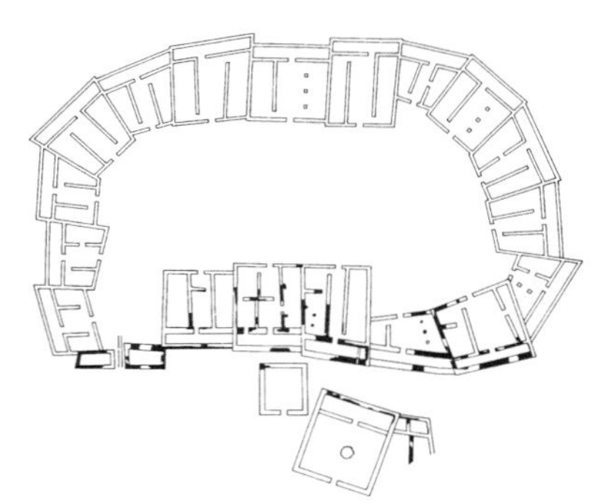

Tel Beer-Sheva

Similar elliptical "courtyard sites" have been found in various regions of the country—western Galilee, the central hill country, the Judean Desert (and perhaps Transjordan) and even the Negev Highlands. At Tel Beer-Sheva, for example, adjacent four-room houses arranged perpendicular to the periphery compose an 11th-century B.C.E. courtyard site found in stratum VII (middle plan). Another 11th-century site in the Beer-Sheva Valley, Tel Esdar, consists of independent structures built parallel to the periphery (bottom plan). The majority of these sites date from Iron I or early Iron II.

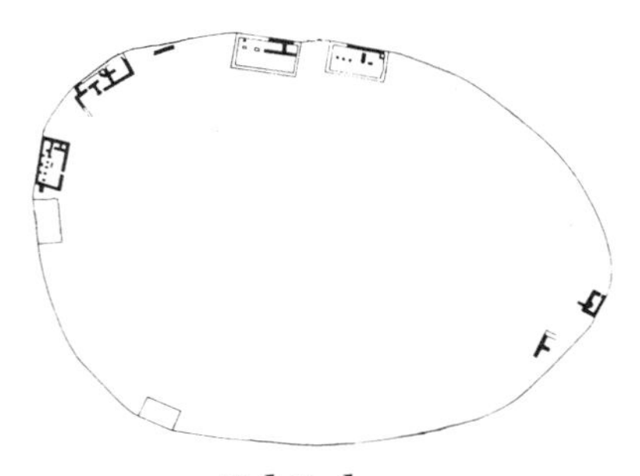

Tel Esdar

The outstanding feature of these sites is the dominant position of the courtyard, which occupies anywhere from 65 to 80 percent of the settlement area. Large courtyards obviously played a central role—figuratively as well as literally—in the lives of the inhabitants, undoubtedly as shelters for their flocks.

The inhabitants of these courtyard sites were primarily herders. Neither ethnic nor chronological factors are necessary to explain the configuration of these settlements. The reasons for the layout are strictly socioeconomic. The

architectural form reflected the subsistence base—pastoralism—of the inhabitants and their social organization.

Most scholars agree that nomads in the process of sedentarization retain pastoral traditions, at least in the early stages. An obvious example is transference of the tradition of portable tents made of perishable materials to permanent structures. This process has also been noted in modern cases.[32] Literature dealing with the lifestyle of nomads in the 19th and 20th centuries indicates that, in cases of enclosed encampments, the tents were either arrayed linearly, in the shape of a crescent, or pitched in a circular or elliptical arrangement. In some regions this arrangement was even called *duwwar* (circle in Arabic).

The early 20th-century encampment in the Judean Desert shown in the photo above is rectangular or trapezoidal in shape.[33] Note the surface area and number of tents, which open onto the large central courtyard. There were one or two entrances into the encampment.

If the early Israelite settlement sites originated in nomadic encampments like this, it follows that the individual unit of construction—the broadroom or "casemate"—originated in the desert tent. The tradition of the tent shape, which was extremely strong, was rooted in centuries of unchanging lifestyle and geographical setting. The tent was a broad structure—that is, with the opening on the broad side—and it generally opened to the east because the prevailing winds blow from the west. The dimensions varied according to the size and means of the family. A large tent might be 40 feet broad and 15 feet deep. A small tent might be 20 feet broad and 8 feet deep.

The similarities between individual tents and isolated broadrooms in oval settlement sites are striking. So is the similarity in the arrangement of the *duwwar* tent camp and the elliptical courtyard sites of the Israelite settlements.[34] The resemblances are evident in general layout, details of plan, function of units and dimensions. The inhabitants of the courtyard sites must have only recently become sedentary, and their customs, as well as their subsistence base, were still connected to their former pastoral mode of living.

a number of stimuli that are likely to set the process of sedentarization in motion.[35] These include improved security, the influence of adjacent cultures, the existence of external economic alternatives to a subsistence based on herding, military pressure exerted by a central authority, climatic changes, the difficulties of subsistence based on pastoralism, and the breakdown of the sociopolitical organization of the sedentary dwellers alongside whom the nomads lived.

Iron I was characterized by the weakening of Egyptian and Canaanite authority, political instability and worsening security conditions. There is, at present, no evidence of climatic change. But there does appear to have been a breakdown of the sociopolitical organization of the sedentary settlers beside whom the pastoralists lived, and alternatives to pastoral subsistence apparently presented themselves to the nomadic population. The circumstances remain somewhat vague, but we can not expect to come up with a rigid monocausal model for the process of sedentarization; most likely other factors, which have escaped our notice, were at work too.

For our purposes, the end of the Late Bronze Age was singular in that this relatively short span of time marked the culmination of a series of trends and events, which together had far-reaching consequences for the history of the land of Israel. Egyptian military campaigns, economic exploitation of Canaan by Egyptian overlords, conflicts among the Canaanite city-states, perhaps long periods of drought and, finally, the pressure exerted by the Sea Peoples (among whom were the Philistines) shook the foundations of the political and economic order of Canaan and weakened the fabric of urban and rural life to an unprecedented degree. These same factors fostered the settlement of nonsedentary groups.

In a dimorphic society, nomadic pastoralists supply sedentary dwellers with animal products in exchange for surplus grain; this, in fact, is the basis of the symbiotic relationship between the two components of the social structure. In this kind of society, the nomads cannot afford to cause a major reversal in the fortunes of the sedentary inhabitants unless they settle down in their stead,[36] because the destruction of agriculture would undermine their continued specialization in herding. In short, the disintegration of permanent settlements (or, at a minimum, the inability of sedentary dwellers to produce surplus grain) necessarily brings about a gradual transition from pastoralism to dry farming, which leads to sedentarization.

Even if this model is not the only valid one, it does help explain the reasons for the settlement of groups of pastoralists starting at the end of the 13th century B.C.E. The internal dissolution and collapse of the Canaanite city-states dealt a crushing blow to agriculture, thus destroying the fragile balance between nomadic pastoralists and the sedentary population and setting in motion the forces that led to sedentarization. The most crucial factors in this process may have been Egyptian economic exploitation of the urban centers, which apparently reached its peak in the 13th century B.C.E.,[37] and long periods of severe drought, which might have made it impossible for the Canaanite sedentary population to produce surplus grain and forced the pastoralists/nomads to engage in seasonal grain-growing agriculture, the beginning of sedentarization.[38] The settlement process was probably gradual and lengthy. As the proportion of sedentary inhabitants increased, the number of nomads dwindled. But only toward the end of the 11th century and beginning of the 10th would the majority of the population have become sedentary.

The material culture of Iron I sites in the hill country, therefore, reflects, partly at least, the character of the people who lived there prior to sedentarization. The influence of the pastoralist mode of existence is still evident, especially in architecture. But certain connections with the material culture of the Canaanite cities are also perceptible, especially in the pottery; this is best understood as the result of the long symbiotic coexistence of nomadic and sedentary elements of the population.[39]

The finds from Israelite settlement sites reflect the first stage of sedentary life in the "frontier zones," when the Israelites lived in small isolated groups and wrestled with less-than-ideal topographical and environmental conditions to eke out their daily sustenance. The absence of luxury goods was undoubtedly related to both basic economic conditions and the general decline in the economy and material culture of the country in Iron I.

Like most scholars, I accept that there must be a kernel of historical veracity in the deeply rooted biblical tradition concerning the origins of Israel in Egypt. Certain elements among the settlers may have come from outside the country, perhaps from the south, and some may even have come from a desert background. At the same time, we cannot brush aside the possibility that some groups that settled in the hill country in Iron I originated directly from the Canaanite urban society of the lowlands; unfortunately, archaeological evidence to support this view is vague, at best.

The vast majority of the people who settled in the hill country and Transjordan during the Iron I period, must have been indigenous; but they were not, as proponents of the Mendenhall-Gottwald model (which, in this context, they often refer to as the "peasant revolt" model) suggest, *direct* dropouts from the Canaanite cities of the lowlands or a nonexistent rural network in the hilly regions. These people had dropped out of the framework of permanent settlement back in the 16th century B.C.E., at the end of the Middle Bronze Age, and had lived in pastoralist groups throughout the Late Bronze Age. Although they may have been active all over the country, their presence would have been most keenly felt in the sparsely inhabited "frontier zones" that were suitable for pasturage—the Transjordanian plateau, the Jordan Valley, the desert fringe and the hill country. They had traversed these areas as part of a transhumant seasonal pattern and had established economic relations with the sedentary inhabitants, especially the residents of the few centers in the marginal regions in the Late Bronze Age—for example, Shechem and Bethel. At the end of the 13th century B.C.E., these groups began to settle down. The process lasted about two centuries and culminated in the political consolidation of the national identity of Israel.[40]

This article was adapted from The Archaeology of the Israelite Settlement *(Jerusalem: Israel Exploration Society, 1988).*

Afterword

The social setting is also the subject of Jesus and the Spiral of Violence: Popular Resistance in Roman Palestine,"[1] *by Richard A. Horsley. Reviewer David Rhoads of the Lutheran School of Theology said this about the book:*

Occasionally a book appears that rearranges the historical landscape. Richard Horsley's *Jesus and the Spiral of Violence*, with its fresh reconstruction of Roman Palestine and the ministry of Jesus, does just that.

The author counters the traditional view that a sect of Zealots came to dominate first-century Israel and drew the nation into war with Rome (66-70 C.E.). According to Horsley, "zeal" was a minor factor, and the people who called themselves "Zealots" did not form a group until 68 C.E. Without the Zealot hypothesis, a complex picture emerges, which Horsley paints with the aid of sociohistorical studies of violence, terrorism and revolution. He describes an agrarian society with a wealthy elite and impoverished peasants, a tense "colonial situation," dominated politically, economically and culturally by imperial Rome through Jewish rulers, and a breakdown of village life, which led to widespread popular resistance.

Horsley analyzes the history of the period in terms of stages in the spiral of violence: (1) institutional exploitation by the rulers; (2) popular protests; (3) severe repression by the establishment; (4) revolution. He describes the various forms of popular resistance to Roman domination, including: protests by intellectual groups, such as the Fourth Philosophy, the offshoot Pharisaism founded by Judas the Galilean that advocated "No lord but God"; popular mass demonstrations under Archelaus, the Emperor Gaius and several procurators; and "apocalyptic" movements expressing hope for an historical transformation–the main religious impetus for rebellion. These popular protests were met with repression, which in turn led to revolution.

Horsley portrays Jesus in light of these sociohistorical realities and rejects the picture of Jesus "sketched with the Zealot movement as a foil." In Horsley's scenario, Jesus' movement was similar to the prophetic movements of Judas the Galilean and Theudas. His apocalyptic outlook was historically oriented, and he addressed economic and political problems. He was not a pacifist in an abstract, individualistic sense; he "actively opposed violence," particularly institutional oppression, in nonviolent ways. The charges against Jesus–that he claimed to be a king, that he stirred up the people and opposed paying tribute to Rome–"were not totally false."

The focus of Horsley's analysis is on Jesus' proclamation of the Kingdom of God, which called for social revolution in the villages. Jesus' renewal included healing, forgiveness and exorcism. He did not recruit tax collectors, prostitutes and the poor in order to form a following apart from Galilean society. Rather, he advocated social renewal in village life through egalitarian family relations, nonhierarchical communities, cancellation of debts, love for one's enemies (cooperation at a local level), nondefensive sharing, mutual assistance and reconciliation. Renewal was to be based on repentance, trust and humility.

At the same time, Horsley argues, Jesus spoke out and took action against the corrupt Jewish hierarchy that contributed to the breakdown of village life. In fact, he condemned the whole Temple system, which, he said, would soon be destroyed and the vineyard given to others, making way for a popular kingship unmediated by either a "hierocracy or a temple system." Jesus' prophetic social revolution was preparation for the kingdom of God—an imminent political revolution in history by which God would break the spiral of violence, end the established order, liberate Israel with justice and bring salvation to the nations.

My disagreements with Horsley's analysis are vastly overshadowed by my appreciation for his fresh analysis of first-century Israel and for the bold new strokes he adds to the portrait of the historical Jesus. This is an even stronger work than his *Bandits, Prophets, and Messiahs,*[2] which was a co-winner of the 1986 BAS Publication Award for the best scholarly book relating to the New Testament and early Christianity. ***BR*** *4:2 (1988), p. 4*

In a review of Carolyn Osiek's book, What Are They Saying about the Social Setting of the New Testament?[3] *Dennis R. MacDonald of Iliff School of Theology made these comments:*

[Osiek's] book is fair, balanced, unpolemical, lucid, suggestive and uncondescendingly kind to the reader. The author uses modern sociological analogies to illustrate and illuminate the ancient social setting, but these analogues are seldom cute, forced or anachronistic. The structure of the book is inspired by Galatians 3:28 and includes: Jew and Greek Merging Cultures; Slave and Free Economic and Social Status; Male and Female Family Structures; and Church Organization.

In the first section, Osiek explains that the terms "Jewish" and "Hellenistic" are not agonistic, that is, they are not mutually exclusive, competitive concepts. The two cultures became profoundly merged, although not into a new monolith, but rather into a wide stream of undulating social experience. Despite differences between Jews and Greeks, the two peoples had many cultural patterns in common—status derived from honor or shame, awareness of social interrelatedness, presumptions about limited material wealth, patriarchal kinship networks and concern for what was clean and unclean.

In the second part of the book, Osiek explains how perceptions of powerlessness and economic injustice, apocalyptic expectations and missionary vagabondism were combined to provide early Christianity in Palestine with a religiously powerful and distinctive social world construction. Osiek contrasts the early Palestinian form of the movement with urban Pauline churches, which welcomed slaves and plutocrats, the dishonorable and the honorable as determined by birth. The mode of apostolic support is related to economic issues. For example, we are told that Paul broke with the practice of itinerant begging as commanded by Jesus when he sent the disciples out. Paul preferred to support himself by working with his own hands–as contemporaneous philosophical preachers did.

In the final section of the book, Osiek discusses authority, structure, charismatic legitimacy and domestic hierarchy. She ends with an appeal for "the merger of social science method and liberation theology, one of the most important directions in which social study of the Bible is moving."

Osiek warns the reader of the perils of sociological reductionism, that is, of limiting the experiences of early Christians to predictable responses to social conditions and overlooking the influences of intellectual traditions, religious symbols and the divine.

> In spite of the potential difficulties which must be constantly kept in mind by scholars using these methods, the social and social science approaches to the New Testament and early Christianity are providing new and valid insights into the life and experience of the first Christians, and, even more important, into how we can today better understand and live their faith.

Those of us who want to understand and live this faith owe Professor Osiek thanks for a fair, balanced and inviting overture to the symphony being performed by investigators into the social setting of the New Testament. ***BR*** *1:3 (1985), p. 12*

CHAPTER 10

The Question of Israelite Literacy

Alan R. Millard

How literate were the ancient Israelites? The Bible says that Moses wrote down the Ten Commandments and that Joshua erected inscribed monuments, but until recently scholars believed that literacy was rare. Now a different picture is developing.

Monumental inscriptions, such as the one commemorating the completion of Hezekiah's water tunnel, show that there was at least a class of trained scribes and some educated citizens who could read them. But literacy must have been widespread to account for the number of private documents and graffiti–names and notes scratched on pots and jars or scribbled on tombs and houses. The large number of bullae–lumps of clay used to seal documents–attests to the existence of many contracts, deeds and letters written on papyrus and other perishable materials.

Writings on potsherds seem to be spur of the moment jottings, sometimes in times of crisis, or "banal information of passing interest." As Millard observes, there is nothing to suggest that potsherd inscriptions were intended for archives or libraries. Moreover, biblical requirements that bills of divorce be written and that certain religious texts be written "on the doorposts of your house" presuppose the ability to comply. "We may conclude," Millard says, "that most ancient Israelites were within reach of the written word."

If Millard is right, a good deal of standard biblical scholarship needs to be reappraised. Written prophetic literature, for example, may have existed alongside oral traditions, and written documents are not as easily altered as oral presentations.–Ed.

How widespread was literacy in ancient Israel? Until recently, the answer usually given was "not very." Writing, it was said, was restricted to a class of professional scribes whose skills were considered almost magical. Because writing was so rare, the argument goes, reading must have been equally rare.[1] Recent archaeological discoveries, however, reveal a different picture.

Everyone agrees that skilled professional scribes were responsible for writing and/or copying many important texts. Professional scribes certainly served monarchs, officials and the gentry around the royal court. Scribes wrote letters, such as Queen Jezebel's order to kill Naboth so that Ahab could seize Naboth's land (1 Kings 21), recorded deliveries of produce, such as the famous Samaria ostraca discovered in the capital of the northern kingdom of Israel, and preserved the pronouncements of prophets like Jeremiah (Jeremiah 36). But other people were also writing.

Ancient Hebrew inscriptions can be divided into three classes—monumental, formal and occasional.[2] Monumental inscriptions are rare, but they do turn up from time to time. For example, in 1982, workers preserving an ancient wall in Jerusalem came upon a fragment of stone with elegantly carved Hebrew lettering on it that appears to date to the seventh century B.C.E. Unfortunately, it is so fragmentary that we can only remark about the beautifully chiseled letters. In Yigal Shiloh's excavations in the area of Jerusalem known as the City of David, he found another fragment of a monumental inscription,[3] which was dated, on the basis of the form of the 15 clearly readable letters, to the eighth or seventh century B.C.E.

These two fragments may now be placed beside the two most famous monumental inscriptions in Jerusalem—the Siloam inscription and the Royal Steward inscription. The Siloam inscription commemorates the completion in the late eighth century B.C.E. of King Hezekiah's tunnel under the city bringing water from a spring outside the walls in preparation for a siege by Sennacherib, king of Assyria. The entire episode is described in the Bible (2 Kings 20:20; 2 Chronicles 32:2-4). The three-line Royal Steward inscription, from the doorway of a tomb in the village of Siloam, inscribed about 700 B.C.E., informs the reader that the tomb belongs to a royal steward whose name ended in *-yahu* (*-iah* in the traditional English rendering of Hebrew names). The inscription says the tomb contained only his bones and that anyone who opened it would be subject to his maid's curse. The late Professor Nahman Avigad of Hebrew University suggested that the steward may have been Shebna, whom Isaiah condemned for his ostentatious tomb (Isaiah 22:15ff.), whose full name was, perhaps, Shebaniah.[4]

The fragments of monumental inscriptions that have been recovered, although they are rare, indicate that monumental inscriptions could be seen not only in the capital of Judah, but probably in other major cities as well. These public inscriptions were visible to people of all social classes, although, admittedly, we still do not know how widespread the ability to read them was.

The second class of inscription, formal inscriptions, includes inscribed seals and bullae (impressions on lumps of clay used to seal documents and letters) and ostraca (singular, ostracon; written accounts on broken pieces of pottery). The most famous collection of ostraca is the Samaria hoard, which was found in 1910. By recent count, there are 102 of them, now in Istanbul,

25 of which are illegible.[5] These ostraca are mundane records of goods delivered: "In the ninth year from Quseh to Gadyaw, one jar of old wine"; "In the tenth year from Yasit, a jar of pure oil from Adoni'am."

The second largest corpus of formal ostraca, from Arad in the Negev, was recovered through the late Yohanan Aharoni's insistence that before discarding excavated potsherds they should be "dipped," that is, immersed in water, and carefully examined to see if they bore inscriptions. The Arad corpus includes letters addressed to and from the commander of the fort at Arad and a variety of brief notes. Most of these pieces date to the early sixth century B.C.E.

Formal inscriptions have also been found on various other objects, for example, a remarkable inscription on an ivory pomegranate that reads "Holy of the priests, the hou[se of Yahweh]."[6] The part in brackets is missing and has been reconstructed by André Lemaire, who discovered the pomegranate in a Jerusalem antiquities shop. Other reconstructions are possible, although Lemaire's is probably correct.

The third class of inscriptions is what I call occasional documents—graffiti consisting of names or notes written in ink or scratched on pots or scribbled in tombs. Occasional inscriptions are also sometimes found on potsherds (ostraca) and can be distinguished from formal inscriptions by the content and style of writing. Occasional inscriptions were often written on the spur of the moment or in isolation. Two brothers wanted to make sure their mugs did not get mixed up, so one of them had his name scratched on his. Someone waiting outside the governor's office at Lachish scratched the first several letters of the alphabet on the step. Were these occasional inscriptions written by professional scribes? In theory, one might argue that scribes on special missions from Jerusalem and Samaria, the capital cities, wrote all of the ostraca that have been recovered. But, given the "occasional" nature of most of them, it is difficult to imagine that anyone would undertake a long journey by ancient standards to write notes of local and ephemeral interest.

It could also be argued that professional scribes were active in towns outside Samaria and Jerusalem. At major places like Lachish this would come as no surprise. But Hebrew ostraca have been unearthed at more than 15 other sites, some of which are relatively small settlements, forts or caravanserais like Horvat 'Uza and Kuntillet 'Ajrud.[7] Should we assume there was a professional scribe operating at each of these sites, or can we suppose that the inscriptions were written by military or government employees, or even private citizens?

The question becomes more urgent with regard to the inscriptions I have described as occasional. It is possible, of course, that some were carried from major cities like Jerusalem, but it is hard to believe they all were. According to my count, more than two dozen sites in Israel have yielded occasional ostraca and graffiti, including letters scratched or pecked on pots! Were all of these written by professional scribes?

SILOAM INSCRIPTION. When the Assyrian king Sennacherib marched on Jerusalem, King Hezekiah prepared for the siege by diverting water through a 1,750-foot-long tunnel (2 Chronicles 32:2-4; 2 Kings 20:20). The inscription was incised on the rock wall near the southern end of the tunnel: "...while there were still three cubits to be he[wn, there was hear]d a man's voice calling to his fellow for there was a crack (?) in the rock on the right and [on the lef]t....And at the end of the tunneling...there flowed the waters from the spring toward the reservoir...." ***Photo: Hershel Shanks***

Let us set aside for the moment the larger collections of ostraca—from Samaria, Arad and Lachish—which were skillfully written and could easily be the work of professional scribes. If the remainder of inscriptions, which are scattered across so many sites, were made by professional scribes, they speak poorly for scribes as a profession. Can we really suppose that Israelite scribes wrote such trifles as the list of names from Tel Masos[8] or the incoherent complaint about a sequestered cloak from Mesad Hashavyahu[9] or scribbled notes about the class of wine in various jugs?[10] I think we can conclude from these examples that the knowledge of writing was widespread in ancient Israel, not just in the cities, but also in remote outlying areas and that the ability to write was not limited to professional scribes, but was available to private citizens.

These conclusions are reinforced when we examine the most common material on which inscriptions were written. Some scholars have argued that potsherds were the normal writing material in Israel,[11] but the growing number of bullae coming to light refutes this theory. Obviously, bullae were used to seal papyrus documents, not potsherds. Indeed, impressions of papyrus fibers have been found on the backs of many clay bullae, as well as the marks of the cords used to bind the folded sheets. The bullae are identical in application to clay sealings found in Egypt still attached to papyri of the Persian period.[12] They clearly attest to the common use of papyrus in Israel. In Egypt many papyri have survived; in Israel only one scrap has survived (see box on p. 149).

Potsherds were used as a writing material in Egypt, as they were in Israel, but from the beginning of Egyptian history, papyrus was the normal medium for administrative records and literature. Scribes wrote short messages, memoranda, scribal exercises and notes of all kinds on potsherds or flakes of stone, which were easy to find, cost nothing and could be discarded freely.

The same was probably true in Israel. Only information of passing interest was consigned to ostraca. On the other hand, papyrus would have been used in Israel for legal documents settling matrimonial affairs, proving ownership of property and establishing rights of inheritance. Letters from rulers, officials and private citizens would also have been written on papyrus, as were all documents meant to be preserved for future consultation, such as the deed of sale for the field in Anathoth, which Jeremiah bought from his cousin (Jeremiah 32). Neither in Egypt nor in Israel has a single ostracon been found

THE SAMARIA OSTRACA, potsherds inscribed in ink, were invoices or labels for wine and oil shipments. This example from the eighth-century B.C.E. hoard of 102 ostraca found in the storerooms of the Israelite royal palace in Samaria is the work of a skilled hand, probably a professional scribe. The text says: "In the tenth year (Belonging) to Shamar/iau of *Ttl*. A *nbl* of / fine oil." A *nbl* was a vessel that held a standard quantity. *Photo: Israel Antiquities Authority*

A SUPPLICANT'S PLEA, this ostracon from the late seventh century B.C.E. was found in the gate guard room of Mesad Hashavyahu, a small coastal fortress near Yavne-yam, ten miles south of Tel Aviv. The petitioner tells his story with many repetitive locutions: "Before the rest, when your servant had finished his reaping, and gathered as usual, Hoshaiahu son of Shobai came and took your servant's garment." The plea concludes, "Let your servant's garment be returned and do not dismiss him." The cursive script indicates that the reaper dictated the letter to a professional scribe. The location of the letter in a guard room suggests that it never reached the governor. *Photo: Israel Antiquities Authority*

that was obviously written to be kept in an archive or library or for someone to consult in the future.[13]

All this evidence combined makes a strong case for widespread literacy during the Israelite monarchy. The bulk of the extant material, however, dates to 750 B.C.E. or later, the last 150 years of Judean history. Earlier texts are rare. Only the Samaria ostraca witness the use of writing in the administration of the northern kingdom of Israel. Faced with this pattern, we might assume that during the early monarchy–say from 1000 B.C.E. (David's reign) to 750 B.C.E.–writing was limited to the courts and did not touch the lives of most Israelites.

It is a mistake, however, to deduce from the absence of an element in an archaeological horizon that the element did not, or could not, have existed. Texts from the earlier period are seldom found because it is a general archaeological truth that only the last phase of occupation of a building and the last decades of a prosperous town yield large numbers of artifacts. Objects and texts dating from more than three generations before the end are rare. If a structure was rebuilt after a number of years, little will be left from the first period of use, and even less from the initial period. Even in Assyria, where the evidence of writing is frequently on indestructible cuneiform clay tablets, very few ordinary legal or administrative deeds survived at major sites like Assur, Kalah and Nineveh from the ninth century B.C.E., although that was the age of the powerful kings Ashurnasirpal II and Shalmaneser III. Details of their reigns have been found in monumental inscriptions on stone and in foundation deposits. But there is no reason to doubt that Assyrian scribes were drawing up deeds on clay tablets then as they did for the next two centuries; in fact, a handful of examples proves that they did.

We have no reason to imagine a different situation for Israel on this score. And indeed we have a few examples of writing in Israel from the United Monarchy and even from the early days of settlement in Canaan. Graffiti from Hazor demonstrate the currency of writing there before the Assyrian conquest in 720 B.C.E. The most outstanding specimen from the United Monarchy is the Gezer calendar from the tenth century B.C.E. This small limestone tablet, which can be held in one hand, lists the duties of the farmer's year in seven lines of slightly uneven letters. It is impossible to be sure if the language is Hebrew or a local Canaanite dialect.

An earlier example is a potsherd found in a storage pit in the little village of 'Izbet Sartah in the hills east of Aphek.[14] About 1100 B.C.E., someone passed the time tracing the letters of the alphabet in different directions on this piece of pottery. Unfortunately, the incisions are faint, and it is impossible to be certain why they were made. But this potsherd attests to someone's knowledge of writing in the days of the Judges, presumably someone who lived in this village (unless the sherd was brought from somewhere else). There is no distinctive feature to prove that the writing or the writer was Israelite, although we can make that assumption on the basis of the pattern of early Iron Age settlement.

Based on these examples, we can trace the same pattern of writing in Israel as in Egypt. Papyrus was the normal writing material, and potsherds were used for what I have called occasional inscriptions. With the physical evidence before us, we can no longer doubt that writing was possible in Israel throughout the period of the monarchy. Also beyond dispute is that writing was widespread; courtiers saw Hebrew writing on monuments in Samaria and Jerusalem; peasants saw it on seal impressions, jars and jugs in country towns, and even on remote farmsteads.

Everyone had seen the alphabet, but how many could actually read or write it? Theoretically at least, writing was within the competence of any ancient Israelite, and we can be sure the ability to write was not limited to a

A Hebrew Papyrus from the Days of the Prophets

In addition to the potsherds and stone surfaces on which ancient Hebrew writing has been found, two other materials were used—wooden tablets and papyrus. No wooden tablets have come to light in Israel or Judah. However, they are mentioned in the Bible (e.g., Isaiah 8:1, 30:8), there are pictures of them on ancient sculptures, and some fragments have been found in Assyria. Evidence from archaeological discoveries, notably clay bullae with imprints of papyrus fibers on the back, supported by analogies with other regions, confirm that papyrus was in common use, despite the fact that none has survived at Palestinian sites.

One piece of Hebrew papyrus (shown below) from the time of the later kings of Judah, a ragged sheet 7 inches wide and 3.5 inches high, was found by Bedouin in a cave in 1952. The cave was almost certainly in the Wadi Murabba'at, which runs into the Dead Sea some ten miles south of Qumran, where the Dead Sea Scrolls were found. Other objects recovered from the Wadi Murabba'at caves and the paleographic characteristics of this unique papyrus indicate that it dates to the seventh century B.C.E., the century that began in Isaiah's time and ended in Jeremiah's.

This piece of papyrus is a palimpsest, that is, material that was written on twice. Originally the papyrus bore a letter with at least five lines of writing, but only parts of the first two lines are legible. They read, "—iah says to you, 'I sent with great concern to ask the welfare of your household. Now don't pay any attention to all that X says to you....'" After that message had been read, someone erased most of it and wrote a list of men's names with an amount beside each one. The amounts are marked with a sign that might denote the *seah* measure, a unit for measuring grain: "Nimtar (son of) Hoshea 14; Abi (son of) Sebi 10; Eleadah (son of) Karshon 5; Shemaiah (son of) Joezer 6." This single fragment is evidence that papyrus was in use in Judah.

The Wadi Murabba'at papyrus. *Photo: Israel Antiquities Authority*

small scribal clan. The variety of ancient Hebrew inscriptions—from monumental texts on buildings, tombs and public works, to letters, seals, lists and names scratched on pots—suggests that writing was widespread, considering that the vast majority of documents were written on papyrus, which did not survive in Israel's damp climate. But especially important to our argument are the casual or occasional texts, names on vessels and notes on potsherds. Here the hands of schoolboys and workmen are visible, as well as the hands of trained scribes. This is the physical evidence that writing by private citizens was fairly common, even in outlying areas.

What evidence is there for the writing of books? Were books in circulation at the time of the Israelite monarchy? Except for the fragments of monumental inscriptions, the only extant examples of Hebrew writing of this period are mundane survivors from daily life. They reflect writing as a utilitarian skill, as it was when writing was invented sometime before 3000 B.C.E. Some have argued that "the oral mode of communication [for wisdom literature] was preferred even by those who could read and write."[15]

THREE IVORY WRITING-BOARDS dating to the late eighth century B.C.E., found in a well at Nimrud, in Assyria, give us an idea what writing-boards—a kind of early book—looked like. The boards were coated on one side with wax, on which notes could be inscribed and later erased by smoothing the surface. These ivory boards still bore part of the wax coating inscribed with an Assyrian divinatory text in tiny cuneiform script. Wooden writing-boards, fragments of which were also found in the well, were often hinged in pairs. Ivory boards were hinged, probably with gold, in sets of 12. Hinged boards could accommodate lengthy texts, which would otherwise have required many separate clay tablets. *Photo: British Museum*

THE GEZER CALENDAR, a small limestone tablet inscribed in an awkward hand, perhaps by a schoolboy, contains seven slightly crooked lines describing the cycle of farm life: "The (two) months of harvest. The (two) months of so/wing. The (two) months of late planting./ The month of reaping flax./ The month of reaping barley./ The month of reaping and measuring./ The (two) months of (vine-)tending./ The month of summer (-fruit)." In the lower left corner, the first three letters of the Hebrew alphabet are incised. Dated to the tenth century B.C.E., this is the oldest known inscription of significant length that can be called Hebrew. The Gezer Calendar suggests that writing was in use among the Israelites of the United Monarchy and that it was not limited to professional scribes. ***Photo: Zev Radovan***

There is no reason to believe, however, that there was ever a limit to what could be written after the initial stages in the invention of Near Eastern scripts. In Egypt, literary texts were created at least as early as the Pyramid Age (c. 2700 to 2200 B.C.E.), and in Babylonia in the Jemdet Nasr period (c. 3000 B.C.E.). Nothing suggests that the alphabet had a smaller scope among the Israelites who settled in Canaan.[16]

Indeed, in the last decade or so, two discoveries have proved that there was writing and copying of literary texts during the monarchy. The first is the Balaam text from Tell Deir 'Alla,[17] where excavators found a painted prophetic literary text that refers to "Balaam, son of Beor," who is known to us from Numbers 22-24, on the plaster wall of some kind of cult center. The text on the wall was copied in columns and is apparently a reproduction of scroll columns, a superb illustration painted on plaster of the papyrus scrolls that did not survive the centuries.

The second text that hints at widespread awareness of literary texts is Ostracon 88 from Arad,[18] a mere snippet of text. Enough survives, however, that we can tell it refers to a king who reigned and is strengthened. Whether this is a royal statement, a proclamation, a copy of an existing royal inscription or a school exercise,[19] it is evidence that someone had access to such a document, someone who was not in a palace or major temple but was stationed at the frontier fortress of Arad.

Archives belonging to private individuals, including both legal deeds and literary compositions, often without distinction by category, have been found in Mesopotamia from the 17th century B.C.E., at Ugarit in Syria from the 14th century B.C.E. and at Elephantine on the Nile from the 5th century B.C.E. If they existed there, they probably also existed in Israel, although examples have not survived.

We may conclude that most ancient Israelites were within reach of the written word, a situation facilitated by the simplicity of the alphabet, especially in comparison with the more cumbersome writing systems in Mesopotamia and Syria (cuneiform) and Egypt (hieroglyphics). Wherever there was alphabetic writing, there was the possibility of literature and of reading that literature.

In light of all this evidence, passages in the Bible that mention writing gain credibility. A man divorcing his wife should have a written document; this was no doubt a job for a scribe, but it was a written document of which both parties must have been aware (Deuteronomy 24:1,3). The Israelites were commanded in Deuteronomy to learn and teach the commandments, to talk about them always and to "write them upon the doorposts of your house and upon your gates" (Deuteronomy 11:20, cf. 6:9).

Is it credible that these commands were issued to a people incapable of carrying them out? The evidence of ancient Hebrew epigraphy suggests the answer is *no*; the lawgiver's commands could be fulfilled to a large degree. Apparently the people did have the technical ability to comply.

The prophetic books must also be reappraised in this light. Written oracles may have existed alongside oral traditions from the time the oracles were uttered. The prophets, indeed, may have recorded and edited their own words. Assumptions about the relationship between written and oral traditions should also be reexamined; once something was put in writing, it may have been harder to alter it or add to it than many experts have assumed.

Ancient Hebrew written documents recovered by archaeologists demonstrate that there were both readers and writers in ancient Israel, and that they were not rare. Most places would have had access to someone who could write, and most Israelites would have been aware of writing.

This article has been adapted from "An Assessment of the Evidence for Writing in Ancient Israel" in Biblical Archaeology Today *(Jerusalem: Israel Exploration Society, 1985).*

PART V

Linguistics and the Bible

Linguistics and the Bible
Introduction

In the beginning was the word." "The Word of God." "A proclamation, the word of God through my messenger." "Now these are the words that Moses spoke...."

Words–language–are central to the Bible. The Bible was composed in Hebrew, Aramaic and Greek over the span of a thousand years. Long before the last book was written, the biblical community had ceased to speak the language of the earlier books; perhaps they did not even understand some of the words. With the help of modern linguistics, we now have new insights into how language in the Bible works.

Wordplay and etymological puns, both explicit and implicit, are everywhere in the Bible. The *mayim* (waters) below and above the firmament are separated by an expanse called *shamayim* (heaven), possibly a play on *sham mayim* (water is there). The first man, *'adam*, is created from *'adamah* (earth), which is *'adom* (red) like *dam* (blood). Adam's partner is called *'ishah* (woman) because she is created out of *'ish* (man). Hagar's son is named *Yishma-el* (God will listen). Leah exclaims at the birth of her firstborn, *Reu ben* (Look, a son!). And Rachel, as she lies dying in childbirth, names her son *Ben-oni* (child of my suffering); but Jacob renames him *Ben-yamin* (child of strength).

These linguistic refinements were obvious to the original audience, which was immersed in the same language and culture as the authors. But as time passed, language and culture changed, and later audiences had to be told the meaning of earlier texts. Thus, in the Gospels, which obviously incorporate earlier traditions, Jesus speaks Aramaic in a few scenes, but the authors are careful to include translations in the text. Jesus raises the dead girl with the words *Talitha cum*, which is interpreted, "Arise, my child" (Mark 5:41); he heals the deaf with the word *Ephphatha*, that is, "Be opened" (Mark 7:34); he says on the cross *Eli, Eli, lema sabachthani*, which is interpreted "My God, my God, why have you forsaken me?" (Matthew 27:46; Mark 15:34).

Later biblical authors themselves sometimes had trouble understanding earlier ones. New Testament authors regularly quoted the Hebrew Bible in the

Greek translation (the Septuagint), which, like any other translation, cannot capture all the wordplay of the original language. And the Hellenized authors of the later biblical period, who were steeped in the conventions of Greek literature, seem not to have understood the workings of Hebrew poetry, like the function of parallelism. In one famous incident, from Matthew 21:2-7, Jesus borrows a donkey and her foal and rides them both at the same time to fulfill the prophecy of Zechariah 9:9:

> Behold, your king comes to you,
> triumphant and victorious,
> riding on an ass,
> on a colt the foal of an ass.

According to the convention of Hebrew poetic parallelism, however, the last two lines should be understood as synonyms, not as two distinct animals.

Since Sumerian, Akkadian and other ancient languages of the Near East have been deciphered, our knowledge of biblical Hebrew and Aramaic has increased, as has our knowledge of Koine Greek, the language of the New Testament authors. We now know, for example, that New Testament Greek ranges from something like careless speech in Revelation to polished prose in Hebrews. Unfortunately, the distinction seldom comes across in translation. But basic linguistic questions remain unanswered.

All languages change over time. Because the Bible is a collection of books written over a period of a thousand years in which earlier sources have been combined to create the final text, it is difficult to pinpoint the meaning of particular words and concepts in particular texts. Moreover, words that meant one thing to the original audience may have meant something else to the author who appropriated the text and may mean something else again to us.

Advances in linguistic science have also enhanced our appreciation of biblical writing. Scholars used to assume that ancient Hebrew had a small vocabulary, and for this reason some translators believed they could make the text more precise and literary in English by rendering single Hebrew words in a variety of English words. Rather than the quaint or archaic "Adam knew Eve" of the King James Version for Genesis 4:1, they prefer Adam "lay with" or "had intercourse with" Eve, which is more idiomatic in modern English.

But studies have shown that even so-called primitive peoples develop complex languages and sophisticated literary sensibilities. In his 1989 presidential address to the Linguistic Society of America (LSA), William Bright observed that "all societies seem to use a variety of patterns for discourses which serve distinct functions–such as songs, prayers, mythic narratives, ceremonial performances, sermons, political speeches, debates, autobiographical reminiscences, jokes or riddles." And articles in recent issues of *Language*, the LSA journal, have been devoted to such topics as phonetics and semantics in Damin, a special language used only in rituals by the Lardil-speaking aborigines of Australia, and the poetics of Nahuatl, the Mayan language. Evidence suggests that the biblical authors–whose culture can hardly be called primitive–may have consciously and creatively adopted a literary idiom. Thus, scholars have debated whether particular words or constructions were used for literary effect or were the only words or constructions available.

More than 50 years ago, Martin Buber and Franz Rosenzweig, who were working on a German translation of the Hebrew Bible, argued that the recurrence of key words in Hebrew was an artistic technique that created cohesion in seemingly artless prose. If repetition is a sign of art, and not a reflection of poverty of the lexicon, the treatment of the verse we just examined has to be completely different.

The Hebrew word used in this verse, *yada'*, as in "Adam knew Eve," means "know" or "experience." If *yada'* were the only Hebrew word for sexual intercourse, and it happened to be a homonym with the word for "know," then "Adam knew Eve" would convey the wrong tone in English because the Hebrew is unexceptional, while the English has introduced a strange locution. But there were other Hebrew words for sexual union–such as *šakab* and *šagal*–so the use of *yada'* in Genesis 4:1 must have been a deliberate attempt to echo the same root as in the Tree of Knowledge and the serpent's words, "God knows you will be like gods, knowing good and evil." In this case, "Adam knew Eve" captures the sense of the Hebrew better than idiomatic modern English.

Orthography also raises questions for modern linguists. Just as *bow* is two distinct words in English (as in the girl wearing a bow took a bow on stage), R. David Freedman suggests that Hebrew *'-z-r* stood for two different Hebrew words. Eve, he argues, was mistakenly taken to be Adam's "helper" when the word can also mean "partner." In addition, as Harvey Minkoff explains in his essay, there are no capital letters in Hebrew; and in ancient Hebrew manuscripts, there was no punctuation. Thus, a refrain in the Song of Songs has been variously translated as "Do not wake love until it is ready" and "Do not wake Love until it is ready." Moreover, because interpretation of a passage depends on the phrasing, the placement of a comma or colon can be crucial. "A voice cries out, 'In the wilderness prepare a path for the Lord'" is worlds away theologically from "A voice cries out in the wilderness, 'Prepare a path for the Lord'" (Isaiah 40:3).

For more than 15 centuries, literal translations of the Bible were considered the most authentic. The literalists based their claim on Jerome, author of the Latin Vulgate, who said that in Holy Scripture "even the word order is sacred." The literal argument also fit in nicely with the Renaissance reverence for classical sources and the Protestant commitment to the preeminence of the biblical text. Thus, over the years English has inherited "biblical" diction characterized by *thee* and *saith*, *verily* and *behold*, as well as Hebrew syntax like "And God saw the light, that it was good" (Genesis 1:4).

Eugene Nida and other modern linguists now strive for "dynamic equivalence" rather than word-for-word transfer. Dynamic equivalence means going beyond thought-for-thought translation to extract the meaning and present it in words and syntax that produce the same effect as the original.

Let's return, then, to the quotation with which we began this section. Instead of the traditional, literal opening of John 1:1, "In the beginning was the Word, and the Word was with God, and the Word was God," the translators of this verse in The Good News Bible–Today's English Version assumed the original was colloquial rather than literary: "Before the world was created, the Word already existed; he was with God, and he was the same as God." Modern linguists hope to recover the original meaning of the text and the whole universe of associations and reactions to the "Word."

CHAPTER 11

The Man Who Wasn't There
Hebrew Textual Mysteries

Harvey Minkoff

Does Satan exist? The answer to this serious theological question may hinge on Hebrew orthography, the conventions of spelling and punctuation. But the reader of an English translation would not know this.

Most names in ancient Hebrew are also common nouns, like Rose and Singer in English; but unlike English, there are no capital letters in Hebrew to set names apart. Thus, there are many ambiguities in the Bible, like "The cooks/Cooks are friends with the bakers/Bakers." An example is the word satan, *which simply means "adversary." Another instance of the same kind of ambiguity is the name of the prophet Malachi, who may not have existed; the only sentence in which he is named–"The word of the Lord...through Malachi"–may actually mean "The word of the Lord...through my messenger." Even using* Lord *or* lord *is a decision for the editor, as is the personification of certain English words, which can change the meaning of a text radically–"Do not rouse Love" in contrast to "Do not rouse my love" in the Song of Songs.*

Without commas and quotation marks, we don't know for sure if Adam or the narrator says, "Therefore shall a man leave his father and mother and cleave to his wife." And the absence of punctuation can create theological problems. "A voice cries out in the wilderness, 'Prepare the way of the Lord'" or "A voice cries out, 'In the wilderness prepare the way of the Lord.'"–Ed.

Who was Masek? Where is Calneh? What do Adam, Satan, Malachi and Shiloh have in common? What did Adam say when he saw Eve for the first time? The answers to these questions may be disconcerting to some students of the Bible.

Masek, according to the Septuagint, a third-century B.C.E. Greek translation of the Bible, is the mother of Abraham's servant Eliezer (Genesis 15:2):

> The word of the Lord came to Abram in a vision, saying, "Fear not, Abram. I shield you; your reward shall be great." And Abram said, "Master, Lord, what will you give me? I will depart without a child, but the son of Masek my home-born female slave, this Eliezer of Damascus."

Calneh, according to the King James Version (KJV), is a city in Shinar (Genesis 10:10) in the realm of Nimrod, the "mighty hunter before the Lord":

> And the beginning of his kingdom was Babel, and Erech, and Accad, and Calneh, in the land of Shinar.

The disquieting aspect of these simple answers is that when we look at other translations we find neither Masek nor Calneh—nor, for that matter, Damascus. Thus, in the New Jewish Publication Society (NJPS) translation, Abraham's response to God's promise is:

> O Lord God, what can You give me, seeing that I shall die childless, and the one in charge of my household is Dammesek Eliezer.

And in the New English Bible (NEB), this is the description of Nimrod's realm:

> His kingdom in the beginning consisted of Babel, Erech, and Accad, all of them in the land of Shinar.

How did Masek become a nonperson and Calneh disappear? The explanation is that modern scholars consider the appearance of these names in the Hebrew Bible to be misunderstandings of Hebrew spelling conventions, and new translators, therefore, read them out of the text. The same is true for many—if not all—of the occurrences of the names Adam, Satan, Malachi and Shiloh, just a few of the textual mysteries created by ancient Hebrew orthography, a writing system very different from modern English.

First of all, in the Hebrew alphabet there are no capital letters. Therefore, there is no difference between the appearance of "He tells the truth" and "He tells the Truth." Consequently, the translator must decide which words to capitalize. In the Song of Songs, for instance, there is a recurring phrase (2:7, 3:5, 8:4) that is translated in the NEB as follows:

> I charge you daughters of Jerusalem:
> Do not rouse her, do not disturb my love
> until she is ready.

But the NJPS reads:

> I adjure you, O maidens of Jerusalem:
> Do not wake or rouse
> Love until it please!

The first translator interprets the Hebrew word *'ahavah* as a common noun, "love"; the second understands it as a proper noun, "Love."

Second, most proper names in the Hebrew Bible are also meaningful words, like the English family names Bush and Baker or the place names Green Bay and Little Rock. Thus, when Jephthah was driven from his home in Gilead and settled *be'ereṣ tob* (Judges 11:3), he was either "in the land of Tob" or "in a good land." Here is still another example–either "a voice was heard in Ramah" or "a voice was heard on high" precedes "lamentation and bitter weeping, Rachel weeping for her children" (Jeremiah 31:15).

David fled Jerusalem during the rebellion of his son Absalom and stopped at *bet hamerḥak* (2 Samuel 15:17). In the 1917 Jewish Publication Society translation, he tarries at "Beth-merḥak," as a place name. Seizing on the root RḤK (far), in the word *merḥak*, in the more recent NJPS and the Jerusalem Bible (JB), David stops at "the last house." The NEB translator adopted a middle approach through creative capitalization. In this version, David stops at a place called "the Far House."

This brings us to the name Malachi. The only reference in the Hebrew Bible to a prophet named Malachi is found–perhaps!–in the first verse of the book that bears his name: "The word of the Lord to Israel through Malachi." But in the absence of other occurrences of the name, we cannot be sure that the Hebrew word *mal'akhi* is a name at all; a note in the NEB offers the alternate reading, "The word of the Lord to Israel through my messenger." Like the disappearing Masek, then, Malachi becomes a man who wasn't there.

Ambiguity also arises because in ancient Hebrew manuscripts–like most modern Hebrew books–vowels are not indicated. The absence of vowels does not usually bother readers fluent in Hebrew.

Vowels in Hebrew commonly carry grammatical nuances, like the tense differences between take and took. Unlike English, however, Hebrew vowels rarely distinguish Hebrew words–as in, for example, English *Joan/Jane/Jan* or *bat/bet/boat/bait*. If we omit the vowels in the English sentence *Jn tk th bt t th prk*, only *Jn* and *bt* are ambiguous. A reader who knows English will expect *Jn* to be the subject of the sentence; it is clearly not the article *the* or a plural noun, so it must be a name. But we can not know if it is Joan, Jane or Jan. Given a singular subject, *tk* must be a verb in the past tense because it does not end in -*s*. Only *took* is possible. After a verb, *th* must be *the*. And so on. Because Hebrew has very few sets of the *Joan/Jane/Jan* type, the absence of vowels causes less difficulty than in this English example. In an analysis of Hebrew words chosen at random from a modern advertisement, only 30 percent had more than one possible reading, even in isolation; in context none was ambiguous.[1]

But problems do occur, especially in poetry, which often includes rare words, innovative images and poetic license. For example, in Jacob's death song, the section about his son Naphtali reads (Genesis 49:21): נפתלי אילה שלחה הנתן אמרי שפר, and like this when the Hebrew components are replaced by equivalent English letters: *nptly 'ylh šlḥh hntn 'mry špr*.[2] The traditional reading of the vowels is *naptaliy 'ayalah šeluḥah hanoten 'imrey šaper*, which the KJV renders:

> Naphtali is a hind let loose: he giveth goodly words.

But the NEB reads *'ylh* as *'eylah* not *'ayalah*, and *'mry* as *'amirey* rather than *'imrey*, that is, keeping the same consonants but hypothesizing different vowels.[3] Consequently the NEB translation reads:

> Naphtali is a spreading terebinth putting forth lovely boughs.

Disagreements also have arisen over unfamiliar names. In 1 Chronicles 6:28 (6:13 in the Hebrew text), the sons of the prophet Samuel are listed as *hbkr wšny w'byh*, which the KJV takes to be *habekor wašniy wa'abiyah*, "the first-born Vashni, and Abiah." But Samuel's elder son is called Joel just five verses later (and in 1 Samuel 8:2), so the NEB reads these words differently, inserting Joel as a name implied. NEB reads *wšny* as *wešeniy*, "and the second." The entire phrase then becomes *habekor [yow'el] wešeniy 'abiah*, "[Joel] the eldest and Abiah the second."

Similarly, the letters *klnh* in the description of Nimrod's domain in Genesis 10:10, are translated as a city named Calneh in the KJV. In the NEB and JB, in contrast, different vowels change the word to *kulanah* (all of them). By this change, the city named Calneh disappears.

Another example. Ignoring several occurrences of the Hebrew prefix *ha-* (the), the KJV introduces a heavenly being named Satan, *hasatan* in Hebrew, into the famous opening chapter of Job (1:6-7):

> Now there was a day when the sons of God came to present themselves before the Lord, and Satan [*hasatan*] came also among them. And the Lord said unto Satan [*hasatan*], Whence comest thou?

But the definite article "the" does not normally precede personal names, so there is nobody named Satan in the NJPS rendering; *hasatan* is taken as a title, not a name:

> One day the divine beings presented themselves before the Lord, and the Adversary [*hasatan*] came along with them. The Lord said to the Adversary [*hasatan*], "Where have you been?"

Ignoring *ha-* affects another passage as well. "To" in Hebrew is the word *'el* or the prefix *le-*. This prefix is a single letter, *l*, attached to the word that follows. The combination *le-ha-* (to the) is contracted to the prefix *la-*, also indicated by the single letter *l*. What then is the correct reading of *l'dm*? Assuming the pronunciation *le'adam* instead of *la'adam* and thus overlooking *ha-* in Genesis 2:19-20, the KJV story features a man named Adam instead of "the man."

> and out of the ground the Lord God formed every beast of the field, and every fowl of the air; and brought them unto Adam [*'el ha'adam*] to see what he would call them; and whatsoever Adam [*ha'adam*] called every living creature, that was the name thereof. And Adam [*ha'adam*] gave names to all cattle, and to the fowl of the air, and to every beast of the field; but for Adam [*le'adam*] there was not found an help meet for him.

A Glossary of Bible Translations

Septuagint (LXX). A Greek translation of the Hebrew Bible. The Pentateuch (Five Books of Moses) was translated in Alexandria, Egypt, in the third century B.C.E. Other books were added during the following few centuries. Septuagint is Greek for "seventy" (hence the abbreviation LXX) and refers to the belief that 72 Jewish scholars, 6 from each of the 12 tribes, collaborated in the work.

King James Version (KJV). A translation commissioned by James I of England; a committee of 54 scholars worked on the project from 1604 to 1611. Although translated from the original Hebrew and Greek, about 60 percent of the KJV wording comes from earlier English versions, in particular William Tyndale's translation (1525) and the Bishop's Bible (1568). Thus, the language was archaic when the KJV appeared in Shakespeare's time. For more than three centuries the KJV was the Authorized Version (AV) for the Anglican and many other Protestant churches. The language was somewhat modernized for the British Revised Version (RV) in 1881-1885 and the American Standard Version (ASV) in 1901. The Thomas Nelson company published the New King James Version between 1979 and 1982.

Revised Standard Version (RSV). An update of the American Standard Version (see above). The New Testament translation first appeared in 1946; both Old and New Testaments appeared in 1952, with the Apocrypha in 1957. The New Revised Standard Version (NRSV), incorporating such advances in biblical studies as the discovery of the Dead Sea Scrolls, was published in 1990.

Jewish Publication Society (JPS). A translation of the Hebrew Bible first published in 1917. Based on the traditional Hebrew text (the Masoretic text) and incorporating Jewish interpretation, the JPS is nevertheless strongly influenced by the KJV. The new Jewish Publication Society Version (NJPS), a completely new translation based on MT, was issued between 1962 and 1982.

Jerusalem Bible (JB). A Catholic translation that appeared between 1959 and 1966. Produced in Jerusalem but first published in French in Paris, this scholarly version contains numerous footnotes and alternative readings. The JB was originally intended as a study Bible and not a liturgical replacement for the Douay Bible (1582-1609), the standard Catholic English translation based on the fourth-century Latin Vulgate. An update, the New Jerusalem Bible, appeared in 1985.

New English Bible (NEB). Sponsored by British Protestant denominations and published between 1961 and 1970. The NEB consciously rejected the KJV tradition. With updated language, innovative scholarship and many textual emendations, the NEB has elicited both praise and criticism. A modified version in loftier liturgical language appeared in 1989 as the Revised English Bible.

In the NEB, however, *la'adam* is translated "to the man," and therefore no Adam appears in this version of the story:

> So God formed out of the ground all the wild animals and all the birds of heaven. He brought them to the man [*'el ha'adam*] to see what he would call them, and whatever the man [*ha'adam*] called each living creature, that was its name. Thus the man [*ha'adam*] gave names to all cattle, to the birds of heaven, and to every wild animal; but for the man [*la'adam*] himself no partner had yet been found.

Besides the absence of capital letters and vowels, scholars believe that in some ancient manuscripts there were no spaces between words. The reader must recognize prefixes and suffixes and hypothesize meaningful words and phrases. Surprisingly enough, thisisnotveryhard. But as a popular experiment in psychology illustrates, readers tend to see what they expect or want to find. GODISNOWHERE can be read "God is now here" or "God is nowhere."

In the case of Hebrew *šylh*, this ambiguity allows the reading *šiyloh* (Shiloh), as in the KJV rendering of Genesis 49:10, a poetic passage from Jacob's death song:

> The sceptre shall not depart from Judah, nor a lawgiver from between his feet, until Shiloh come; and unto him shall the gathering of the people be.

But the letters could also be divided into *šay loh* (tribute to him), as proposed by the translators of the NEB:

> The sceptre shall not pass from Judah, nor the staff from his descendants, so long as tribute is brought to him and the obedience of the nations is his.

The reading *šay loh* also seems to underlie the JB rendering, "until he come to whom it belongs," which is explained in a footnote as referring to the Messiah or "to David as a type of the Messiah."

Coupled with the absence of periods and commas, equivocal word divisions create uncertainty in Genesis 20:16. Because Abraham and Sarah have passed themselves off as brother and sister, King Abimelech has taken Sarah into his harem. God appears to Abimelech and tells him to return Sarah to Abraham. Abimelech does so and also gives them generous presents. In the KJV, the story continues (Genesis 20:16):

> And unto Sarah he said, Behold, I have given thy brother a thousand pieces of silver: behold, he is to thee a covering of the eyes, unto all that are with thee, and with all other: thus she was reproved.

In the NEB the sentence reads:

> To Sarah he said, "I have given your brother a thousand pieces of silver, so that your own people may turn a blind eye on it all, and you will be completely vindicated."

The crux here is that, in the KJV, the Hebrew words are separated into *w't kl wnḳht* (pronounce *ve'et kol venokhahat*), "and with all [other]; and [she was] made right." In the NEB, the same letters are separated into *w't klw nḳht* (pronounced *ve'at kulow nokhahat*), "and you will be completely made right."[4]

There is another textual conundrum in this passage. Where does Abimelech's statement end? There are no quotation marks in manuscripts of the Hebrew Bible. In the KJV, the last clause in the sentence is the narrator's comment; in the NEB, it is spoken by Abimelech. The Hebrew verb *nḳht* agrees with an unnamed feminine subject, but does not specify first, second or third person, so in the KJV, "she" is inserted to make it a statement *about* Sarah; in the NEB, *w't* is *ve'at* (you), making it a comment *to* Sarah.

The same problem arises in Adam's reaction to seeing Eve for the first time. According to the KJV, when Adam rejects all the animals of the earth as partners and finally finds Eve "an help meet for him," he makes an observation and a prediction (Genesis 2:23-24):

> This is now bone of my bone, and flesh of my flesh: she shall be called Woman, because she was taken out of Man. Therefore shall a man leave his father and his mother, and shall cleave unto his wife: and they shall be one flesh.

But in both the NEB and JB, the man (*ha'adam*) says only the first sentence; the second is the narrator's comment. In the NEB, the verses read:

> [A]nd the man said:
> "Now this, at last—
> bone from my bones,
> flesh from my flesh!—
> this shall be called woman,
> for from man was this taken."
> That is why a man leaves his father and mother and is united to his wife, and the two become one flesh.

Sometimes even favorite quotations can be called into question. The Hebrew of Isaiah 40:3 can be rendered word for word into English as "a voice calls in the wilderness prepare a path for the Lord." Because of the absence of quotation marks, however, we may wonder what, exactly, is in the wilderness. According to the time-honored phrasing of the KJV, following the interpretation popularized by the Septuagint, a lone, outcast voice is in the wilderness:

> The voice of him that crieth in the wilderness,
> Prepare ye the way of the Lord....

But almost all modern translators recognize a poetic parallel with the following phrase and place the adverbial phrase "in the wilderness" in the quoted speech. When this is done, the way of the Lord, rather than the voice, is in the wilderness. The JB thus reads:

> A voice cries, "Prepare in the wilderness a way for Yahweh. Make a straight highway for our God across the desert."

And the JB–which is not averse to finding messianic prefigurations, as we saw in Jacob's death song–is moved to comment on the loss in a footnote:

> The evangelists quote this text in its LXX [that is, Septuagint] form: "A voice of one who cries in the wilderness....": for them this is the voice of John the Baptist, the forerunner of the Messiah.

As the JB translation shows, however, in this verse John the Baptist is another man who wasn't there.

Afterword

Alan Millard takes issue with Minkoff's statement that there are no spaces between words in some ancient Hebrew manuscripts in "Were Words Separated in Ancient Hebrew Writing?":

Writing without word divisions is called *scriptio continua*, or continuous writing. Ancient Greek was commonly written like that. Stone monuments from Athens and other Greek cities, Greek papyri found in Egypt, as well as classical and biblical manuscripts in Greek all show line after line of letters in unbroken sequences. Some scholars have assumed that Hebrew scribes also wrote in *scriptio continua*. But even a superficial look at ancient Hebrew documents proves that this is untrue.

Before the Babylonian Exile (that is, before 586 B.C.E.), Hebrew was written in a script variously called Old Hebrew, paleo-Hebrew or Phoenician. Although this script continued to be used in some circles (the Samaritan alphabet is a descendant) after the exiles returned, it was replaced, for the most part, with the square Aramaic script the exiles brought back from Babylonia. Incidentally, the same square script is still used in printed Hebrew today. But even in early Hebrew inscriptions written in the old Hebrew script, dots between words were used as dividers. Word dividers are clearly visible in the famous Siloam tunnel inscription, an eighth-century B.C.E. inscription engraved in the wall of the tunnel that the Judahite king Hezekiah dug under the city to bring water into Jerusalem during the siege of the Assyrian king Sennacherib (2 Kings 20:20; 2 Chronicles 32:2-4,30).

Word separators can also be seen in an eighth-century B.C.E. inscription from Nimrud. This fragmentary ivory plaque was found in the ruins of an Assyrian storehouse at Nimrud (ancient Kalhu), south of Nineveh, where it was probably brought as booty, perhaps from Samaria. The words that survive are part of a curse on the person who would destroy the inscription, or possibly the object to which it was affixed.

Ostraca, brief notes scribbled on potsherds (singular, ostracon), scores of which have been found, are the everyday literary remains of the early Israelites. Even here, dots as word dividers are usually present, although they are not always easy to see. Sometimes dots as word dividers were even included on ancient Hebrew seals. Moabite and Ammonite scribes in Transjordan also used them.

When Jewish scribes adopted the Aramaic script during the Babylonian Exile, they found word division was customary in that writing as well. Instead of a dot, however, scribes left spaces the width of narrow letters between words. The famous fifth-century B.C.E. Aramaic papyri left by the Jewish community of Elephantine (an island near the first cataract of the Nile) clearly show this word division. The practice applied to letters and legal deeds, as well as to literary works such as the Proverbs of Ahiqar, an Aramaic story and collection of aphorisms preserved on pieces of a papyrus scroll found at Elephantine. These are the oldest known examples of a book written in a Semitic language on a scroll.

Separating words continued to be the custom in Hebrew manuscripts. The Dead Sea Scrolls (230 B.C.E.- 68 C.E.) and the Bar-Kokhba documents (from the time of the Second Jewish Revolt against Rome, 132-135 C.E.) are fine examples.

Of course, scribes did make mistakes, and one of the easiest was running words together. Scribes reading exemplars and copying them phrase by phrase could easily make this mistake; so could scribes writing from dictation. Many run-ons were probably corrected long ago. Nevertheless, scholars have detected a few places in the Bible where the Hebrew text is best explained, even today, by correcting the text.

The best example is Amos 6:12, which reads in the Hebrew text, "Do horses run upon rocks? Does one plough with oxen?" The Hebrew word for oxen is *bqrym*. But the singular *bqr* (ox) can also be used for the plural. If this is done, the letters *ym* can be read as a separate word, namely "sea." By taking the last two letters as a separate word, "sea," one obtains the sense "oxen the sea." As the text stands, the first line asks a question to which the expected answer is no; in the second line, read as "Does one plow with oxen?" the reasonable answer is yes. Yet the sense of the verse as a whole suggests negative answers to both questions. When *bqrym* is separated into two words, the verse is properly rendered: "Do horses run upon the rocks? Does one plough the sea with oxen?" To both questions one may answer no. It is easy to see how a copyist ran the two words together, because the resulting word is a perfectly good Hebrew word meaning "oxen."

In some cases, scribes mistakenly split one word into two, especially if the word was unusual. Minkoff cites an example from Genesis 49:10, where the Hebrew *šylh* may be read either as *šiyloh* (Shiloh) or *šay loh* (tribute to him).

But contrary to popular opinion, word division was normal in early Hebrew writing and was passed down as good scribal practice in Jewish tradition. Mistakes were made (and usually corrected), but they were relatively rare. ***BR*** *8:3 (1992), p. 44*

CHAPTER 12

Woman, a Power Equal to Man

R. David Freedman

The passage in Genesis describing Eve as a "helpmate" for Adam has long been used to define woman's place. But, in his analysis of Hebrew orthography, Freedman argues that two different words accidentally came to have the same spelling. The correct translation in this verse, he says, should be "partner."

The phrase in question is ʿezer kenegdo. *Though* ʿ-z-r *was originally pronounced differently from the unrelated root* g-z-r, *"when the Bible was written, what originally had been two roots...one with an ʿayin and one with a ghayyin...merged into one." One meant "save," the other "strong." But the merger of spelling was eventually followed by a merger of meaning, and "in time the root* ʿ-z-r *was always interpreted as 'to help.'" In addition,* kenegdo *is usually wrongly translated "fit," meaning "a helper fit for him." The phrase is properly rendered "a power equal to him."–Ed.*

In the second account of creation in Genesis,[1] woman is created after man has been placed in the Garden of Eden and commanded not to eat of the tree of knowledge of good and evil. God then decides that it is not good for man to be alone and creates a "suitable" "helper" or "helpmate" for him. At least that is the customary translation.

The verse in this story on which I would like to focus is Genesis 2:18b. With minor variations in translation, the woman is supposed to be an assistant, fit or appropriate for the man. Here are a few translations of the verse; God is the speaker in all of them:

> I shall make him a helper fit for him. (Revised Standard Version)
> I will make him a helpmate. (Jerusalem Bible)
> I will make a fitting helper for him. (New Jewish Publication Society)
> I will make him an aid fit for him. (Anchor Bible, *Genesis*)

The two Hebrew words that describe the position of the about-to-be-created woman vis-à-vis the man are *ʿēzer k*^{e}*negdô*. I believe the customary translation

"THE FALL OF MAN" by German artist Albrecht Dürer (1471-1528).

of this phrase, despite nearly universal acceptance, is wrong. That is not what the words are intended to convey. The phrase should be translated instead to mean, approximately, "a power equal to man."[2] That is, when God decided to create another creature so that man would not be alone, he decided to make "a power equal to him," someone whose strength was equal to man's. Woman was not intended just to be man's helper. She was intended to be his partner.

A careful study of the two Hebrew words involved will prove my point. The Hebrew word *ʿēzer* is a combination of two roots, one *ʿ-z-r* (to rescue or to save), and the other *ǵ-z-r* (to be strong). The only difference is in the first sign. The raised ʿ stands for the letter ʿayin, which in modern Hebrew is often silent. But in ancient times, it was a guttural sound in the back of the throat. The symbol ǵ stands for the letter ghayyin, a guttural much like the ancient Hebrew ʿayin but produced higher up in the throat. Some ancient Semitic languages distinguished between the two signs; others did not. For example, Ugaritic maintains a distinction between ʿayin and ghayyin. Hebrew no longer does.[3]

In Phoenicia about 1500 B.C.E., these two phonemes, or sounds, began to be written the same way; that is, they were represented by the same written sign. As scholars would say, the two phonemes merged into one grapheme. Later, the pronunciations also merged. In Hebrew the merger appears to have taken place somewhat later, around 1200 B.C.E. Thus, by the time the Bible was written, the two original roots of *ʿēzer*, one with an ʿayin and one with a ghayyin, had merged.

With the merger of writing and pronunciation came a merger of meaning. The word *ʿēzer* could mean either "to save" (*ʿ-z-r*) or "to be strong" (*ǵ-z-r*).[4] But in time the root *ʿ-z-r* was always interpreted "to help," a combination of both meanings.

The noun *ʿēzer* occurs 21 times in the Hebrew Bible. In eight instances, the word means "savior." These instances are easy to identify because the word is used with other expressions meaning "save" or with associated ideas. For example, in Psalm 70:5 we read:

> I am completely destitute;
> O God, hurry to my rescue [*ʿezri*].
> You are my deliverer [*mᵉfallᵉti*].
> O Lord do not delay.

The context and especially the word *mᵉfallᵉti* (deliverer) make the meaning *ʿezri* (my aid or my help) clear. The other seven examples are similar.[5]

Elsewhere, the root *ʿēzer* means "strength." For example, in Deuteronomy 33:26 we read:

> There is none like God, O Jeshurun,
> The Rider of the Sky in your strength [*beʿezreka*],
> in the heavens in your majesty [*ga'avah*].

And in Deuteronomy 33:29:

> Happy are you, Israel! Who is like you,
> a people delivered by the Lord,
> The shield of your strength [*ʿezreka*]
> and the sword of your majesty [*ga'avah*].

The conclusion of verse 29 tells of the defeat of Israel's enemies—a clear indication that *ʿēzer* in these examples means "strength." In several instances in the Bible, the concept of majesty is paralleled with the concept of strength. In these examples the word for strength is clear. Thus, in Psalm 68:34 we find a parallel between majesty and strength:

> Ascribe strength [*ʿoz*] to God:
> His majesty [*ga'avah*] is upon Israel,
> and his strength [*ʿuzzo*] is in the heavens.

And in Psalm 93:1:

> The Lord reigns,
> He is clothed in majesty [*ge'ut*, a variant of *ga'avah*]
> He is girded with strength [*ʿoz*].

Because strength is the parallel of majesty in these cases (where *ʿoz* is used to mean "strength"), we should also expect strength to be the parallel of majesty in Deuteronomy 33:29 where a form of *ʿēzer* is used (*ʿezreka* meaning "your strength") instead of *ʿoz*.

Furthermore, the phrase found in Deuteronomy 33:29, "the shield of your strength," must be compared to a similar phrase in Psalm 28:7, "the Lord is my strength [*ʿuzzi*] and my shield." The juxtaposition of shield and strength (*ʿoz*) suggests that the word *ʿezreka* juxtaposed with the word for "shield" in Deuteronomy 33:29 means "my strength" rather than "my aid" or "my savior."

Finally, the fact that one king of Judah had two names, *ʿzryh* and *ʿzyh* (Azariah and Uzziah, both referring to God's strength), demonstrates that a root (*ʿ-z-r*) meaning "strength" was known in Hebrew. Instances in which the forms of *ʿēzer* mean "strength" could be multiplied and the meaning demonstrated in the same way.[6]

Thus, forms of *ʿēzer* in the Bible can mean "to save" or "to be strong." In Genesis 2:18b, when God announces that he will create a being to relieve the man's loneliness, he surely does not intend this being to be the man's savior. This makes no sense. God intends this new being to be, like the man, a power (or strength) superior to the animals. This is the true meaning of *ʿēzer* as used in this passage.

The second word from Genesis 2:18b that we must examine is *k*^{e}*negdô*, a word that appears in the Bible only once. (Scholars call such a word a *hapax legomenon* or *hapax* for short.) In later Mishnaic Hebrew, the root *k*^{e}*neged* means "equal," as in the famous saying that "The study of Torah is equal [*k*^{e}*neged*] to all the other commandments."

In my opinion, there is no basis for translating the word *k*^{e}*neged* as "fit" or "appropriate," as traditional translators do when they describe the woman as a "fit helper." When God created Eve from Adam's rib, his intent was that she would be–unlike the animals–"a power [or strength] *equal* to him." I think there is no other way to understand the phrase *ʿēzer k*^{e}*negdô* that can be defended philologically. The traditional translation is based on a late nuance of *ʿēzer* (help), which can not be justified in this context.

Note that my translation is consonant with the account of creation in Genesis 1 where man and woman are created at the same time. In chapter 1, man and woman are both created "in the image of God." In my interpretation, *ʿēzer k*^{e}*negdô* fills the literary function of two phrases in Genesis 1–"in the image of God" and "male and female He created them." Eve is created in Adam's image to the degree that she is his equal–just as man is created in God's image to the degree that he fulfills an analogous role. Moreover, "male and female he created them" does not imply the superiority of either one.

Reflections of this essential equality are found elsewhere in the Bible. Even in the covenant code (Exodus 21 and 22), which is so patently early that even some modern scholars have attributed it to Moses, men and women are consistently subject to the same punishment for the same crime (equal pay for equal work), and crimes committed against a man or a woman are punished identically. Clearly, the concept in Genesis 2 of Eve's having been created to be Adam's equal informs the spirit and underlies the legal provisions of the covenant code.

But the equality of punishment shows up much earlier, in Genesis 3, in the punishment of Adam and Eve for disobeying God and for eating the forbidden fruit. The equality of their punishments can been seen in the chart on the following page.

	Role	***New Attitude***	***Partner***	***Punishment***
Adam	farmer	toil	Earth	willful production of thorns and thistles instead of grain (frustration)
Eve	child-bearing	pain	Adam	Adam's willful dominance over Eve despite her desire for him (frustration)

Moreover, in both instances the temporary nature of the punishment is evident. The curse imposed on the earth as punishment for Adam's sin is removed with the birth of Noah:

> This one [Noah] will bring us relief for the earth cursed by the Lord.
> Genesis 5:29

The woman's punishment was also temporary. In Genesis 30:14-16, Leah and Rachel determine Jacob's sleeping arrangements for the night in his absence. Clearly, the text takes for granted that the patriarch was not "master" over his wives in this regard. What is more, in Exodus 21:10, a first wife is guaranteed food, clothing and conjugal rights in the event that her husband takes a second wife. This ancient interpretation of the verse is proof that man's sexual mastery over woman was temporary.

Still more evidence of the equality of Adam and Eve can be found in Genesis 2:23, where Adam says of Eve:

> This one at last
> Is bone of my bones
> And flesh of my flesh.

In this passage both meanings of this *double entendre* are evoked.[7] Eve was literally created from Adam's bone and flesh. But the idiomatic meaning in the Bible of "bone and flesh" is "very close relative," "one of us"—in effect, "our equal." For example, Jacob, who is "my bone and my flesh" of Laban in Genesis 29:14, means Jacob is entitled to free hospitality. But once Jacob is demoted to *aḥ* (brother, kinsman) in verse 15, he has to work for his keep.[8] Adam reinforces the double meaning of the phrase "bone and flesh" in Genesis 2:23:

> She shall be called "woman" [*iššah*] because she was taken out of "man" [*iš*].

The idiomatic meaning of "bone and flesh" as "equal" retains its force, however, alongside the literal meaning.

So God made up for the inadequacy of his original creation of man—an inadequacy he admits when he says "It is not good for the man to be alone"—by creating the female of the species, who is intended to be *ʿēzer kᵉnegdô*, "a power equal to him."[9]

Afterword

Norman M. Meskin of Forest Hills, New York, feels that the concluding paragraph of Freedman's article requires clarification:

I am troubled by the ambiguity of the words "my interpretation" as they appear in endnote nine: "My interpretation has been anticipated in medieval Jewish Midrashim, especially the *Alfabeta d'Rabbi Akiva* and *Pirkei d'Rabbi Eliezer.*" If Professor Freedman is referring to his rendering of *'ezer kenegdo* as "a power equal to him," then his statement is correct–there is support for such a notion among traditional Jewish commentaries–but this should have been pointed out the first time the phrase was used, which is in the first paragraph of the article. No less a scholar than Rabbi Samson Raphael Hirsch concurs:

> And *'ezer kenegdo* certainly expresses no idea of subordination, but rather complete equality, and on a footing of equal independence. Woman stands to Man *kenegdo*, parallel, on one line, at his side.[1]

If however, as I suspect, the words "my interpretation" refer to the concluding paragraph in its entirety, then I must take strong exception to this statement. No classical Jewish thinker would lend credence to the notion that God's original creation of man was "inadequate" or that God "admitted" such an inadequacy. God does *not* change his mind! He doesn't vacillate! He doesn't create by trial and error!

This misguided thinking was, indeed, "anticipated" by classical Jewish commentators, and I would like to share with Professor Freedman and your readers two explanations intended to pre-empt this line of reasoning:

> ...the Torah earlier described how man was created in a very concise manner. This is not very different from the description of the creation of the heaven, earth and trees, which was also very concise. The Torah then backtracks and describes how the world was before it was created. The same is true of the creation of man. The statement "It is not good for man to be alone," was therefore made before man was created. Thus, it was all part of God's plan.[2]

> This does not imply that God changed His mind, but rather to draw our attention to the precious nature of this partnership and to teach us that it is not good for man to be alone. For this reason, the Holy One Blessed be He willed it that man should be without woman for a brief period and then afterwards introduced her so that she would be dear to him after he had felt something was lacking without her.[3]

***BAR** 9:3 (1983), p. 26*

R. David Freedman replies:

Mr. Meskin can rest easy. The note that concerns him refers to my rendering of *ʿēzer kᵉnegdô*. I saved it for the end because I tend to hold trump cards for the end of the game. Mr. Meskin is welcome to move it, if he wishes, to wherever he feels it is appropriate. Mr. Meskin is also cordially invited to add the word *kivyakol* (Hebrew for "so to speak") to bring the article up to the level of his philosophical understanding. ***BAR*** *9:3 (1983), p. 26*

Pastor William W. Bennett of Edwards Corners Bible Church in Marcellus, Michigan, believes Freedman's interpretation is not consonant with other biblical passages:

Let me first say that I enjoyed the insights of the etymology of the Hebrew words. If one were to translate and interpret on the basis of this argument, I might find myself in complete agreement with Freedman's point of view.

However, I believe that when one interprets Scripture, a basic rule is that the interpretation be in agreement with the rest of Scripture. When I read the article in question, I was immediately drawn to three New Testament writings on the subject: Corinthians 11:3-16; Ephesians 5:22-33; and 1 Peter 3:1-7, especially verse 7.

In light of these passages, I believe that the traditional view is most credible. Also, because an etymological study traces a word through history, I am convinced that Professor Freedman made the error of taking a later meaning for the original. I am sure that in time the word came to mean exactly what Professor Freedman suggests. That does not necessarily suggest that it was understood as such at the time Genesis was written. ***BAR*** *9:3 (1983), p. 26*

Freedman replies:

Since the New Testament is not scripture for me, I am not faced with Pastor Bennett's problem. More to the point, however, the New Testament is at least 500 years later than the Genesis passage (even by the reckoning of the critics), and must therefore take second place to philology as a way of arriving at the intent of the words in question.

Finally, if part of the punishment of Eve was that Adam was to rule over her, it is obvious that this was not the status quo beforehand.

Incidentally, I do not claim that *ʿēzer kᵉnegdô* came to mean "a power equal to man" but that it came to mean something like "a helpmate fit for him" by way of back-reading a later social norm into an earlier text. ***BAR*** *9:3 (1983), p. 27*

PART VI

The Bible as Literature

The Bible as Literature
Introduction

In *Approaches to Teaching the Hebrew Bible as Literature in Translation*,[1] a guidebook for teachers published by the Modern Language Association, Barry N. Olshen asks how treatment of the Bible "as literature" differs from treatment as history, theology or "divine revelation"? One answer can be found in *Congregation*,[2] a collection of essays about the Bible by professional writers rather than biblical scholars. As editor David Rosenberg observes, "many of the contributing novelists read the Bible in the same spirit of intimacy they would bring to a novel, and many of the poets here have bared their innermost poetic instinct in the presence of the Bible's poetry." Ideally, a literary approach to the Bible is an appreciation of the artistic medium that conveys or embodies the message.

But the idea of applying techniques of literary criticism to the Bible sends shivers up many spines, and objections have arisen from many quarters. Some still confuse the historical, source-critical approach of the past century–which was often called literary criticism–with new literary approaches. Historical source-critics seemed to take pleasure in debunking traditional views about the authorship, authority and historicity of the Bible. Even as Olshen describes the contemporary literary-critical approach as "arguably the most exciting recent development in Bible scholarship," he notes the number of "apologia for the study of the Bible 'as literature'" intended to allay the fears of people who believe the Bible is more than, or different from, literature.

Some serious students of the Bible harbor unpleasant memories of ill-defined or vacuous college courses called "The Bible as Literature." Perhaps, as Richard Coggins suggests in *Introducing the Old Testament*,[3] literary analysis implies excessive subjectivity, which raises questions that may undermine or denigrate adherence to a particular creed. Readers who believe the Bible is the word of God consider it sacrilegious to classify the Bible as literature and are put off by suggestions, like Meir Sternberg's in *The Poetics of Biblical Narrative*, that "[t]o offer a poetics of biblical narrative is to claim that biblical narrative is a work of literature. Not just an artful work...not a work resorting to so-called literary devices...but a literary work."[4] The appeal of the Bible to Western civilization as a whole and to each of us as individuals is not, after all, primarily literary.

Nevertheless, acknowledging that, whatever the sacred content or intent of the Bible, the text is literary need not create problems. Consider, for a moment, that the Torah, the "Law" of the Jews, logically leads the uninitiated to expect a legal code, a tome filled with case histories, precedents and decisions instead of the epic story of Noah and the Flood, the family sagas of Abraham, Isaac and Jacob, the drama of the Exodus, the poetry of the Song of the Sea and Moses' Death Song. But the laws in the Bible (even the code of priestly behavior and the laws of inheritance) are embedded in a narrative framework. Those who object to exploring the Bible as literature may be more comfortable with the approach of Northrop Frye in *The Great Code: The Bible and Literature* that the Bible is "as literary as it can well be without actually being literature."[5]

In *The Literary Guide to the Bible*, Robert Alter observes that in some circles considering the Bible as literature means "turn[ing] it around to an odd angle from its own original emphases, which are theological, legislative, historiographic and moral." He argues, however, that "opposition between literature and the really serious things collapses the moment we realize that it is the exception in any culture for literary invention to be a purely aesthetic activity."[6] Coggins, for example, maintains that the "characteristic manner of expressing belief about God in the Old Testament is by means of stories." He points out that the abstract "maker of heaven and earth" is brought to life in the creation stories of Genesis 1 and 2, that the God of promise is embodied in stories of the patriarchs, and that the "nature of the relationship between God and humanity is explored by means of a story–the Book of Job."

Stories are the building blocks of religion. Few people engage sterile philosophy without the mediating presence of heroes and role models, rituals and poetry. The Hebrew prophets declaimed their messages in poetry, with tangible images of nature, common occupations and family life. And the authors of Jonah, Ruth and Esther knew the importance of character development, dialogue and plot turns. Thus, there is much to be gained by paying close attention to biblical language, imagery, characterization and other literary concerns such as genre, theme, diction and narrative point of view.

The publication in 1946 of *Mimesis* by Erich Auerbach was a defining moment in modern literary criticism of the Bible.[7] Until that time, biblical scholars had been dominated by historical concerns; they had treated the text as a kind of ore from which a persistent scholar might mine an occasional nugget of historical truth or original folk literature. When the Bible was subjected to literary analysis, the result was usually a negative comparison to classical Greek literature as epitomized in Matthew Arnold's famous description in *Culture and Anarchy* of Hebraism as conduct and Hellenism as culture.

"Educate and humanize the Philistines," he pleaded. "Remedy their excessive Hebraism by a dose of Hellenism."[8]

Auerbach disagreed with Arnold's reductive description of Hebraism. He analyzed Hebrew and Homeric narratives and championed biblical realism as a major aesthetic achievement. Not all scholars accepted Auerbach's argument, but he succeeded in changing the way critics read the Bible. After Auerbach, the focus, which had been on the underlying sources of the received text and the intentions of the original authors, shifted to the text itself, as it existed, and the editors who left their marks on the final product.

David Noel Freedman, for example, has written a number of works exploring the structural coherence of the Bible. He claims that excessive concern with original sources caused scholars to overlook the importance of the actual text and to trivialize the work of the final redactor(s). In his essay on the Book of Job in this section, Freedman argues that, even though an existing folk story was adopted as the framework of a philosophical poem, and despite the likelihood that the Hymn to Wisdom in Job 28 was originally a separate work, what really matters is the meaning of the book before us.

According to Olshen, "[t]he most notable advances in recent years have been in the area of biblical narrative." This is reflected in the questions being asked about plot, theme, motivation and genres, like epic, saga, folktale and story. In his article, Kenneth R. R. Gros Louis tries to explain why Matthew and Luke chose to tell the same story in different ways. "What questions go through a writer's mind as he considers his sources and subject?" Gros Louis asks. The author must decide which events to emphasize, which characters should speak and what they should say. These are concerns common to all narratives, whether sacred or secular.

Jonathan Culler, in *Identity of the Literary Text*,[9] bases his argument on the venerable axiom of criticism that "a literary masterpiece was inexhaustible in that new readings–including one's own rereading of a text–could always uncover new beauties that belonged to the work's identity but had not thitherto been revealed." Interestingly, the ancient rabbis also believed in the eternal newness of the Torah, as expressed in the words of Deuteronomy 6:6, "these words, which I command you this day." And the idea of the inexhaustible text informs the saying from Mishnah Avoth 5:25, "Turn it [the Torah] this way, turn it that way, everything is in it." In this sense, literary readings of the Bible are at least as old as Jewish Midrash (creative, sometimes fanciful, expositions of the Bible by rabbis and scholars who tried, among other things, to demonstrate the significance of the Bible for their generation).

Great literature is great because it is forever fresh and relevant. As Coggins says, "Our sympathies are engaged, our imagination stimulated, we are invited to reflect upon our own situation in the light of the story." A case can be made that literary critics capture the essential strength of the Bible, an inherent theological openness.

Events in the Bible are presented from a particular point of view, with a particular interpretation, but not the only possible interpretation. To the author of Samuel, David is a noble hero hounded by mad King Saul; the same events could be interpreted to mean that the ruthless outlaw David drives the patriotic Saul to his death. As Coggins has noted, Abraham's willingness to sacrifice Isaac in Genesis 22 is intended to portray exemplary religious faith; in a modern telling of the story, Abraham might be portrayed as an abusive parent who should be barred from contact with his children.

In this same spirit, Freedman asks if it is possible to understand the book of Job. For, as Alter says of Job, "the literary medium is not merely a means of 'conveying' doctrinal positions but an adventurous occasion for deepening doctrine through the play of literary resources, or perhaps even, at least here, for leaping beyond doctrine." Rather than undermining sacred intent, Alter says, literature makes "meanings more memorable, more satisfyingly complex, so that what is well wrought in language can more powerfully engage the world of events, values, human and divine ends."

CHAPTER 13

Understanding the Book of Job

David Noel Freedman

The Book of Job is better known for raising questions than for answering them. Readers have agonized over the sequence of speeches, their logic and coherence. Scholars have suggested that some sections were added by authors with different world views from the original writer's. Nevertheless, argues Freedman, we must respect the work of the final editor. Whatever its compositional history, the book before us "is not an accidental assemblage of disparate and disconnected materials." Our obligation as readers is not to tear the work apart but to understand its unity–"the story of an upright, God-fearing man...who endures great suffering, but who nevertheless perseveres in his integrity and fidelity."

Many readers dismiss the opening description of Job's suffering as a narrative device to facilitate the debate that comprises 95 percent of the book. Freedman, however, believes "testing" is the unifying theme of the work. Job is tested by the loss of his family and again by the inflammation that attacks his body. The lengthy dialogue is a third test, more painful than the others, as Job must defend his integrity against the conventional pieties of his friends. The fourth test is the accusation of the brash Elihu, who comes from nowhere and immediately disappears, a sign, Freedman believes, that he is really Satan in disguise.

While "carefully positioned by the author/editor to be fully aware of both scenes" in heaven and on earth, the reader is nonetheless caught up in the suspense. Will Job maintain his integrity, or will he mouth pious platitudes to recoup his former status? What is the truth? What does God want of Job–and us?–Ed.

The Book of Job, a masterpiece of world literature, is better known for posing problems and raising issues than for answering questions or resolving dilemmas. To the untutored eye, Job (at least in translation) reads smoothly from beginning to end. But critical investigation reveals seams, if not rents, in the fabric of the text. There are rough passages and rougher transitions, and a good case can be made that various passages are intrusive and were not part of the original work. Questions have also been raised about the sequence of speeches and their integrity and completeness.

Nevertheless, we must respect the final editor or compiler of the book. Job is not, after all, an accidental assemblage of disparate or disconnected materials. Regardless of where the various pieces originated, the editor or compiler worked them into a whole, and if seams and gaps are visible, then Job is no different from other great works of literature and art. It is reasonable and legitimate for us to consider the book as a whole.

Job does have an overall unity, including all the parts. It is the story of an upright, God-fearing man–Job of the land of Uz–who endures terrible suffering but who, nevertheless, maintains his integrity and fidelity and is, ultimately, rewarded for his faith by being restored to his former state and compensated for his losses. From the start, Job is presented as a virtuous and righteous man (Job 1:1). This is the premise of the book, with which any valid interpretation must begin. Enter now the Adversary, or the Satan (*ha-satan* in Hebrew), who challenges Yahweh's assertion that there is no one else on earth like Job, "a blameless and upright man who fears God and shuns evil" (Job 1:8).

Satan argues that Job's righteousness is calculated piety based on his special relationship with God. In other words, Satan says, Job serves and reveres God not for God's sake alone, which is the true measure of faith. Job's faith, he says, is based on God's care and protection. This reciprocal relationship may be beneficial to both parties, Satan suggests, but it hardly proves that Job is inwardly righteous; it only shows that Job responds to divine grace and thereby reaps rich rewards. Satan argues that Job has actually hoodwinked God, who wants to believe that Job's righteousness is pure and disinterested. Satan contends that if God were to take away Job's material possessions and blessings he would soon see what Job really thinks and would realize how superficial Job's piety is.

God is intrigued by Satan's proposal, and because he is convinced that Job is

JOB "FEARED GOD AND SHUNNED EVIL" (Job 1:1). Yet he was made to suffer outrageous torment, as is dramatically portrayed in this 16th-century wood relief by Alonso Berruguette (c.1468-1561), a Spanish sculptor and painter and a pupil of Michelangelo. This Job was sculpted for the cathedral of Toledo, Spain. *Photo: Joseph Martin*

truly righteous–namely that he reveres God for himself alone and will adhere to his faith regardless of his personal misfortune–God allows Satan to inflict a series of devastating blows on Job, destroying not only his material possessions, but also his servants and children. (Only his wife is spared, an interesting point, but one not discussed in the story.)

Like Job's righteousness, Yahweh's responsibility for what transpires is a given. No one ever questions that God is ultimately responsible for what happens to Job. Even though the idea was Satan's and Yahweh only granted him permission to proceed, Satan is only an agent of God. He plays the role of prosecuting attorney in the divine court, a member of Yahweh's entourage who prosecutes humans who have broken the divine rules. Although there is no valid charge against the holy and upright Job, Satan invents one, thereby raising a serious theological question for which there is no simple answer.

Even when Job loses his material possessions and blessings, he does not break. But Satan is still not satisfied that Job has vindicated Yahweh's position. He argues that the test has been insufficient and that Job himself must be attacked. That, he says, is the true test. At that point, according to Satan, Job will surely abandon his faith and curse God openly, thereby vindicating Satan. God, who acknowledges the possibility that Satan may be right, gives Satan permission to inflict a terrible disease on Job to convince him he has been abandoned by God. But even then Job does not reject God or blaspheme, which might be regarded as appropriate or, at least, understandable under the circumstances.

At this point, the heavenly debate is suspended while the drama continues on earth. Job goes outside the village to suffer in solitude. But he is joined there by three companions, Eliphaz, Bildad and Zophar, and a lengthy dialogue ensues about Job's physical and spiritual condition. The dialogue, which fills the gap between the second test and Job's restoration and reward at the end of the story, is the bridge between the prologue (Job 1:1-2:10) and the epilogue (Job 42:7-19). After Satan afflicts Job's body with a severe inflammation from the soles of his feet to the crown of his head, he disappears from the story.

The dialogue occupies 95 percent of the book and can best be understood as another test of Job's faith. Whatever his friends may have intended by coming to console Job, their visit and conversation turn out to be part of the testing process, a more severe test, perhaps, than the suffering inflicted by Satan. Although Satan's presence in the dialogue is not explicit, we may conclude that the friends, especially their arguments, constitute Satan's third attempt to bring Job down.

The main thrust of the argument is that Job should concede that he must have unknowingly broken his compact with God and that, if he confesses and repents, he will be forgiven. In other words, repentance is a panacea, and it is better to repent than to compound the original sin by challenging God and, in effect, defying him by self-justification. This argument sounds reasonable but, in fact, plays into Satan's hands. By accepting undeserved blame, Job might be granted grace but only at the cost of his innocence and integrity.

You will recall that the main premise of the book is that Job is honorable and innocent, a good and just man. That is a given, assented to even by Satan. If Job were to throw in the towel, he would prove Satan right and God wrong. This explains God's anger toward the friends (Job 42:7-9), who, he understands, are agents of Satan trying to convince Job to compromise his integrity. Job withstands the friends' arguments in three cycles of speeches and replies.

A. First Cycle
  1. Job: first speech, chapter 3
  2. Eliphaz: first speech, chapters 4-5
  3. Job's reply: chapters 6-7
  4. Bildad: first speech, chapter 8
  5. Job's reply: chapters 6-7
  6. Zophar: first speech, chapter 11
  7. Job's reply: chapters 12-14

B. Second Cycle
  1. Eliphaz: second speech, chapter 15
  2. Job's reply: chapters 16-17
  3. Bildad: second speech, chapter 18
  4. Job's reply: chapter 18
  5. Zophar: second speech, chapter 20
  6. Job's reply: chapter 21

C. Third Cycle
  1. Eliphaz: third speech, chapter 22
  2. Job's reply: chapters 23-24
  3. Bildad: third speech, chapter 25
  4. Job's reply: chapter 26
  5. Job's reply: chapter 27

Nothing is gained or lost in these speeches, except that, by the end of the third round, the friendships have been badly frayed. The dialogue is a dramatic demonstration of the futility of debate, except to strengthen one's own resolve.

Interestingly enough, the three friends never speak to one another; they never question each other or discuss strategy or goals. Their only interaction is with Job, who remains impartial and responds in the same spirit to each of them. As the dialogue winds down, the speeches become shorter, and the orderly sequence seems to wobble, become fragmented and fall apart as though the three friends had finally worn themselves out. This development, in effect, increases the drama and refocuses attention on the beleaguered Job.

The debate is followed by a digressive allocution on the subject of wisdom (Job 28). Although this digression may appear to be part of Job's last speech, it is in fact an independent composition not addressed to anyone in the story but clearly aimed at the reader. The digression is a kind of intermezzo on the scarcity and extraordinary value of wisdom advising the reader that the preliminaries are over, and the important issues are about to be addressed. And the reader will be required to exercise that rare, prized faculty, namely wisdom, to grasp the points at issue and understand the proposed resolutions.

Job's final speech (Job 29-31) is a detailed affirmation of the original premise, that he is an upright man whose actions had met with divine favor until the sudden and inexplicable change in God's behavior. Job is adamant that the problem is with God, not with him. For the third time, the friends fail to budge Job from his position. The issue throughout has been Job's insistence on his innocence and righteousness, which is precisely the core of the conflict between God and Satan.

Before Yahweh himself re-enters the drama, Elihu, a fourth friend, appears on the scene. Previously unannounced and unaccounted for, the brash Elihu is a comparative youngster who speaks to and at everybody, criticizing the friends for inferior debating and attacking Job for his stubbornness. Elihu argues vigorously, brooking neither interruption nor rejoinder, in four consecutive speeches that fill six chapters (Job 32-37). The fact that Job and his friends do not respond suggests that communication among the human parties has now ended and that Elihu speaks for the record and, possibly, the reader. Men have become completely alienated from each other. They talk, but no one responds, probably because they are no longer listening to each other.

Elihu is highly critical of everyone who preceded him and scornful in an excessively polite and prolix fashion, but he adds little to the sum of human knowledge. In spite of his insistence on being heard and his rapid-fire loquaciousness, he is ignored, not only by the people he addresses, but also by the Almighty. I believe that Elihu–who appears out of nowhere and disappears from the scene as soon as he finishes talking–is not a real person at all. Like the other participants in the dialogue, he is given a name and a profession, but, as is often the case in Greek epic, he is in disguise. Elihu is the form assumed by Satan to press his case one last time.[1] His speeches are Job's fourth test.

Satan's personal intervention (through Elihu) prompts God to intervene directly. Hence the next and last speech is by Yahweh. Because he cannot risk Job replying to Elihu (because Job may be at the point of resignation and repudiation), God himself answers Elihu, thus settling the wager and all associated issues. Nevertheless, Yahweh, like Satan, is limited by the rules of the original arrangement and can not offer Job consolation or encouragement, which would reinstitute the same situation Satan had complained about in the first place. For the test to be valid, Yahweh must stay out of it.

But for Yahweh to be kept out of the picture totally doesn't seem fair either. So he, too, makes a statement. Beginning in chapter 38, he delivers a powerful and brilliant two-part speech addressed to the group, but especially to Job. At last, Job has a worthy antagonist, and he concedes that he has, at last, met his match. Indeed, he is overmatched. God's first speech (Job 38-39) is followed by a brief response:

> See, I am of small worth; what can I answer You?
> I clap my hand to my mouth.
> I have spoken once, and will not reply,
> Twice, and will do so no more.
>
> Job 40:4-5

Yahweh then launches into a second major address (Job 40-41), and Job, in turn, gives his final response, in which he confesses his failure to understand and his lack of wisdom. Job then repents on dust and ashes (Job 42:1-6).

Although Yahweh's speeches barely address Job's grievances directly, a genuine dialogue is established, and Job is satisfied that Yahweh, who professes to be entirely occupied with running the universe and too busy to intervene in the petty affairs of human beings, nevertheless has responded to Job's urgent appeals. Moreover, by responding he has demonstrated that, excessively busy or not, he is aware of the human predicament and can and will intervene if there is a compelling reason to do so. But, in general, God is too busy with important matters to pay much attention to human beings, and hence Job should not make such a fuss because things have gone wrong.

Job is abashed by the divine intervention and ashamed of his complaints. In fact, Yahweh is not very helpful, as most scholars have observed, and, if this is the author's point, he is at odds with most of the rest of the Bible, which reflects God's intimate concern and attention to what people do.

But the editor of Job has a different strategy. Just as Satan may not finally kill Job, God may not reassure Job of his interest in frail human beings. That would completely spoil the test. Yahweh can not allow himself to say more without violating the terms of the wager. But Job receives the right message even from the wrong words.

What God denies in words is affirmed by the very fact of his speaking them. Job understands that Yahweh's blast from heaven is the very message he needs–that Yahweh has his eye on him and has expressed concern for him. That is enough. Job responds, "With the hearing of the ear I had heard you. But now my eyes have seen you" (Job 42:5). Once he knows that God cares for him, he can freely repent, thus paving the way for the conclusion of the book–his restoration and reward.

Both Satan and God have pressed their case upon Job, who finally makes the necessary move to end the struggle between the opposing forces. He withdraws his charges and does what the friends had arrogantly and insultingly insisted he do from the beginning. He repents on dust and ashes: "Therefore, I recant and relent" (Job 42:6). The way is thus cleared for the resolution of Job's predicament. God judges that Job has vindicated his faith in him and can now be restored to his former state and compensated for his suffering.

Yahweh cheerfully concedes that Job has been wronged and that he has a just cause and claim against him. This concession is implicitly confirmed by compensation over and above simple restoration. Job is given double his former possessions, which is one of the specified damage awards for victims of unjust confiscation of property. Job's children are also restored, a miracle that confirms the potent goodness of Job and the surpassing grace of God. In the end, everything is as it was before, only better.

The story of Job begins on the ragged edge of heresy and lurches and sags in a variety of directions away from the central biblical tradition, which is characterized by absolute commitments and historical certainties. The drama of Job is twofold. One scene is played out on earth with the unfortunate Job and his household (or what is left of it—his wife), providing the framework for the dialogue. The other is played out in heaven by an entirely different cast of characters, an all powerful, willful deity surrounded by servitors. These subordinates are neither echoes nor sycophants of the Almighty. They are intelligent, serious and significant actors whose participation in heavenly decision-making is positively alarming.

The two stories intertwine with palpable effects on one another, but the levels are separated, as it were, by tinted glass that permits vision and knowledge to flow in only one direction. The heavenly participants understand what is happening and why, but their earthly counterparts wander in confusion; their earthly assumptions and assertions play against the contrary realities revealed in the heavenly scenes. The reader is carefully positioned by the author/editor so as to be fully aware of both scenes and of the calculated ironies and paradoxes arising from their juxtaposition. Suspense builds as the audience, within and without the story, wonders not only what will happen to Job and his interlocutors, but also whether or not any of them will learn the truth. Will they peel the onion to its core, or will they, in the end, be forced to settle for conventional wisdom, pious platitudes and the subterfuge that pervades the dealings of the heavenly sphere with the human sphere.

As it turns out, the issues are resolved only at the level on which they began. Job, the innocent and righteous sufferer, is restored to health and happiness and recovers his family and his fortune, but he is no wiser in the end than he was at the beginning. His ordeal satisfied his testers, and he passed the test with flying colors and reaped great rewards for his pains. But in the end, he may be more perplexed than satisfied, more disturbed than complacent—and he remains ignorant of the workings of the heavenly court.

Paradoxically, because the question of Job's integrity is at the heart of the story, even God does not know how matters will turn out. Will Job stand fast, or will he succumb to the pressures of his undeserved suffering and give in to the temptation to curse his maker? If God remains uncertain about the outcome, how much more so are the other characters, especially the human ones, who are not privy to the terms of the wager between God and Satan—the central secret of the drama. How would Job, who is ignorant of the truth but deeply disturbed and badly upset by the course of events, behave if he had any inkling of the truth?

From one perspective, the central issue is the strength and purity of Job's integrity and faith. From the point of view of someone on earth, however, matters look very different. From that vantage point, the central issue is God's righteousness and faith. Is there a moral law in the universe? Does God have any ethical integrity? Or is the universe totally amoral? The reader is shown a single human situation from two sides, and perhaps the author's intention was not to resolve the issues but to explore and exploit them.

The explanation and solution in the prologue and epilogue provide a framework, starting and stopping points. But long after the fate of Job has been resolved, the issues raised in the dialogue persist. All of the participants express deep concerns, fundamental religious questions, about the nature of God and his relationship to the created universe; the plight or position of humanity in relation to God and his world; the problem of suffering; and the responsibility of human beings toward God and toward each other.

Finally, the question must be raised about why God accepted Satan's challenge to Job's righteousness. Satan questioned Job's integrity because, he said, Job's devotion was merely a ploy to win Yahweh's blessing, and he was confident that Job would break under pressure and reveal his true motives. Satan had no way of knowing this in advance, however, and ultimately he was proved wrong.

But what about God? Why didn't he know in advance? Doesn't he know everything, including what goes on inside a man's heart and mind? It is axiomatic in both Christianity and Judaism that God is omniscient and omnipotent and that he has a monopoly on the attributes reflecting his absolute divinity, in which case there is no question as to whether he knows the outcome in advance or enters into the test in good faith.

There are actually two problems here. If God knows everything, and in particular he knows that Job is truly faithful, as God states, why does he allow Job to be tested? Why does he subject Job to terrible trials, tribulations and outright suffering, if there is no point except, perhaps, to show up Satan's false pretensions? If God knows his victory is a sure thing, is it fair for him to enter into a wager with Satan?

The truth is, despite theological claims of divine omniscience, the God of the Hebrew Bible is not omniscient. He has a great deal of knowledge about most things that count, but there is, apparently, a self-imposed limitation when it comes to his knowledge of the inner workings of the human soul. Determining what makes human beings decide ultimate questions and make ultimate commitments requires scrutiny and testing. Several examples in the Bible demonstrate this.

Exegetes have tried for centuries to prove that the story of Abraham's near sacrifice of Isaac (Genesis 22) does not imply a limitation in God's knowledge of Abraham's faith. But the story clearly says otherwise. God calls on Abraham to sacrifice his son Isaac (as is explicitly stated in Genesis 22:1) in order to determine whether or not Abraham is willing to obey the divine command to surrender his only son, whom he loves, to God's demand for such a sacrifice. The clear implication is that God imposes the test in order to find out something he does not know. Moreover, in Genesis 22:11-12, after Abraham passes the test, God says, "Now I know." The same limitation on God's knowledge is reflected in Deuteronomy 8:2-3, where God explains that he kept the Israelites in the wilderness for 40 years to test them (among other things), to find out what was in their hearts, to see if they would prove faithful.

The same is true of Job. The test is imposed so that God, as well as Satan, will know who is right about Job. Is he faithful to God for God's sake or his own? The determination cannot be made without putting Job to the test. God might have created human beings so that they could be known and understood without being tested, but it was essential to his purpose that human beings be responsible for their decisions and answerable for their actions. Therefore, they must be free of divine control and foreknowledge. Although this question has been hotly debated in both Judaism and Christianity, the evidence in the Hebrew Bible indicates that there is a mystery at the center of the human person, a mystery that even God respects. The ultimate truth of human commitment can only be decided by time and testing.

It may seem paradoxical, but God cannot proceed with the test if he knows the outcome beforehand. He can be as confident as Satan, which makes the challenge meaningful and the wager legitimate, but it must also be possible to prove him wrong. The fact that God proceeds with the test proves that he isn't sure of the outcome.

The argument of Job's three friends—who are in essential agreement on the main points—is based on the principle that it is sacrilegious to hint, much less to say, that God's dealings with the world and human beings may not be just. From that premise, the friends argue back to the logical inference about Job's suffering. If it is axiomatic that God is the source of bane as well as blessing, and if God is, by definition, just, it follows that Job must have done or said or thought something blameworthy. According to this argument, he makes things worse by stubbornly insisting on his righteousness. The solution to the dilemma, they say, is repentance. If Job were to concede that the root of the trouble is his unwillingness to confess, make amends and repent, the friends are confident that his present agonies will cease and he will be restored to divine favor, with appropriate restitution and recompense.

Job does not accept their analysis or their prescription for resolving the problem. He refuses to repent or ask forgiveness for sins or crimes he did not commit. What happens to him is intended to be outrageous, and Satan makes sure that the experience is so unbearable that Job will ultimately curse God—as his wife strongly recommends (she presumably is not taken from Job along with the rest of his family because she, like the friends, is an agent provocateur who furthers Satan's purpose by pushing Job toward disillusionment and frustration and thus into cursing God).

The friends' argument is based on an impeccable premise that is central to biblical religion—the God who created an orderly universe and made the laws by which it is run does not violate those laws and act unjustly toward upright human beings who uphold his law. If Job is treated badly by God, there must be evidence to justify his treatment. Hence, Job must be guilty of some grave offense, and his denial only compounds the original crime and makes punishment more certain and more severe.

Job rejects the inference and, ultimately, in one sense at least, the central premise. His starting point is his innocence, and on this point he will not budge. In fact, this is the linchpin of his argument. The reader is advised by the author-editor from the very beginning of the story that Job's righteousness is not in question. His innocence is the primary given of the story and the point on which divine, satanic and human opinions converge. Job is an honest and honorable man whose integrity is vouched for by God, Satan and Job himself.

Job's experience leads him to conclude that God is unjust. Everyone acknowledges that what happens to him results from deliberate decisions and executive actions by God. Because he knows his sufferings are undeserved, Job reasons that the system of just rewards and punishments has broken down and that God is in violation of his own code of ethics. In short, God has no right to punish Job, and his friends are wrong. From premise to conclusion, Job's argument is as impeccable as the argument of his friends.

If the premises of both are correct, the logical inferences must also be correct. Doubt and confusion arise over the basic premises, and there are repeated efforts in the story to reinterpret or misinterpret events to reach a satisfying conclusion. In the end, both arguments are shown to be one-sided and simplistic. The premises may be correct and the reasoning impeccable, but the inferences are wrong. And that is where the additional speeches by Elihu and God come in.

In the three cycles of speeches by Job and his three friends, the positions do not change. In the speeches of Elihu (Job 32-37) and Yahweh (Job 38-41), however, things do change. However we choose to explain the appearance of Elihu and his intrusive monologues, their placement in the text reflects on what has preceded them. Elihu is critical of all the participants, especially Job, for their assumptions and inferences about God's relationship with human beings. Although he acknowledges the presence of the friends, Elihu directs most of his remarks to Job.

The final entry in the debate, however, is the voice from the whirlwind, which addresses Job directly and does not seem to acknowledge the existence of Elihu. The voice from the whirlwind is concerned about the conclusions Job draws from the premise and supporting data—that Job must condemn God in order to exonerate himself. The two are linked, but Job hasn't made the right correlations or deductions. He must go back to the proverbial drawing board.

At the end of God's second speech, Job repents–as his friends had urged him to do–but for entirely different reasons and in an entirely different connection. Although he has not budged on the question of his innocence, he recognizes that his reasoning was faulty and his logical inferences were wrong; and these he is willing to modify. The link between Job's suffering and divine malevolence is no longer clear, nor, presumably, is the necessary contradiction between his righteousness and his suffering.

In the story, everything is resolved when the *status quo ante* is restored, with compensation. But at the end of the dialogue, confusion remains. We might call this the beginning of wisdom. Up to this point, all the humans have been wrong in greater or lesser measure. Now they know that, although the ways of God remain mysterious, it is possible to maintain faith and integrity in the face of trying, even inexplicable, circumstances.

Afterword

Many readers have tried to resolve the problems raised by Job. Raymond Campbell of Monticello, Kentucky, suggests that the injustice of Job's suffering is not the main point:

Job can be understood, but not in terms of unjust suffering. When Job put the question of unjust suffering to God, he only got God to admit that he (Job) had spoken about something he didn't understand.

We too speak without true understanding if we claim to be able to explain how Job's suffering, which appears to us *unjust*, can be *justified*. One can't deal with suffering by believing it is just (therefore explainable and justified) or by believing it is unjust (therefore must be explained and justified). The central point of Job is that the concepts of justice and injustice are inadequate to resolve the central mystery of humanity. ***BR** 4:4 (1988), p. 6*

And Donald N. McKay of Fayetteville, New York, believes that Job's story is a Greek myth:

Job is a variation-in-theme of a Greek myth, that is, one god-type pitted in battle against another; and, of course, the battleground for this contest always happens to be a hapless human being. The God whom I experience, however, doesn't play games with people as he does with Job. If he did, then He would be a candidate for the celestial insane asylum.

Where did the Job episode come from? It came from the same place myths come from–human beings. I sense that Freedman would like to have come out and said the same thing, but I feel he's restrained by professionalism. I, on the other hand, gave up restraint long ago. The God of Job is as fickle and insecure as human beings are. Satan has all the earmarks of a sly, excellent lawyer. Job is a pseudonym for the author after he's been on the receiving end of life's kicks in the teeth. ***BR** 4:4 (1988), p. 6*

CHAPTER 14
Gospel Versions of the Birth of Jesus

Kenneth R. R. Gros Louis

The application of literary criticism to Bible study has changed the questions we ask and the insights we discover, according to Gros Louis. "A literary critic is interested in such matters as how a narrative begins, the significance of parallels and contrasts, and of repetition....changes in characters or images or setting; information withheld from the reader as well as information provided." Literary critics also examine artistic techniques, language, imagery, and author and narrator's point of view. To illustrate the value of this approach, Gros Louis examines "narrative strategies" in the accounts of the birth of Jesus by Matthew and Luke.

Scholars long ago noticed discrepancies between the two gospel accounts but addressed them as aspects of history or theology. A different understanding of their significance emerges when we ask the questions that go through a writer's mind as he considers his sources and subjects. Who are his readers? What do they already know? Do they need to be persuaded or reassured? If so, what is the best way to accomplish this?

The narratives of Matthew and Luke differ in structure, emphasis and point of view. In Matthew's story, men–namely Joseph and Herod–play key roles; in Luke, women–notably Elizabeth and Mary–are central characters. In Matthew, history "reflects a divine plan," events are prophesied and fulfilled by people "who act simply as instruments of that plan"; in Luke, people may be motivated by fear, belief, delight or wonder, and events become important after the fact.

The issue is not truth or error, Gros Louis stresses. Witnesses often describe the same events differently because they have different ideas about what matters or is meaningful. By putting human sensibilities in the foreground, a literary critic can deepen and broaden our appreciation of the Bible.–Ed.

Biblical scholars have long recognized significant differences between the accounts of Jesus' birth in the Gospels of Matthew and Luke–the only two

Gospels that contain birth narratives. Rarely, however, have biblical scholars gone beyond the basic observation that the narratives differ, as indeed, the Gospels as a whole differ. The recent focus in biblical studies on literary criticism has opened new ways of considering the rich literature of the New as well as the Old Testament. And applying principles of literary criticism to these texts has considerably expanded our understanding of the strategies of biblical narratives and, indeed, significantly influenced the teaching of the Bible as literature in secondary schools, colleges and universities.

Literary criticism reveals strikingly different approaches by the Gospel writers of Matthew and Luke to a description of what is, in the end, the same event. (We may be reminded that witnesses to an event—an automobile accident or an argument, for example—may describe it in very different ways.) Literary critics are interested in such matters as how a narrative begins, the significance of parallels and contrasts, and the frequency and significance of repetition. They also examine changes in characters, images or settings; information withheld from or provided to the reader; changes in the physical, material, psychological or spiritual situation of the characters; interaction among the characters and the effect of chance or planned encounters; the revelation of character by what the characters say and, more importantly, how they say it; and the plausibility of events within the narrative, even if in "real life" the events are implausible.

Seventeen years ago, in an article in *Commentary* that was later expanded in *The Art of Biblical Narrative*, Robert Alter expressed surprise that there had been no serious literary analysis of the Bible, that no one had paid serious attention to the artful use of language, the shifting play of ideas, conventions, tones, sounds, images, narrative points of view, compositional units and so on.[1] In the past decade, Alter and others have shaken up conservatives and liberals alike with startling new readings of biblical narratives.

The remarkable differences between the infancy narratives in Matthew and Luke are naturally of great interest to literary critics. The differences are demonstrative of the fact that the same events can be described in vastly different ways, that writers, even when depicting well known events, like the events surrounding the birth of Jesus, select and augment their material. We must be alert to the narrative voice, a voice that, whether we like it or not, influences the meaning or significance we derive from the narrative.

Our two writers, Matthew and Luke, describe the same event, the miraculous birth of someone they believe is very important—the King of the Jews, the Savior, the Son of God. Our question is really their question—how do they go about their task? Many stories must have circulated about this man Jesus—conflicting versions of his birth and life and death, of his family and disciples, of his sayings and influence. How did Matthew and Luke decide which elements to include? What questions went through their minds as they considered their sources and subjects?

Jesus' Birth in Matthew and Luke

MATTHEW	LUKE
OPENING	
Genealogy of Jesus *(Matthew: 1-17)*	Statement of intention addressed to "most excellent Theophilus." (Luke 1:1-4) (Genealogy appears in 3:23-38, when Jesus is 30 years old.)
PROMISE OF JOHN'S BIRTH	
NOT INCLUDED IN MATTHEW	Gabriel appears to Zechariah to tell him that his aged, barren wife Elizabeth will bear a son. Elizabeth conceives. (Luke 1:5-25)
THE ANNUNCIATION	
NOT INCLUDED IN MATTHEW	Gabriel appears to the Virgin Mary in Nazareth to tell her she will conceive a son who will be called Jesus. Mary is told about Elizabeth's pregnancy. (Luke 1:26-38)
MARY VISITS ELIZABETH	
NOT INCLUDED IN MATTHEW	Mary visits Elizabeth and remains with her for three months. (Luke 1:39-56)
BIRTH OF JOHN THE BAPTIST	
NOT INCLUDED IN MATTHEW	Elizabeth bears a son who is named John. (Luke 1:57-80)
BIRTH OF JESUS	
Mary bears a son as the fulfillment of prophecy. (Text does not explain how Mary came to Bethlehem.) He is named Jesus. (Matthew 1:18-25)	Mary and Joseph leave Nazareth for Bethlehem. Son is born in a manger because there is no room in the inn. (Luke 2:1-7)
VISIT OF THE MAGI	
Wise men from the East come to Jerusalem and are summoned by King Herod, who tells them to bring him word of where the child is in Bethlehem. They find Mary and the child and present their gifts but do not return to Herod. (Matthew 2:1-12)	NOT INCLUDED IN LUKE

MATTHEW	LUKE
VISIT OF THE SHEPHERDS	
NOT INCLUDED IN MATTHEW	An angel appears to the shepherds in the field and tells them of the birth of the child in Bethlehem. They find Mary, Joseph and the baby in the manger. (Luke 2:8-20)
FLIGHT TO EGYPT	
Joseph, afraid that Herod will destroy Jesus, flees with his family to Egypt. Herod orders all male children two years old or younger in Bethlehem to be killed. After Herod's death, the family returns to Nazareth. (Matthew 2:13-23)	NOT INCLUDED IN LUKE
CIRCUMCISION OF JESUS	
NOT INCLUDED IN MATTHEW	At the age of eight days, the baby is circumcised and named Jesus. (Luke 2:21)
PRESENTATION IN THE TEMPLE	
NOT INCLUDED IN MATTHEW	Joseph and Mary bring Jesus to the Temple in Jerusalem to present their firstborn and to offer sacrifices. They are blessed by Simeon. The prophetess Anna thanks God when she sees Jesus. Jesus, Mary and Joseph return to Nazareth. (Luke 2:22-40)
JESUS AT AGE 12	
NOT INCLUDED IN MATTHEW	Jesus goes up to Jerusalem with his parents for Passover. He spends three days in the Temple listening and questioning teachers, who are amazed at his understanding. Jesus returns with Joseph and Mary to Nazareth. (Luke 2:41-52)

Matthew and Luke might have asked themselves questions like these: How should I describe the birth? Who are my readers? How much do they know? Do I need to persuade them of the importance of Jesus' birth? If so, how can I do this best? Must I make the birth of a child to a virgin believable? How can I do that best? Into what narrative context should the birth be set? Which events should I emphasize? Which characters should I include, and which ones should I highlight? Who should speak? What should they say? Should my sources be made known? In what ways should the birth set the pattern and tone for the rest of the narrative, for this is, after all, the introduction to a longer account of Jesus' life? We will attempt to determine how Matthew and Luke answered these questions–the questions every writer must ask–by examining the narratives and then asking why certain choices were made.

Matthew tells of the birth of Jesus in the first two chapters. He begins by tracing Jesus' genealogy back through Joseph to King David and then to Abraham (Matthew 1:1-17). By contrast, Luke postpones his genealogy until the end of chapter three, when Jesus is 30 years old.

Matthew begins with, "Now the birth of Jesus Christ took place in this way" (Matthew 1:18). (All quotes are from the Revised Standard Version.) But instead of recounting the birth, Matthew tells us that Joseph does not divorce Mary after she becomes pregnant because she has become pregnant by the Holy Spirit. Then we are told that this fulfills a prophecy in Isaiah 7:14 that a virgin shall bring forth a child who shall be called Emmanuel, "God is with us."

Chapter two of Matthew begins with the birth of Jesus in Bethlehem during the reign of Herod the Great. Wise men from the East arrive in Jerusalem on their way to visit the child. King Herod is troubled, especially when he learns from his chief priests and scribes that the prophet Micah has prophesied that a ruler of Israel will be born in Bethlehem (Matthew 2:3-6). Herod summons the wise men and instructs them to complete their journey and then let him know where the child is so that he too may worship him. They continue to Bethlehem where they find the child, to whom they present gifts of gold, frankincense and myrrh. The wise men are then warned in a dream, however, not to obey King Herod's instructions and to return home by a different route.

Joseph also is warned in a dream that Herod plans to destroy the child and is told to flee to Egypt. This flight, Matthew tells us, was prophesied in Hosea (Hosea 11:1). Herod, in a rage, orders that all male children in Bethlehem two years old or younger be killed (Matthew 2:16); thus is fulfilled the terrible prophecy of Jeremiah 31:15, which Matthew quotes in 2:18:

> A voice was heard in Ramah,
> wailing and loud lamentation,
> Rachel weeping for her children;
> she refused to be consoled,
> because they were no more.

When Herod dies, Joseph, again following instructions in a dream, returns to Israel (Matthew 2:20). In another dream, he is instructed to settle in Nazareth, rather than in Judea where Herod's son now rules (Matthew 2:22). Matthew concludes by noting that thus were fulfilled the words of Isaiah, which he quotes in 2:23: "He [Jesus] shall be called a Nazarene."

As a literary narrative, Luke is far different from Matthew. Luke opens with a formal preface addressed to the "most excellent Theophilus," in which the author announces his intention to write an "orderly account" of things about which Theophilus has only been "informed" (Luke 1:4).

The narrative proper begins not with the story of Jesus but with the story of Zechariah, a righteous priest, whose wife Elizabeth is barren. Both of them, we are told, are now advanced in years (Luke 1:7). While Zechariah is serving in the temple, the angel Gabriel appears to him and tells him that his wife Elizabeth, though old and barren, will bear a son, who shall be named John and who will "make ready for the Lord a people prepared." When Zechariah questions Gabriel's prediction, he is struck mute. Zechariah returns home, and Elizabeth soon conceives.

In the sixth month of Elizabeth's pregnancy, the angel Gabriel appears before Mary–the first mention of Mary–who is living in Nazareth. Gabriel announces that Mary, although she is a virgin, will bear a son, who shall be named Jesus and who "will be great, and will be called the Son of the Most High" (Luke 1:32). Gabriel explains that nothing is impossible for God, as is evidenced by Elizabeth, who was barren until old age and is now pregnant. Mary decides to visit Elizabeth, her kinswoman, in Judea. When Mary greets Elizabeth, the unborn John stirs in her womb, and Elizabeth cries out, "Blessed are you among women, and blessed is the fruit of your womb!" (Luke 1:41-42).

When her time comes, Elizabeth gives birth to a son. Neighbors and relatives gather at the mute Zechariah's house for the child's circumcision, urging that the child be named for his father. Elizabeth, however, indicates that the boy will be named John. Everyone is surprised because no one in the family has had that name, and they ask what Zechariah would like the child to be called. Unable to speak, he asks for a tablet, and, to the amazement of the crowd, he writes on the tablet, "His name is John." At that moment, his ability to speak is restored. He praises the Lord and prophesies that his son "will be called the prophet of the Most High." When John has grown strong in age and spirit, he goes into the wilderness (Luke 1:80). Thus ends the first chapter of Luke.

The story then returns to Joseph and Mary, who leave their home in Nazareth and journey to Bethlehem in accordance with the decree of Caesar Augustus that everyone must be "enrolled." For the enrollment, Joseph must return to Bethlehem, because he is of the house of David, and David was a Bethlehemite. Although Mary is pregnant, she returns with him. When the time comes for Mary to give birth, the inn is full, so she wraps the child in

Prophecies and Dreams in Matthew

PROPHECY	FULFILLMENT
Prophecy of Isaiah 7:14 "Behold, a virgin shall conceive and bear a son, and his name shall be called Emmanuel." (Matthew 1:23)	*Mary conceives and gives birth to Jesus.*
Prophecy of Micah 5:2 "And you, O Bethlehem, in the land of Judah, are by no means least among the rulers of Judah; for from you shall come a ruler who will govern my people Israel." (Matthew 2:6)	*Jesus is born in Bethlehem.*
Prophecy of Hosea 11:1 "Out of Egypt have I called my son." (Matthew 2:15)	*Joseph, Mary and Jesus go to Egypt.*
Prophecy of Jeremiah 31:15 "A voice was heard in Ramah, wailing and loud lamentation, Rachel weeping for her children; she refused to be consoled, because they were no more." (Matthew 2:18)	*Herod murders all male children two years old or younger in Bethlehem.*
Prophecy of Isaiah 11:1 "He shall be called a Nazarene." (Matthew 2:23)	*Joseph takes his family to live in Nazareth.*

swaddling clothes and lays him in a manger. An angel of the Lord appears to shepherds in the surrounding fields to tell them the "good news" of the birth of a "Savior, who is Christ the Lord." The shepherds decide to visit the child, and when they find him (they do not give gifts), they tell Mary and Joseph what they have been told by the angel.

The baby is circumcised after eight days, and his parents name him Jesus, in accordance with the angel Gabriel's instructions when he first made known to Mary that she would conceive a son by the Holy Spirit. Later, Mary and Joseph take Jesus to Jerusalem "to present him to the Lord" (Luke 2:22), in accordance with the Levitical law relating to the firstborn (Leviticus 12:1-8).

DREAM	FULFILLMENT
Joseph's Dream An angel of the Lord appeared to him in a dream, saying, "Joseph, son of David, do not fear to take Mary your wife, for that which is conceived in her is of the Holy Spirit." (Matthew 1:20)	*Then Joseph...did as the angel of the Lord commanded him; he took his wife...* (Matthew 1:24)
Wise Men's Dream And being warned in a dream not to return to Herod... (Matthew 2:12)	*...they departed to their own country by another way.* (Matthew 2:12)
Joseph's Dream An angel of the Lord appeared to Joseph in a dream and said, "Rise, take the child and his mother, and flee to Egypt..." (Matthew 2:13)	*And he rose and took the child and his mother by night, and departed to Egypt.* (Matthew 2:14)
Joseph's Dream When Herod died, behold, an angel of the Lord appeared in a dream to Joseph in Egypt, saying, "Rise, take the child and the mother, and go to the land of Israel." (Matthew 2:19-20)	*And he rose and took the child and his mother, and went to the land of Israel.* (Matthew 2:21)
Joseph's Dream When he heard that Archelaus reigned over Judea in place of his father Herod, he was afraid to go there, and being warned in a dream... (Matthew 2:22)	*...he withdrew to the district of Galilee.* (Matthew 2:22)

What strikes the reader of these two narratives is that, even though they describe the same basic event, they are totally different from each other, not only in the details, but also in the essentials–structure, emphasis, point of view toward the birth and point of view toward the participants. In Matthew, Joseph and Herod play central roles, but in Luke they are only names. Mary, who is only a name in Matthew, is a central character in Luke. Zechariah, Elizabeth and John do not even appear in Matthew. Bethlehem is the site of Jesus' birth in both accounts, but the circumstances differ greatly; wise men visit Jesus in Matthew, shepherds visit him in Luke. The list could be extended by noting details unique to one narrative or the other.

The only things the two narratives have in common, in fact, are some names and places and two important details–the mother is a virgin and the child's name is given as Jesus by an angel of the Lord. Clearly, the same momentous historical event is being reported in two markedly different ways. Finally, it is important to note that neither account is an elaboration of the other–nothing in Matthew's version suggests what is in Luke's, or vice-versa.

What are we, as readers of literature, to make of these two stories? What does each reveal about the narrator's attitude toward the implications of the birth of a man both present as the Son of God? Surely such questions are provocative, if only because of our surprise at discovering that the nativity story, with which we are all familiar, is really a composite of stories in two different Gospels.

To begin with, in Matthew, we notice the importance of dreams and prophecies. In two short chapters, we find five dreams and five prophecies fulfilled. By contrast, in Luke, neither dreams nor prophecies are mentioned. We must decide if the dreams and prophecies in Matthew are there because of clumsy narration or are there for a purpose. Re-reading Matthew with the dreams and prophecies in mind, we see that everything that happens, every action, begins or ends as the result of a dream or the fulfillment of a prophecy. The *only* act that is not directly related to dreams and prophecies is the journey of the wise men, but even they, after calculating astrological changes, follow a star. So their decision about the proper time to seek Jesus is predetermined.

What does this apparently purposeful emphasis on dreams and prophecies suggest about the narrator's concept of history and the role of individuals in history? This is, after all, a narrative describing a major historical event. By describing actions as the outcome of dreams or the fulfillment of prophecies, Matthew invites us to view history as a series of predetermined patterns and not individual choices. This kind of narrative is not going to place much emphasis on individual personalities. The pattern, the fulfillment of the plan, is what is important.

Further analysis of Matthew confirms this. The dreams always *alter* human decisions–Joseph had quietly resolved to divorce Mary until he was told to do otherwise in a dream. The wise men had presumably planned to return to Jerusalem to report to Herod until they were warned not to in a dream. Joseph presumably had decided to remain in Bethlehem until the angel in his dream told him to take the child to Egypt to escape Herod's massacre. And Joseph does not leave Egypt until he is told to do so in another dream.

Moreover, the prophecies are always given *after* facts and events have been described. We are told that Mary, a virgin, is pregnant before the narrator recalls the prophecy in Isaiah. We are told that Jesus is born in Bethlehem before Herod's chief priests and scribes tell him the news, and then we are told that Jesus' birth fulfills a prophecy. We learn of the family's flight to Egypt, of Herod's mass murder and of Joseph's return to Nazareth before the prophecies that these events fulfill. The narrator obviously could have reversed the pattern, but the effect of recalling prophecies after the events is to make the prophecies seem like afterthoughts confirming what we already know from the narrative.

Additional evidence for the narrator's view of history as predetermined pattern comes from the long genealogy at the beginning of Matthew. Here we are told that there are 14 generations from Abraham (the first in the genealogical line) to David, 14 generations from David to the Exile in Babylon following the destruction of the Temple in 586 B.C.E., and 14 generations from the deportation to the birth of the Messiah, Jesus (Matthew 1:17). The history of humanity follows a plan, as is demonstrated by Abraham's line and the triple-14 pattern; and history is still being directed from elsewhere, as is demonstrated through the devices of dreams and prophecies.

The genealogy further suggests that history is dominated by males, a logical conclusion if central historical importance is given to Abraham, David and Jesus. This may explain why Matthew is also heavily male-dominated. The angel instructs *Joseph* to name the baby Jesus (Matthew 1:21), *Herod* plays a central role, the *wise men* journey to Bethlehem, an angel appears to *Joseph* four times in dreams. Mary is barely mentioned. The narrative ends with *men*—Joseph, the wise men, Herod, Jesus, Jesus' forefathers.

This male-dominant view of history explains, perhaps, why Herod's mass murder is emphasized—the killing of all *male* children in the region of Bethlehem was an event of major historical importance. This may also explain why so few women are mentioned in the genealogy and why the narrator does not even allude by name to Bathsheba, the woman who caused David's downfall—she is only "the wife of Uriah." After several dozen repetitions of the pattern, "X the father of Y," we cannot help but be struck when we read in 1:16: "Joseph *the husband of* Mary, of whom Jesus was born, who is called Christ." Alert readers should then know who the subject of this narrative will be.

A narrative based on history as divine plan and men as instruments of that plan makes for a special kind of literature, one that describes major events and largely ignores dramatic action, human emotions and responses and other details. Matthew offers few descriptions of individual responses, and the few that are mentioned are not much more than narrative fillers between a dream and the next prophecy.

Turning from Matthew to Luke, we realize how complex the differences between the two narratives are. Instead of a structure dominated by dreams, prophecies and events on a large canvas, the structure in Luke is controlled by carefully worked out parallels between the births of John and Jesus and the varied responses of people connected with them. Instead of a male-dominated narrative, Luke, if not female-dominated, is, at least, more balanced. Luke informs us of the responses and emotions of Elizabeth and Mary as well as those of Zechariah and Joseph.

Furthermore, instead of characters suddenly appearing or being directed to go elsewhere, as they do in Matthew, characters in Luke move from place to place for logical reasons. Zechariah, a priest, has a reason to be in the temple when he is confronted by the angel Gabriel. Mary's trip to Judea to visit Elizabeth is described in detail. We are told that the neighbors and kinfolk are as excited about the birth of the child as Elizabeth is and that they urge that the newborn child be named after Zechariah (Luke 1:58-59). Joseph has a logical reason for going to Bethlehem—the census. After the angel tells the shepherds to look for Jesus in the manger, the shepherds discuss their decision to visit him (Luke 2:15).

Events in Luke are logically connected. In other words, in Luke, history, or the reporting of history, or the creation of literature, involves not only recording events and causes, but also describing what happens to people in time and space as events unravel. Matthew, by contrast, tells us simply that "the birth of Jesus Christ took place in this way" and proceeds to describe Joseph's decision not to divorce Mary and the fulfillment of the prophecy concerning the virgin birth. The birth itself is not described at all. The next thing we are told—another event—is that Jesus has been born in Bethlehem. Immediately after Matthew reports that the angel directs Joseph to go to Egypt, he shifts to an account of Herod's rage. The author's interest, in other words, is in the *instructions* to Joseph and not in the human problems and difficulties he encounters in carrying them out.

Luke, on the other hand, is much more interested in human emotions and responses—Zechariah's fear and disbelief at Gabriel's announcement that he and Elizabeth will have a son; the bewilderment of the crowd at Zechariah's delay in coming out of the temple; Elizabeth's delight with the baby in her womb; Mary's wonderment at Gabriel's announcement that she too will bear a son; Elizabeth's ecstatic response to Mary's visit; and so on. History may be worked out in advance, as the songs in Luke suggest—the Magnificat recited by Mary (Luke 1:46-55) and the Benedictus recited by Zechariah (Luke 1:68-79)—but Luke is as interested in the characters as he is in the history that results from what they do.

The tight parallel structure in Luke indicates that, like the author of Matthew, Luke believes in the ordering and patterning of human events. But Matthew does not include details about human responses and movements or asides, which are typical of Luke and which fill out the narrative. For example, Luke mentions that Zechariah is a member of the division of the priesthood named after Abijah (Luke 1:5), that the angel Gabriel appears on the right side of the incense altar when he tells Zechariah he and Elizabeth will have a child (Luke 1:11), that the friends and neighbors of Zechariah gossip about what will become of his son John (Luke 1:66), that the enrollment for which Joseph goes to Bethlehem is the "first enrollment" (Luke 2:2). Matthew omits these details and responses, which seemed irrelevant to the larger patterns of history.

A different sensibility is at work in Luke, creating a different kind of literature. Even the preface to Theophilus suggests that the narrator has a strong sense of self; he conceives of his function in time and space–*he* will be the reliable narrator, writing an "orderly account" of recent events. He seems aware of his audience–an official, someone in power, a skeptic perhaps, but someone knowledgeable and interested in the human details of a remarkable event. Luke's personal voice addressing a specific auditor differs markedly from Matthew's impersonal, somewhat majestic voice recounting the long genealogy from Abraham to Jesus.

Although dreams and prophecies do not determine or alter human decisions and actions in Luke's account, this does not mean that his characters do not fulfill prophecies or follow divinely inspired instructions. It means that the narrative centers on human beings as they participate in history instead of on prophecies being fulfilled and instructions being followed. Mary's song to the Lord (the Magnificat, Luke 1:46-55), for example, may be an independent hymn that was inserted later at this particular point in the narrative, but it accurately reflects Mary's wonder at having been selected to be the mother of the Son of God. Similarly, although Gabriel's song praising John (Luke 1:14-17) may have been inserted for instructional purposes, the narrator refers back to the part of the song where we are told that John "will be filled with the Holy Spirit, even from his mother's womb," when he tells us that the unborn John leaped in his mother's womb when Mary greeted Elizabeth (Luke 1:41). Luke insists on recording these human responses.

Different sensibilities are at work in Luke and Matthew, with different concepts of history, of the individual in history and of the function of self in the creation of art. For Matthew, the birth is one event in a series of major events beginning with the birth of Abraham. History is the sum total of these significant moments and is determined by announcements and instructions from angels and the fulfillment of prophecies. The characters do not move in time and space as we know them. For Luke, however, the birth of Jesus suggests a different kind of emphasis. Luke is interested in how people respond to events, how they get from place to place, what they are doing when they are not present in the narrative.

Notice the narrative neatness of Luke. The scene at the temple–where Zechariah goes, meets Gabriel, becomes mute, and emerges–has a beginning, a middle and an end. Mary goes to and from Elizabeth's house. When Zechariah writes "His name is John," the neighbors are amazed and discuss the incident throughout the countryside (Luke 1:63-66). John is in the wilderness when he is not in the narrative. Joseph is required to go to Bethlehem.

There are several obvious reasons for Luke's parallel narratives of the births of John and Jesus. Because something comparable happened to the old and barren Elizabeth, what happens to the virgin Mary is more believable. This is the pattern for much of the narrative that follows. Gabriel's announcement to

Zechariah that he and Elizabeth will have a child prepares us for Gabriel's announcement to Mary that she, a virgin, will conceive. The same pattern is repeated by having John, the son of Elizabeth, prepare the way for Jesus, the son of Mary. Zechariah's skepticism at Gabriel's announcement sharply contrasts with Mary's humble acceptance.

But one major difference between the parallel accounts of John and Jesus may shed some light on Luke's interest in human emotions and specific details. The events surrounding the birth of John are heavily publicized. Many people are involved—the multitude is perplexed at Zechariah's delay in coming out of the temple, the neighbors and kinfolk marvel when Zechariah recovers his speech at John's circumcision, the country people gossip about "What then this child [John] will be."

By contrast, the birth of Jesus is private and isolated. Gabriel appears to Mary when she is alone. The news is shared only with Elizabeth and, presumably, with Joseph. The narrative takes Joseph and his family away from their hometown, and therefore away from their neighbors and kinfolk, to be enrolled in Bethlehem. And even there, the child must be born in a manger, out of sight, unnoticed by the people staying at the inn. The good news of the birth is told to shepherds in the fields, not to multitudes in the temple or assemblies in the city or court. In fact, we know from Luke 1:65 that the big news in Judea (where Jesus is born), "talked about through all the hill country," is the birth of John. Only when Jesus goes to Jerusalem does he begin to receive public attention. The difference between the multitudes who know about John and the few who know about Jesus is striking.

Thus Luke emphasizes the privacy and isolation of Jesus' birth, and Matthew emphasizes that Jesus' birth is a fulfillment of Old Testament prophecies. In Matthew, the event has an enormous public impact on King Herod as well as on the entire city of Jerusalem.

This contrast may shed light on Luke's understanding of the birth and its significance for the individual in history. Perhaps for Luke, events become major events, become "history" in other words, only after the fact. History is made up of seemingly minor events involving people we do not know; history is the result of millions of births we do not hear about. In Luke, people marvel at John's conception and birth, not realizing that, unknown to them, a more important conception and birth are taking place elsewhere.

This irony is similar to the literary device of the "still, small voice," a strand that runs through the Old Testament, for example in 1 Kings 19, when Elijah covers his face with his mantle at the sound of the still, small voice of the Lord, which is ironic because he did not cover his face when the storm and whirlwind raged around the mountain. Another example is Isaiah 53, when the suffering servant, who is despised and rejected, is later exalted as king.

The differences between the birth narratives in Matthew and Luke are not just different versions of an oral tradition. The characters in Luke wonder, exclaim, rejoice, marvel and ponder; they are troubled, perplexed and filled with fear. By contrast, only the wise men rejoice in Matthew, and only Herod expresses emotion of any kind. For Luke, Jesus' birth alters the meaning of individual actions and responses, any one of which might become significant for history and for literature. For Matthew, Jesus' birth is part of a predetermined plan that prophets have predicted and that instructions given in dreams will help to fulfill. Jesus' birth in the Gospels is not one, but two, stories told in profoundly different narrative styles, based on different interpretations of history and the individual's role in history. They represent different ways of depicting reality.

By asking appropriate literary questions of the birth stories in the Gospels of Matthew and Luke, we realize how important the selection of narrative strategy is for a reader's understanding of the text. Biblical scholars have long explained differences between the two accounts by focusing on historical and cultural circumstances at the time the narratives were composed as well as on the audiences to which they were addressed. These explanations, of course, follow important and legitimate avenues of scholarly research. A literary approach to the Gospels, however, requires one to ask different questions than the ones posed by biblical scholars. Literary critics can illuminate the strategies of the narratives in ways that enhance and broaden our appreciation of the artistry of the New Testament.

Afterword

William H. Richardson of Potomac, Maryland, argues that the differences between Matthew and Luke reflect different target audiences:

As pointed out by Dr. Gros Louis, Jesus' birth appears in only two of the four Gospels, and that is as it should be–one for the Jewish world and one for the gentile world. Matthew was written primarily for the Jews of Israel. Luke was written for, and directed to, Greeks, whether they were gentile Greeks or Hellenistic Jews. This distinction is basic to any meaningful comparison of the literary treatments of the story of Christ's birth.

Saint Paul, in 1 Corinthians, reminds us that the Greeks seek wisdom and the Jews seek a sign. Had Dr. Gros Louis recognized the respective readerships of Matthew and Luke, his critique would have been considerably different, and many of the problems he raises would have been resolved. The obvious differences should have been clues that the authors may have been writing for different audiences.

Matthew cited Old Testament scripture because the Jews he was writing for would either already know the references or would seek them out. That was Matthew's primary objective–Jewish facts, not literature as we like to think of it. Matthew knew if his message was to be believed, given the nature of the Jewish world view, he had to tie events surrounding Jesus' birth to specific prophecies in scripture.

Matthew was also aware that Jews were awaiting the messiah, for whose coming they had been praying for more than 300 years, and were seeking signs. Jews were not interested in the effects on or the emotions of people close to events. As a Roman tax collector, Matthew was in daily contact with the entire spectrum of Jewish society. Of all the apostles, he was best equipped to write a gospel to the Jews. In brief, Matthew's audience was concerned with what happened, and not with related esoteric factors.

Luke's problem was entirely different. He had to prepare a gospel that started even before the main story in order to satisfy Greek readers and hearers. As they teach in journalism school, wherever possible, the writer should provide the who, what, when, how, where and why of events. By 200 B.C.E., educated Greeks wanted all of these questions answered. They were more interested in the human effects of events on people than they were in the events themselves. That is why most of our psychological terms are derived from Greek. The more background data there was, the greater the impact.

Whether Luke's personal background was culturally Jewish or Hellenistic has not, to my knowledge, been clearly established. In any event, he knew his problem and wrote his gospel accordingly. Further, his training as a physician also shows throughout his gospel. Detailing the emotional effects of events on observers and participants alike was necessary to depicting the full significance of the event to Greek readers. Cultured and educated Greeks were convinced they already had answers to mankind's most nagging questions. Knowing this, Luke had to make a supreme effort to write a gospel on as high a literary level as his education would permit. His narrative had to contain much more than anecdotal and prophetic material. He had to demonstrate his erudition and organizational skills and create an accurate chronology.

That Luke chose to address his gospel to the prominent and highly regarded Greek official Theophilus tells us much about Luke's awareness of the formidable effort he had undertaken. To convince the Greeks who Jesus was, i.e., God's son incarnate who had come to earth among the Jews of Palestine, was indeed a stupendous literary assignment. Some biblical historians believe that Theophilus was appointed by Rome to serve in one of the Greek provinces at about the level of procurator because he was able and could be trusted.

Dr. Gros Louis did about as well as one could expect comparing literary styles. Unfortunately, a comparison of literary styles alone is probably the least fruitful basis for such an analysis. Sometimes we strive so valiantly to achieve our immediate and personal goals that we overlook the obvious. ***BR*** *1:2 (1985), p. 5*

Gros Louis replies:

Like Mr. Richardson, I believe that no single approach can describe all the intricacies of a text. His focus on the different audiences of Matthew and Luke brings to light interesting and well known aspects of these gospels. Similarly, a literary critic, while recognizing the intent of the authors, examines additional characteristics that affect the reading of the texts. Thus, excluding either approach may limit our understanding. ***BR*** *1:2 (1985), p. 6*

John S. O'Connor of Seattle, Washington, appreciates Gros Louis' literary approach to the Gospels but wonders whether he can answer the following question:

Why do Matthew and Luke place so much emphasis on Joseph's genealogy? According to the Gospels, Joseph had nothing to do with Jesus' birth because Mary was a virgin who had become pregnant by the Holy Spirit, and Jesus is the Son of God. ***BR*** *1:3 (1985), p. 22*

Gros Louis responds:

I believe this question can be answered from a literary perspective in both instances. Matthew, as I noted, sees history as dominated by male characters who follow a predetermined course of action. Therefore, it comes as no surprise that he places the birth of Jesus in the context of male characters. Jesus is seen as the son of Joseph, who in turn is posited in the line of Abraham and David.

Luke, on the other hand, waits to present the genealogy until just before Jesus begins his ministry. As I noted in the article, perhaps for Luke, events become major events, that is, "history," only after the fact. Luke may have wanted to show that prior events that seemed unimportant at the time had become part of the history of mankind. Thus, his narrative switches to a more historical tone or genre. The change from Luke, whose account revolves around two women and whose narrative explores personal relationships, to Matthew's straightforward genealogy that makes no mention of women and does not expand on personal relationships, highlights the switch to a historical perspective. To a literary critic, a change in mode signals an additional message; in this case, it draws attention to the affirmation of a series of personal events as part of history.

Perhaps I should note that other approaches to the text might suggest different answers to the question. For example, a historical critic might say that the genealogies focus on Joseph because he would later be considered the legal progenitor of Jesus. An analysis from a higher critical perspective might indicate that other sources and documents list the genealogies of Joseph but not of Mary. I, however, chose a different way of looking at these narratives and in so doing, arrived at different conclusions. ***BR** 1:3 (1985), p. 22*

PART VII

Structuralism and the Bible

Structuralism and the Bible
Introduction

Literary approaches to the Bible are at least as old as Jewish Midrash, but literary appreciation of the Bible in the modern sense began only in the middle of this century. As recently as 1981, Robert Alter wrote in *The Art of Biblical Narrative* that "literary analysis of the...sort I have tried to illustrate here...is only in its infancy."[1] What approach did he have in mind?

Analyses of plot, theme and character may be new to biblical studies, but for hundreds of years they have been standard ways of analyzing plays, novels and short stories. Recently, innovative—often controversial—methods of study have been applied to literature in general and to the Bible, the most productive of which focus on the structure or form of the text, under the label structuralism, form criticism or something else. Defenders of a mild form of this approach contend that structure is an important aspect of a work and a component of meaning. Advocates of an extreme version claim that meaning is "encoded" in the structure, which is therefore the source of the true meaning—which is often different from the obvious surface meaning.

Linguists studying American Indian languages at the turn of the century discovered that meaning-based grammatical definitions of the Greco-Latin tradition were not always helpful. Although in the languages of Europe and the Near East nouns usually identify people or things and verbs show action in time, in American Indian languages these concepts overlapped in unexpected ways. For example, in Potawatomi, a native language of Michigan, the "past" suffix *-pun* appears in *nkušatuspun* (I used to be happy), *nospun* (my dead father) and *nčimanpun* (my former canoe). Faced with the awkwardness of explaining this linguistic trait in traditional terms, linguists hit upon the idea of describing language in terms of structure, that is, how words and phrases are put together. In physics we might say *fire* is an action, but in English *fire* is a noun if it takes the plural marker -s and a verb if it takes the past tense marker *-ed*. In structuralist terms, past tense was defined as the ending *-ed*, not the meaning "in past time": *stopped* is past tense even in the sentence "I think it's time you stopped watching TV."

Ferdinand de Saussure carried the argument a step further when he contended that the significance of units in a structure cannot be explicated in isolation but must be analyzed in terms of each other.[2] For example, a person who is compelled to answer questions but knows only the word *yes* cannot communicate meaningfully, even if an affirmative response is the one he wants to communicate. The answer *yes* is meaningful only if the person chooses it instead of *no* or can choose not to say anything. In a sense, Saussure's argument is that to know *what* something means we must first discover *how* it means. The influential linguist Roman Jakobson considered the essence of scientific structuralism the focus on the inner workings of language.[3] And, as the philosopher Jacques Derrida has noted, this approach to language has become the model for other "human sciences."[4]

Investigating how meaning is conveyed led linguists to think in terms of larger units of discourse, such distinctive patterns as songs, prayers, sermons, debates, jokes, riddles, mythic narratives, ceremonial performances, political speeches, and autobiographical reminiscences. A parallel development in biblical studies is called form criticism. Hermann Gunkel, impressed by Jakob and Wilhelm Grimm's classification of folktales as fairy tales, myths, sagas and legends, argued that much of the patriarchal material in Genesis originated as independent family sagas.[5] Sigmund Mowinckel classified psalms according to their cultic functions.[6] Gerhard von Rad believed that the description of the presentation of the first fruit in Deuteronomy 26:1-11 incorporates a credo, a ritual affirmation of God's hand in Israelite history:[7]

> You shall say to the priest in charge at that time, "I acknowledge this day before the Lord your God that I have entered the land which the Lord swore to our fathers to give us."
>
> The priest shall take the basket from your hand and set it down in front of the altar of the Lord your God. You shall then recite as follows: "My father was a wandering Aramean. He went down to Egypt with a small number and lived there. The Egyptians dealt harshly with us and oppressed us; they imposed heavy labor on us. But we cried to the Lord, the God of our fathers, and the Lord heard our plea and saw our plight, our misery, and our oppression. And the Lord freed us from Egypt...."

Form critics like von Rad isolated genres such as hymns, blessings, legends, laments, fables and covenants, the last of which was discussed in an essay by Kevin G. O'Connell.[8]

As Gene M. Tucker explains in *Form Criticism and the Old Testament*, form criticism is both historical and exegetical.[9] Form critics try to discover the conventions available to biblical writers in order to understand their message. When we hear a story that begins with the words *once upon a time*, we have certain expectations about what follows–whether or not the story is literally true, who the intended audience is and how the meaning should be extracted. Similarly, if two letters both contain descriptions of a trip to Paris or ideas for estate planning, we immediately understand that the one beginning *Dear Sir* has different applications and implications from the one beginning *My Dearest Love*. Form critics maintain that the conventional form of a biblical passage tells us how to interpret the content. If, for example, we take for granted that poetry is understood differently from prose, it is essential that we recognize the parallel structure of Hebrew verse embedded in a prose passage.

Acknowledging the influence of Roman Jakobson, Claude Levi-Strauss championed "structural anthropology" and "structural mythology."[10] Vladimir Propp, in *Morphology of the Folktale*, posited 31 "functions" or "constant features of plot structure" in Russian heroic folktales.[11] These ideas have influenced biblical critics, such as Edmund Leach and D. Alan Aycock, in *Structuralist Interpretations of Biblical Myth*,[12] and Jack M. Sasson, who applies Propp's types to the Book of Ruth.[13] Opinions vary, of course, as to the value of this approach and the specific applications of form criticism. Barry N. Olshen, in *Approaches to Teaching the Hebrew Bible as Literature in Translation*,[14] believes that Isaac M. Kikawada and Arthur Quinn "make credible use" of structural analysis in *Before Abraham Was*;[15] on the other hand, in a review reprinted in volume 1 of this series, P. Kyle McCarter finds their argument (that the structure of Genesis 1-11 can best be explained as the careful artistry of a single author) unconvincing.[16] And in the following chapter, John Dominic Crossan–editor of *Paul Ricoeur on Biblical Hermeneutics*, a collection of essays about the influence of Ricoeur's structuralism[17]–faults Kenneth R. R. Gros Louis for explicating the wrong structure in his analysis of the nativity narratives in Matthew and Luke in the previous chapter, "Gospel Versions of the Birth of Jesus." Applying the literary study of "sources and analogs" to the form of the stories, Crossan argues that Matthew consciously modeled his account on the story of the infant Moses.

One of the most influential applications of a structural approach to the Bible is Alter's *The Art of Biblical Narrative*. Alter takes issue with the "new narratology" and "elaborate taxonomies," but he too focuses on structure, "the biblical writer's articulations of narrative form," rather than "merely on an imaginative impression of the story." His analysis entails "minutely discriminating attention to the artful use of language, to the shifting play of ideas, conventions, tone, sound, imagery, syntax, narrative viewpoint, compositional units and much else." Alter is especially impressive when he tracks verbal and thematic echoes throughout the text of a story, showing, for example, how the plea *recognize this* links the deception of Jacob by Judah to the subsequent deception of Judah by Tamar. This theme and other structural aspects of the Jacob cycle are explored in Richard Elliott Friedman's article, "The Cycle of Deception in the Jacob Tradition."

Alter's approach has affinities to rabbinic exegesis, as he acknowledges. Contrasting modern biblical scholarship to Midrash in *The Art of Biblical Narrative*, he claims that "the difference between the two is ultimately the difference between assuming that the text is an intricately interconnected unity, as the midrashic exegetes did, and assuming it is a patchwork of frequently disparate documents, as most modern scholars have supposed."[18] He elucidates that unity in *The Literary Guide to the Bible*:

> ...the telling has a shapeliness whose subtleties we are only beginning to understand, and it was undertaken by writers with the most brilliant gifts for intimating character, defining scenes, fashioning dialogue, elaborating motifs, balancing near and far episodes, just as the God-intoxicated poems of the psalmists and prophets evince a dazzling virtuosity in their arabesques of soundplay and syntax, wordplay and image.[19]

We get a taste of Alter's insightful reading of "the God-intoxicated poems of the psalmists" in his article, "Psalms: Beauty and Poetic Structure," adapted from *The Art of Biblical Poetry*.[20]

An interesting question raised by structural or form critics is whether or not the Bible is a unified book, or, to put this another way, what it means to say that the Bible is a single book. If form is the key to meaning, it is axiomatic that having chapters in the right order and knowing where a book begins and ends are crucial. Historical critics attempt to discover or reconstruct the original or "real" Bible. But as Richard Coggins writes in *Introducing the Old Testament*:

> If Amos, for example, is to be regarded primarily as a witness to the social and economic conditions of eighth-century Israel, then it is clearly of fundamental importance to eliminate any material in the book which comes from a later period....[but] some would...say that Amos ought to be regarded as an important "chapter" in a larger book, the collection of the 12 Minor Prophets, and that to rearrange these prophetic "chapters" in their supposed historical order is to miss an important part of their collective impact....Just as the beginning of Amos shows links with the book of Joel which precedes it...so the end of Amos provides a link with the book of Obadiah which follows it.[21]

Moreover, the Christian and Jewish Bibles have different endings. Leonard Thompson observes in "From *Tanakh* to Old Testament" that:

> ...when *Tanakh* (Jewish Scriptures) is reproduced as Old Testament (Christian Scriptures), the text remains exactly the same, but the meaning is dramatically changed. *Tanakh* loses its autonomy and becomes subordinated as Old to New. Without the text's changing, *Tanakh* is transformed into a book of promises and scenes of expectation that are fulfilled in the Christian community and the life of the Christian Savior.[22]

Thus, in reference to Isaiah 7:14, "Behold a young woman shall conceive," Thompson says:

> No student of the Christian Bible can read the passage in Isaiah without making the association with Jesus, and, more important, the link with Jesus is often unreflectively assumed as essential in the interpretation of Isaiah 7:14. When Isaiah is read in the context of *Tanakh*, however, the connection with Jesus is inconceivable...In fact, from a historical perspective the Christian reading becomes impossible.[23]

This is a clear case of structure influencing meaning. "*Tanakh* does not need the New Testament to be understood...If one stops reading at the end of the Hebrew Bible, there is no sense of incompleteness." On the other hand, while "[n]othing intrinsic to Hebrew Scriptures requires that they be placed in relation to the Christian New Testament," in the context of Christian theology they are and must be understood in relation to each other. This analysis may offend some readers, but it demonstrates that form criticism of the Bible is not just an academic exercise.

CHAPTER 15

From Moses to Jesus: Parallel Themes

John Dominic Crossan

The difference in emphasis between literary appreciation of a biblical text and structural analysis is clearly illustrated in Crossan's reaction to Gros Louis' analysis of the narrative strategies in the Gospel accounts of Jesus' birth. Crossan does not refute Gros Louis' arguments, but he does fault him for concentrating on "minor tactics" and "completely ignoring the dominant strategy of the text... parallelism with the story of Moses' infancy." The story of Moses, Crossan says, "controls the general sequence and even the details of the Matthean text."

Going beyond the bare-bones narrative in Exodus 1-2, Crossan examines elaborate versions of Moses' birth and infancy stories that he believes were circulating at the time Matthew wrote his Gospel. Crossan argues that specific details in these popular stories, which have been preserved in the works of Josephus, pseudo-Philo and others, have narrative elements in common with the Gospel account; more importantly, he says, they have the same "narrative structure" and the same "narrative function." For example, Pharaoh's plan to murder the Hebrew children puts the infant Moses in jeopardy and is thus a narrative element similar to Herod's plan to murder Hebrew children in his attempt to murder the infant Jesus. But whereas Herod's slaughter of the innocents was intended to kill the unknown messiah of the Jews, in the Exodus story Moses is not the object of Pharaoh's hostility. In the elaborated versions, however, Pharaoh kills the children in order to kill the unidentified savior of the Israelites. This is the version, Crossan says, that influenced Matthew.

Crossan analyzes the structures of these two stories as dramas in three acts with parallel scenes and themes. Act 1 is "The King's Plot," Act 2 "The Father's Action" and Act 3 "The Child's Deliverance." Within each act, Matthew has included both obvious and subtle allusions to the story of Moses. Keeping in mind that the revelation at Sinai was the apex of Moses' career, "No one should be surprised," Crossan concludes, "that Matthew, and only Matthew, has Jesus deliver his inaugural sermon 'on the mountain.'"–Ed.

In an article in *Bible Review,*[1] Kenneth Gros Louis discusses what he calls "narrative strategies in New Testament infancy narratives." It seems to me that he analyzes only minor tactics and completely ignores the dominant strategy of the text–or at least the text of Matthew. (A similar case could be made for Luke, but I shall leave that for another occasion.)

The dominant strategy of the infancy narrative in the Gospel of Matthew is parallelism with the infancy story of Moses, a parallelism that determines the underlying structure of Matthew's entire account of Jesus' infancy. Matthew's parallels are based, however, not on the concise biblical account of Moses' infancy in Exodus 1-2, but on expanded, popular accounts of Moses' infancy that were circulating at the time and are reflected in Midrashim (the plural of Midrash, a nonliteral elaboration of a biblical text) and other Jewish sources of the time.

As we shall see, this parallelism determines not only the overall structure of Matthew's infancy narrative, but it also dictates and controls the general sequence and even the details of the Matthean text. A simple comparison between the infancy narrative in Matthew 1-2 and the infancy narrative in Exodus 1-2 reveals more differences than similarities. Both have, to be sure, a massacre of male children (Exodus 1:16, 22 and Matthew 2:16), but in the Exodus account the purpose of the massacre is to kill the Israelites. Moses just happens to be born in the wrong place at the wrong time. In Matthew's infancy narrative, the purpose of the massacre is precisely to kill Jesus. Similarities between the gospel account and the biblical story in Exodus are at the level of narrative elements and not at the level of narrative function or structure and could easily be dismissed as coincidence. But the situation is quite different if we take into account other developments in the story of Moses' infancy that had taken place by the time Matthew wrote.

More than 30 years ago, Renée Bloch collected expansions of Moses' infancy story dating from the first to the 12th century C.E.[2] Some of the traditions, however, go back much further than the sources and manuscripts that have survived. Unfortunately, critical studies of these sources have not yet provided us with definitive dates for the histories of various traditions.[3]

Two of the sources, however–Josephus and pseudo-Philo–indisputably go back to the first century C.E., so we can be certain that this material was circulating at the time Matthew wrote. The Jewish historian Flavius Josephus wrote *Antiquities of the Jews* in 93-94 C.E.[4] The man we know only as pseudo-Philo wrote shortly after the Roman destruction of Jerusalem in 70 C.E. Philo himself wrote in about 45 C.E., but pseudo-Philo, who wrote in Philo's name–a common practice at the time–wrote *Liber Antiquitatum Biblicarum* about 30 years later.[5]

Josephus contains an account of the king's (or Pharaoh's) plot, in which Moses is the cause of the massacre. Pseudo-Philo contains an account of Moses' father's action, which includes his participation in a general divorce by all Hebrews of their wives. My assumption is that these represent separate,

Moses' Infancy Story in Exodus and Later Sources and Jesus' Infancy Story in Matthew

MOSES			JESUS
ACT I The Plot against the Children			
by Pharaoh			***by King Herod***
SCENE 1:			SCENE 1:
A Sign in the form of a prediction (Josephus *Antiquities* and *Sefer ha-Zikronot*) dream (*Sefer ha-Zikronot*)			A sign in the form of a star (Matthew 2:1-2)
SCENE 2:			SCENE 2:
Pharaoh and his courtiers' fear (*Sefer ha-Zikronot*)			Herod's fear (Matthew 2:3)
SCENE 3:			SCENE 3:
Pharaoh consults with courtiers (*Sefer ha-Zikronot*)			Herod consults with priests and scribes (Matthew 2:4)
SCENE 4:			SCENE 4:
Pharaoh decides to massacre male Hebrew children (Exodus 1:16,22)			Herod decides to massacre all male children two years old or younger (Matthew 2:16)
ACT II The Father's Action			
by Amram			***by Joseph***
SEFER HA-ZIKRONOT	***JOSEPHUS***	***PSEUDO-PHILO***	
SCENE 1:			SCENE 1:
Amram refuses divorce	Amram's prayer	General divorce	Divorce (Matthew 1:18-19)
SCENE 2:			SCENE 2:
Reassurance by God in Miriam's prophecy	Reassurance by God through Amram in a dream	Remarriage	Reassurance by God through an angel in Joseph's dream (Matthew 1:20-21)
SCENE 3:			SCENE 3:
Remarriage		Reassurance by God to Amram through Miriam in a dream	Remarriage (Matthew 1:24)
ACT III The Deliverance			
of Moses			***of Jesus***
Infant Moses is rescued from the Nile (Exodus 2:3-10) Moses, directed by God, leads the Hebrews out of Egypt (Exodus 14)			Joseph, directed by an angel of God, takes Jesus and Mary to Egypt (Matthew 2)

selective abbreviations of a story already fully developed in structural outline by the first century. I also assume that minor narrative details added in a 12th-century C.E. manuscript in Bloch's collection, the *Sefer ha-Zikronot* (*Book of Memory*), record a narrative structure already present in the first century.

Now let us compare Jesus' infancy narrative in Matthew with Moses' infancy narrative in Exodus as expanded by these later Jewish sources. In Matthew and in the rabbinic sources preserved in Josephus, pseudo-Philo and *Sefer ha-Zikronot*, we have dramas in three acts. As we shall see, each act in one is paralleled in the other.

Act 1. The King's Plot–Pharaoh and Herod

In Exodus, the king's plot to massacre the Hebrew male children is based on the following observation by Pharaoh:

> Behold, the people of Israel are too many and too mighty for us. Come, let us deal shrewdly with them, lest they multiply, and, if war befall us, they join our enemies and fight against us and escape from the land.
>
> Exodus 1:9-10

Pharaoh's first solution to this problem was to work the Hebrews to death: "Therefore, they set taskmasters over them to afflict them with heavy burdens." This solution, however, failed: "But the more they were oppressed, the more they multiplied and the more they spread abroad" (Exodus 1:11-14). So he tried another solution, which was no more successful than the first:

> Then the king of Egypt said to the Hebrew midwives, one of whom was named Shiphrah and the other Puah, "When you serve as midwives to the Hebrew women, and see them upon the birthstool, if it is a son, you shall kill him; but if it is a daughter, she shall live." But the midwives feared God, and did not do as the king of Egypt commanded them but let the male children live.
>
> Exodus 1:15-20

Then comes the final solution: "Then Pharaoh commanded all his people, 'Every son that is born to the Hebrews you shall cast into the Nile, but you shall let every daughter live'" (Exodus 1:22).

In this version of the story, Pharaoh makes no personal attack against Moses. Moses just happens to be born at the wrong time, in the midst of a general extermination of male Hebrew children. His life is in jeopardy, but his existence is not the cause of the massacre. Some thoughtful readers of the biblical account might find this "coincidence" disconcerting, even inappropriate. Shouldn't Moses play a more central role in the extermination process? Wouldn't the story be more effective if the general extermination were intended to eliminate Moses?

This is exactly what happens in Josephus' version of the story, which begins with the unsuccessful attempt by the Egyptians to work the Israelites to death and continues as follows:

> A further incident had the effect of stimulating the Egyptians yet more to exterminate our race. One of the sacred scribes–persons with considerable skill in accurately predicting the future–announced to the king that there would be born to the Israelites at that time one who would abase the sovereignty of the Egyptians and exalt the Israelites, were he reared to maturity, and would surpass all men in virtue and win everlasting renown. Alarmed, the king, on this sage's advice, ordered that every male child born to the Israelites should be destroyed by being cast into the river.[6]

Josephus smoothly integrates into the story a significant cause of the massacre of Hebrew male children *relating to Moses*, although the biblical narrative contains none. In the biblical narrative, the threat to Moses' life is the effect. In Josephus, Moses' existence is the cause of the threat.

Josephus records not only the earliest, but also the simplest, version of the transition from Moses as effect to Moses as cause of the massacre. Obviously, the tradition may have originated much earlier. A much later–and fuller–version of the story is preserved in the medieval *Sefer ha-Zikronot*.[7] It is possible that this version includes some details that are even earlier than Josephus; Josephus was as capable of abbreviating a text as he was of expanding it. Here is the account from the *Sefer ha-Zikronot* (italics added):

> In the 130th year after the descent of Israel into Egypt, Pharaoh *dreamed* that he was sitting on the throne of his kingdom. He looked up and saw an old man standing before him with a balance like those of a merchant in his hand. The old man grasped the scales and held them up before Pharaoh. Then he took all the elders of Egypt, her princes and her nobles and put them on one scale of the balance. After that he took a tender lamb and put it on the second scale and the lamb outweighed them all. Pharaoh wondered at this terrible vision, how the lamb outweighed them all and then Pharaoh awoke to find *it was only a dream*. Next morning, Pharaoh arose and when he had summoned all his courtiers and narrated his dream, they were extremely frightened. Then one of the royal princes answered, "This can only mean that a great evil shall come on Egypt at the end of days." "And what is that?" the king asked the eunuch. So the eunuch replied to the king, "A child will be born in Israel who will destroy all the land of Egypt. If it pleases the king, let a royal statute be written here and promulgated throughout all the land of Egypt to kill every newborn male of the Hebrews so that the evil be averted from the land of Egypt." And the king did so and he sent to call the midwives of the Hebrews....

The heart of this much fuller version is still, of course, a prophecy of Moses' destiny, which is the direct cause of the massacre of male Israelite children. But the story has become an act with four scenes: (1) a sign in the form of a dream; (2) fear of Pharaoh and his courtiers; (3) consultation with the courtiers; and (4) the decision to massacre the Hebrew male children.

Once the shift is made from Moses as effect to Moses as cause, the parallelism with the Jesus infancy narrative in Matthew is much closer. Moreover, all four scenes in the *Sefer ha-Zikronot* are paralleled in Matthew, with one significant exception–the magi, which is unique to Matthew. But I shall return to this point later; let us first look at the parallels:

Scene 1: *A sign.* In Matthew 2:1-2 we read, "Now when Jesus was born in Bethlehem of Judea in the days of Herod the king, behold, wise men from the East came to Jerusalem, saying, 'Where is he who has been born king of the Jews? For we have seen his star in the East, and have come to worship him.'" The sign in the infancy story of Moses is in Pharaoh's dream rather than a star.

Scene 2: *Fear.* The fear of Pharaoh and his courtiers is neatly paralleled in Matthew's infancy narrative. In Matthew 2:3 we read, "When Herod the king heard this, he was troubled, and all Jerusalem with him."

Scene 3: *Consultation.* The consultations are similar in both cases. Just as Pharaoh consulted his courtiers, in Matthew 2:4 we read that Herod "assemb[led] all the chief priests and scribes of the people [and] he inquired of them where Christ was to be born. They told him, 'In Bethlehem of Judea....'"

Scene 4: *The decision to massacre.* Herod first tries to trap the magi into betraying the child in Matthew 2:7-15; only when this plan fails does he issue the decree of extermination of the male children in 2:16. The presence of the magi introduces a difference between the two stories, just as it did in the first scene; but again I shall turn to this later.

Act 2. The Father's Action–Amram and Joseph

In the Bible, Moses' father is initially an unnamed individual. A necessary prerequisite to any parallelism in Matthew is the elevation of Moses' father to a named protagonist. That is exactly what happens in the later Jewish sources we have been examining.

In Exodus, Moses' father is mentioned only in passing (Exodus 2:1-2a): "Now a man from the house of Levi went and took to wife a daughter of Levi. The woman conceived and bore a son." Only later–in Exodus 6:20–is he given a name, Amram.

In the later traditions, the role of Moses' father (and of Moses' sister, Miriam) becomes increasingly important. Behind this development, one can see the same careful and thoughtful reading of the biblical account that was evident in the development of "The King's Plot," where Moses became the cause of the massacre. Why, early readers no doubt asked themselves, did the Israelites go on having children if the Egyptians had condemned them to death? Josephus gives the answer:

> Amaram(es), a Hebrew of noble birth, fearing that the whole race would be extinguished through lack of the succeeding generation, and seriously anxious on his own account because his wife was with child, was in grievous perplexity. He accordingly had recourse to prayer to God...And God had compassion on him, and, moved by his supplication, appeared

> to him in his sleep, exhorted him not to despair of the future and told him..."This child, whose birth has filled the Egyptians with such dread that they have condemned to destruction all the offspring of the Israelites, shall indeed be thine; he shall escape those who are watching to destroy him, and, reared in marvellous wise, he shall deliver the Hebrew race from their bondage in Egypt, and be remembered, so long as the universe shall endure, not by Hebrews alone but even by alien nations; that favour do I bestow upon thee and upon thy posterity."[8]

The role of Amram has grown considerably. This act has two scenes: (1) Amram's prayer and (2) God's reassurance.

Pseudo-Philo reflects a further development in the role of Amram:

> Then the elders of the people assembled the people with mourning and mourned and lamented saying...let us appoint us an ordinance, that no man come near his wife...for it is better to die childless, until we know what God will do.
>
> And Amram answered and said...I will not abide by that which ye ordain, but will go in and take my wife and beget sons, that we may be made many on the earth...Now therefore I will go and take my wife, neither will I consent to the commandment of the king....
>
> And the word which Amram had in his heart was pleasing to God...And Amram of the tribe of Levi went forth and took a wife of his tribe, and it was so when he took her, that the residue did after him and took their wives....
>
> And the spirit of God came upon Maria [Miriam] by night, and she saw a dream, and told her parents in the morning saying: I saw this night, and behold a man in a linen garment stood and said to me: Go and tell thy parents: behold, that which shall be born of you shall be cast into the water, for by him water shall be dried up, and by him will I do signs, and I will save my people, and he shall have the captaincy thereof always...[9]

Here we have three scenes instead of two: (1) the divorce whereby husbands are to refrain from relations with their wives. In Josephus, Amram prays his son will survive; in pseudo-Philo, Amram's prayer is overshadowed by the general divorce decreed by the leaders of Israel, which Amram refuses to accept; (2) the remarriage, which reverses the divorce; (3) the reassurance by God. In Josephus, reassurance is given by God directly to Amram in a dream; in pseudo-Philo, the message is mediated through Miriam, but still in a dream.[10]

Here is the account of the same events in the *Sefer ha-Zikronot*:

> Then, when the Israelites heard the decree ordained by Pharaoh that their male children be thrown in the river, part of the people divorced their wives but the rest stayed married to them...
>
> And there was a man of Levi in the land of Egypt whose name was Amram, son of Qahat, son of Levi, son of Jacob, and the man married Jochebed, a daughter of Levi and his own aunt, and the woman conceived and bore a daughter and called her name Miriam....
>
> And then at the end of three years the Spirit of God descended on Miriam and she went and prophesied in the center of the house saying,

> "Behold, the son will be born to my father and my mother at this time who will save Israel from the power of Egypt." So when Amram had heard the words of the child he went and remarried his wife whom he had divorced after the decree of Pharaoh ordering the destruction of every male of the house of Jacob. And in the third year of the divorce he slept with her and she conceived by him. And at the end of six months from the time of conception she bore a son and the house was filled with brightness like that of the sun and moon at their rising.[11]

Again, there are three scenes: (1) divorce; (2) reassurance; and (3) remarriage. But here even Amram is involved in the general divorce. The same three scenes are the structural elements of "The Father's Action" in Matthew's account of the infancy of Jesus.

Scene 1. *Divorce*. Matthew 1:18-19 reads:

> Now the birth of Jesus Christ took place in this way. When his mother Mary had been betrothed to Joseph, before they came together she was found to be with child of the Holy Spirit; and her husband Joseph, being a just man and unwilling to put her to shame, resolved to divorce her quietly.

Scene 2. *Reassurance*. This occurs in a dream, just as in the Moses tradition the reassurance is given in a dream to Amram or Miriam. In Matthew 1:20-21 we read:

> But as he [Joseph] considered this [divorce], behold, an angel of the Lord appeared to him in a dream, saying "Joseph, son of David, do not fear to take Mary your wife, for that which is conceived in her is of the Holy Spirit; she will bear a son, and you shall call his name Jesus, for he will save his people from their sins."

Notice the salvational role promised the child in Matthew just as it is promised of Moses in Josephus ("He shall deliver the Hebrew race"), in pseudo-Philo ("By him...I will save my people") and in *Sefer ha-Zikronot* ("He...who will save Israel").

Scene 3. *Remarriage*. Matthew 1:24 concludes: "When Joseph woke from sleep, he did as the angel of the Lord commanded him; he took his wife, but knew her not until she had borne a son, and he called his name Jesus."

Act 3. The Child's Deliverance–Moses and Jesus

The basic story of Moses' deliverance is the well known story of the basket in the Nile bulrushes and the rescue by Pharaoh's daughter, as recounted in Exodus 2:3-10. This story is fully developed in the Bible, so there was little need for popular or midrashic expansion. Early readers had the good taste to recognize that the biblical account did not need structural amplification.

On the surface, the story of Jesus' deliverance in Matthew 2 is completely different from the story of Moses' deliverance in Exodus. Nevertheless, the parallelism that was so obvious in the first two acts of the drama is also present in this act, but on a deeper and ironic, if not sardonic, level. At this point we see what it means for Matthew to describe Jesus as a "new" Moses.

In the earlier article in *Bible Review* to which I referred at the outset, Gros Louis correctly noted the five prophecies that are fulfilled and the five dreams that give warnings in the first two chapters of Matthew. The double five presumably points subtly towards Moses and the Pentateuch (the five books of Moses). Second, in contrast to the Hebrew Bible, dreams are rare in the New Testament. The Matthean emphasis on action controlled by God through dreams links those dreams to the dreams of Pharaoh and Amram or Miriam that control the Mosaic infancy narrative at crucial points. Third, and most important, Hosea 11:1 is fulfilled in Matthew 2:13-15. Hosea 11:1 reads: "When Israel was a child I loved him, and I called my son out of Egypt." The fulfillment or repetition of this event is Matthew 2:13-15:

> Now when they [the magi] had departed, behold, an angel appeared to Joseph in a dream and said, "Rise, take the child and his mother, and flee to Egypt, and remain there till I tell you; for Herod is about to search for the child, to destroy him." And he rose and took the child and his mother by night, and departed to Egypt, and remained there until the death of Herod. This was to fulfill what the Lord had spoken by the prophet, "Out of Egypt have I called my son."

Later, in Matthew 2:19-21, we read:

> But when Herod died, behold, an angel of the Lord appeared to Joseph in Egypt, saying, "Rise, take the child and his mother, and go to the land of Israel, for those who sought the child's life are dead." And he rose and took the child and his mother, and went to the land of Israel.

One might have expected that the fulfillment of Hosea 11:1 (leaving Egypt) would be mentioned after Matthew 2:19-21 (leaving Egypt) rather than after 2:13-15a (entering Egypt); that is, it should have been mentioned when Jesus was coming out of Egypt rather than going down to Egypt. This could be explained as a simple flash-forward, but I think there is something more subtle at work. Matthew wants us to think *simultaneously* of Jesus fleeing Israel and taking refuge in Egypt and of Moses fleeing Egypt and taking refuge in Israel. The supreme irony is that the "new" Moses moves in the opposite direction, not from but towards the gentiles. The parallelism here is no longer between the infant Jesus and the infant Moses but between the infant Jesus and the grown Moses who, as had been foretold, saved Israel from Egypt. For Matthew, Jesus is the Moses of the gentiles, and his destiny is to "save his people from their sins" as had been foretold in Matthew 1:21. In retrospect, this explains the sharp contrast between the gentile wise men (magi) who came from the east to worship Jesus, and that "when Herod the king heard this, he was troubled and all Jerusalem with him" (Matthew 2:1-3). For Matthew, Jesus is the "new" Moses, the Moses of the gentiles, who saves them not from Egypt, but from sin.

Of course, Matthew's infancy story also contains given, traditional material about Jesus. The most important elements of this material can be seen in the few places where Matthew's narrative coincides with Luke 1-2. Two key elements are the virginal conception of Jesus in Matthew 1:23 and Luke 1:31-35, in fulfillment of Isaiah 7:14, and the Bethlehem birth of Jesus in Matthew 2:1 and Luke 2:4, 11, presumably in fulfillment of Micah 5:2, "Truly, He will leave them [helpless] until she who is to bear has borne; then the rest of his countrymen shall return to the children of Israel."

The major strategy of Jesus' infancy story in Matthew is dictated, however, by Mosaic parallelism, which accounts for the close structural similarities between the first two acts in Matthew and the extrabiblical versions of Moses' infancy story. But in the third act, "The Child's Deliverance," the parallelism becomes ironic or even satiric. Jesus is the "new" Moses who is accepted by the wise men of the gentiles (the magi); Jesus flees for safety not *from*, but *to* the gentiles (in Egypt). And he saves his people from spiritual rather than physical bondage. This is the message embedded in the structure of the Matthew infancy narrative.

No one should be surprised that in Matthew, and only in Matthew, Jesus delivers his inaugural sermon "on the mountain" (Matthew 5:1). In Luke, where there is no concern for Mosaic parallelism, Jesus delivers this sermon, not on the mountain, but after "he came down with them [the disciples] and stood on a level place" (Luke 6: 17). Furthermore, in Matthew, but not in Luke, the Mosaic parallelism continues in the six antitheses to the Sinai commandments, "You have heard that it was said to the men of old," which Jesus counteracts with his absolute and apodictic "But I say to you" (Matthew 5:21,27,31,33,38,43). This is the new Moses speaking from the new mountain delivering new commandments.

CHAPTER 16

The Cycle of Deception in the Jacob Tradition

Richard Elliott Friedman

The structure of some biblical narratives is as subtle as the structure of a modern novel or poem, inhering in lexical echoes, muted refrains and ironic repetitions. Friedman shows that the theme of "deception for deception" lends coherence to the entire Jacob cycle in Genesis, although this underlying structure may not be obvious. As Friedman says, "The writer did not hit his readers over the head with it." As a result, each generation of readers has been granted "the burden of seeking it out–and the pleasure of discovering it."

It is obvious to any reader that the members of Jacob's family constantly deceive one another. Jacob and Rebecca deceive Esau and Isaac to attain the blessing of the firstborn; Laban deceives Jacob by marrying Leah to him instead of Rachel; Jacob deceives Laban in the matter of the spotted and striped herds; Jacob's sons deceive him with Joseph's bloody coat; Tamar deceives Judah in order to conceive his child; Joseph deceives his brothers when they come to Egypt for food.

Friedman notes that "for every act of deception, an ironic recompense occurs later in the story." And this, he argues, is the key to the meaning of the story, which is not, as some scholars have suggested, a rollicking picaresque tale of trickery told around nomad campfires. Friedman contends that the tale teaches a moral lesson. "The consistency of this recompense indicates that the biblical author is specifically developing the theme of deception and recompense to a denouement"–when Joseph forgives the brothers who sold him into slavery. The cycle of deception and revenge ends "when one family member puts family above revenge, when one who is manifestly entitled to retribution chooses not to take it."

Friedman characterizes his essay as "an example of the literary study of the Bible being used in the present generation of biblical scholars," but contends that his approach also yields theological rewards. In this case, "by not glorifying human heroes, the authors glorify the other central figure, the deity."–Ed.

The biblical story of Jacob is an exquisite artistic creation, an intriguing psychological portrait and an interpretive religious treasure trove—but it has always presented problems. Even Sunday school children recognize that the hero Jacob, the great patriarch, withholds food from his own brother Esau, to get his brother's birthright and then lies to his blind father Isaac on his deathbed to steal his brother's blessing. Why did the ancient Israelite author portray his own ancestor as manipulative and deceitful?

Moreover, Jacob is not the only one who is portrayed as a deceiver. His mother Rebekah, his uncle Laban, his wife Rachel, and most of his sons become involved in deception as well. Why was such a story conceived? And why was it included in sacred literature?

Complex and infectious intrafamily conflict has long—perhaps always—been a powerful literary theme. A comedian used to summarize the plot of "Hamlet" this way. At the end of the play, Ophelia has drowned, her father Polonius, has been run through with a sword, her brother Laertes and her lover Hamlet lie dead onstage from poisoned swords, Hamlet's mother Gertrude lies dead of a poisoned drink, Hamlet's uncle Claudius lies dead from Hamlet's thrust of Laertes' sword. The comedian suggested that the ghost of Hamlet's father who opened the play should walk onto the stage and say to the audience with a sigh, "You see? Go try and raise a family."

"Hamlet" is only one example of the family conflicts portrayed in literature and drama. The list includes families from the house of Atreus to the Karamazovs. In our Freudian age, it hardly seems necessary to explain why this subject lends itself to powerful dramatic portrayals. It should not surprise us, therefore, that one such story appears in the Bible.

The story of Jacob is the story of a family divided geographically. Half of the family lives in Canaan, half in Mesopotamia. The Bible focuses first on the branch in Canaan, then, because of the conflict within the family, on the branch in Mesopotamia; after 20 years, the story returns to Canaan; and events culminate, in Joseph's time, in Egypt.

From the very beginning, the story of Jacob is a story of conflict. Jacob and his twin brother Esau fight in their mother Rebekah's womb. Esau is born first, but Jacob reaches out from the womb to hold him back. Esau's birth priority is a central fact of Jacob's life, and the conflict with his brother requires that he find a way to circumvent that fact. The means he finds is *deception*.

The story soon becomes an account of family members constantly deceiving one another. Jacob, with Rebekah's help, deceives Esau and Isaac in order to get Esau's birthright and blessing for himself. Jacob's uncle Laban deceives Jacob by substituting his elder daughter Leah for his younger daughter Rachel, whom Jacob loves. Jacob, in turn, deceives Laban over ownership of their livestock. Rachel deceives her father Laban over possession of the family icons. Jacob's sons deceive him about the disappearance of their brother Joseph. Joseph deceives his brothers about the fate that awaits them in Egypt. Jacob's sons Simeon and Levi deceive the people of Shechem over an injury to their sister Dinah. Jacob's son Judah deceives his own daughter-in-law Tamar by reneging on his promise to allow her to marry his youngest son. Tamar, in turn, deceives her father-in-law Judah to expose his wrongful deception. Go try and raise a family.

The theme of deception in these stories has not gone unnoticed. Literary and theological interpreters of Genesis have commented on it for centuries—and have been troubled by it. What are we to think of Jacob's behavior—and Rebekah's and Rachel's and Judah's? Interpreters have tried to vindicate Jacob, to rationalize his actions, to disparage Esau, or to come to terms in other ways with Jacob's actions. But how is this matter treated in the biblical text? How does the biblical author present the story of deception and its consequences? In fact, for every act of deception there is an ironic recompense later in the story. The consistency of this pattern indicates that the biblical author deliberately developed the theme of deception and recompense, which comes to a denouement at the end of the story.

Jacob first deceives his brother Esau in order to obtain his birthright, which entitles him to a double portion of their father's property after his death. The story is well known. Esau returns from hunting, famished, and asks his brother for food; Jacob insists that Esau sell him his birthright in return for some lentil stew. Esau says that the birthright will do him no good if he dies of hunger; he capitulates and sells Jacob his birthright. Jacob then gives him bread and lentil stew (Genesis 25:29-34).

Jacob's recompense comes years later in an equally famous story. Jacob loves his cousin Rachel, and he agrees to work for her father Laban for seven years in exchange for Rachel's hand in marriage. But at the end of seven years, on the morning after the wedding night, Jacob finds that Laban has substituted Rachel's older sister Leah for Rachel. Jacob asks his uncle/father-in-law, "Why have you deceived me?" Laban answers: "It is not done thus in our place, to give the younger before the *firstborn*" (Genesis 29:26).[1]

Note that the text does not say "the younger before the elder," but "the younger before the *firstborn*."[2] The man who wrongfully took the firstborn privilege of his brother suffers because of the firstborn privilege of his beloved's sister. Is the reference to Leah as the firstborn a chance detail based on a coincidence of language, or is it an essential development in the structure of the story?

Jacob's second deception is done in order to obtain the blessing that his father Isaac intends for Esau, a blessing of both prosperity and dominion. Isaac, now old and blind and aware that he will soon die, asks Esau to hunt some game and prepare a meal for him, after which he will bless him. Isaac's wife Rebekah loves Jacob, however. She overhears what Isaac told Esau, sends Jacob to the flocks to bring back two choice goat kids and prepares a meal for Isaac like the meal he asked Esau to prepare. She then sends Jacob, her preferred son, to pose as Esau and receive Isaac's blessing. To deceive his father, Jacob wears Esau's clothes that smell of his hunter brother and covers his arms with goatskins to simulate his brother's hairy skin. Thus attired, Jacob brings Isaac the meal Rebekah has prepared. When Isaac asks who has come to him, Jacob replies, "I am Esau, your firstborn." Isaac draws Jacob to him and feels his hairy skin: "The voice is the voice of Jacob, but the hands are the hands of Esau," he says. Then he eats the meal and draws Jacob to him once again. He smells the clothes Jacob is wearing–Esau's clothes. Jacob kisses his father, who then blesses him with the blessing meant for Esau.

When the deception is revealed, Isaac trembles, and Esau weeps in bitter anguish, "Bless me too, father." Jacob answers, "Your brother came with deception and took away your blessing." Esau cries out, "Isn't his name Jacob (*to catch*)! He's caught me these two times! He took away my birthright and now he has taken away my blessing" (Genesis 27:34-36).

Years later, Jacob is paid back for this deception, too, when his own sons, jealous of Jacob's preferred son Joseph, sell him into slavery in Egypt. They dip Joseph's coat of many colors in the blood of a goat and take it to the now elderly Jacob. "We found this," the brothers say, bringing it to Jacob. "Recognize this!" they tell Jacob. Jacob *recognized* it, the text notes: "It is my son's coat; a wild animal has eaten him" (Genesis 37:33). Jacob rends his clothes and wears sackcloth in mourning for his son. The other children try to comfort him, but he refuses to be comforted. "Thus his father bewailed [Joseph]." And thus was Jacob deceived.

Note the specific parallels. Jacob once deceived his father with his *brother's clothing* and the meat and hide of a *goat*. Now his sons deceive him with their brother's *clothing* and the blood of a *goat*. Worse, Jacob deceives *himself* in response to his sons' request that he *recognize* the coat. Worse still, the word used for *goat* in the Joseph story is *śēʿîr*, and *Seʿir* is the name of the place where *Esau* settles (Genesis 33:16). We are thus subtly reminded of the connection between the two stories. This is actually a double pun; Esau is described as a *hairy man*, which was the reason for the goatskin deception in the first place, and *hairy* in Hebrew is *śāʿir* (Genesis 27:11).

I have already described how Laban deceives Jacob by substituting Leah for Rachel. Laban is repaid in the same coin years later, when Jacob asks for all the spotted, striped and brown sheep and goats among Laban's flocks in return for his work. Laban agrees, and Jacob, who is in charge of the flocks, connives (by magic? miracle? paragenetics?) to produce colored sheep and goats in great numbers, making him rich in ewes and rams (Genesis 30:28-43). Thus Jacob deceives Laban in turn. Laban deceived him over *Rachel* and *Leah*; Jacob has paid Laban back by getting his ewes and rams.

In Hebrew, ewes and rams are *rᵉḥēlîm* and *ʾêlîm* (Genesis 32:14, 31:38). That is, Rachel (*rāḥēl*) in Hebrew means ewe, and the word for ram (*ʾayil*) is a twist of the name Leah. Laban, who deceived Jacob by substituting Leah for Rachel, is repaid by losing his ewes and rams (his Rachels and Leahs). Here again, the payback subtly refers back to the original offense.

Like father, like daughter! Next Rachel deceives her father Laban. This may be another recompense for Laban substituting Leah for her at the wedding. But Rachel, too, is paid back, as we shall see. When Jacob leaves Laban's house, he departs secretly with his wives and children, his flocks and his belongings. Unknown to Jacob, his beloved Rachel steals her father's household icons, the *teraphim*. Three days later, when Laban discovers that Jacob and his family have fled and that his icons are missing, he pursues Jacob and charges him with stealing his *teraphim*. Jacob, not knowing that Rachel has stolen the icons, allows Laban to search the camp and tells him "With whomever you find your gods, let that person not live" (Genesis 31:32). Laban searches all the tents, but when he comes to Rachel's tent, she hides the stolen gods in her camel saddle and sits on it. She tells her father, "I cannot get up before you because the way of women is with me" (Genesis 31:35).

Thus Rachel deceives her father and successfully appropriates his *teraphim*, perhaps in recompense for denying her her wedding night with the husband who had labored for her for seven years. But Rachel's deception proves to be the costliest of all. Jacob, not knowing that she has stolen the icons, has unwittingly cursed his wife: "With whomever you find your gods, let that person not live." Rachel deceived her father by claiming to be menstruating. Four chapters later, she dies in childbirth—which involves the cessation of menstruation.

Like father, like sons! We have already seen how Jacob's sons, after they sold Joseph into slavery in Egypt, deceived their father by taking Joseph's coat of many colors and dipping it in goat's blood, thus deceiving Jacob into believing that Joseph, the first son of his beloved Rachel, had been devoured by wild beasts. Years later, when Joseph has risen to a position of extraordinary power in Egypt, he, in turn, deceives his brothers. Jacob sends the brothers to Egypt to buy food, for the famine in Canaan is severe; in Egypt the storehouses are bulging, thanks to Joseph's wise administration, to say nothing of his ability to foresee the seven-year drought.

When the brothers arrive, Joseph interrogates them. He recognizes them, but they do not recognize the chief dispenser of grain as their long-lost brother. Ironically, they refer to themselves as "your slaves" (Genesis 42:10-13, 44:9,16,21,23,31). Again, the deception-for-deception theme is subtly developed in the text.

The ten brothers (excluding Benjamin) had sold Joseph into slavery for 20 measures of silver, and when they come to Egypt to buy grain, they are repaid with 20 measures of silver. The story is a bit complicated, but the point is clear. Joseph first accuses them of being spies from Canaan. They, of course, deny this. They are, they say, 10 of 12 sons of a man from the land of Canaan, one son having died (Joseph) and another (the youngest, Benjamin) having remained at home with his father.

Supposedly testing the truth of this story, Joseph keeps Simeon and sends the other nine back to Canaan to return with Benjamin. To confuse them further, Joseph secretly orders that the silver they paid for the grain be put back in the sacks of the nine brothers. When they later return with their youngest brother, Benjamin, to buy more food, Joseph releases Simeon and sends all 11 brothers off; again he secretly returns the silver, this time of 11 brothers. Thus Joseph returns a total of 20 measures of silver–the same amount the brothers received when they sold Joseph into slavery (Genesis 37:28, 42:3-25, 43:15-44:1). The brothers thus receive 20 measures of silver a second time, but this time, under very different circumstances, they learn what it means to be victims of injustice. And, just as they once deceived, they are now deceived.

Reuben, the oldest brother, had originally opposed selling Joseph and was not present at the time of the deed. Simeon, the second oldest, was responsible–and it was he who was imprisoned to assure the return of the other brothers with Benjamin. Thus Simeon, too, apparently was repaid for his part in the sale and deception.

The theme of deception–and recompense–continues. Jacob's son Judah deceives his daughter-in-law Tamar. Judah has three sons, the oldest of whom he marries to Tamar. But the son soon dies without children. The second son marries Tamar to provide offspring for the deceased brother, but the second son also dies. Judah promises Tamar that he will give her his third son Shelah, but he is afraid that Shelah, too, may die if he marries Tamar. Judah therefore deceives Tamar by telling her that Shelah is still too young for marriage and that she must wait a while. She waits until Shelah grows up, but Judah makes no wedding plans. Tamar poses as a veiled prostitute on the road. Judah, now a widower, is attracted to her, sleeps with her and promises to pay her one goat. As a pledge for the payment he leaves, among other things, an article of his clothing. When Judah tries to redeem his pledge, she is nowhere to be found. Some time later, he learns that his daughter-in-law is pregnant. Since Tamar is still officially bound to Judah's son Shelah, this is the equivalent of adultery. Judah says that Tamar should be burned for the offense, but Tamar produces Judah's pledge items and says, "Recognize these." Judah then acknowledges that he has wronged her.

Like father, like son! The deceiver has again been deceived. Judah deceived Tamar; Tamar deceived him. And the retribution is fitting for the original deception. He denies her a man; she makes him her man. Moreover, this deception involves clothing (the pledge) and a goat (the payment)–just as Jacob deceived his father Isaac by donning his brother's clothing and giving him the cooked meal of a goat and just as the brothers deceived Jacob with Joseph's coat dipped in the blood of a goat. Moreover, the story of Judah and Tamar ends with the word *recognize*, just as Jacob was told to *recognize* Joseph's coat of many colors. Thus clothing and a goat are thrice involved.

Tamar gives birth to twins who, like Jacob and Esau, fight each other to be first out of the womb! Because they are Judah's sons, not Shelah's, they are replacements, as it were, for the two sons who died after marrying Tamar (Genesis 38).

Three other sons of Jacob also commit costly acts of deception. Jacob's firstborn son Reuben deceives his father by sleeping with Jacob's concubine Bilhah, but Jacob finds out (Genesis 35:22). Jacob's second and third sons Simeon and Levi deceive the people of the city of Shechem. After the prince of that city, whose name is also Shechem, sleeps with their sister Dinah and only later asks for her hand in marriage, her brothers respond to the proposal with a deception, saying that they will only permit intermarriage with the Shechemites if all the males undergo circumcision. The Shechemites agree to the surgery, and when they are immobilized from the pain of the circumcisions, Simeon and Levi enter the city and massacre the inhabitants. Jacob criticizes them for this act, but they answer, "Shall he treat our sister like a prostitute?" (Genesis 34).

Reuben, Simeon and Levi pay a high price for their deceptions. On his deathbed, Jacob explicitly takes away Reuben's preeminence because he has slept with Bilhah ("When you mounted your father's bed you brought disgrace" Genesis 49:3-4) and condemns the descendants of Simeon and Levi to dispersal ("When angry they slay men" Genesis 49:5-7). The honor of the birthright goes to the fourth son, Judah ("The sceptre shall not depart from Judah" Genesis 49:8-10). The first three are deprived of their succession to the birthright. So every deception has been paid back, and all of the deceivers have been deceived in turn.

When did this chain of deception begin? And when will it end? It is difficult to say how the chain of events got started. The biblical authors may have considered it a matter of destiny, a complex series of twists and turns to explain how the people of Israel came to reside in Egypt. Or perhaps we should look for the root of the family inclination for deception before Jacob. After all, Jacob's father Isaac tried to deceive the Philistine king Abimelek into believing that Isaac's wife Rebekah was his sister (Genesis 26). And Isaac's father Abraham had tried the same trick on the same king and again on the Egyptian king (Genesis 12 and 20). Did the chain of deceptions begin with Rebekah who helped her preferred son Jacob deceive Isaac? Or did it begin with Isaac? Or with Abraham? Or perhaps with the snake in the Garden of Eden?

It is easier to pinpoint what brings the chain of deceptions to an end—forgiveness. The sequence that has caused this family so much suffering finally comes to an end when Joseph chooses not to take revenge on his brothers. He causes them discomfort to the point of their recognizing their past wrong, but he does not repay them in kind for what they did to him, although he clearly has the power to do so. Much of the Book of Genesis is about deception, but the last chapter is a touching portrayal of forgiveness. After Jacob dies, the brothers say to one another, "He [Joseph] will certainly pay us back all the harm that we did him." But their younger brother is no longer the naive teenager who once offended them by telling them his grandiose dreams. The adult Joseph rejects deception and retaliation:

> And Joseph said to them, "Do not be afraid, for am I in the place of God? You intended harm for me. God intended it for good: in order to do as it is today, to keep a large people alive. And now do not be afraid. I shall provide for you and your children." And he comforted them, and he spoke on their hearts.
>
> Genesis 50:15-21

However the deception began, it ends when a family member puts family above revenge, when someone who is manifestly entitled to retribution chooses not to exact it. Joseph, who was once a thoughtless teenager, has become a powerful, sensitive man. No equivalent character development takes place in Adam, Noah, Abraham, Sarah, Isaac or Rebekah, who all remain basically constant figures.

The only other figure whose character develops like Joseph's is Jacob. Here the matter of deception is intimately related to character development. As Esau points out, Jacob's very name, which means "to catch," connotes deception. The name also recalls his earliest conflict with Esau because the name Jacob is related to the Hebrew word for heel (*ăqēb*). We are told that Jacob is given this name because he reached out from the womb to try to grab his twin brother Esau's heel–ostensibly to pull him back so he could be the firstborn (Genesis 25:26).

But after his experiences in Mesopotamia, Jacob changes. He has been both deceiver and deceived. He has hurt and been hurt. Now a husband and father, he is a man who has struggled and prospered. For the rest of the story, he is no longer portrayed as a man of action but, more often, as a somewhat passive man who tries to appease his brother and avoid further strife. At precisely the juncture that marks this change in Jacob's character, he encounters God (or an angel?) at Penuel.

When Jacob is about to reenter the land of Canaan after his long journey from Laban's house, he wrestles alone with this extraordinary being until the break of day, after which the angel blesses him and tells him, "Your name shall no longer be Jacob, but Israel [*Yisră-'ēl*], for you have struggled with Elohim [God] and men, and prevailed." In this verse, the name Israel is understood to mean "the one who has struggled with God." The Hebrew word for struggled (*s-r-h*) is related to the first two syllables of the Hebrew word for Israel (*Yisră-'ēl*).

Is this divine encounter the signal or the cause of the change in Jacob's character? In either case, when he ceases to be a deceiver, he sheds the name Jacob, the one who catches, and becomes instead Israel, the one who has struggled with God (Genesis 32:25-29).

The Bible does not "clean up" Jacob the way some Sunday school teachers, Midrashim and modern interpreters do. Biblical writers seem to have been content with imperfect heroes. But why? Why did the author even conceive of such a story? Perhaps he recognized deception in the world around him or, for that matter, in his own family, and wanted to warn that one deception always leads to another. Perhaps he meant to send a message to his people? To his wife? To his children? To his in-laws?

Or perhaps he conceived the story as a literary protest against the ancient Near Eastern tradition of glorifying national heroes. As has been frequently observed, from ancient reports one would think that Near Eastern kings never lost in battle. In this respect, it is tantalizing to compare the Jacob cycle to the court history of David in 2 Samuel. The similarities in style, subject and description of events between these two works is so striking that some scholars have suggested they were written by the same author.

One striking similarity is that the court history, like the Joseph cycle, manifestly develops the idea of deception for deception. For example, after King David sleeps with Uriah's wife Bathsheba, she becomes pregnant, and David tries to deceive Uriah into thinking he (Uriah) is the father of the child. When this fails, David plots successfully to have the devoted Uriah killed in battle. The prophet Nathan then deceives King David by concealing the underlying message of a story about a rich man with a large flock who steals from a poor friend with but one lamb in order to get food to entertain a guest. David flies into a rage at Nathan's story and proclaims that the rich man deserves to die. "And Nathan said to David, 'That man is you!'" (2 Samuel 12:1-7). Nathan thus exposes David's crime with a deceitful story that tricks David into condemning himself.

For his deception of Uriah, David pays a price involving a series of deceptions among his children. Here again a Judean author describes the founder of the national dynasty critically. Whatever the purpose of the author of the Jacob cycle, the fact is that he, like other biblical writers, had a realistic impulse, a sense of the psychological complexity of families–sibling rivalries, conflicts between fathers and sons, mothers forced to find channels of influence in male family structures, women torn between fathers and husbands. Would idealized heroes have been more effective or more inspiring?

There is another value in keeping heroes realistically human–a theological value. By not glorifying human heroes, the authors glorify the other central figure, the deity. The message, which is repeated through the generations described in the Hebrew Bible, is that, apparently, God can work through any human being–a deceiver, an errant king or a man with a "heavy mouth and heavy tongue" (Exodus 4:10). His prophet may be a layperson (Isaiah), a priest (Jeremiah 1:1) or a cowboy (Amos 7:14). The principles of divine selection are inscrutable. God gives Rebekah an oracle while she is still carrying the twins Jacob and Esau in her womb that her younger son will dominate the elder. Does the oracle reflect divine *foreknowledge* or divine *control*? When she takes a hand in affecting the outcome herself, is she acting in pious obedience to the oracle or out of loyalty to her preferred son? As usual, the literary and theological ambiguities in the biblical text are as interesting as the articulated facts.

The deception-for-deception pattern is subtly woven into the language of the text. Instead of hitting readers over the head with it, the writer developed his point through story, not pronouncement. And he wove it into the fabric of his story, so that each generation of readers would have the burden of seeking it out—and the pleasure of discovering it.

And so the Bible conceals treasures of art and ideas, some intended by the authors and some not, for successive generations to discover. Splendid puns embedded in the Book of Jonah for millennia have been gradually identified, until the work is now recognized as an elaborate fabric of wordplay.[3] The Song of Deborah (Judges 5) has been identified, after millennia, as the poetic source of the prose history of Deborah in Judges 4.[4]

New generations of readers bring new methods, new interests and new sensitivities to the ancient texts. This article is an example of the literary study of the Bible favored by the present generation of biblical scholars. Literary criticism, enriched with historical, theological and psychological studies, is now helping bring to light some of the Bible's concealed treasures. But the Bible at its richest has yet to be read.

CHAPTER 17

Psalms
Beauty and Poetic Structure

Robert Alter

Any approach to the Bible is valuable if it helps us see new dimensions and gain meaningful insights into the text. Robert Alter asks what difference it makes to the content of the psalms that they are poems and then demonstrates how a sensitive reader of poetry uses literary techniques to appreciate the beauty–and therefore the enduring power–of the psalms.

In the past, some scholars have characterized the biblical psalms as "poetry of the heart," the spontaneous overflow of irresistible emotion. But Alter argues that they are "artful poems" that incorporate "a system of complex linkages of sound, image, word, rhythm, syntax, theme, idea...for conveying densely patterned meanings." In one respect, however, the psalms differ from other poems, and that is their "reliance on the conventional, the familiar, in imagery, in the sequence of ideas, in the structure of the poem" so that they could easily be chanted by pilgrims or recited by people offering sacrifices or praying for divine intervention.

Nevertheless, Alter says, the Hebrew psalms, like all great poems, "exert a subtle pressure on convention" in order to create something unique. In this case, the cultic hymn common to the Near East was transformed into a medium for expressing "a distinctive, sometimes radically new, sense of time, space, history, creation and the character of individual destiny." For example, the "idea of neatly retributive justice" in Psalm 1 "derives its force from the fact that the language of the poem makes it seem built into the very structure of reality." And Psalm 8 "is a luminous instance of how poetic structure was made to yield a picture of the world that eloquently integrates underlying elements of Israelite belief."

The insightful readings that follow are adapted from Alter's book, The Art of Biblical Poetry, *which reviewer Baruch Halpern called "an index of the contemporary rapprochement between biblical studies and literary criticism."–Ed.*

Of all the books of the Bible in which poetry plays a role, Psalms is the one set of texts whose poetic status has been most strongly felt throughout the generations—regardless of the vagaries of translation, typographical arrangement of verses or notions about biblical literary form.

The unwavering perception that the psalms are formal poems—even in ages when most readers imagined that the prophets spoke emphatic figurative prose—was reinforced by explicit musical indications in the texts themselves. Many of the psalms are presented, in introductory notes, as liturgical songs to be intoned to the accompaniment of the lyre, cymbals, drums or whatever other instruments once filled the temple courts with melody and rhythm. The name of the book in Western languages, which comes from the Greek *psalmos*, meaning a song sung to a plucked instrument, stresses the musical character of the psalms, as does the full Hebrew title, *mizmorei tehillim* (songs of praise).

Symptomatic of the general response to these poems is that many poets in Renaissance England, who were ignorant both of Hebrew and of biblical poetic structure, tried producing metrical English versions. No matter how biblical versification was thought to work, it was almost universally assumed that the psalms exhibited the rhythmic regularity, symmetries and cadenced repetitions of artful poems.

A countervailing assumption, however, has also enjoyed a great deal of currency down to our own time—that if the Book of Psalms is poetry, it is quintessentially "poetry of the heart," spontaneous outpourings of feeling expressed directly and simply, almost without artifice; in fact, the poignancy and universal appeal of psalms derive from the lack of conscious artifice. An extreme, but by no means uncharacteristic, instance of this view is expressed by the Israeli *littérateur* Yeshurun Keshet, who says, "In the Book of Psalms everything is said in a primary fashion, without any 'literariness.' What characterizes the poetic expression of Psalms is that the poet allows objects and nature to speak for themselves without explaining them to us as modern poets do."[1]

This statement strikes me as fundamentally misconceived in that Keshet imagines that any kind of literary expression can escape "literariness," but of course, one sees the features of psalms the writer has in mind. Whereas in Job, for example, one encounters daring leaps of invention in the imagery or, in the prophets, intricate elaborations of rhetorical figures, the psalms generally stick to something more "primary"—which does not mean something less literary but, on the contrary, more reliant on the conventional and familiar in imagery, in the sequence of ideas and in the structure of the poems. Reliance on the conventional is perfectly understandable here because poems meant to be chanted by pilgrims in procession on their way up to the Temple Mount or recited by supplicants at the altar or by people offering thanksgiving sacrifices after recovering from grave illnesses do not require fancy imagery and syntax; more appropriate, in fact, are eloquent rehearsals of traditional material, even traditional ways of ordering that material.

Psalm 1

Happy is the man

1. **a** Who has walked not in the council of the wicked,
   b nor stood in the way of sinners,
   c nor sat in the seat of fools.
2. **a** Rather, in the Lord's teaching [is] his delight,
   b In his teaching he meditates day and night.
3. **a** He shall be like a tree planted by streams of water,
   b that gives its fruit in season,
4. **a** Whose leaf does not wither
   b and all it puts forth, prospers.
5. **a** *Not so the wicked:*
   b rather are they like the chaff the wind blows.
6. **a** Thus the wicked will not stand up in judgment,
   b nor sinners in the council of the righteous.
7. **a** *For the Lord embraces the way of the righteous,*
   b *But the way of the wicked is lost.*

The conventional nature of the psalms may be conceded; literary convention gives writers of both verse and prose a solid framework for constructing their own discourse. But good writers always exert subtle pressures on convention, in certain ways remaking it even as they build within it. So it is with the psalms.

The modern emphasis on originality in literature may lead to a certain perplexity about how to think of a collection where, in any given psalmic genre—thanksgiving psalms or cultic hymns, for example—a dozen or more poems seem to say the same thing, often with more or less the same metaphors and sometimes even with some of the same phrases. As modern readers, we need to be attuned to the nuanced individual character—"originality," in fact, may not be the relevant concept—of poems that reflect the same genre and use many of the same formulaic devices. There are abundant examples in later poetic tradition, Arabic and Hebrew poetry of medieval Spain or Petrarchan love poetry for instance, where the power of the individual poem is felt precisely in fine recastings of the conventional. And that is what we ought to be able to discern more minutely in the psalms.

Let me state the question about the form of Psalms in the most basic fashion. What difference does it make to the content of the psalms that they are poems? Simply this—poetry, working through complex linkages of sounds, images, words, rhythms, syntax, themes and ideas, is an instrument for conveying densely patterned meanings, sometimes contradictory meanings, that are not readily conveyed in other modes of discourse. On the evidence of countless poems, ancient and modern, we may say that poetry is a way of using language strongly oriented toward the creation of minute, multiple, heterogeneous and semantically fruitful interconnections in the text.

The psalms are, of course, poems written out of deep, often passionate faith. I am proposing that the poetic medium made it possible to articulate the emotional freight, the moral consequences, the altered perception of the world that flowed from monotheistic belief in compact verbal structures that can, in some instances, seem simplicity itself.

The psalm, at least in the guise of a cultic hymn, was a common poetic genre throughout the ancient Near East. But when the form was adapted by Hebrew poets, it often became an instrument for expressing, in a collective voice (whether first person plural or singular), a distinctive, sometimes radically new, sense of time, space, history, creation and the character of individual destiny. In keeping with this complex expressive purpose, many psalms, when scrutinized, prove to have a finely tensile semantic weave that one would not expect from the apparent conventionality of the language.

An instructive case in point is the very first psalm in the traditional collection (see box on p. 239). The ancient editors must have felt, with considerable justice, that this psalm was characteristic and thus fitting to set at the beginning of the collection, perhaps as an introduction to the rest.

The opening formula, "Happy is the man," occurs in a series of psalms, as does praise of God's teaching (*torah*) and the assured sense that wickedness will be requited with evil, righteousness with success. There is, in fact, not much that seems "poetic" about Psalm 1 and certainly nothing that appears original. The poem contains very little figurative language, and the agricultural similes could scarcely be more conventional—fruit-bearing trees over against wind-driven chaff. Where, then, does the power of the poem lie, and in what way might it be, for all its simplicity and conventionality, more than the versification of an ancient monotheistic moral cliche?

The poet insists on a neat contrast between the wicked and the righteous. Structurally the poem is fashioned around a tight logical antithesis. The psalmist takes pains to place explicit indicators of logical transition from the righteous to the wicked or vice versa at the beginning of four different verses: "rather" (verse 2a), "not so" (verse 5a), "rather" (verse 5b), "thus" (verse 6a). Reality is thus made to yield an exact moral calculus. There are things the just man will not do; indeed, he does something antithetical instead; the fate of the wicked man is the contrary of the fate of the just man.

The poetic formulation of this idea of neatly retributive justice derives force from the language of the poem, which makes it seem built into the very structure of reality. As a result, the didactic movement from "not so" to "thus," in the context of the poem, is something more than preaching insistence.

Note that the righteous man stands still—indeed, his righteousness may depend on his ability to stand still and reflect upon true things. In the first verse—

the only triadic verse in the poem—we are told what the righteous man does not do. He does not walk...stand...or sit. If he actually performed these actions, he would be constantly on the move. When, in line 2a, the righteous man is characterized by what he actually does, at first he is given no verb; in line 2b, he meditates, a verb of contemplative activity or conning a text. Next he is described not with an active verb but with a past participle that denotes the opposite of movement—he has been "planted" (line 3a). From this firmly anchored position, the tree—not the man—can put forth fruit and grow unwithering leaves. (Thus, the verb is applied to the referent, the tree, rather than the man.)

The wicked, by contrast, are in constant, restless motion. Without direction, they are carried hither and thither by forces over which they exert no control. Psychologically, to be wicked is to give oneself over to conflicting and insatiable desires, hence to a condition of rudderlessness; in terms of moral consequences, one makes oneself absolutely vulnerable to retribution.

The poem closes, in the last two lines, with what scholars call an envelope structure, of which biblical writers are particularly fond. The end formally echoes the beginning. The poem begins with sinners and the wicked; it ends with the same agents of wrongdoing, into whose midst, however, the righteous—mentioned explicitly for the first time—are introduced. The poem begins by invoking evil councils and assemblies; it concludes with the mention of proper councils and legal assemblies, where the wicked cannot hope to prevail or presume to join.

The syntax of the final line articulates the contrast between the just and the unjust with a further complication of meaning. Line 7a is the only place in the poem where God appears as a grammatical subject. God "knows" (a verb that implies a special intimacy, as in the sexual sense; hence my translation, "embraces") the way of the righteous. Line 7b then pointedly swerves away from syntactic parallelism and pursues an antithesis—and the way of the wicked is lost (or perishes). The very "way" of evildoers, on which, at the beginning of the poem, we are told the happy man does not stand, is at the end seen to be a way that leads either nowhere or to perdition. The wicked themselves are not even accorded the dignity of being the grammatical subject of an active verb. They are windblown like chaff, and whatever way they go on is trackless, directionless, doomed.

The effectiveness of the whole poem surely has a good deal to do, as many readers have recognized, with the archetypal simplicity of the contrasted images of tree and chaff. But the study in movement and stillness that underlies the poem provides an added dimension that helps explain the power of the poem. We may even wonder whether we are justified in considering this evocation of impotent kinetic movement in contrast to fruitful stasis in terms of moral psychology, and not merely as a matter of reward and punishment. That is, the essence of wrongdoing is to miss the mark (that is

Psalm 8

For the leader on the *gittit, a psalm of David**

1. **a** O Lord, our master,
   b how majestic [is] Your name in all the earth.
2. **a** You, whose splendor was told[2] over the heavens,
   b out of the mouth of babes and sucklings.**
3. **a** You have founded a strength because of Your foes,
   b to put an end to enemy and avenger.†
4. **a** When I look at Your heavens, the work of Your fingers,
   b the moon and the stars You established,
5. **a** What is man that You are mindful of him,
   b humankind, that You pay him heed?
6. **a** You have set him little lower than the angels,
   b with honor and glory You have crowned him.
7. **a** You have given him dominion over the work of Your hands,
   b You have placed all at his feet.
8. **a** Sheep and oxen, all of them,
   b and also beasts of the field.
9. **a** Bird of the air and fish of the sea,
   b whatever passes along the paths of the sea.
10. **a** O Lord, our master,
    b how majestic [is] Your name in all the earth.

* A musical instrument whose precise nature is no longer known.

** Though "out of the mouth of babes and sucklings" has become a proverbial phrase, it is far from clear what these infants are doing in this poem.

† The relevance to the context of foes and avengers is obscure.

etymologically what the Hebrew word for "sinners" means), to pursue foolish or unattainable objects of desire, which leads a man to frustration; by contrast, the man whose delight is in the Lord's teaching knows the art of sitting still in the right place, of finding fulfillment within the limits of the law and his human condition.

The psalms contain no real nature poetry because, in the psalmist's view, there is no independent realm of nature. But there are creation poems, evocations of the natural world as the embodiment of the creator's ordering power and quickening presence. The justly celebrated Psalm 8 is a luminous instance of how poetic structure can be made to yield a picture of the world that eloquently integrates underlying elements of Israelite belief. The poem might be described as a kind of summarizing paraphrase of the account of creation in Genesis 1, more or less following the same order and stressing, as does Genesis 1, man's God-given dominion over the created world. The difference in form, however, between the two texts is crucial and instructive.

Genesis 1, being a narrative, describes creation as a sequence–indeed, as a regulated procession moving from the division of light and darkness and the making of heaven, earth and sea, through the creation of the animal kingdom and man, to God's rest on the seventh day. It is all forward movement, from origins through time to fulfillment. Psalm 8 assumes this narrative process as background. The psalm begins when creation is complete. Like many lyric poems, this psalm is the complex realization of a moment–the moment the speaker marvels at the created world and man's place in it.

All literary texts are, of course, serial; they unroll in time like the scrolls on which they were once written. A narrative may, to a limited extent, qualify this temporal thrust by suggesting, through repetition and analogy, that the reader shuttle back and forth mentally along the text continuum as he reads. Short lyric poems, however, have the greatest potential for neutralizing the temporal movement inherent in verbal texts. Within a small compass, through the use of intricate and closely clustered devices of linkage and repetition, lyric poems can sometimes create the illusion of simultaneity, offering to the mind's eye a single panorama with multiple elements held closely together. Psalm 8 is an excellent example of this illusion, although lines 2 and 3 are not very intelligible in the Hebrew text that has been passed down to us.

Psalm 8 is an example of envelope structure–the refrain of the first line reappears in the last line. This ending device is common in many bodies of poetry but is used only occasionally in biblical verse. The refrain in this poem is clearly appropriate–it closes a perfect circle. The majesty of God, which is affirmed at the beginning, is restated verbatim at the end, but with the sense accrued through the intervening eight lines that the meaning of his name is majestic throughout the earth. The Hebrew says specifically *all* the earth, thus framing the whole poem between symmetrical *alls*. His dominion is over all, heaven and earth, angels and men, creatures of the field, air and sea; and he places *all* (line 7b) at the feet of men.

After the resounding formula of introduction and address to God in line 1, we may be able, tentatively, to rescue a few fragments from the enigma of lines 2 and 3. The heavens tell God's glory, which is intelligible enough; this leads directly to the assertion in line 4 of the awe-inspiring sight of heaven, the moon and stars. *Heaven* in line 2a also links up with *earth* at the end of line 2, thus recalling the creation story and reinforcing the idea of allness. Heaven and earth is a good biblical idiom for all of creation.

I have made a hesitant guess that "out of the mouths of babes..." is a parallel verse to the one in which the heavens tell God's splendor, because it would also seem to be an indication of praise–that is, the whole range of creation, from the beauty of the heavens to the prattle of infants, bears witness to God's magnificence.

Any interpretation of line 3 is bound to be conjectural. I suggest that the notion of laying low enemies and *founding* something strong, in the context of a creation story, is an allusion to mythic imagery borrowed from the Canaanite tradition, in which God, like Baal, is said to have subdued a primordial sea beast in order to secure the world on dry land.[3] If my guess is right, this would also introduce the sea at the beginning of the poem, forming a cosmological triptych of heaven, earth and sea. At any rate, *founded* at the beginning of line 3 would seem to be linked with *established* at the end of line 4, both pointing to the completed work of creation, whose perfection the speaker now beholds.

In line 4, the speaker introduces himself explicitly into the frame of the poem with the words *I see*. We are invited to stand with him, an individual human being looking up at the splendor of the night sky and marveling at man's place in the intricate scheme of things. The next six lines leading to the final refrain constitute a special kind of "focusing," a common feature of biblical verse. In other words, although the two halves of a line are often more or less parallel in meaning, the second half of the line typically intensifies the first (for example, from *break* to *smash*) or concretizes it (from *wrath* to *flaming fury*) or, in the case of spatial and geographical images, adopts a kind of zoom-lens effect (from *the cities of Judea* to *the courtyards of Jerusalem*).

In this poem, the focusing process governs the whole structure. First, the speaker, the *I*, beholds the heavens; then, he sees, according to a common pattern, what is contained within the heavens–the moon and the stars. The heavens are *the work of Your fingers*–an elegant variant of the standard phrase, *the work of Your hands*, which we find in line 7. This is the only place in the whole Bible this variant appears, so we may expect to find in it an indication of especially delicate work, as the speaker scans the exquisite tracery of the night sky.

Next, in line 4, the speaker moves from heaven to man, who is a little lower than the heavens and the celestial beings (*'elohim*). Below man is the rest of God's handiwork, *all* that is *at his feet*. (The Hebrew says literally "under his feet," thus reinforcing the downward vertical movement in the picture of the cosmic hierarchy.)

Next comes the famous cry of amazement that God has singled man out (line 5). This is a striking example of the intuitive counterpoint that often guides biblical poets. In every line of the poem except this one, there is dynamic movement between the two halves of the line–the second half of the line specifies what is general in the first half; or the second half focuses or heightens what is referred to in the first half; or the second half forms a miniature narrative sequence following the first half of the line. But not in line 5. Here, at the exact thematic center of the poem, semantic movement slows to allow for the strong, stately emphasis of virtual synonymity, noun for noun and verb for verb, in the same syntactical order: *What is man that You are mindful of him,/ humankind, that You pay him heed?*

In the lines that follow, the poet makes this stasis the basis for dynamic movement–as in the first section of the poem (lines 1-4)–creating a parallelism of specification and sequentiality in the second half of the lines. God has set this human creature only a little lower than the divine, crowning him with honor and glory (line 6), quite like the attributes he himself possesses (parallel to lines 1-2). Line 7 then specifies the meaning of this coronation as man's having been given dominion over earthly things. This line thus makes a transition in the vertical scheme from heaven through man to the world below.

Lines 8 and 9, just before the refrain, reiterate the inventory of living creatures, loosely recalling Genesis 1 (in different terms), then specifying what is contained within the *all...work of Your hands*, referred to in line 7. These two lines concisely invoke both domestic and wild animals and all three spheres of terrestrial life–field, air and sea.

The second half of line 8 focuses the first half. *Fish of the sea* becomes, in the second half of the line, *whatever passes along the paths of the sea*. Interestingly, *passes* is the only active verb in the poem attached to a created thing. Otherwise God acts on all realms of creation; man beholds the various realms; but until now, the created things have been listed as objects of God's attention and that of his surrogate, man. Now, in the final detail of the catalogue of creation, we find an image of movement, a nice intimation in this panoramic view of the teeming vitality that surges through the most inaccessible reaches of the created world, over which man has been appointed to rule.

The God of biblical faith is not only a God of the cosmos, but also a God of history. Many psalms–including the ones that refer explicitly to the Judean king, which are classified as "royal psalms," are responses to urgent pressures of the historical moment–either pleas to God to save his king and people at a time of national danger or celebrations of a recent or remembered military victory. Poems of this sort were common in the pre-monotheistic world, where every nation was presumed to have a particular god whose intercession was solicited in time of need. Even in monotheistic guise, this may seem one of the less edifying forms of worship. Remember Voltaire's bitter mockery at the beginning of *Candide*, when both sides simultaneously celebrate a *Te Deum* over the smoking battlefield for having been vouchsafed the grace to slaughter thousands of their enemies.

But the best of the "political psalms" are neither as narrow nor as crudely pragmatic as modern preconceptions might lead us to expect. The composers of political psalms were confronted with expressing in poetic form a paradox at the heart of biblical religion–the universalistic belief in a single God of all the earth who had chosen, as the medium of his relations with humanity, the particularism of a compact with one people.

This paradox had a major geographical corollary. The psalms were intended for use in and around the temple cult in Jerusalem. So how were the Israelites to imagine the capital city of a nation-state, which was first conquered by David for strategic and political reasons, as the "city of our God," the God who was master of all the nations of the world? The poetic medium, I would suggest, with its extraordinary capacity for interlocking disparate elements and establishing intricate progressions of images and ideas, was a unique instrument for expressing meanings held in high tension.

Here is Psalm 48, which seems to be a song sung by—or perhaps to—pilgrims making their way up the steep ascent to the ramparts of Jerusalem. The first two lines of the poem lock together the particularist and universalist poles of the psalmist's vision. God's greatness is acclaimed in the one city in the world that is uniquely his, but the high-bastioned city itself, viewed from below by the celebrants climbing up to it, is a *joy to all the earth* (line 2). This sense of the looming importance of Jerusalem is enhanced by its designation as the mythological *peak of Zaphon*. In Canaanite tradition, Mount Zaphon was the abode of the gods, and that is how Mount Zion is imagined here. If we may mix mythologies, Mount Zion is viewed as a kind of Mount Olympus.

If I am right that each part of the triad of line 2 builds on a heightening movement, the reference to the *great King* at the end of line 2 is to God, not the reigning Davidic monarch, and thus the rising pitch of assertion culminates in the following fashion: (a) lofty Jerusalem is a joy to all the world; (b) Mount Zion is a veritable dwelling-place of the gods; (c) in fact, it is the chosen capital of the world's king.

Line 3 nicely summarizes what has preceded and leads into the narrative of lines 4 through 11. One has only to look up at the impregnable citadels of Jerusalem to realize how, in historical fact, God has become a stronghold and a fortress for his people.

The speaker then launches into the story of a spectacular defeat inflicted on allied forces that, at some point in the near or distant past, tried to invade Israel by sea (lines 4-7). The precise historical reference is probably not recoverable, but the vivid language describing the naval victory shows how the poet locates Jerusalem in historical time and space. Clearly, there is a pointed antithesis between the *great King* of line 2, who becomes *known* in line 3, and the conspiring kings of line 5, who assemble, or join, forces. The antithesis is heightened in Hebrew by the word *nod'a* in line 3 (the great King becomes "known") and *no'adu* in line 4 (the kings "join forces" or "assemble").

Perhaps, as some scholars have proposed, the *ships of Tarshish* in line 7 refer not to the port of embarkation but to a particular kind of low-keeled, oar--propelled warship. Be that as it may, the invasion fleet must have come from the west, across the Mediterranean, and Tarshish is a far-off port (it is the destination of the fleeing Jonah). In other words, as our gaze now swivels around from the ramparts of Jerusalem down over the coastal plain to the Great Sea beyond, and as we move at the same time from present to past, we are invited to imagine hostile forces assembling from the ends of the earth to attack the Land of Israel.

The link between Mount Zion and an attempted invasion by sea may at first seem tenuous, depending on the implicit notion that the capital city would

Psalm 48

A song. A psalm of the sons of Korah

1. **a** Great is the Lord and greatly to be praised,
   b in the city of our God, His holy mountain.
2. **a** Beautiful in its height, it is a joy to all the earth,
   b Mount Zion, peak of Zaphon,
   c city of the great King.
3. **a** God through its bastions
   b has become known as a stronghold.
4. **a** For, look, the kings assembled,
   b advanced together.
5. **a** When they saw, indeed, they were dismayed,
   b were panicked, were shaken.
6. **a** Trembling seized them there,
   b shaking, like a woman in labor.
7. **a** With an east wind
   b You smashed the ships of Tarshish.
8. **a** Just as we heard;
   b now we see.
9. **a** In the city of the Lord of hosts,
   b in the city of our God,
   c may God keep it firm-founded forever. Selah.
10. **a** We have glimpsed, O God, Your steadfastness [or loving kindness]
    b in the midst of Your temple.
11. **a** Your name, O God, like Your praise,
    b [reaches] to the ends of the earth
    c Your right hand is filled with justice.
12. **a** Let Mount Zion rejoice,
    b let the daughters[4] of Judah exult
    c because of Your judgments.
13. **a** Go round about Zion, encircle it,
    b count its towers.
14. **a** Note its ramparts,
    b scale[5] its bastions,
15. **a** So you may recount
    b to the last generation:
16. **a** That this is God, our God, for ever and ever.
    b He will lead us evermore.*

* Asterisk indicates difficulty in the Hebrew.

have been the invaders' ultimate goal. The juxtaposition, however, of Mount Zion and the sea makes perfect sense when one realizes that the description of an easterly gale overturning the enemy fleet is a phrase-for-phrase allusion to the Song of the Sea in Exodus. Compare lines 6 and 7 of this psalm with Exodus 15:14-16:

> The peoples hear, they tremble;
> Agony grips the dwellers in Philistia.
> Now are the clans of Edom dismayed;
> The tribes of Moab–trembling grips them;
> All the dwellers in Canaan are aghast

Moses' victory song in Exodus ends with a stanza contrasting the sanctuary God will build in Israel's future land with the engulfing sea that destroys Israel's enemies. Psalm 48 starts from the other end of the geographical perspective, that is, from the concluding verses of the poem in Exodus 15–the solid mountain sanctuary established for Israel, from whose rocky heights one can see God's enemies perishing in unstable water.

As we move back, in lines 8 and 9, from the defeat of God's enemies to *the city of our God*, the allusion to Exodus 15 continues, for the poet's prayer for the city is that it be forever *firm-founded* (*konen*, the same verb that dominates the last lines of the Song of the Sea in Exodus 15).[6] Thus, we can appreciate the poetic perception of victory over a particular sea-borne foe as a reenactment of the triumph at the Red (or Reed) Sea. The earlier geographical setting, superimposed on the later–the mountainous eminence of Jerusalem over against the watery expanse of the Mediterranean–is a symbolic pairing depicting God's dominion over the earth and the power of his presence in history. Just as the spatial imagery of the poem moves from Jerusalem to the far reaches of the known world, the temporal indications unite the present with the relatively recent past (the sea victory) and the distant past (Moses' victory) as well as with the indefinite future. Jerusalem, God's city, will continue *for ever and ever* to the *last [or, a future] generation, evermore* (lines 15-16). Thus the towering ramparts of the fortress-city become a nexus for all imagined time and space.

Beginning with line 10, the psalm comes back to city and temple, at which point the paradox of the God of all the earth who has chosen a local place and habitation is flaunted–God's *steadfastness*, or *loving kindness* (*ḥesed*), can be discerned within *the midst of [his] temple*, while his praise reaches *to the ends of the earth*. The last four lines of the poem then revert, in a loose envelope structure, to the perspective with which the poem began–the spiritual tourist approaching the city from below. Visitors to the city are invited to take in the entire imposing circumference, to *count* the towers deployed in space so that they may *recount* God's greatness for all future time (the pun is there in the Hebrew also).

This juggling of time and space around the idea of Jerusalem will hardly allay the doubts of modern readers who may be nervous about mixing politics and faith, but with even a grudging suspension of disbelief, we see how the finely regulated sequence of images and actions translates the monotheistic belief in a world-embracing God who chooses a place and takes sides in the large sweep of history.

The personal and penitential psalms are the ones that speak most directly to a wide range of readers, despite the transformations of Judaism and Christianity since biblical times. In religious poems that do not have a strong national context, there is usually no poetic redefinition of space, because geography and geopolitics are not at issue. In some of them, however, time is strikingly refashioned, as the imagination stretches to gauge the abyss between the creaturely temporality of man and the eternality of the creator. Awareness of the fleeting nature of human life is, of course, not limited to monotheistic or religious poetry, but the biblical poets deepened this perception in a distinctive way by rendering the ephemerality of human life against the background of God's eternity. Because poetry—especially biblical poetry—often works out meanings through an interplay of polarities, the brevity of human life also provides a certain imaginative access, through contrast, to the inconceivable timelessness of God.

Perhaps the most remarkable expression of juxtaposed time—man's and God's—is Psalm 90 (see p. 250). The poem is composed of four segments, which are successive stages in a pronounced rhetorical structure: (1) proem (lines 1-3), addressing God and invoking his eternality; (2) characterization of human transience (lines 4-7), referring to man in the third person; (3) confession of man's sinfulness (lines 8-13), in the first person plural; (4) man's prayer for wisdom and God's grace (lines 14-19).

This poem is a collective penitential supplication. The community has apparently been suffering some unspecified ill for a considerable length of time. God's *wrath* is repeatedly mentioned and more concretely, affliction and years of evil are referred to in line 17, whether famine or plague or military defeat or a combination of disasters. The recurrent formula of psalms of supplication, *O Lord! How long?* is introduced in line 15, at the beginning of the plea for a change of heart (*hinaḥem*, rendered here as *take pity*).

In most supplication poems, the structure intensifies the speaker's anguish, but here the poet transforms supplication into a haunting meditation on human transience. The proem, framed by *Lord, You...* (line 1a) and *You are God* (line 3b), invokes the beginnings of the world through conventional birth imagery (line 2, literally, says the mountains *were born*). Conventional imagery is especially effective here because the language of biological reproduction, when focused on the birth of the world, simultaneously points forward to ephemeral man born of woman and underscores the contrast with the creator, whose existence is *from everlasting to everlasting* (line 3).

After the proem, the poet strikes a penitential note when God urges men to *turn back*, that is, to repent. The actual agency of this urging, however, is a deed as well as an utterance. In line 4a, God has turned man back (the same verb) to dust through suffering. (In some translations, God brings man back to contrition, rather than dust.) Man's suffering reminds the poet of the painful mortality of humankind—and that is the burden of the rest of the poem. The *turning back* is thus already embodied in the chastened self-knowledge of the poetic discourse.

Line 5 is triadic in form, in keeping with its function as the beginning of the meditation on human transience. We glide swiftly from *a thousand years* in God's sight, to *yesterday* that has just passed, to a brief *watch in the night*—an exquisite example of focusing within a single verse. In this line, time is viewed

Psalm 90

A prayer of Moses, the man of God

I

1. **a** Lord, You have been our dwelling place
   b in every generation.
2. **a** Before the mountains were brought forth,
   b or even before You formed the earth and the world,
3. **a** From everlasting to everlasting
   b You are God.

II

4. **a** You turn man back to dust,
   b You say, "Turn back, humankind."
5. **a** For a thousand years in Your sight
   b are but as yesterday when it is past,
   c like a watch in the night.
6. **a** You engulf them with sleep,*
   b in the morning they are like grass, renewed,
7. **a** In the morning it sprouts anew,
   b by evening it withers and dries.

III

8. **a** For we are consumed in Your wrath,
   b in Your anger we are overwhelmed.
9. **a** You set our transgressions before You,
   b our hidden faults [revealed] in the light of Your face.
10. **a** All our days slip away in Your fury,
    b we use up our years like a sigh.
11. **a** The days of our years [are] but seventy,
    b or if in great strength, eighty years–
12. **a** Their span is trouble and grief,
    b for swiftly [they are] cut down,* and we fly off.
13. **a** Who can know the power of Your wrath?
    b As the fear of You, so is Your fury.

IV

14. **a** So teach us to number our days,
    b that we may get a heart of wisdom.
15. **a** Return, O Lord! How long?
    b Have pity on Your servants.
16. **a** Sate us in the morning with Your kindness,
    b that we may sing and rejoice all our days.
17. **a** Give us gladness, as the days You have afflicted us,
    b the years we saw evil.
18. **a** Let Your deeds be seen by Your servants,
    b Your glory by their children
19. **a** Let the favor of the Lord our God be on us.
    b the work of our hands firmly founded for us,
    c the work of our hands firmly found!

* Asterisk indicates difficulty in the Hebrew.

from God's end of the telescope, but the last image–*like a watch in the night*–takes us down into the human world. In a beautiful overlap, *watch in the night* carries us into line 6, to man engulfed by sleep. In other words, a thousand years to God are a fleeting moment of wakefulness in the dark of eternity, and man's whole existence is little more than a fluid, fitful sleep. God's time is indicated by the poetic device of focusing. By contrast, man's time is represented through narrative movement, limited to a 24-hour framework that, by implication, cyclically recurs for each individual–from *night* (line 6a) to *morning* (6b-7a) to *evening* (7b).

In Part III, the poet switches to the first person plural and proceeds to the confession proper (lines 8-13), which is bracketed by an internal envelope structure–God's *wrath* and *anger* in line 8 become God's *wrath* and *fury* in line 13. Part III is characterized by an underlying image of insubstantial, combustible humanity incinerated in the heat of God's wrath. The effect is reinforced by likening man's life to a *sigh* (line 10), an ineffectual breath of sound in contrast to God's consuming blast.

Unlike the units of time linked to God in line 5, the units of man's time move progressively, advancing from *days* (line 10a), to *years* (10b), to a compound, *days of our years* (11a), but never getting beyond 70 or 80 years, certainly not to a thousand, which is a brief interval for God.

The final prayer (Part IV), which carries the accumulated weight of the poem, begins with a petition for the wisdom to *number our days*. God, who urged man to turn back, is now entreated to respond by turning back to man. The temporal terminology is taken up again, but in keeping with the hopeful prayer, the poet envisions that God will *Sate us in the morning with Your kindness,/ that we may sing and rejoice all our days.// Give us gladness as the days You have afflicted us,/ the years we saw evil.* The narrative progression, from morning to days and from days to years, looks beyond transience to life as a movement from lesser to greater joy. Significantly, the only temporal terms not repeated here are evening and night, the terms symbolically associated with fitful sleep and death.

The final line of the poem, which concludes the prayer for divine favor, is once again a triad repeating the final climactic clause: *Let...the work of our hands [be] firmly founded for us,/ the work of our hands firmly found.* The verb, *firmly found*, is used in the context of solid foundations, like the foundations of houses or temples. The special force of the repetition at the end of Psalm 90 provides a contrast to the images of withering grass, sighs, things burnt up by God's wrath and humanity engulfed by sleep. Only with God's blessing can human endeavor be solid, lasting and well founded. Our lives are fleeting–and the poet never loses sight of this painful truth, even in the hopeful piety of his conclusion–but our works, when performed with proper awareness of mortality, can have substance and become vehicles of continuity and renewal from one generation to the next.

The structure of the poem makes possible a remarkably multifaceted sense of temporal permutations. By a subtle sequence of fairly simple conventional images and basic units of time, backward and forward and forward again, the poet imaginatively realizes three different perceptions of time in rapid succession–from the divine perspective of eternity, from man's vanishing vantage point and, reversing that view, from the perspective of a community that sees a prospect of happy persistence.

God manifests himself to man partly through language, and his deeds are necessarily made known by one man to another, and perhaps to himself, through the mediation of language. Psalms, more than any other group of biblical poems, highlights awareness of the linguistic medium of religious experience. The ancient makers of devotional and celebratory poems were keenly aware that poetry is the most complex ordering of language, and perhaps the most demanding. Within the formal limits of a poem, the poet can take advantage of emphatic repetitions dictated by a particular prosodic system–symmetries, antitheses and internal echoes intensified by a closed verbal structure, the fine intertwinings of sounds, images and reported acts. These poetic devices lend coherence and authority to his perceptions of the world. The psalmist's delight in the supple serendipities of poetic form does not detract from the spiritual seriousness of the poems; in fact, poetic form is the chief means of realizing his vision and a source of their continuing power.

This article was adapted from "Forms of Faith in Psalms" in The Art of Biblical Poetry *(New York: Basic Books, 1985).*

PART VIII

Feminism and the Bible

Feminism and the Bible Introduction

Feminism is unapologetically ideological. A basic feminist argument, in fact, is that all scholarship is ideological and that feminists, at least, are honest in declaring their ideology and exposing ideologies implicit in the work of others. The fundamental goal of feminism is to change society so that women and men can be equal. In pursuit of this goal, feminists have developed political and legal theories, as well as distinct approaches to science and literature. Feminists have studied and reevaluated many texts from a feminist perspective. Two subjects of particular importance in feminist literary scholarship are canon formation and empowerment, both of which have implications for biblical criticism.

Canon formation is the process by which certain texts achieve status in a community, whether that community is defined by religion, nationality, culture, ethnicity, gender or some other criterion. Inspiration, morality, insight, patriotism, literary merit, social cohesiveness, political correctness–have all been proposed as reasons for reading or teaching particular books. All of these criteria imply that someone has determined that the chosen books convey these ideas better or more effectively than competing books and that the values they reflect are universally acceptable.

Both of these assumptions, however, can be, and have been, questioned. What one person praises as patriotism another may decry as fascism or radicalism; someone else may attack patriotism itself as atavistic chauvinism. Moreover, just as ideological criteria are controversial, literary merit is notoriously hard to pin down. And disagreements about inspiration, which account for the differences among the biblical canons of the Jewish, Catholic and Protestant communities, may be the most controversial of all.

Modern feminist literary criticism emerged from the Women's Liberation Movement in the 1970s, at the same time as ethnic, minority and non-Western studies. Feminist critics argue that the literary canon–that is, the set of books sanctioned by critics, dignified by articles in academic journals and taught in schools and universities–is dominated by and reflects the values of white,

Protestant, upper middle-class men, and they are determined to reveal the ideological underpinnings of portrayals of women in this tradition. They also champion lesser known or ignored women writers. In *Sexual Politics*,[1] an influential early feminist work, Kate Millett argued that the existing literary canon validates widespread misogyny and the subjugation of women; Nina Baym, in *Woman's Fiction*,[2] resurrected a group of popular nineteenth-century writers whom Nathaniel Hawthorne, a contemporary cultural icon, dismissed as a "damned mob of scribbling women."

Feminist critics also investigate the criteria by which works are elevated to the canon or dismissed. Their arguments are based on the premise that value systems are not natural but cultural, and on that basis, they reject the hegemony of what Adrienne Rich calls "the false male universal" of abstraction and objectivity. Feminists demand equal recognition for female rhetoric, which is grounded in experience and emotion. And they point out that despite general agreement that great literature addresses universal truths of the first order the settings of critically sanctioned works are more often whaling ships and battlefields than homes and family circles, the aspects of life women are most likely to know and write about. Moreover, even when men and women address the same issues in the same settings, the literary canon has favored men. Henry James, for example, is virtually an academic industry, while Edith Wharton, who was immensely popular in her day, is often dismissed as an imitator of James. Men who recreate regional life are included on reading lists as realists; women writing about the same subjects are often dismissed as local colorists.

Some feminists—as well as African-American, Native American, Hispanic and other ethnic critics—have set about creating countercanons of works by forgotten and ignored writers. In the meantime, however, support is growing for dropping the idea of a literary canon altogether in favor of an ethic of diversity. The result is reflected in the titles of books like *American Women Writers: Diverse Voices in Prose since 1845*,[3] *The Madwoman in the Attic: The Woman Writer and the Nineteenth-Century Literary Imagination*,[4] *Beyond Stereotypes: The Critical Analysis of Chicana Literature*,[5] an antidote to the prevailing image of Hispanic women, and *All the Women Are White, All the Blacks Are Men, But Some of Us Are Brave*,[6] a study of black women.

The sense of urgency attached to revisionist criticism derives from the conviction that a literary canon represents power and that reading, therefore, is an act of empowerment. Early on, feminist critics identified women as an oppressed minority naturally allied with other oppressed groups, whether on the basis of race, class or sexual orientation. Feminist literary critics, therefore, found promise in theories that changed the balance of power, especially poststructuralist philosophy and reader-response theory.

Poststructuralist theorists reexamine the relationship of language to reality and, by exposing implicit prejudices, often undermine accepted truths. By analyzing linguisitic structures, forms of thought, ways of knowing–in effect, making the unconscious conscious–poststructuralists have generally concluded that these are also culturally determined. If they are correct, feminist critics argue, we must rethink our comfortable assumptions about human nature and social values. Feminists need no longer argue, for example, that women's writing is as objective as men's; they can now insist that so-called female subjectivity is the literary equal of so-called male objectivity.

For many years, the regnant theory of Western literature, as well as what we might call the commonsense view, was that texts are autonomous, that is, they have structure–or "being"–that determines the range of possible meanings. In some cases, traffic signs for example, the range is very small; in other cases, poems for example, the range is much larger. But the structure always determines the acceptable interpretations because, as Jonathan Culler has noted, "interpretation is always interpretation of something."[7] This view, however, has recently come under attack.

In *Identity of the Literary Text*, Robert Weimann posits a connection "between the decline of the approach to the poem as a self-contained organic whole and the crisis, culminating in the late 1960s, of the traditional definition of the cultural function of the humanities."[8] In other words, when society lost faith in its coherence and rejected traditional standards, when "high" culture was replaced by "popular" culture, critics also lost faith in the coherence of literature, the literary canon and even in language itself. It was argued that readers create meaning through their experience, expectations and assumptions and that there is no right or wrong interpretation of a text. Every reader finds in a given text what he or she is preconditioned to find–and all interpretations, being equally personal, are equally valid. Reader response theory denies that the text places any restraints on the reader's predisposition to interpretation. The result is a loss of authority by any and all texts–including, of course, texts in the literary canon–and the consequent empowerment of readers.

All of these theories and debates are reflected in feminist biblical studies. In "Reading as Empowerment: The Bible from a Feminist Perspective," Mieke Bal analyzes and rejects three feminist approaches to the Bible. The first idealizes the Bible by ignoring misogyny, which may enable some women to remain faithful to a religious community. The second blames the Bible for modern sexism (and other problems), sometimes slipping into intellectualized anti-Semitism. The third tries to strip away later sexist impositions to reveal the nonsexist truth of the original Bible. Bal's preference is that we "change the presuppositions," reexamine the "dependence of text on context," "step over from 'truth' to 'relevance' as a basis for understanding" and encourage "empowering reading that will leave room for both technical accuracy and personal commitment."[9]

Not surprisingly, many feminist critics focus on portrayals of women and explicit and implicit assumptions in the biblical text about virginity, marriage, chastity and "woman's place" generally. A recurrent theme is that the Bible—especially later interpretations–suppressed or distorted the true contributions of women in order to demonstrate their folly, weakness, treachery or sexual threat, thereby validating the patriarchal hierarchy.

As far back as the early nineteenth century, champions of women's rights, many of whom were active abolitionists, argued that the Bible was misused to justify the inferior position of women, just as it was perverted to justify slavery. Feminists who remained within the religious community argued for a metaphorical reading of Genesis, especially the Adam and Eve story. Many early feminists studied Hebrew and Greek in an attempt to discover the original meaning of the Bible. And they emphasized the role and character of positive female biblical heroines, like Miriam, Deborah and Priscilla, to counter the negative images of Eve, Jezebel and others.

Some early feminists, however, concluded that the Bible itself was the problem. In 1893, Matilda Joslyn Gage published *Woman, Church and State: The Original Exposé of Male Collaboration against the Female Sex.*[10] And between 1895 and 1898, Elizabeth Cady Stanton published *The Woman's Bible*,[11] a systematic analysis of scriptural contributions to the oppression of women. These "radical" feminist studies were dismissed by male scholars and kept at arm's length by most feminists, who, Stanton noted, were afraid "they might compromise their evangelical faith by affiliating with those of more liberal views" and that it was "not politic to rouse religious opposition."

When feminist biblical scholars reappeared in the 1970s, the emphasis was on "reclaiming" the Bible for women, finding a true, positive image of women behind centuries of male misinterpretation. Phyllis Trible, a pioneer in this field, maintains that the role of Miriam as prophet and leader of the Exodus was minimized in favor of Moses, who is even credited with composing *her* Song of the Sea. Mieke Bal argues that the story of Samson and Delilah is more often popularized than the stories of Yael and Sisera or Judith and Holofernes because Delilah betrays "our" hero to the enemy. And Carey A. Moore suggests that Judith may have been omitted from the canon because she was too independent, and therefore threatening to males, as a role model for women.[12]

Interestingly enough, feminist readings of the Bible have led to renewed study of some earlier nonsexist, or philo-female, commentaries. In "Rereading Eve and Other Women: The Bible in a Women's Studies Course," Ruth Adler recounts how the works of Alter, Trible and medieval rabbinic commentaries enabled her to harmonize the supposedly conflicting accounts of creation in Genesis 1 and 2. Adler notes that Rashi, the most popular medieval Jewish exegete, took the idea of *'ezer kenegdo* (a power equal to him) one step further and observed that *sela'* means "side" as well as "rib." Therefore, "Adam and Eve may be seen to have been created simultaneously as an androgynous being that was later separated."[13]

In "Was the First Feminist Bible in Yiddish?" Harvey Minkoff and Evelyn B. Melamed show that *Tzenah Urenah*, a Yiddish biblical paraphrase popular with Jewish women since the 16th century, incorporated older Midrashim that explicitly reject patriarchal interpretations. For example, the passage after the Song of the Sea in which Miriam is called a prophet is described this way:

> Miriam, the sister of Moses, was already a prophet before Moses was born; she prophesied that her mother would have a son who would lead Israel out of Egypt. And...one should not wonder that a woman prophesied, for a woman is also man[kind] since she was created from man. And Sarah was a greater prophet than her husband Abraham....moreover one should not denigrate women, for a pious woman is as worthy as a pious man.

The Garden of Eden story, about which Pamela Milne claims "No biblical story has had a more profound negative impact on women throughout history," is also paraphrased in *Tzenah Urenah*:

> Adam did not admit or repent the sin he committed. Instead, he blamed "the woman you put with me." In essence, Adam repudiated the favor he had been done–the favor of having been given a wife.[14]

Despite attempts to salvage women's role, some feminist critics have concluded that portions of the Bible cannot be reclaimed. In *Texts of Terror*,[15] Trible retells biblical stories of rape, murder and mutilation "on behalf of the victims," memorializing them through repentance and a "dialectic of redemption." Others have exposed insidious portrayals of women as deceptive, devious and dangerous, as well as the cultural assumption that women are–or should be–dependent, subordinate and passive. Some have even demanded that these stories be removed from the Bible. As Pamela Milne warns, unless an acceptable solution is found, feminists may be forced "to choose rejection of the Bible and the faith traditions within which it is preserved."

CHAPTER 18

Eve and Adam
A Feminist Reading

Pamela J. Milne

To generations of Christians, Eve was a temptress who brought sin and death into the world. But, Milne asks, is this what the Bible really says? "Can this story be reclaimed for women? Can feminist analysis recover it from centuries of patriarchal interpretation and make it a positive spiritual resource for women?" The issue is not just academic. The perception of sexism in the Bible raises the "question of the Bible's authority for women," and an unsatisfactory answer may lead to "rejection of the Bible and the faith traditions" that call it sacred.

The story of Eve, Milne says, "provided an important basis for the development of deprecatory Christian theologies of woman" as a secondary, inferior, subordinate, evil and seductive being who was "defective by nature...born female because of some defect in the active force or maternal disposition." The biblical text, however, is open to other interpretations. In the 19th century, Elizabeth Cady Stanton claimed that "[t]he conduct of Eve from beginning to end is...superior to that of Adam," exhibiting "the courage, the dignity and the lofty ambition of the woman." More recently, Phyllis Trible has argued that Eve is an "intelligent, informed, perceptive...theologian, ethicist, hermeneut, and rabbi."

Nonetheless, feminist hermeneutics has been almost completely ignored by mainstream scholars. Even scholars who are sympathetic to women's issues wonder who, in "a patriarchal culture like the one that produced the Bible...would have composed a feminist story" that portrays Eve as superior to Adam. This leads to the unfortunate conclusion that, perhaps, the Bible itself, and not just later appropriations of it, is sexist. We may even be forced to acknowledge, Milne says, "that some parts might be so thoroughly patriarchal that they might have to be excluded from the canon."–Ed.

Scholars have identified two different creation stories at the beginning of Genesis. The first story (Genesis 1-2:4a) is attributed to the "P" source (the Priestly tradition) and the second (Genesis 2:4b-3:24) to the "J" source (the Yahwist tradition).[1]

These accounts differ in many ways. The language and style are obviously different. The P account is repetitive and filled with set formulas (for example, "it was evening and morning, the first day" and "and God saw that it was good"). The J account, on the other hand, flows along like a good story. The P account begins with lifeless, watery chaos from which dry land must emerge before life can begin; the J story moves in the opposite direction, with lifeless, dry land to which water is added, which permits life to begin. In the P account, God creates by speaking; in the J account, God acts like a potter, a gardener and a builder.

The two accounts also differ with respect to the creation of human beings. In the first version, the P account, God creates woman and man at the same time, as the last act of creation. We are not told what material they are made from, only that they are made in the image of God. In this account, no names are given to the woman or the man. In the second story, the J account, it seems as though man is created at the beginning of creation and woman at the end. The man is fashioned from the earth, while the woman is created from the man's rib to overcome the man's loneliness in the garden. In neither story, however, is the man or woman given a name. They are identified only as "woman" (*ishah*) and "man" (*ish*). The second story is generally thought to be much older than the first. Most scholars think that the J source was composed in the tenth century B.C.E. during the United Monarchy, most likely during the reign of Solomon.

The story of the expulsion from the Garden of Eden in Genesis 3 also belongs to the J source, the earlier of the two traditions. There is no parallel account of this story in the P source. At the beginning of the expulsion story, we are introduced to the serpent, who questions the woman about the divine commandment regulating the fruit that may or may not be eaten by the human couple. The woman explains that the fruit of only one tree may not be eaten. The serpent questions God's motives for this injunction, and the woman realizes that the fruit of that tree is also good for food. And so she eats this fruit and offers some to the man, who accepts and eats it.

As a consequence of disobeying the divine commandment, the man and the woman become aware and ashamed of their nakedness. When God learns of their disobedience, he drives the man out of the Garden of Eden. Only at this point in the story–just before the expulsion–does the man name the woman "Eve." She is called Eve because she is the mother of all living things (Genesis 3:20). This explanation of the name is a popular etymology linking the Hebrew *Ḥavva* (Eve) to the word for life (*ḥayyim*). The actual root meaning of the name Eve is uncertain.

The story of Eve in Genesis 2-3 has given rise to many difficulties for women and has been, therefore, of major interest to feminist critics of the Bible, who have studied it extensively in the last 15 years. At the heart of the issue is whether the story is irretrievably patriarchal or whether the patriarchal elements can be overcome through feminist interpretation. In other words, can this story be reclaimed for women? Can feminist analysis recover it from centuries of patriarchal interpretation and make it a positive spiritual resource for women?

No biblical story has had a more profound negative impact on women throughout history than the story of Eve. The long tradition of patriarchal and, in some cases, misogynistic (characterized by hatred of women) interpretation has made this text thoroughly unacceptable to many women and men from all religious backgrounds.

In early Christian writings, Eve is usually depicted as secondary and inferior to Adam because she was created after Adam and from Adam. She is also regularly portrayed as weak, seductive and evil—the one who caused Adam to disobey God's command.[2] At the same time, Eve came to be regarded not only as the mother of all living things, but also as the paradigm for all women. A unique exception is Mary, the mother of Jesus, who later became, in her own right, a paradigm of idealized womanhood to Christians.

The combination of the negative image of Eve and the idea that she is the model of what it means to be a woman was one basis for the development of deprecatory patriarchal Christian theologies of woman. In 1 Timothy 2:11-14, for example, we are told that women should not speak in the assembly or teach or tell men what to do because Eve was formed after Adam and led Adam astray:

> Let a woman learn in silence with all submissiveness. I permit no woman to teach or to have authority over men; she is to keep silent. For Adam was formed first, then Eve; and Adam was not deceived, but the woman was deceived and became a transgressor.
>
> 1 Timothy 2:11-14

The early church father Tertullian (c. 160-240 C.E.) taught that all women share the ignominy of Eve:

> And do you not know that you are each an Eve? The sentence of God on this sex of yours lives in this age: the guilt, of necessity, must live too. You are the devil's gateway; you are the unsealer of that forbidden tree; you are the first deserter of the divine law; you are she who persuaded him whom the devil was not valiant enough to attack. You destroyed so easily God's image, man.[3]

In the traditional understanding of the text, Eve was created to be a "helper" (Hebrew *'ezer*) to the man. Because Eve is thought to be secondary and inferior to Adam, her role as "helper" is said to be limited. Early interpreters often suggested that Eve was a helper to Adam only for the purpose of procreation.

Listen to Ambrose, a fourth-century bishop of Milan and one of the four great doctors of the Latin church:

> [E]ven though man was created outside Paradise (i.e., in an inferior place) [In Genesis 2:15 we are told that "The Lord God took the man and placed him in the Garden of Eden."], he is found to be superior, while woman, though created in a better place (i.e., inside Paradise) is found inferior...[I]ndeed, after woman was made, she was the first to violate the divine command. She even dragged her husband along with her into sin and showed herself to be an incentive to him. [God] said, "Let us make for him a helper like unto himself" (Genesis 2:18). We take this to mean a helper for the purpose of generating human nature...This then is the way in which a woman is a good helper of less importance.[4]

By Augustine's time (354-430 C.E.), Genesis 23 was the well established cornerstone of a theology that women were secondary, and thus inferior and subordinate, to men; women were also considered evil and seductive.

Extending the biblical analysis, Thomas Aquinas (1225-1274 C.E.), adapted Aristotelian ideas to develop further the idea of women's inferiority. Women, he urged, are defective by nature. They are "misbegotten males," born female because of a defect in the active force or maternal disposition or because of an external force such as a moist south wind.[5]

A work entitled *Malleus Maleficarum* (*Hammer against Witches*), written by two Dominican priests, Heinrich Kraemer and Jakob Sprenger, published in 1486 for use during the Inquisition, uses Genesis 3 among other biblical texts to depict women as evil, feebleminded and lustful. This work provided the principle theological justification for the persecution of women as witches. In the years following publication, thousands of women were accused of, and executed for, practicing witchcraft.[6]

The themes of inferiority, evil and seductiveness are repeatedly emphasized in Christian writings from Luther, Calvin and Knox all the way to 20th-century papal encyclicals and the broadcasts of TV fundamentalist preachers.[7] In our own day, some men appeal to Genesis 2-3 as a theological basis for their "right" to "discipline" physically a wife who is not properly subordinate. Some battered women actually accept physical abuse because they think abuse is a husband's divinely sanctioned "right" and "duty."[8]

Until recently, the traditional interpretation of Genesis 2-3 was virtually unchallenged. The American activist Elizabeth Cady Stanton toward the end of her life focused her feminist critique on organized religion. After years of political struggle, she had come to appreciate the role of religion, especially the Bible, in the oppression of women. In 1895 she published a feminist commentary on the Bible called the *Woman's Bible*, which contains a feminist reinterpretation of the story of Eve and Adam. Stanton directly challenged the centuries-old patriarchal reading of this text:

> The unprejudiced reader must be impressed with the courage, the dignity, and the lofty ambition of the woman....Reading this narrative carefully,

> it is amazing that any set of men ever claimed that the dogma of the inferiority of woman is here set forth. The conduct of Eve from the beginning to the end is so superior to that of Adam.[9]

But biblical scholars and feminists largely ignored Stanton's pioneering efforts at "depatriarchalizing" the Bible.

Not until the rise of feminist theology in the 1960s did anyone seriously question the traditional image of Eve or her function as a theological paradigm for women in Christian tradition. The most extensive and sustained feminist analysis and reinterpretation of the Eve and Adam story was undertaken in the 1970s by feminist Bible scholar Phyllis Trible.[10]

Like a number of other feminist exegetes, Trible argued that the problem with the Eve-Adam story is not in the text but rather in centuries of sexist, patriarchal interpretations of the text. She readily concedes that the Bible is largely a "man's book" but is still certain the Eve-Adam story can be liberated from patriarchal interpretations. Trible contends that when this is done, the liberating essence of the story for women can be revealed and appropriated.

According to Trible, none of the traditional patriarchal claims is altogether accurate and most are simply not present in the story itself. Some patriarchal claims, she argues, actually violate the rhetoric of the biblical account. For example, in the traditional interpretation, man is said to be superior because he is created first (Genesis 2:7), and woman is deemed inferior because she is created last (Genesis 2:22). But these same patriarchalist interpreters never argue that humans are inferior to animals, which were created first in the Priestly creation account (Genesis 1:27). On the contrary, they regard the creation of humans, the final creative act in Genesis 1, as the pinnacle of creation. If this interpretative principle is applied consistently, the creation of the woman in Genesis 2 is the crowning achievement of divine creativity.

Traditional interpreters often focus on the fact that the serpent speaks to the woman and not to the man. They explain this in a variety of ways: the woman is morally weaker than the man and thus easier prey for the serpent; the woman is simpleminded, gullible, untrustworthy; the woman is more sexual, and her sexuality can be used by the serpent to ruin the man. Trible stresses that all of these explanations are speculative, that the text does not say why the serpent speaks to the woman. She pokes fun at such eisegesis (reading into a text what is not actually there) by suggesting how women might indulge in the same kind of speculation. For example: the serpent speaks to the woman because she is more intelligent than the man; the woman has a better understanding of the divine command and, therefore, she is in a better position to act as theologian and translator; she is more independent than the man, who is portrayed as silent, passive, bland and belly-oriented, a creature that thinks with his stomach instead of his brain. In a similar vein, another feminist exegete has noted that even Eve's "temptation" of Adam is not in the text but has been read into the story by patriarchalist interpreters.[11]

Trible advocates re-reading and reinterpreting the story based on exegesis, reading out of the text, rather than eisegesis, reading into the text. Her reinterpretation is based on a recently developed, widely used methodology of biblical interpretation known as rhetorical criticism. Rhetorical critics analyze the literary devices of style and rhetoric used by biblical authors to convey meaning.

Trible's combination of rhetorical criticism and a feminist point of view (a critique of culture in light of misogyny) produces fresh insights that frequently challenge traditional interpretations of the Eve-Adam story. She finds in the story a circular or symmetrical pattern, and the creation of woman last is part of that symmetry. Trible argues that the creation of woman completes the creative process begun with the creation of *ha-'adam* in Genesis 2:7 (variously translated as "man," "the man" or "Adam"; *ha* is the definite article "the"). The *'adam* created at the beginning of the story should not, however, be thought of as necessarily male. Rather, she argues, the Hebrew text presents us with a pun–an earth creature (*ha-'adam*) who has been created from the earth (*ha-'adamah*) who remains basically sexless until the differentiation of female and male occurs in Genesis 2:21-23. Only with the advent of sexuality does the term *ha-'adam* acquire the secondary meaning of male, and even then it is ambiguous.

When the woman is created, she is created as an *'ezer kenegdo*. This phrase is usually translated as "a helper/helpmate for him." The words "helper" and "helpmate" have a pejorative sense in English, and, as we have seen, traditional interpreters assume this pejorative sense in describing the relationship of the woman to the man. Trible translates the phrase as "a companion corresponding to it." She notes that *'ezer* is a relational term, the meaning of which is totally absent from the English word "helper." The relation implied is a beneficial one, not one of inferiority. In fact, in some biblical passages, the same Hebrew word is used to describe God (e.g., Exodus 18:4; Deuteronomy 33:7; Psalm 33:20), but in these passages translators use the word "help" rather than "helper" to avoid the pejorative connotation. Trible argues that the concepts of mutuality and equality are conveyed by the word *kenegdo*.[12]

Trible also challenges the patriarchal assertion that the superiority of the man over the woman is established by the man "naming" the woman in Genesis 2:23 ("She shall be called woman") as he had previously named the other creatures in the garden. Trible points out that the usual naming formula–"to call the name" (used, for example, in Genesis 2:19,20, 4:17,25,26)–is not used in Genesis 2:23. Moreover, the "calling" of the woman by the man does not signify the establishment of man's power over woman but rather his joy in their mutuality.

The man does, eventually, name the woman "Eve" (in Genesis 3:20), and only then does he assert his rule over her. But at that point sin has already corrupted the mutuality and equality between them. Thus, the man's naming of the woman, his domination of her, is not part of the goodness of creation but is an indication of his sinfulness. Accordingly, male domination is not by divine intention but is a consequence, and a sign of, sinfulness. Therefore, male domination should not to be held up as an ideal but should be deplored as a condition to be overcome in order to recover our full humanity. The story reread in this way, Trible says, liberates both women and men rather than continuing to enslave them.

The feminist approach taken by Trible and others is a "reformist" approach.[13] The reformists believe that the biblical traditions contain a reformable, recoverable core. The counterparts of the reformists are the "revolutionaries," feminists who maintain that the core biblical symbols of Judaism and Christianity are male and unreformable. Most feminist biblical scholars and theologians are "reformists" who have remained within the Jewish and Christian traditions and have developed exegetical and hermeneutical strategies for reclaiming the Bible as a positive spiritual resource for women.[14]

Recently, however, a growing sense of uneasiness can be detected among the reformists, who are becoming less optimistic that the whole Bible can be recovered. They now acknowledge that some parts of the Bible might be so thoroughly patriarchal that they might have to be excluded from the canon (the collection of biblical books that are authoritative or sacred). This, in turn, has led to questioning the whole notion of canon and biblical authority.[15]

But the Eve-Adam story is not among these texts. Genesis 2-3 is widely regarded by feminists as a text that can be reclaimed and understood as having a positive message of sexual equality. In Trible's rereading of the story, the traditional view of Eve is overturned, and Eve is no longer a simpleminded, gullible female who seduces the male to sin. Instead, she is an "intelligent, informed, perceptive...theologian, ethicist, hermeneut, and rabbi" who speaks with "clarity and authority" and acts independently but without deception.

Is optimism on the part of feminist reformists about Genesis 2-3 well founded? Feminist exegetes have certainly mounted an important challenge to traditional interpretation, but have they been successful in reforming the way the Eve-Adam story is understood? The answer seems to be no, or at least not yet. Mainline biblical scholars have mostly ignored the work of feminists on this text. For example, Howard N. Wallace's 1985 study, *The Eden Narrative*,[16] a survey of recent trends in interpreting Genesis 2-3, does not contain a single reference to any feminist study of this text. Clearly, Wallace did not think feminist reinterpretations were significant.

Another interesting example is Jerome T. Walsh's article, "Genesis 2:4b-3:24: A Synchronic Approach."[17] Like Wallace, Walsh seems completely unaware of feminist critiques when he reasserts many traditional patriarchal interpretations of the story. What makes this particularly ironic is that Walsh uses the same critical method as Trible, rhetorical criticism, to arrive at diametrically opposite conclusions about the relationship between man and woman.

Walsh assumes that *ha-'adam* is male from the beginning of the story. He interprets Genesis 2:23 as "a decree of naming" and the woman as a "matching helper." Like Trible, Walsh finds in the story a concentric ring pattern, although he does not identify the pattern the same way. He divides the story into seven scenes, six of which are balanced around the central (fourth) scene. Scene 2 (Genesis 2:18-25), he argues, "establishes a type of hierarchy among the characters: Yahweh God is supreme, the man is the highest of the creatures, with the woman closely associated but subordinated to him; least of all are the animals."

By the central scene (Genesis 3:6-8), where the man and woman eat of the fruit and suddenly realize they are naked, the proper social hierarchy has been inverted, according to Walsh. The woman is presented here as superior to the man, and he is now presented as "her man/husband" (Genesis 3:6). The woman was "named for her derivation from him" in Genesis 2:23, but now the man is "designated in terms of his relationship with her"; he has become "an adjunct" to the woman, who was supposed to be "a matching helper" to the man. The proper order is restored in scene 6 (Genesis 3:14-19) when "man's superiority over the woman is explicitly stated in the woman's punishment"—"in pain shall you bring forth children" (Genesis 3:16). With Walsh, we seem to be back where we started.

Critics who use one of the newest approaches to the study of the Eve-Adam story, structuralist analysis, also largely ignore feminist reformist studies. Structuralism *per se* is not a methodology but rather a perspective, a point of view, a way of looking at the world that is essentially independent of the subject matter.[18] The structures of various kinds of relationships that structuralists investigate lie below the surface of the text (the level investigated by rhetorical critics) and, therefore, cannot be apprehended directly. Using structuralist analytical techniques, structures that operate at the unconscious or subconscious level can be identified and described.

The first structural study of the Eve-Adam story was undertaken by British anthropologist Sir Edmund Leach in 1961.[19] In the introduction to his analysis, Leach notes that binary oppositions are intrinsic to human thought. For example, objects are either alive or not alive; and human beings are either male or not male!

This binary opposition is the one that interests us in connection with Leach's analysis of the Eve-Adam story. Leach notes that for males, non-males are divided into women of two kinds: (1) our kind, with whom sexual relations are incestuous; and (2) the other kind, with whom sexual relations are allowed. Every human society devises rules to regulate incest and exogamy (marrying outside one's group). A logical problem arises, however, with respect to human beginnings. If the original human parents were of the same kind, then their relationship was incestuous. But if they were of different kinds, then what kind exactly was the other member of the original pair? Myths of human origin, according to Leach, mediate this paradox by introducing a third category that is anomalous or abnormal in terms of ordinary rational categories.

The rational categories that form a binary opposition in Genesis 2 are, according to Leach, man (i.e., *ha-'adam*, which Leach assumes is male) and animal. None of the animals, however, can mitigate man's loneliness. The woman is the anomalous/abnormal "other" introduced to mediate this opposition. She belongs to a paradigmatic set of mediating terms that consists of the creeping things in Genesis 1 and the serpent in Genesis 3. All members of this set belong to the "confused category" of mediator between the rational categories man and animal. Thus, for Leach, in the order of creation, Eve apparently belongs neither to the category (kind) animal nor to the category (kind) human.

Leach completed his study before the feminist reformist analyses appeared, so he may, perhaps, be forgiven for his androcentric conclusions. More recent structural analysts, however, are just as unaware of the feminist reformist critics and can not be as easily forgiven. In 1980, an entire issue of *Semeia*, a highly regarded scholarly journal, was devoted to structural studies of the Eve-Adam story. Nowhere in the publication was there a direct reference to the work of Trible or any other feminist exegete. Not surprisingly, most ended up supporting the familiar patriarchal interpretations, although they arrived at this point by a variety of analytical routes.

Among structuralist studies, David Jobling's recent analysis of Genesis 2-3 stands out as the first serious attempt to respond to feminist concerns in general and Trible's interpretations in particular.[20] In an earlier article, Jobling had concluded that the Eve-Adam story is "male mythology striving to deal with the complexity of social life and in particular with women."[21] This is not a story with a universal perspective on human existence; nor is it a story produced by a generic human mind. Jobling's study shows that the story is the product of a male mind.

Jobling is sympathetic to feminist concerns and would like to be able to agree with Trible that Genesis 2-3 is a feminist story. But the results of his analysis do not allow him to do so. There is, first of all, a practical problem. In a patriarchal culture like the one that produced the Bible, Jobling wonders who would have composed a feminist story. And if the Eve-Adam story is a feminist story, how could it have been accepted in ancient Israel as a basic myth of human origins?

Despite the fact that Jobling does not find that Genesis 2-3 is a feminist story, he remains convinced that a feminist reading is both possible and necessary. He argues that the positive feminist aspects of the story are not in the surface features, as Trible tries to prove, but are present at a deeper level–in the tension between the main narrative program (getting man to till the earth) and the dominant theological theme (the fall).

In the main narrative program we find two opposed "logics," according to Jobling–the logic of "inside the garden" and the logic of "outside the garden."

Inside the garden, humanity is solitary and male; he is born autochthonously and is immortal. Outside the garden, humanity is both male and female, born sexually and mortal. In Jobling's words:

> "Inside," woman does not exist—the solitary "earth-creature" is male.... "Outside," she shares the hardness of life, indeed has more than her share of it. But the hardness is defined for her wholly in terms of her sexual/generative function; it includes being subordinated to the will of man.

In the dominant theological program, the opposed logics are "before the fall" and "after the fall." The fall theme is a typical myth of transformation from the "other world," where only the male exists, to "this world," where both male and female exist. The cultural mind-set that fosters thinking in terms of such oppositions is, according to Jobling, male-centered, patriarchal, even misogynistic.

Ultimately, according to Jobling's analysis, a middle semantics is necessary to mediate the oppositions. Woman represents the possibility of the "after" in the "before" and thus precipitates the transformation from "inside" to "outside." In the "after," the woman suffers subordination to the man. To make this appear logical, she must be made to do something in the "before" that is worse than what the man does. That "worse" thing is instigating man's disobedience. It is intolerable to the male mind-set that the responsibility for evil be placed either on the deity or on the man. And so woman (and the animals) is made to assume the guilt.

Despite his sympathetic awareness of feminist scholarship, Jobling arrives at essentially the same conclusion as other structuralists about how the story portrays the woman. But Jobling's study is not just another patriarchal interpretation. The way he applies his conclusions marks his work as feminist. Ultimately, Jobling says, the story explains nothing. Superficially, the male dream world prevails (male only and immortal), but actually it fails to replace the real world of male and female.

At this point, Jobling sees a possibility for a feminist reading of the story. Deconstruction of the text, he says, lays bare the effects of the patriarchal mind tying itself in knots to account for woman and femaleness in a way that makes sense and still supports patriarchal assumptions. Feminists, he suggests, should neither reject the Bible because it is wholly patriarchal nor deny that it is wholly patriarchal. Once they accept that the Bible is wholly patriarchal, through the effective use of deconstruction they can expose it as the attempt of a bad conscience to make sense of patriarchy.

Much depends, of course, on what Jobling means by "accept." If he means that feminists should accept the challenge to expose the patriarchy of the Bible as an academic, intellectual exercise, then he is unquestionably correct. But if he is suggesting that feminists accept a patriarchal Bible as a spiritual resource, then his analysis raises some fundamental hermeneutical problems. Jobling has, after all, demonstrated that the patriarchal interpretations of the Eve-Adam story that have accrued over the centuries did not originate solely from the bias of interpreters but are derived from the underlying structures of the biblical text itself. His deconstruction of these patriarchal structures has laid bare their illogic and unsensibleness. (This is not unlike what Trible has done with the stories of Hagar, the Levite's concubine, Jephthah's daughter and others in *Texts of Terror*.)[22] But is patriarchy exposed as illogical and unsensible more acceptable than before? If anything, Jobling's work has made it even more difficult, if not impossible, to reclaim the biblical tradition as a positive spiritual resource for women.

There are some who suggest that one way around the problem is to recognize the sexist presuppositions of the Eve-Adam story, indeed, of the whole Bible, but also to recognize that these presuppositions are descriptive of the patriarchal society from which they arose and not prescriptive for today. The challenge for us is to transcend the sexism of the biblical text.[23]

For a growing number of feminists, neither approach offers much comfort. The fact is that there is little evidence that there is much interest, either in scholarly or popular circles, in transcending the sexism of the text. Most recent studies of the Eve-Adam story continue to reinforce, even to sanctify, sexism.

It seems that the recognition by many feminist interpreters, including Jobling, that the text is patriarchal and that the inherent sexism cannot be fully overcome by rereading it from a feminist perspective has intensified the question of the Bible's authority for women. We are now forced to come to terms with the idea that the sacred text is patriarchal and continues to communicate patriarchal values both directly, on the surface, and indirectly, through deep structures and narrative strategies.

To keep more feminists from rejecting the Bible and the faith traditions within which it is preserved, there will have to be better solutions to this dilemma than the ones that have been proposed thus far. It is not enough to ascribe sexism to the ancient culture as long as the modern culture continues to preserve it with such dedication. We must explore more deeply why faith traditions and biblical scholars remain committed to maintaining and emphasizing the patriarchal aspects of stories like Genesis 2-3 and why most biblical scholars continue to turn a blind eye to the work of feminist scholars. They must begin to listen more sensitively to women, who, throughout history, have suffered from the subordination and inequality that have been justified on the basis of such texts. This is not to say that the Bible is to blame for all the sexism and discrimination women have suffered. But it is time we began to look honestly and directly at what it means to call apparently non-reformable, patriarchal texts like the story of Adam and Eve "sacred."

Afterword

Pinchas Lapide, in "Eve and Adam: Touching the Forbidden Fruit," compiles rabbinic commentary to show that in the Hebrew text Adam is at fault and not Eve:

> Now the serpent was the shrewdest of all the wild beasts that the Lord God had made. He said to the woman, "Did God really say: 'You shall not eat of any tree of the garden'?" The woman replied to the serpent, "We may eat of the fruit of the other trees of the garden. It is only about fruit of the tree in the middle of the garden that God said: 'You shall not eat of it *or touch it*, lest you die.'"
>
> Genesis 3:1-3

There is one problem here. Eve tells the serpent that God proscribed *touching* the fruit of the tree of knowledge of good and evil. We know what God said. We've already been told what God said. He said nothing about *touching* the fruit of the tree.

This is what God said: "And the Lord God commanded the man, saying, 'Of every tree of the garden you are free to eat; but as for the tree of knowledge of good and evil, you must not eat of it; for as soon as you eat of it, you shall die'" (Genesis 2:16-17). Note that God communicated this prohibition to Adam, not to Eve. At the time, Eve hadn't even been created. (That occurs in the second half of chapter 2.) Eve must have learned from her husband about the prohibition against eating the fruit. The question is–did Adam add the bit about not touching the fruit when he told Eve of the prohibition? Or did Eve add it herself when she told the snake about the prohibition?

Traditional exegetes are divided on the question. One group says that Eve added it herself, that she tended to exaggerate, that she was simply too garrulous. Another group argues that Adam quoted God incorrectly when he told Eve about the tree; as a safety measure, Adam added, on his own initiative, the prohibition against touching. This view is disputed by the interpreters of the first school, who cannot believe that Adam had such a vivid imagination.

In any event, the addition of the prohibition against touching proves fatal, for it provides an opening for the snake–leading Eve to believe that God had not really meant what he said about punishing a transgression of the proscription. Actually, the snake appears to have been looking for a way to suck Eve into his nefarious plot (he is the craftiest animal in the garden–Genesis 3:1), and the bit about touching gives him the opportunity.

The snake opens the conversation with a provocative question. "Did God *really* say: 'You shall not eat of any tree of the garden'?" (Genesis 3:1). We have already quoted Eve's reply, which includes the prohibition against touching as well as eating. The passage ends with her questioning God's threat of death as punishment for transgression: "You shall not eat of it or touch it, lest you die" (Genesis 3:3).

The snake then tells Eve: "You are not going to die" (Genesis 3:4). The text is silent on the matter, but there are those who believe that the snake demonstrates that she would not die for violating the prohibition against touching the fruit. Because nothing happens when she touches the fruit, she supposes she can also eat it with impunity. In this way, the snake is able to entice her.

Just think, if Eve hadn't added the prohibition about touching, we might all still be living in paradise. "You will be as God, knowing good and evil," the snake promises (Genesis 3:5). Adam and Eve had everything they needed to live a carefree life in harmony with God and his creation. But Eve aspired to higher things. Was her thirst for knowledge, her yearning for self-development, part of the basic stuff of humanity?

Eve understands the snake's words as a promise of greater achievement, more knowledge, a more intense life, equality with her own prototype, God. As a bearer of God's image, she is, in fact, already like God. But to be equal to God—that is worth careful consideration! None of this, however, does she discuss with Adam. Although their common fate is involved, she does not ask his counsel.

By deciding to go it alone, Eve reveals herself as the first theologian. She explains God's will to the snake, but she also knows the consequences of transgressing the prohibition. "Then you will die," God had said. On the other hand, there is the prospect of omniscience—a promise that attracts the clever Eve but apparently leaves Adam cold.

Adam, in fact, reveals himself to be rather reserved, taciturn and, to put it mildly, not terribly energetic. Throughout the story, he plays a miserable, walk-on role, which the Bible refuses to embellish one iota. While Eve acts independently and takes on responsibility, Adam sits idly somewhere off by himself. There is not a single word to suggest that he hesitates, weighs his options or even reminds his wife of God's omnipotence.

The fall reaches a dramatic peak in a short laconic sentence, which is, in its very terseness, suggestive: "And she took of the fruit and ate and gave her husband of it as well, and he ate" (Genesis 3:6). Adam neither participates in the debate with the snake nor makes the slightest attempt to influence his wife. He follows his wife blindly, without question; idle, taciturn and passive, Adam is portrayed as a silent fellow-eater.

For almost 2,000 years, the fruit of the tree in this passage has been painted, sculpted and described as an apple. But the text speaks only of an undefined "fruit." How did we get to the apple, of all things, which was not known in the Near East until a century ago? In Jerome's fifth-century Latin translation of the Bible, the Vulgate, the word for "evil," with which the snake's speech ends (Genesis 3:5), is *malum*, which can also mean "apple." This false apple was projected back three lines and ended up ultimately in Eve's hands, where it never was in the first place.

But this isn't the end. God takes a walk in the garden; Adam tries to hide in the undergrowth. God asks him, "Where are you?" (Genesis 3:9). Adam replies, "I heard the sound of You in the garden, and I was afraid because I was naked, so I hid" (Genesis 3:10). God replies, "Who told you that you were naked? Did you eat of the tree from which I had forbidden you to eat?" (Genesis 3:11). Note Adam's reply: "The woman You put at my side–she gave me of the tree, and I ate" (Genesis 3:12).

This answer should make every man blush with shame. Although Adam neither impressed God's prohibition on Eve nor made the slightest attempt to steer her away from her purpose, when it comes to settling accounts, he pushes his guilt aside in an instant and looks for a scapegoat to take on his responsibility; and immediately, with no difficulty, he finds two. First, the woman. She led me astray, he tells God. Still more. "The woman You gave me," he adds in the same breath, intimating that you (God) pushed her on me. Eve bears the blame, he protests, and he attempts to make God an accessory, while he, Adam, remains a pure, innocent lamb.

Rabbinic tradition deduces from this passage that Adam was a coward who was guilty of four offenses: (1) eating the forbidden fruit; (2) default for not stopping Eve; (3) resorting to threadbare excuses that convince no one; and, not least, (4) lacking insight and repentance. ***BR*** *4:4 (1988), p. 42*

CHAPTER 19

The Mothers of Israel

J. Cheryl Exum

The so-called "reformist" approach to feminist biblical hermeneutics is exemplified in Exum's statement that "within the admittedly patriarchal context of the biblical literature, we find strong countercurrents of affirmation of women: stories that show women's courage, strength, faith, ingenuity, talents, dignity and worth." Among these are the stories of Sarah, Rebekah, Rachel and Leah, women who are portrayed in the ordinary role of mothers but who "are not so ordinary after all."

Although the defining events in the narrative of Israel's ancestors are centered on men, women are the ones who set them in motion and determine their outcome. For example, God promises Abraham many children, but Sarah takes the initiative and fulfills the promise when she gives her maid Hagar to Abraham as a surrogate and he "hearkens to her voice." Similarly, God's promise was destined to be fulfilled through Jacob, as his Israelite descendants knew, but Isaac intended to bless Esau; therefore, Rebekah instigated the plot by which Jacob tricked Isaac.

One of the major insights of biblical feminist critics, Exum says, is that the women are acknowledged to be victims of the patriarchal system. Because a woman's value was determined by her ability to bear sons, Sarah had to share her husband with Hagar, who in turn challenged her position. "It is a vicious circle," Exum says, "in which women are played off against each other in the quest for status." The same sequence of events was repeated in the rivalry between Rachel and Leah, two sisters in "a childbearing contest" to win and retain the love of Jacob, the husband they share.–Ed.

When one thinks of the narratives of Genesis 12-50, one thinks of the patriarchs–Abraham, Isaac and Jacob–and their special role as the bearers of God's promise to his chosen people. But what about the matriarchs–Sarah, Rebekah, Rachel and Leah? What role do they play in the dramatic saga of Israel's origins? They fill the familiar roles of wife and mother, roles that often defined and determined the meaning of a woman's life in biblical times. What happens when we examine the role of Israel's mothers from a feminist perspective? In the following article, I do not attempt to defend the Bible or to deny its patriarchal bias. I only attempt to subject the biblical narratives to a feminist critique.

Recently, some scholars have begun to examine biblical material from a nonandrocentric (non-male-centered) perspective; much remains to be done, however.[1] A variety of methods will be used in this task. Sociological and anthropological studies shed light on women's status in biblical times.[2] Literary studies reveal attitudes toward women and reflect a variety of opinions about their contributions, real or idealized, to the community of faith. My approach here is primarily literary, a method of close reading paying careful attention to the portrayal of women in selected texts.

Within the admittedly patriarchal context of biblical literature, we find strong countercurrents of affirmation of women, stories that show women's courage, strength, faith, ingenuity, talents, dignity and worth. Such stories undermine patriarchal assumptions and temper patriarchal biases, often challenging the very structures that dominate the narrative landscape.

It is worthwhile to look at the matriarchs only in their role as mothers, not only because motherhood so often defines a "woman's place," but also because of the ordinariness of the role—mothers *per se* are not major characters. These women derive their significance from the fact that they gave birth to famous sons. But closer examination reveals that these mothers are not so ordinary after all, and their influence is far-reaching. A striking paradox emerges in these stories. Although the important events in Israelite tradition are experienced by men, they are often set in motion and determined by women.

I hope that my comments here will be suggestive of what can and should be done on a larger scale. The same patterns and paradoxes can be found in the Exodus narrative, in the period of the Judges and the monarchy. During the Exile and restoration, the pattern is disrupted, and in New Testament times, the familiar themes are reappropriated (Luke 1:5-25) and reshaped (Matthew 1:18-25; Luke 1:26-56).

The stories of the patriarchs and matriarchs in Genesis 12-50 are stories about a promise, the threefold promise to Abraham that (1) he will have numerous descendants, who will (2) inhabit the land of Canaan and that he, Abraham, is the (3) mediator of God's blessing to all humanity. This promise was passed from Abraham to his son, to his son, and so on down the male line. Numerous obstacles threaten the promise and postpone fulfillment—the barrenness of Sarah (Genesis 11:30, 16:1), Rebekah (Genesis 25:21) and Rachel (Genesis 29:31); the potential loss of the matriarchs when the patriarchs pass off their wives as sisters and the women are threatened with being taken into a foreign ruler's harem (Genesis 12, 20, 26); the fact that Abraham and Sarah are too old to bear children (Genesis 17:17, 18:12); or the command that

Abraham sacrifice his son, his "only son Isaac, whom you [Abraham] love" (Genesis 22:2).

Everyone knows the outcome of these stories in advance, for the patriarchs are personifications of the collective memory of Israel, and the listeners are heirs to the promise. The delight is in the telling. In the figures of the patriarchs, the special relationship between Israel and God is reaffirmed, and Israel is revealed, holding up for scrutiny both positive and negative aspects of its character.

What, then, is the role of the matriarchs? Obviously, they must bear the children of the promise—thus the importance of finding the "right" wife—Abraham's wife Sarah, not his concubine Hagar, must be the mother of the rightful heir; Isaac and Jacob may not marry Canaanite—that is, "foreign"—wives (Genesis 24:3, 27:46, 28:1). Not only must the "right" woman be the mother of the chosen people, but the "right" son must be the bearer of the promise—of Abraham's sons, Isaac and not Ishmael; of Isaac's sons, Jacob and not Esau.

In the patriarchal world, males are the significant figures—Abraham follows the divine call to the Promised Land; Sarah, on the other hand, is "taken" with him. "Abraham took his wife Sarah...and they set out for Canaan" (Genesis 12:4,5). Indeed, she is repeatedly "taken" elsewhere in chapter 12 (verses 15, 19). Sarah is thus treated as an object or a possession.

Women are simply ignored in numerous scenes. The Genesis narrators are interested in Abraham's faith, not Sarah's (see, for example, Genesis 22, dealing with Abraham's near sacrifice of Isaac). Jacob wrestles with God in "face to face" combat (Genesis 32:30), while Rachel's "mighty wrestlings" are with her sister (Genesis 30:8). Typically, the matriarchs are omitted from recitals of faith. We hear only of "my father" (Deuteronomy 26:5), or "your fathers lived of old...I took your father Abraham...I gave him Isaac; and to Isaac I gave Jacob and Esau" (Joshua 24:2-4). In Psalm 105, we read:

> The covenant which he made with Abraham,
> his sworn promise to Isaac,
> which he confirmed to Jacob as a statute,
> to Israel as an everlasting covenant.
>
> verses 9-10

An exception to the general rule is Isaiah 51:2, where Sarah is included. "Look to Abraham your father/ and to Sarah who bore you./ For when he was but one I called him,/ And I blessed him and made him many."

When the matriarchs do appear as actors, however, they come to life as fully developed personalities whose struggles and determination are deftly sketched and whose joys and sorrows become real for us. In these stories, they are not just appendages of the patriarchs, but persons in their own right—women participating in a patriarchal culture who sometimes stand over or against it. This is the paradox: *though frequently ignored in the larger story of Israel's journey toward the promise, the matriarchs act at strategic points to move the plot, and thus the promise, in the direction of fulfillment.*

The major events in the lives of the matriarchs center around their sons. The barren matriarch (Sarah, Rebekah, Rachel) is a common theme because barrenness could mean the needed son might not appear; barrenness also offers God an opportunity to intervene. In Genesis 16, Sarah speaks for the first time, thus coming to life for the first time as a character. She initiates the action and controls events throughout the six verses in which she appears.

In contrast to what has gone before when Abraham was the active figure, Abraham is passive here. In fact, he obeys Sarah. (The Revised Standard Version translates "hearkened to the voice of" Sarah [Genesis 16:2].) He even acknowledges her authority over Hagar. When Hagar becomes pregnant and treats the barren Sarah with disdain, Abraham tells Sarah, "Your maid is in your power" (Genesis 16:6). For the first time we see things from Sarah's point of view.[3] The situation, however, is rather complex because the narrator of the tale is our source for Sarah's point of view, and the narrative point of view is androcentric (male-centered) and uncritical of patriarchy.

To be childless in a patriarchal society represents a loss of status. The childless Sarah, who recognizes God's ultimate responsibility, offers a concrete solution to the lack of an heir. She gives Abraham her Egyptian maid Hagar, not simply so that Abraham might have an heir. (He could take another wife to bear him children if he wished, but he does not. Only after Sarah dies does he take another wife, Keturah [Genesis 25:1].) Sarah gives Hagar to Abraham because, according to custom, Hagar's child would be considered Sarah's. This particular means of obtaining children is for the woman's sake and not the man's, which is made clear in Genesis 29-30, where Rachel and Leah give their maids to Jacob, even though he already has sons.

Sarah's plan backfires, however, when the pregnant Hagar becomes arrogant, thus presenting a different kind of challenge, a threat to Sarah's superior status as primary wife. Again Sarah must act, this time to guarantee her position. She treats Hagar harshly, and Hagar flees. Thus, another threat to the promise–that Hagar the Egyptian might become the mother of Israel–is thwarted. God, however, in one of the few theophanies to a woman, instructs Hagar to return and submit to Sarah, which poses the threat anew.

The story gives us poignant insight into the plight of both women. Hagar, in particular, when approached from a feminist perspective, is revealed as a paradigm of the oppressed woman with the courage to seek freedom. (Notice the odd reversal of the Exodus paradigm, for here an Egyptian flees oppression by Israel.) Hagar becomes the mother of a great nation characterized by the refusal to submit.[4]

Although the story is told with sympathy for Sarah and sensitivity toward Hagar, feminist critics will recognize its painful limitations. Both Sarah and Hagar are victims of a patriarchal society that stresses the importance of sons, and of a narrative structure that revolves around the promise of sons. Sadly, but not surprisingly in this context, the women make victims of each other.

In the story, the privileged woman exploits her subordinate. Sarah uses Hagar (how Hagar feels about being given to Abraham as a wife is not stated), and Hagar apparently covets Sarah's position–the oppressed woman who attempts to change places with the oppressor. Thus, Sarah must oppress Hagar in order to assert herself.

Both women are caught in a vicious circle in which they are played off against each other in the quest for status, a situation we shall see repeated in the conflict between Rachel and Leah. From a critical feminist perspective, Sarah's anger at Abraham when Hagar becomes arrogant–"May the Lord judge between you and me" (not "between Hagar and me" [Genesis 16:5])–becomes an indictment of the patriarchal system, which pits women against each other and challenges their intrinsic worth with patriarchal presuppositions about the role of women.

In Genesis 17 and 18, attention is focused on Sarah and the promised birth of her son: "I will bless her, and she shall be a mother of nations" (Genesis 17:16). Finally, Sarah bears the long-awaited heir. Genesis 21 resolves once and for all the threat posed by the presence of Hagar and Ishmael. Earlier, Sarah had acted to secure her own position; now she moves to protect Isaac's inheritance by having Hagar and Ishmael sent away. Although Abraham is displeased, Sarah's position receives divine approval; the threat must be removed, and God works through Sarah to remove it: "Whatever Sarah says to you," God orders Abraham, "do as she tells you, for through Isaac shall your descendants be named" (Genesis 21:12).

From a feminist perspective, both women suffer. One is cast out but becomes the mother of a great nation excluded from the covenant; the other stays within the patriarchal hearth and almost loses her only child to the father, who is prepared to offer him to God as a sacrifice (Genesis 22). Sarah does not appear in the story of the near sacrifice of Isaac. This is, after all, a test of Abraham's faith, just as Genesis 12:1-3 was a call to Abraham to go to Canaan. The entire divine experiment hinges on Abraham's faith, not Sarah's. In a later Midrash (a postbiblical commentary on the Bible), Sarah dropped dead upon hearing what Abraham was prepared to do.[5]

Isaac, Sarah's son, is comforted after his mother's death by his marriage to Rebekah (Genesis 24:67), a brief but touching testimony to the bond between mother and son. In Genesis 24, Rebekah's generosity and initiative are revealed when Abraham's servant comes looking for a wife for Abraham's son Isaac. We must skip over the details of this delightful tale, however, in order to focus on Rebekah's pivotal role in obtaining for her son Jacob the patriarchal blessing.

Like Sarah, Rebekah is barren at first; but when Isaac offers an intercessory prayer, she conceives twins (Genesis 25:21-24). The struggle between Jacob and Esau begins even before their birth, and the anxious mother-to-be seeks a divine oracle without benefit of either patriarchal or priestly intercession. She receives an answer to which she alone is privy: "The elder shall serve the younger" (Genesis 25:23). Rebekah knows from the outset—as we know and as the ancient listeners knew—how things will turn out. And thus she loves and favors Jacob (Genesis 25:28).

Is it coincidence that Rebekah is listening when Isaac reveals his intention to bless Esau (Genesis 27:1-5)? She immediately sets her plan in motion, and her favorite son has only to follow her instructions: "Obey my word," she tells him twice (Genesis 27:8,13). Jacob is afraid that discovery of the ruse by his father might bring him a curse rather than a blessing, an understandable fear given the seriousness of the curse, which, once uttered, proceeds immutably toward realization. Rebekah's response, "Upon me be your curse, my son," demonstrates her remarkable resolve.

What does Jacob have to lose? Rebekah is the one who risks everything. She prepares the food Isaac loves so that Jacob can present it to him as if he were Esau. She dresses Jacob in Esau's clothes and outfits him with animal skins so that he will both smell and feel like his older brother and thereby deceive his blind father. With all the details arranged by his mother, Jacob carries out the ruse and succeeds in getting the coveted blessing for himself—only moments before his brother Esau returns to claim what is rightfully his. Clearly, Jacob owes his success to the timely and decisive action of his strong-willed and resourceful mother, Rebekah.

Justifiably angry, Esau resolves to kill Jacob. Rebekah—typically well informed—learns of his plan and again acts decisively, this time to preserve Jacob's life. Again she gives him all-important instructions: "Obey my voice," she says (Genesis 27:43). She tells Jacob to flee to her brother Laban until Esau's anger subsides, at which time she will send for him. Rebekah even manages to get Isaac to send Jacob off with his blessing to take a wife from Rebekah's family (Genesis 27:46-28:5). Jacob, who will one day become Israel, sets out on his journey toward the fulfillment of Israel's destiny, on a course charted by his mother.

Jacob acquires two wives (Leah and Rachel), but he loves one (Rachel) more than the other (Genesis 29:30). This situation gives rise to a variation of the barrenness motif. Only the favored wife Rachel is initially barren; God blesses the other, Leah, with fertility, compensation for being unloved by her husband. Genesis 29-30 describes a childbearing contest (Genesis 30:8) between the rival sisters through which Jacob/Israel is built up. The 12 sons of Jacob represent the 12 tribes of Israel, and the promise of numerous descendants moves toward fulfillment. Again, from the androcentric perspective, women are valued for their ability to produce sons; Dinah, the daughter of Jacob and Leah, is mentioned only in passing (Genesis 30:21).

Leah believes that by mothering Jacob's firstborn son she will gain the patriarch's affection: "Surely now my husband will love me" (Genesis 29:32). In quick succession, she bears three more sons. Rachel envies her sister's fruitfulness and vents her frustration on Jacob (Genesis 30:1). Like Sarah's anger at Abraham (Genesis 16:5), a woman's dissatisfaction with her position receives recognition in the text, but the real source of the problem, the patriarchal system, remains unrecognized. The matriarchs can only vent their frustration on the patriarchs. (Rachel says to Jacob, "Give me children or I shall die" [Genesis 30:1].) Both Rachel and Leah give their maids, Bilhah and Zilpah, to Jacob in order to obtain children, and each bears two sons.

Although the narrative encourages us to feel sympathetic toward Leah, who is not loved, and toward Rachel, who longs for children but has none, it also invites us to laugh. There is something ludicrous in their preoccupation with producing sons. But the real butt of our laughter is the patriarch himself. Rachel, in search of an aphrodisiac, asks her sister Leah for some mandrake roots that belong to Leah's son Reuben. Leah agrees to give Rachel the mandrakes in exchange for Rachel's allowing Jacob to sleep with Leah that night. Jacob's sexual services are thus traded for aphrodisiacs. Imagine Jacob coming in from a day's work in the field to be met by his triumphant, unloved wife Leah with the words, "You must come in to me, for I have hired you with my son's mandrakes" (Genesis 30:16). Is this any way to treat the great patriarch of Israel?

Not unexpectedly, Leah bears another son and, later, a sixth. At this point, she seems to have given up all hope of winning Jacob's love (Genesis 29:32) and settled for the more modest goal of gaining his respect, "Now my husband will honor me, because I have borne him six sons" (Genesis 30:20). When at last "God remembered Rachel" and "hearkened to her and opened her womb" (Genesis 30:22), the contest between the sisters comes to an end. But this occurs only after Rachel takes the initiative to solve the problem of barrenness with the mandrakes. (Perhaps they were effective?)

Eleven of the twelve tribes are now accounted for–six from Leah, two each from Bilhah and Zilpah and one (Joseph) from Rachel. Later in the Genesis narrative, Rachel bears the twelfth son, Benjamin. But because she dies in childbirth, this last son is not a source of joy (see Genesis 35:16-20).

In this quick survey, I have focused on a recurrent theme in the matriarchal stories. Israel becomes a people numerous and blessed because of the mothers. Sarah guarantees Isaac's inheritance against the threat of Ishmael. Rebekah sees to it that Jacob, rather than Esau, obtains Isaac's blessing. And Rachel and Leah, in their competition to give Jacob sons, build up the house of Israel. At the same time, reviewing these stories makes us aware of the limitations placed upon the matriarchs by the patriarchal system taken for granted in the Bible. Bearing sons is of the utmost importance, and the major accomplishments of the matriarchs are for the sake of their sons. In the end, Israel is personified in the sons, not their mothers.

Afterword

In a study of ancient polytheism, In the Wake of the Goddesses: Women, Culture, and the Biblical Transformation of Pagan Myth,[1] *Tikva Frymer-Kensky also explores the status of women in the Bible. Reviewer Ronald S. Hendel of Southern Methodist University believes she may be too forgiving:*

Books about ancient goddesses are popular these days. Many of them promise that, if the worship of nurturing goddesses is restored, we will return to a more harmonious and peaceful existence. According to some feminist writers, the rise of biblical monotheism sounded the death knell of goddess-religions, and rigid patriarchy has been dominant in the Western world ever since. The recovery of prebiblical goddess-religions signals a return to paradise–a time when people were nurturing, nonsexist and ecologically balanced. Is the Bible really to blame for the loss of this ideal? Will a return to prebiblical goddesses solve the problems of the modern world?

Tikva Frymer-Kensky, a Bible scholar and professor at the Reconstructionist Rabbinical College in Philadelphia, has taken up the challenge of these issues in an ambitious and thought provoking book. As a scholar and feminist, Frymer-Kensky casts a critical eye on popular trends and attempts to set things straight. The result is a learned and passionate book in which she examines the worship of goddesses in ancient Sumer and traces religious transformations in biblical Israel. There are virtually two books here–one on goddesses and the other on biblical monotheism. At stake is the compelling question of which is better suited for life in the late 20th century. Frymer-Kensky concludes, after much detailed discussion, that biblical monotheism is better, although it "has never been truly tried."

At the heart of Frymer-Kensky's argument is the problem of the transition from Near Eastern polytheism (including goddess-worship) to biblical monotheism. What happened to the world of the goddesses when the many were replaced by the One? Frymer-Kensky's answer is striking: "The biblical system had to replace both goddesses and gods, and as it did so, it transformed its thinking about nature, culture, gender and humanity." As a result, humans became active participants in the workings of the cosmos, taking over many functions of the gods. "In every aspect of biblical thought, human beings gain in prominence in–and because of–the absence of the goddesses."

Frymer-Kensky argues that the Bible envisions "a radically new concept of gender" in which male and female are equal partners. Whereas the mother goddess in Mesopotamian literature creates a male, Enkidu, to be Gilgamesh's true companion, God in the Bible creates a woman, Eve, to be Adam's true counterpart. In Mesopotamia, "the truest bonding, the truest similarity possible is between two members of the same gender," whereas the Bible envisions a "gender-free concept of humanity." In other words, monotheism, not goddess-worship, represents a nonsexist view of humanity, a vision that "makes sense in our more egalitarian world."

It would be nice if this were true and the Bible were a model of progressive, nonsexist thinking. And some passages support the idea. But many more biblical stories and passages suggest the opposite. In Phyllis Trible's powerful book, *Texts of Terror*,[2] she laments some of these misogynist stories (for example, the stories of Hagar, Tamar, Jephthah's daughter and other unnamed women). Other biblical scholars–including Carol Meyers, Jo Ann Hackett and Phyllis Bird–have also clarified the antiwoman bias in many biblical texts. Frymer-Kensky seems to ignore significant implications of these recent studies for her argument (although she cites them often in her notes) and fails to make a convincing case.

Many of Frymer-Kensky's key examples can be interpreted differently. For instance, in the Bible the marriage of Adam and Eve may not be the most revealing comparison to Gilgamesh's bond with Enkidu. David's relationship with Jonathan may be more apropos. Just as Gilgamesh laments the death of Enkidu by calling him "my friend, whom I love deeply," David grieves for Jonathan with the poignant lament, "to me your love was greater than the love of women" (2 Samuel 1:26). The heroic ideal of male bonding is as strong in biblical literature, it seems, as it is in Mesopotamian.

And yet, although Frymer-Kensky's overall argument may be more wishful thinking than not, many of her individual discussions deserve merit. Particularly illuminating is the section on Sumerian goddesses, an area where Frymer-Kensky's interests and expertise shine. Other sections are also valuable, such as her sensitive investigation of the symbolism of Zion and Wisdom as a woman and many striking insights into individual stories and themes.

Frymer-Kensky ends by urging us to purge "Greek" misogyny and return to the egalitarian monotheism envisaged in the Hebrew Bible. I doubt whether the Greeks were quite as "phallic," or the Bible quite as nonsexist, as Frymer Kensky contends, but her challenge is well worth the attempt. ***BR** 8:3 (1992), p. 11*

Tikva Frymer-Kensky, in a review of Bread Not Stone: The Challenge of Feminist Biblical Interpretation,[3] *by Elisabeth Schüssler Fiorenza, argues that women–and feminists–have a stake in the Bible and are following a noble tradition by attempting to find contemporary significance in the ancient text:*

Anyone who believes that the Bible is the literal word of God, which was written once and is henceforth never-changing, will not like this book. For Schüssler Fiorenza's concept of the Bible is very different. She does not view it as inspired by the word of God, but she does see it as a historical prototype that nurtures and sustains ongoing divine inspiration. The Bible is, in other words, bread, not stone. Each generation, each community, reads and has read the Bible through a particular interpretive prism. Often this prism is subconscious, and the reader believes he or she reads the "plain sense" of the text. But there is no way of reading the Bible (or anything else) noninterpretively, and we should make explicit the ways we read and interpret. This is Schüssler Fiorenza's thesis.

Schüssler Fiorenza writes as a Christian, and she addresses herself mainly to the Christian question of the adaptation of Christian scripture to the development of theology. She writes, furthermore, as a woman, for what she calls the women-church, the "gathering of all those women and men who, empowered by the Holy Spirit and inspired by the biblical vision of justice, freedom and salvation, continue, against all odds, to struggle for liberation from patriarchal oppression in society and religion." This is her hermeneutical principle, her interpretive prism, the way she reads the Bible.

In our society, the Bible is read in different ways. There is the doctrinal way—biblical revelation as verbal inspiration. There is the scholastic, or historical-factual, way—the Bible as a collection of more-or-less historically reliable writings. And there is the dialogic-pluralistic way—as a plurality of voices reflecting the multifaceted life of historical communities. This approach is an attempt to locate the "canon within the canon," to find authentic texts that can be used to measure and evaluate other texts.

Schüssler Fiorenza goes one step further and locates the authentic divine voice outside the biblical writings in the experiences of women struggling to free themselves from patriarchal oppression. The Bible is the formative root-model of the struggle for liberation, but revelation is ongoing and takes place for "our salvation." Therefore, we must remember and transform our biblical heritage.

Schüssler Fiorenza approaches the Bible not only as a biblical scholar, but also as a theologian, and, in fact, she believes there should be no separation between the two. All too often, Schüssler Fiorenza says, faith communities have treated the Bible as a miraculous book, and biblical scholars have concerned themselves only with historical factualness, leaving the individual minister with the task of mediating between "value-neutral" exegesis and the fact of the Bible as scripture. She would like to chart a new paradigm of interpretation based on the recognition that there is no such thing as a value-free study of texts and that biblical texts are responses to particular situations, not reflections of timeless principles or journalistic records.

Using a new method of interpretation, which she calls the "pastoral-theological paradigm," Schüssler Fiorenza attempts to translate the meaning and context of biblical texts into today's situation. The Bible is a root-model with many voices, and we should continue to preserve and teach all the biblical traditions. But we should proclaim and preach only the traditions that are meaningful and relevant to the Christian community today.

Schüssler Fiorenza comes out of (and explains to the reader) the newest currents in historical and biblical studies, which have recognized that there is a circle of historical learning (the hermeneutical circle) in which the scholar engages in a dialogue with the material. An interpreter may be convinced and then decide, on the basis of the evidence, that the original interpretation was wrong, and the interpretation may then be modified; but the interpreter is aware that he or she operates within a limited psycho-social mode of thought. If this is true of scholars in general, it is particularly true of biblical scholars, who must pay attention to the questions and needs of faith communities and who must validate or reject these questions.

Another important component of Schüssler Fiorenza's thought comes from liberation theology, which is based on the principle that theology is, by definition, always for or against the oppressed. Just as value-neutral, objective historical scholarship is impossible, so intellectual neutrality vis-à-vis the oppressed is impossible, and one should make one's position explicit. The explicit advocacy stance of liberation theology (and of feminist theology) brings into the open the hidden perspectives of other approaches as well. Liberation theology holds that one must read the Bible through the eyes of the oppressed, for God is the God of the oppressed. But Schüssler Fiorenza argues that liberation theology can present a "hermeneutics of consent" because the God of the Bible is the God of the oppressed poor.

In the case of women, however, there are no clear statements in the Bible in favor of equality. In this case, the standard for evaluating biblical traditions cannot be derived from the Bible or the biblical process of learning but must be derived from the struggle for the liberation of all oppressed people. Feminist biblical interpreters must insist that only nonsexist and nonoppressive traditions of the Bible and biblical interpretation have the theological authority of revelation.

Knowing that the biblical texts are androcentric, we search out the traditions and interpretations that transcend androcentrism. In this way, the Bible can become a resource for solving moral problems and generating moral challenges. This kind of study also enables those seeking gender equality to deal with the fact that the Bible has often been used to justify female subordination.

Feminists should not ignore the Bible, for this assumes that women have no authentic history within biblical religion and deprives them of their history in religion. According to Schüssler Fiorenza, feminists must develop feminist biblical hermeneutics as a critical-evaluative hermeneutic. Being a female Christian is a social, historical and cultural ecclesial process. An evaluative hermeneutics of liberation ultimately aims at "the emancipation of biblical religion from patriarchal structures and ideologies" so that the "gospel" can again be recognized as "the power of God for salvation." We have to mine the Bible, to break through the silence of the texts and find the liberating message. We must be suspicious of all texts and analyze them for what lies behind them, to recover biblical history as memory and tradition for people today and tomorrow.

This is an honest book that addresses the problem of interpreting biblical passages that offend modern theological sensibilities. The author advocates what she calls a "paradigm shift" in attitude towards the Bible in which the Bible ceases to be the final authority against which we measure everything and becomes, instead, a living history and resource in which God's word informed and informs us today. Maintaining texts that are oppressive and used to legitimate ongoing oppression means affirming that God desires oppression. This Schüssler Fiorenza cannot do. The community out of which she comes and for which she writes, the Christian feminist community, must believe in a liberating God and must find the voice of this God in the Bible. Biblical texts in which the voice of God bespeaks submission and inequality must be remembered and taught but not as representing God's word.

Schüssler Fiorenza brings into the open what developing and growing religions have always done as they grow within a tradition but attempt to learn from the tradition, adapt it and grow with it. She calls on biblical scholars, who have an allegiance to the meaning of the text, not to abdicate their important role of interpreting the Bible for today. ***BR** 3:2 (1987), p. 48*

CHAPTER 20

Bringing Miriam Out of the Shadows

Phyllis Trible

The real hero of the Exodus, Trible claims, is Miriam, who not only saved the life of the infant Moses and composed the Song of the Sea, which the Bible ascribes to Moses, but also shared leadership with him in the wilderness and was revered in a "pro-Miriamic tradition" that was suppressed by "patriarchal storytellers."

Trible finds bits and pieces in the Bible of a larger story centered on Miriam. Exodus 2:1-2 begins the story of Moses with the logical opening–a man from the house of Levi took a wife who conceived and bore a son. But two sentences later, after the infant is placed in the river, we are told he has an older sister. Where did she come from? That "the siblings begin their lives together in narrative tension," Trible says, should alert us to a hidden drama.–Ed.

Buried in scripture are bits and pieces of a story waiting to be discovered, a story that highlights a woman, Miriam. To unearth the fragments, assemble them, ponder the gaps and then construct a text requires the interplay of many methods but the dogmatism of none.[1] This enterprise welcomes all lovers of scripture who seek to redeem life from patriarchal death.

At the Riverbank

We begin the search with hints and guesses–textual hints and reader's guesses. The setting is parlous–Egypt, an alien land; the king, a tyrant; his edict, a death decree. When Pharaoh discovers his order has been disobeyed by two midwives who refuse to kill Hebrew sons, he extends the order to all the people: "Every son that is born–into the Nile you shall cast him, but every daughter you shall let live" (Exodus 1:22).[2] In Pharaoh's land, sex determines life and death for Hebrew babies.

Although the royal decree sets the stage for the advent of Moses, the text (Exodus 2:1-10) focuses on three unnamed females,[3] who, like the midwives,

Exodus 15:1-21

Then Moses and the people of Israel sang this song to the Lord, saying,

"I will sing to the Lord, for he has triumphed gloriously;
the horse and his rider he has thrown into the sea.
The Lord is my strength and my song,
and he has become my salvation;
this is my God, and I will praise him,
my father's God, and I will exalt him.
The Lord is a man of war;
the Lord is his name.

"Pharaoh's chariots and his host he cast into the sea;
and his picked officers are sunk in the Red Sea.
The floods cover them;
they went down into the depths like a stone.
Thy right hand, O Lord, glorious in power,
thy right hand, O Lord, shatters the enemy.
In the greatness of thy majesty thou overthrowest thy adversaries;
thou sendest forth thy fury, it consumes them like stubble.
At the blast of thy nostrils the waters piled up,
the floods stood up in a heap;
the deeps congealed in the heart of the sea.
The enemy said, 'I will pursue, I will overtake,
I will divide the spoil, my desire shall have its fill of them.
I will draw my sword, my hand shall destroy them.'
Thou didst blow with thy wind,
the sea covered them;
they sank as lead in the mighty waters.

defy the edict. In the first section of the story, narrated discourse permits us to visualize but not hear these women (Exodus 2:1-6). Each is independent although connected to another.

The first is a married woman who is identified only as a daughter of Levi. A host of active verbs secures her presence. She conceived and bore a son; she saw how good he was; she hid him until she could hide him no longer; she took a basket for him, sealed it, put him in it and placed it at the riverbank. Her actions move between life and death. In cradle or coffin, the living son floats on the waters decreed to drown him.

Opposing the daughter of Levi, in artistic symmetry, is the second woman, the daughter of Pharaoh. A multitude of active verbs also establishes her presence. She came to bathe at the river, saw the basket, sent her maid to fetch it, opened it, saw the foreign child, had compassion on him and hailed his identity: "'One of the Hebrew babies is this!' she said" (Exodus 2:6). Unlike the daughter of Levi, we hear as well as see the princess.

The two women counter each other. One Hebrew, the other Egyptian. One slave, the other free. One common, the other royal. One poor, the other rich.

"Who is like thee, O Lord, among the
gods?
Who is like thee, majestic in holiness,
terrible in glorious deeds, doing
wonders?
Thou didst stretch out thy right hand,
the earth swallowed them.

"Thou hast led in thy steadfast love the
people whom thou hast
redeemed,
thou hast guided them by thy
strength to thy holy abode.
The peoples have heard, they tremble;
pangs have seized on the
inhabitants of Philistia.
Now are the chiefs of Edom dismayed;
the leaders of Moab, trembling
seizes them;
all the inhabitants of Canaan have
melted away.
Terror and dread fall upon them;
because of the greatness of thy arm,
they are as still as a stone,
till thy people, O Lord, pass by,
till the people pass by whom
thou hast purchased.
Thou wilt bring them in, and plant
them on thy own mountain,
the place, O Lord, which thou hast
made for thy abode,
the sanctuary, O Lord, which thy
hands have established.
The Lord will reign for ever and ever."

For when the horses of Pharaoh with his chariots and his horsemen went into the sea, the Lord brought back the waters of the sea upon them; but the people of Israel walked on dry ground in the midst of the sea. Then Miriam, the prophetess, the sister of Aaron, took a timbrel in her hand; and all the women went out after her with timbrels and dancing.

And Miriam sang to them:

"Sing to the Lord, for he has
triumphed gloriously,
the horse and his rider he has
thrown into the sea." (RSV)

One relinquishing, the other finding. One silent, the other speaking. One is one; the other, the other. Who will bring them together?

The answer is a third woman. Narrative structure locates her between the first two, just as content makes her their mediator. Between the placing and the discovery of the newborn child, "stood his sister at a distance to know what would be done to him" (Exodus 2:4). Although she too is a daughter, she is identified as a sister. The designation sister seems odd, however, because in a preface it was implied that the son is the firstborn. First comes a marriage. "A man from the house of Levi went and took a daughter of Levi" (Exodus 2:1). Immediately after comes a birth announcement: "The woman conceived and bore a son" (Exodus 2:2, RSV). These statements in effect elevate Moses over his sister. But except for the preface, nothing in the narrative requires that the son be the firstborn. On the contrary, his sister's appearance shows that he is not. Thus, the siblings begin their narrative lives together in narrative tension.

"And his sister stood at a distance to know what would be done to him" (Exodus 2:4, RSV). References to water surround her. The Hebrew woman has placed her son at the riverbank (Exodus 2:3), and the Egyptian princess has come down to the river to bathe (Exodus 2:5). From afar, not yet approaching the water, the sister waits to see what happens. Although the narrator's phrase may suggest passive watching, it foreshadows the opposite. The child's sister, not the daughter of Levi or the daughter of Pharaoh, will take the initiative that will shape the child's destiny.

In the second half of the story, the still unnamed sister moves into closer view. She speaks to Pharaoh's daughter: "Shall I go and call for you [*lach*] a woman nursing from the Hebrews so that she nurses for you [*lach*] the child?" (Exodus 2:7). By putting the phrase "for you" immediately after the verbs "call" and "nurse," the sister expresses solicitude and offers servitude. She also shapes the future by defining the need of Pharaoh's daughter to secure a Hebrew nurse. Skillfully crafted, her words propose a perfect arrangement for the one and for the other, thereby bringing them together.

The royal command, "Go," is but the desired reply to the sister's question. To report the sister's action, the storyteller plays with vocabulary, repeating crucial verbs and introducing new nouns. "Shall I go and call for you a woman nursing...?" the sister asks, but then "the young woman"—not "his sister"—"went and called" (Exodus 2:8). A description of someone independent has replaced a description of someone derivative. As the one in charge, "the young woman went and called the mother of the baby." The maternal noun makes explicit the beautiful irony of her proposal. "A woman nursing from the Hebrews" is the child's own mother. Thus the story comes swiftly to a climax. The daughters meet to work out a plan. Nursed by his natural mother, the child grows to become the adopted son of Pharaoh's daughter and receives from her the name Moses. If Pharaoh had recognized the power of women, he might have reversed his decree and had daughters rather than sons killed. But God moves in mysterious ways.

Central to the happy solution is the unnamed sister, Miriam. She enters scripture obliquely. No lineage, birth announcement or naming ritual proclaims her advent. Silence gives her birth. Her first appearance is from afar. She stands "at a distance." With speech, she moves closer to unite two daughters for the sake of a male child. Having succeeded, she fades from the story. A model of discretion and timing, the sister negotiates, mediates and leads. She initiates the plan that delivers her brother. Humanly speaking, the Exodus story owes its beginning not to Moses but to Miriam and other women.

In the Midst of the Struggle

The body of the story develops with scant recognition of its female origins. Moses, at times assisted by his brother Aaron, dominates the struggle against Pharaoh. The received tradition turns away from the women who began it. In quiet, secret and effective ways, these women, Hebrew and Egyptian, worked together. By contrast, Moses makes noise, attracts attention and becomes *persona non grata* to both Hebrews and Egyptians.

For many chapters, the text exalts him and ignores his sister. Silence gave birth to Miriam and contains her during the bondage and the battle. Patriarchal storytellers did their work well. They suppressed the women–but not completely. Bits and pieces of the buried story surface at the conclusion of the Exodus narrative.

At the Shore of the Sea

These fragments survived amid jumbled reports of events at the sea. But when the strife is o'er and the battle is done, Israel summarizes the victory won:

> So the Lord saved on that day Israel from the hand of the Egyptians.
> ...
> The people feared the Lord and they trusted in the Lord and in Moses, God's servant.
>
> Exodus 14:30-31

Here the elevation of Moses increases as he appears in a linguistic parallelism to the deity. At this point, the Israelites having crossed the sea dry-shod and the Egyptians having been drowned, the narrative ends. In the poetic passage that follows, Moses becomes musical leader of the sons of Israel.

> Then Moses sang–and also the sons of Israel–this song to the Lord.
> Exodus 15:1

An opening stanza sets the tone for a lengthy poem of celebration:

> I will sing to the Lord
> Most glorious deity!
> Horse and rider
> God has hurled into the sea!
>
> Exodus 15:1

The poem continues by proclaiming the power of God to lead the people and culminates with the ringing affirmation, "The Lord will reign for ever and ever" (Exodus 15:18, RSV). Literarily and theologically, this long litany of triumph climaxes and closes the Exodus story.

How puzzling, then, is the narrative text that follows (Exodus 15:19). In capsule form, it recapitulates the struggle at the sea, thereby returning to the events that preceded the closure. The recapitulation jars. It seems awkward, repetitious and misplaced. An attentive reader begins to suspect tampering with the text, and, as she reads on, the suspicion intensifies. A subsequent unit, ever so small, focuses on Miriam and the women of Israel:

> Then Miriam the prophet, the sister of Aaron, took timbrel in her hand. And all the women went out after her, with timbrels and dances. And Miriam answered them: "Sing to the Lord most glorious deity! Horse and rider God has hurled into the sea!"
>
> Exodus 15:21

After Miriam's brief song, the text moves from the sea to the wilderness (Exodus 15:22). Thus her words become the definitive ending of the Exodus account. And yet they provoke discussion rather than closure.[4]

In this passage, Miriam is named for the first time. She also has a title, "the prophet." Indeed, she is the first woman in all Israel to bear that title, and she acquires it before her brother Moses. That sibling relationship is not even acknowledged here. Instead, Miriam is called "the sister of Aaron." Earlier, Aaron bore the title prophet (Exodus 7:1), though with the specific meaning of spokesman before Pharaoh. As applied to Miriam, the title remains undefined and the meaning open. In fact, the entire line, "Miriam the prophet, sister of Aaron," introduces her in a special way.

Music also signals Miriam's importance. She "took a timbrel in her hand." Joining her are all the women with timbrels and dances. The text tells us Miriam sang responsively to "them." Yet, the Hebrew pronoun "them" is masculine, not feminine, yielding an ambiguous gender referent. Perhaps, under Miriam's leadership, the ritual celebration involved all the people, although the major participants were women.

The song Miriam chants is a repetition, with variations, of the first stanza of the long poem (Exodus 15:1-18) attributed earlier to Moses. The repetition suggests that her contribution is derivative and his original. Furthermore, he sings an entire song, but she cites, and then imperfectly, only the first stanza. By comparison, her performance seems deficient, as does the entire small passage that awkwardly follows the grand Mosaic ending. As a second ending, it is anticlimactic, an afterthought, a token of female presence.

Divergent in length, content and emphasis, the two endings work in tension, not in tandem. The Mosaic conclusion so overpowers the Miriamic that it raises the question of why the second ending ever survived. Ironically, scholarly answers to this question (and they cannot be accused of a feminist bias!) diminish Moses and highlight Miriam.[5] They hold that the very retention of a Miriamic ending, in the presence of a Mosaic avalanche, argues for both its antiquity and authority. So tenacious was the Miriamic tradition that later editors did not dare to eliminate it altogether.

In fact, once upon an early time, before editors got jobs, the entire Song of the Sea, not just the first stanza, was ascribed to Miriam and the women of Israel. Later, redactors (editors) intent upon elevating Moses took the song right out of her mouth and gave it to him—to Moses, the inarticulate one—in company with the sons of Israel. Thus they constructed an ending for the Exodus story that contradicted the older tradition. Unable to squelch the Miriamic tradition altogether, however, the redactors appended it in truncated form (Exodus 15:20-21) to their preferred Mosaic version.

So we now have two endings—the preferred Mosaic version (Exodus 15:1-18) and the truncated version (Exodus 15:20-21) of the original Miriamic ending.[6] To separate the two (as well as to introduce the Miriamic section), the redactors placed between them a recapitulation of the struggle at the sea. The passage reported again the drowning of the Egyptians and the crossing of the Israelites dry-shod (Exodus 15:19). The entire exercise ended up both preserving and destroying the women's story. It kept Miriam but diminished her importance. And it heightened the apotheosis of Moses.

Though carefully done, the redactional work is not perfect. The juxtaposition of endings creates a muted tension. By retaining the tension, scripture provides, even though inadvertently, a critique of itself. The Exodus narrative destroys the power of Pharaoh but also turns inward to challenge the dominance of Moses. But the challenge is subtle, and in the saga of faith, few among the chosen have detected it.

The ending of the Exodus story, like the beginning, belongs to women. They are the alpha and omega, the aleph and taw, of deliverance. The link between the two groups and times is the figure of Miriam. At the bank (s^{e}*phat*) of the river we first meet her (Exodus 2:4); at the shore (s^{e}*phat*) of the sea we find her again (Exodus 15:20-21). The mediator has become percussionist, lyricist, vocalist, prophet, leader and theologian. In both places, narrated, not direct discourse reports tension between her and Moses. What began as sibling tension developed into competing portraits of leadership. Between these narratives of beginning and ending, Moses, along with the men of Israel, dominates the Exodus account.

Within and behind the text, the conflict mounts. The female voice struggles to be heard; the Miriamic presence counters the Mosaic bias. What began as a cloud the size of a baby's hand rising from the waters of the River Nile and grew into a man's hand stretched over the Reed Sea (Exodus 14:21) will in time burst forth in a storm of controversy about authority. To that we now turn.

In the Wilds of the Wilderness

The story moves to the Book of Numbers, which in Hebrew is called b^{e}*midbar*, "in the wilderness." Wilderness symbolizes complaint, confusion and conflict. Moving from site to site, the people of Israel murmur, indeed rebel. Their deity replies with ambivalence, mingling gracious acts with kindled anger. Nothing happens in an orderly way. Entangled in the wilderness, multiple layers of tradition defy source analysis and internal coherence to become much like the chaos they report.[7] The task of the interpreter is to extract Miriam's story from the muddle.

The portrait of Miriam is embedded in controversies about leadership, authority and prophecy. Moses is overwhelmed. Caught between the demands of the people and the blazing anger of the Lord, he protests. After all, he is not the mother of Israel. God is. "Did I conceive all this people? Did I bring them forth that you should say to me, 'Carry them in your bosom as a nurse carries the suckling child'...? I am not able to carry all this people alone; the burden is too heavy for me" (Numbers 11:12-14).

Numbers 12:2-14, 20:1-2

And they said, "Has the Lord indeed spoken only through Moses? Has He not spoken through us also?" And the Lord heard it. Now the man Moses was very meek, more than all men that were on the face of the earth. And suddenly the Lord said to Moses and to Aaron and Miriam, "Come out, you three, to the tent of meeting." And the three of them came out. And the Lord came down in a pillar of cloud, and stood at the door of the tent, and called Aaron and Miriam; and they both came forward. And he said, "Hear my words: If there is a prophet among you, I the Lord make Myself known to him in a vision, I speak with him in a dream. Not so with My servant Moses; he is entrusted with all my house. With him I speak mouth to mouth, clearly, and not in dark speech; and he beholds the form of the Lord. Why the were you not afraid to speak against my servant Moses?"

And the anger of the Lord was kindled against them, and he departed; and when the cloud removed from over the tent, behold, Miriam was leprous, as white as snow. And Aaron turned towards Miriam, and behold, she was leprous. And Aaron said to Moses, "O my lord, do not punish us because we have done foolishly and have sinned. Let her not be as one dead, of whom the flesh is half consumed when he comes out of his mother's womb." And Moses cried to the Lord, "Heal her, O God, I beseech thee." But the Lord said to Moses, "If her father had but spit in her face, should she not be shamed seven days? Let her be shut up outside the camp seven days, and after that she may be brought in again." So Miriam was s hut up outside the camp seven days, and the people did not set out on the march till Miriam was brought in again. After that the people set out from Hazeroth, and encamped in the wilderness of Paran.

...

And the people Israel, the whole congregation, came into the wilderness of Zin in the first month, and the people stayed in Kadesh; and Miriam died there, and was buried there.

Now there was no water for the congregation; and they assembled themselves together against Moses and against Aaron. (RSV)

Moses wants to establish a new kind of leadership, a shared responsibility. At first, the deity appears to consent. He orders Moses to choose "seventy elders" upon whom some of Moses' spirit will rest so they too may bear the burden of leading the people (Numbers 11:16-25). Moses complies, though ironically even his selection of the 70 and receipt of private revelation affirm his unique role. The elders are subordinate to him. Moreover, the entire plan comes to naught. Imbued with some of Moses' spirit, they prophesy, "but they did so no more," according to the text (Numbers 11:25, RSV). There is no shared responsibility or shared authority. The leadership of Moses remains supreme.

The same issue is raised in another incident. Two men, not among the chosen elders, begin to prophesy. Rather than partaking of Moses' spirit, they are independently endowed and thus approach equality with Moses. Some Israelites oppose them, but Moses welcomes the news: "Would that all the Lord's people were prophets, that the Lord would put the divine spirit upon them" (Numbers 11:29). But the matter is far from settled. The elders no longer prophesy; and some among the people want to outlaw the independent prophets. The deity remains ominously silent.

As the Israelites journey to a new site, the power struggle rages.[8] Miriam enters the fray, and for the first time she is not accompanied by other women. Her companion is Aaron, but in a supporting role. Once prophetic and kinship language linked them (both are called prophets, and she is identified as his sister); now prophetic and priestly issues unite them. To be sure, nowhere in the received tradition does Miriam, or any other female, hold the title "priest" or perform cultic functions. Nevertheless, a few scattered clues in the Book of Numbers attest to her priestly connections. They await further attention.

As for Aaron, some traditions proclaim him outright the first priest, even the founder of the priesthood. In fact, the historical picture is exceedingly complex and far from clear. Biblical narratives tantalize us with scant data and mammoth conflicts. In the story at hand, Miriam and Aaron join forces against Moses. Miriam leads and Aaron supports her–in rebellion against Moses' authority.

When she speaks out, a confused text makes hearing Miriam's words difficult. The two problems, priestly and prophetic, are jumbled together.[9] In narrated discourse, we are told of the first challenge. "And Miriam spoke, and Aaron, against Moses because of the Cushite woman whom he married. 'He married a Cushite woman'" (Numbers 12:1). The information and charge appear *in medias res*. We know nothing specific about the matter and can only speculate.

Who is this Cushite wife–Zipporah, as Moses' wife is named elsewhere–or a different woman? Why isn't she mentioned anywhere else in scripture? If she is Zipporah, is the issue a priestly struggle based on her lineage as daughter of Jethro the priest? Putting aside the question of the woman's identity, is the attack racist, suggesting opposition to black Cushite skin? Why does the narrator set woman against woman? Is the conflict ideological resistance to foreign marriages? Are the concepts of cleanliness and uncleanliness violated by the marriage? Are the priestly credentials of Moses being challenged? Whatever the answers to these questions, the text implicates Miriam in cultic affairs.

Cited only once, the problem of the Cushite wife yields quickly to a prophetic matter. If the cultic purity of Moses can be criticized, then his supreme authority can also be challenged. Unlike the first challenge, the second is related in direct discourse. Miriam and Aaron ask, "Has the Lord spoken only through Moses? Has the Lord not also spoken through us?" (Numbers 12:2a-b).

For Miriam, the prophetic task centers not upon a single male (Moses) but embraces diverse voices, female and male. Her questions seem to harmonize with Moses' wish that "all the Lord's people were prophets" (Numbers 11:29, RSV). But Miriam makes clear what Moses' words did not, that "all the Lord's people" includes women. After all, as a "prophet," she has already spoken for God at the sea, even though the Mosaic bias would drown her voice there. Now, in the wilderness she seeks an equal share of prophetic leadership. Hers is a commanding word, and the "Lord hears it" (Numbers 12:2c).

Alas, the price of speaking out is severe. Breaking his ominous silence, the Lord summons Moses, Aaron and Miriam to come forth (Numbers 12:4). In this context, the order of their names hints at the diminution of Miriam. The deity addresses her and Aaron; the divine explanation comes with the power of poetry and the exclusivity of grammatical gender. God addresses the prophetic issue but not the priestly issue:[10]

> Hear now my words:
> If there be a prophet among you,
> In a vision to him I make myself known;
> In a dream I speak with him.
> Not so [with] my servant Moses
> In all my household he [alone] is faithful.
> Mouth to mouth I speak with him.
> In clarity and not in riddles;
> The form of the Lord he beholds.
>
> Numbers 12:6-8

The divine speech requires little commentary. It resolves the issue of leadership and authority by declaring a hierarchy of prophets, and Moses stands alone at the top. Although Miriam is not denied a prophetic role, God undercuts her in gender and point of view. He also undermines Moses' wish for egalitarian prophecy. As if this declaration were not sufficient, the deity then rebuffs Aaron and Miriam: "Why then were you not afraid to speak against my servant Moses?" (Numbers 12:8, RSV). Moses may attack God, even accuse the deity of oppression unto death (Numbers 11:11-15), but God decrees that no one may attack Moses.

After this intimidating question, the Lord speaks to Miriam for the first and only time. She has no opportunity to reply. Instead, to the crushing power of the divine words, the narrator adds a scathing conclusion: "And the nostril of the Lord burned against them and God left" (Numbers 12:9). While the mouth of the Lord glorifies Moses, the nose attacks Aaron and Miriam. This deity is made of stern stuff.

Yet the kindled anger of the deity does not treat targets equally. Miriam is separated from Aaron, making her the true antagonist. When the divine anger departs, Miriam alone is stricken with scales like snow (Numbers 12:9-10). Red hot anger becomes a cold white disease. A searing emotion produces a scarred body. The punishment relates to the priestly issue of the Cushite wife. She who opposed Moses because of his marriage to the black woman stands condemned in diseased white. The irony of the implied contrast seems to set female against female, native against foreigner, white against black, the powerful against the powerless.

But these opposites merge as the irony folds in upon itself. If the Cushite woman stands outside the system of ritual purity, Miriam now stands with her. She too has become an outcast, a rejected woman without voice or power. Although her prophetic authority has only been limited, making her no different from other prophets save Moses, her cultic connections have been irreparably severed. And no such punishment was visited on Aaron. The male is spared; the female sacrificed.

Miriam has become leprous, not with the raw flesh of uncleanliness but with dead flesh, the aftermath of the all-consuming disease.[11] Divine anger has run its course on Miriam. Turning toward her (Numbers 12:10), Aaron beseeches Moses, rather than the Lord, not to "hold against us the sin that we were foolish and that we sinned" (Numbers 12:11-12). Despite efforts to dissociate this priest from the woman, Aaron pleads on her behalf:[12] "Let her not be as one dead, of whom the flesh is half consumed when it comes out of its mother's womb" (Numbers 12:12). Although repulsive, the imagery is also poignant, recalling metaphors used by Moses when he implored the deity to be a responsible mother to the children of her womb. Those reflections led Moses to propose death for himself unless God changed. Now Aaron unites birth and death imagery in describing the horrible punishment God has inflicted upon Miriam.

Long ago at Sinai the pillar of cloud would descend and stand at the door of the tent (Exodus 33:10 f.), and Moses would enter to speak with God. When Moses came out, the skin of his face shone (Exodus 34:29 ff.).[13] Although the people were afraid, they came near. Moses incarnated divine glory. Now, in the wilderness, the pillar of cloud descends again and stands at the door of the tent, and Aaron and Miriam come forward to hear God speak. When the deity departs, Miriam's skin is scaled like snow and her flesh half-consumed. She is separated from the people. Miriam incarnates divine anger.

So Aaron asks for a miracle, the restoration of Miriam to her pre-leprous condition. After all, such a miracle was once visited upon the hand of Moses (Exodus 4:6-7), although in a different context. By appealing now to Moses, Aaron acknowledges his supremacy. Moses answers Aaron's request: "O God, please, heal her now!" (Numbers 12:13). Whatever tensions exist between Miriamic and Mosaic points of view, they have not destroyed sibling affection. Having once been saved through his sister, Moses now petitions God to save her from living death. In a cryptic reply that tempers but does not remove the punishment, the Lord confines her outside the camp for seven days. That period of banishment verifies her cleanliness but does not restore her to wholeness. Miriam remains a marked woman, indeed, she is a warning for generations to come: "Remember what the Lord your God did to Miriam on the way as you came forth out of Egypt" (Deuteronomy 24:9, RSV).

The vendetta continues unto Miriam's death. By silences and juxtapositions the tale unfolds. From the time of her punishment on, Miriam neither speaks nor is spoken to. In fact, for a time, she vanishes from the wilderness narrative. Then, just before her obituary, comes a lengthy passage of ritual prescriptions (Numbers 19:1-22).[14] The content and placement of this passage indict Miriam.

The first prescription concerns preparation of special water for washing away impurity. To the burning of a cow the priest adds "cedarwood, hyssop and scarlet" (Numbers 19:6). Although the meaning of the three ingredients is not specified here, we know from Leviticus (14:4) that they were used to cleanse lepers–a reminder of Miriam's punishment. At the appropriate time, running water is added to the mixture, the use of which is specified in a second prescription pertaining to those who become unclean through contact with the dead (Numbers 19:11-13). Seven days are required for their purification, the same period of time needed for cleansing a leper. In addition, this ritual involves sprinkling the unclean with the water for impurity.

Immediately following these two prescriptions–one alluding to leprosy and the other emphasizing the uncleanliness of the dead–comes the announcement of Miriam's death:

> And the people of Israel, the whole community, came into the wilderness of Zin in the first month, and the people stayed in Kadesh; and Miriam died there and was buried there.
>
> Numbers 20:1 (RSV)

This is no ordinary obituary, but rather the culmination of the vendetta against Miriam.[15] Reasons for the attack may be difficult to discern, but the threat she represented to the cultic establishment is evident. And that threat testifies to her prominence, power and prestige in early Israel. So important was this woman that detractors tabooed her to death, seeking to bury her forever in disgrace.

From Here and There

But the detractors do not have the final word. Miriam survives in fragments embedded in the very scripture that would condemn her. The first fragment appears in the Exodus and wilderness traditions. From the start, Miriam works on behalf of the people. Her role in delivering one of them, Moses, expands to leadership of all Israel at the sea. Thus, a certain poignancy attends the closing narration of the leprosy account.

Miriam was banished from the camp for seven days, and "the people did not set out on the march till Miriam was brought in again" (Numbers 12:15, RSV). No matter that the Lord had decreed the leadership of Moses; no matter that the deity had expressed divine anger in a show of power against the will of the people; no matter that the white-scaled Miriam stands before them as proof of divine indictment and continuing intimidation; no matter.

"The people did not set out on the march till Miriam was brought in again." Those whom she served do not forsake her in her time of tribulation. They wait.

Never do they assail her, as on various occasions they attack Aaron, Moses and God. And their allegiance survives unto her death. Three references in Numbers 20:1–"the people of Israel," "the whole community" and "the people"–attest to their presence when she died and was buried in Kadesh. The steadfast devotion of the people to Miriam hints at a story different from the regnant one.

The symbol of water also supports Miriam's importance. First seen at a distance, she soon moves to the riverbank. In a triumphal appearance, she sings at the shore of the Reed Sea. No life-giving waters appear, however, when the authorities conspire to punish her in the wilderness. Leprous flesh bespeaks arid land. In the ritual prescriptions (Numbers 19:1-22) preceding her obituary, the water symbol reappears but with ambivalence. "The water for impurity" mediates between cleanliness and uncleanliness. Miriam dies, thereby becoming unclean, but at her death no water for impurity is invoked. Instead, the wells in the desert dry up. "Miriam died and was buried there [in Kadesh]. Now there was no water for the community" (Numbers 20:1-2). Nature's response to Miriam's death is immediate and severe. The earth mourns, and the community suffers. Miriam, protector of her brother at the riverbank and leader in the victory at the sea, symbolized life. How appropriate, then, that the waters of life should show reverence at her death. Nature, like the people of Israel, honors Miriam.

After Miriam's burial, the lack of water introduces a long narrative passage (Numbers 20:2-29) critical of Moses and Aaron.[16] In structure, this passage balances the ritual prescriptions (Numbers 19:1-22) preceding Miriam's obituary. In effect, the narrative critical of Moses and Aaron counters the vendetta against her. If the ritual prescriptions implicitly demean Miriam, the account following her obituary explicitly debases Moses and Aaron. Once again, the people attack their leaders because of their overwhelming misery. The two men appeal to God, who instructs them to secure water from a rock (Numbers 20:6-13). Though they are successful, the deity is so displeased that he decrees that neither man shall lead the people into the promised land.[17]

Miriam's death has initiated the demise of Aaron and Moses. And soon thereafter, when the congregation has journeyed from Kadesh to Mount Hor, Aaron dies. In due time, Moses follows. Miriam never reaches the Promised Land, but neither do her brothers. Indeed, the efforts to discredit her backfired and led to censure of Moses and Aaron. The juxtaposition of texts dramatizes the point. When Miriam dies, the wells in the desert dry up, the people rebel, God censures Moses and Aaron, Aaron dies, and Moses' days are numbered. However hard the detractors of Miriam have tried, they can not control the story. There are more interpretations than are dreamed of in their hermeneutics.

Beyond the Exodus and wilderness accounts, fragments of a pro-Miriamic tradition also surface later in the Hebrew Scriptures. The priesthood may have repudiated Miriam forever, but the prophets reclaim her. In fact, Micah states boldly what others worked hard to deny–that in early Israel Miriam belonged to a trinity of leaders. She was the equal of Moses and Aaron. Thus the prophetic deity speaks in Micah 6:4 (RSV):

> For I brought you up from the land of Egypt
> and redeemed you from the house of bondage;
> and I sent before you Moses, Aaron, and Miriam.

In prophecy, the legitimacy of Miriam is acknowledged; she was, in fact, the ancestor who was designated "the prophet" even before Moses. The recognition undercuts a hierarchy of authority with a male at the top.

As the first woman to be called "prophet," Miriam represents a class of females in Israel about whom we know little. From the Exodus beyond the Exile, their erratic and infrequent presence hints at a lost history. In the 12th century B.C.E., Deborah arises to judge Israel, lead armies in battle and sing a song of triumph (Judges 4-5). In the eighth century B.C.E., the unnamed woman of Isaiah gives birth to a prophetic oracle (Isaiah 8:3). In the seventh century B.C.E., Huldah validates the book of the law to initiate a canon of scripture (2 Kings 22:14-20). And in the fifth century B.C.E., the woman Noadiah opposes Nehemiah during the restoration (Nehemiah 6:14). Each of these prophets witnesses a heritage rooted in Miriam. If Moses is the archetype of the male prophetic tradition, Miriam is the archetype of the female tradition.

Another allusion to Miriam is tucked away in the prophecy of Jeremiah.[18] In a vision of the restoration of Israel after the Babylonian destruction of Jerusalem, Jeremiah evokes the vocabulary of the Exodus to describe a new era of grace and joy. The deity addresses the people as female:

> Again I will build you, and you will be built, O virgin Israel!
> Again you will adorn yourself with timbrels, and will go forth in the dance of the merrymakers.
>
> Jeremiah 31:4

The imagery may be read in two directions. It recalls Miriam at the Reed Sea, and it forecasts her restoration. Returned to her rightful place, she and other females will again lead with timbrels and dancing. She participates in the eschatological vision of Hebrew prophecy.

Miriam also animates the musical life of Israel. Jubal is the mythical father (Genesis 4:21), but she is the historical mother. She inaugurates a procession of women who move throughout scripture, singing and dancing in sorrow and joy. In the days of the Judges, the unsuspecting daughter of Jephthah "comes out to meet him with timbrels and dances" (Judges 11:34). Later, the virgin daughters of Shiloh "come out to dance in the dances" (Judges 21:21, RSV). In the days of the monarchy, when warriors return victorious from battle, "the women come out of all the cities singing and dancing...with timbrels, songs of joy and instruments of music. And the women sing to one another as they make merry" (1 Samuel 18:6-7; cf. 1 Samuel 21:11, 29:5).

From these passages, the musical legacy of Miriam passes into liturgical traditions. Although rejected by the priesthood, this woman nevertheless resounds in the cultic experience of the people. A psalm describes a parade entering the temple with "the singers in front, the minstrels last,/ between them maidens playing timbrels" (Psalm 68:25, RSV). Another psalm, based on Exodus and wilderness memories, echoes Miriam: "Raise a song, sound the timbrel" (Psalm 81:2, RSV). A third proclaims: "Let Israel praise God's name with dancing,/ making melody with timbrel and lyre" (Psalm 149:3-4). And in the grand finale of the Psalter, in which everything that breathes is called upon to praise God, the woman Miriam breathes in the line, "Praise the Lord with timbrel and dance!" (Psalm 150:4).

Buried in scripture are bits and pieces of a story waiting to be rediscovered. By unearthing the fragments and reassembling them, we have crafted a mosaic of Miriam. Stepping back to view the whole, we see a story that begins at the bank of the river, moves to the shore of the sea, continues in the wilds of the wilderness, disappears in the new land and is recovered there through prophecy and song. From beneath overlays of patriarchy, Miriam's true portrait begins to emerge. Lo, the fragments that the builders rejected have become tesserae in a mosaic of salvation. Let all women and men who have eyes to behold this mosaic join Miriam in singing an updated version of her song of deliverance: "Sing to the Lord, most glorious deity!/ Patriarchy and its horsemen God has hurled into the sea."[19]

Afterword

Phyllis Trible is a pioneer of feminist hermeneutics. When her book, God and the Rhetoric of Sexuality,[1] *appeared in 1978, Rivkah Harris of the School of the Art Institute of Chicago reviewed it and assessed Trible's place among feminist biblical scholars:*

For generations, the treatment of biblical women by apologists has focused on notable women, such as Sarah, Deborah and Abigail, thereby attempting to sweep under the carpet the unattractive realities of women's legal and economic status in a patriarchal society. At the same time, writers antagonistic to the theocentricity of the Bible have denigrated the quality of Israelite life on all levels, especially the lot of women.

As a result of new theories, broader interest in institutions like marriage and the family, and the feminist movement of the 1960s, women have now become the subject of serious investigation. Scholars and writers have been sensitized to the glaring oversights of earlier studies.

Just as we must avoid the apologetic impulse to justify or cover up the status of women in the Bible, we must also avoid the strident hostility of some feminists who consider the Hebrew Scriptures the culprit for female subordination in Western society. We must also bear in mind the quite different perspectives of the biblical and modern worlds. It is foolish to try to understand biblical accounts of love between the sexes, for example, in terms of the Western tradition of romantic love, which is rooted in 12th-century Europe. Moreover, the Bible covers a period of more than a thousand years and encompasses enormous political, cultural and social changes.

Finally, the central concern of the Hebrew Bible is the covenantal relationship between God and his people, Israel. From that perspective, a great deal about everyday life is irrelevant. Only individuals, events and institutions that relate to this central concern are depicted and, even then, only from the perspective of this concern....

Only by exhaustive probing of the text, applying the methods of the social sciences and comparing the biblical materials with data from other cultures can we understand subtler aspects of women's lives in the biblical period....

In *God and the Rhetoric of Sexuality*, Phyllis Trible provides new insights based on sensitive and careful textual analysis. Traditionally, Eve, who was created from Adam's rib, has been regarded as the temptress and the source of human sinfulness. Trible challenges this deep-seated negative view of Eve, who long ago became the prototype of every woman. Trible convincingly demonstrates that the fact that Eve was formed from Adam's rib does not imply inferiority. Rather, she argues, the phrase "bone of my bones and flesh of my flesh" (Genesis 2:23) bespeaks "unity, solidarity, mutuality, and equality." The real tempter is the serpent. Eve's response to the serpent reveals her as "intelligent, informed, [and] perceptive."

Trible also challenges the traditional view that Yahweh's judgment of Eve is more severe than his judgment of Adam or the snake. After Adam and Eve have eaten the fruit, Trible tells us, "although surrounded by curses, the woman herself is never cursed, directly or indirectly, here or elsewhere in the story." Human obedience and disobedience are the subjects of the story, and woman and man are equal characters.

Woman, then, was not created subordinate to man. Woman, in the biblical tradition is not, as in the Greek philosophical tradition, of lesser intelligence or incapable of being a fitting companion of man. It is interesting that nowhere else in ancient sources is woman created separately from man.

In a chapter on "Love's Lyrics Redeemed," Trible provocatively analyzes the Song of Songs, which, she believes, must be read against the backdrop of Genesis 2-3. In the Song of Songs there is also a garden. Here too the subject is "the love that is bone of bone and flesh of flesh." Once again woman is man's equal.

A small example of Trible's perceptiveness, supported by a careful study of the texts, must suffice. The word *tesuqa* (desire) occurs only three times in the Bible–twice in Genesis (3:16, 4:7) and once in Song of Songs (7:10). For Trible, the word *tesuqa* links the two books. In two of the three occurrences, the word refers to desire between human beings. In one (Genesis 3:16), it refers to a woman's desire for a man. In Song of Songs, it refers to a man's desire for a woman. Female subordination has vanished; mutuality once again characterizes male/female relationships.

Trible analyzes the rich female imagery for God, a long-neglected component of the biblical depiction of God. She traces with remarkable sensitivity the Hebrew root *rḥm*, meaning womb, through a variety of transformations to the ultimate reference to the compassion of God. She also discusses various metaphors that describe God as a mother in labor writhing at the birth of Israel (Deuteronomy 32:18), a tender mother and nurse (Isaiah 66:13; Numbers 11:12) and a seamstress concerned for the nakedness of Adam and Eve (Genesis 3:21).

Although male imagery is more common, Trible maintains that in biblical terms, neither gender is appropriate to describing God's attributes. On the contrary, Israel's leaders stood against their environment in affirming a God of history who transcends both sexuality and nature. ***BR*** *9:1 (1983), p. 70*

In a review of Texts of Terror: Literary-Feminist Readings of Biblical Narratives,[2] *Tikva Frymer-Kensky puts Trible's work in a different perspective:*

There are several ways to study "woman and the Bible" that reveal important insights. The first step is to realize that the Bible, which has shaped so much of our thinking, is to some degree culture bound. It was shaped by men who were "patriarchal," which is to say androcentric (male-oriented), perhaps even misogynistic (women-hating). Biblical "patriarchy" can easily be demonstrated; studies have shown legal subordination of women, their greater vulnerability to impurity, restrictions on women's roles in society and even their inferior monetary value.

It is equally important to realize that not every statement in the Bible is misogynistic, that some portrayals of women are sympathetic, that women are sometimes depicted as playing a more nearly equal role than has been admitted in traditional interpretations. When biblical texts are read with a fresh eye unburdened by traditional interpretations, the portrayal of women does not appear as misogynistic as had been previously thought. "Depatriarchalizing" the Bible means finding sympathetic portrayals of women that have been ignored or reinterpreting stories portraying women or finding the original sense of texts that have been used to justify antiwoman attitudes or actions.

The act of "depatriarchalizing" reveals that the "patriarchy," or "misogyny," of the Bible is not as monolithic or extensive as was later interpreted. Only after the biblical period were biblical tales reread and reinterpreted to accord with misogyny. Recovering the original sense of the text is crucial, not only as an intellectual, "objective," scholarly endeavor, but also because the original sense of the text can undercut "biblical" support for current misogynistic traditions and thereby advance the cause of women in religion today. In this way, a feminist reading of scripture approaches the status of a prophetic movement, providing a critique of history in the light of an oppressed group (in this case, women) as well as calling for purification of the present in the light of a newly authenticated biblical version.

Phyllis Trible's *God and the Rhetoric of Sexuality* is a classic work of "depatriarchalizing," a study of several "familiar" stories in the Bible. Paying careful attention to the nuances of the text, Trible presents a description of God's original intentions for the relationship between men and women, the changes that occurred because of "the fall" of Adam and Eve, and the restoration of ideal relationships embodied in the Song of Songs. The job of depatriarchalizing is not complete, however, and books and articles continue to appear showing the biblical image of women in a more favorable light than interpreters in the intervening millennia have done.

Nevertheless, there remains a corpus of texts in the Bible that are clearly not sympathetic to women. One can declare them culture bound and thereafter ignore them, but they are part of scripture. They refuse to go away, and people continue to read them and continue to be influenced by them. What should the attitude of religious feminists be toward these texts? Modern feminist biblical scholars want to find meaning in all of scripture, and for this reason, Phyllis Trible wrote *Texts of Terror*, in which she retells these stories in order to make them meaningful to us today. We cannot ignore what it is perilous to forget, and *Texts of Terror* is, metaphorically, a book of holocaust studies, stories told so that we will remember and, in remembering, say "never again."

The Bible can be put to many uses, and every faith community–including the feminist faith community–has its own needs and uses for the Bible. There is, nevertheless, a difference between biblical scholarship and preaching. A preacher may use a text freely. His or her primary guide is the message rather than the plain sense of the text. For the preacher, the text is a pretext for the message. But biblical scholars must try to reach some understanding of the text on its own terms. This is not always easy, for we cannot easily divorce ourselves from the quests for truth we bring to the text. There is no such thing as "total objectivity," but biblical scholars must make every effort to focus on the text rather than their personal needs.

The attempt to find an unmotivated, unbiased or objective perspective makes it possible for biblical scholars from different faith communities to communicate and collaborate with one another. This does not mean that we cannot involve ourselves in the message of the text or use the textual message as a guide, but it does mean that we must be strict about our approach to the text, that we must be guided by disciplined methodology in our quest for meaning, and that we must be sure the meaning we read into the text does not violate the sense of the text itself.

One cannot fault Trible in this respect, for she is a serious textual scholar, which makes her books works of scholarship rather than preaching. She approaches the text as a literary critic, which means she searches within the text for artistic "clues"–verbal repetitions, sentence and text constructions and other literary nuances that reveal an author's intention. In *Texts of Terror*, Trible has studied four tales: the story of Hagar, Abraham's concubine who gave birth to Ishmael; the rape of Tamar by Amnon; the concubine in Gibeah; and the daughter of Jephthah.

Hagar's tale (Genesis 16:1-16; 21:9-21) is embedded in the story of Sarah and her son Isaac. Sarah and Hagar were engaged in a power struggle within the limited confines of women's roles in a society that granted real power only to men. Sarah was out to safeguard her prerogatives and those of her son Isaac. First Hagar was used (to bear Abraham a son in Sarah's stead); then she was rejected. Trible finds similarities between Hagar's situation and the situation of the Israelites in Egypt. Similar vocabulary is used in both stories. Hagar is also the prototype of special mothers in Israel, who receive a divine annunciation predicting the birth of a child. But unlike later special mothers, Hagar experienced exodus without liberation. In this contrast is the terror of Hagar's tale. In the passion tale Trible tells, she characterizes Hagar this way: "She was wounded for our transgressions, she was bruised for our iniquities."

Tamar, the daughter of David, was raped by her half-brother Amnon and then expelled by him (2 Samuel 13:1-22). The author reveals a series of inclusive structures in the text that draw a net around Tamar, trapping her structurally as she was trapped in family structures and her brother's lust. The reason and wisdom of Tamar's words were of no avail. The beautiful virgin, once protectively encircled (13:1-2), became the isolated, raped sister. Tamar was "a woman of sorrows and acquainted with grief."

The tale of the concubine in Gibeah is one of rape and murder (Judges 19:1-30). During the premonarchical period of the Judges, a man of Ephraim traveling with his unnamed concubine found shelter in the home of a man of Gibeah. The men of the city came to attack the stranger, much as the men of Sodom had come to attack the angels sojourning with Lot (Genesis 19:4-5). In order to save his male guest, the host (like Lot in the Sodom story) offered his daughter to the attackers. When the attackers declined the offer, the concubine was cast out. She was raped "all night until morning" and finally collapsed (dead or exhausted? Trible wonders) at the door of the house. Her master-husband took her home, dismembered her body and sent pieces to the various tribes–a macabre call to war that rallied the Israelites against Benjamin.

In this war, during which Benjamin was first brought to the brink of destruction and then repopulated, many more women were captured, raped and abducted. Trible points out that there are many possible responses to this story of a woman "whose body was broken and given to many." She calls upon us to redeem the story by retelling it and confessing its present reality, which is that misogyny is still with us, and women are still considered objects and are abused and destroyed with little thought for their personhood or individuality.

Condemned to death by the thoughtless vow of her father, Jephthah's daughter declared her willingness to perish in obedience to that vow (Judges 11:29-40). But first she turned to other females for comfort and asked them to join her in lamenting her virgin death. Although God did not act to save her as he had saved Isaac ("My God, my God, why hast Thou forsaken her?"), this childless woman was not forgotten, for the women of Israel gathered yearly to mourn and remember her. Trible calls on us, too, to hallow her memory by perpetuating our lament for her.

Not everyone will want to retell these stories either as passion tales or as holocaust studies. But Trible's solid scholarship offers fresh perspectives on women and the Bible, extracting a lesson for all of us about what can happen not only to women in a male-dominated society but also to other oppressed or subordinated groups. ***BR*** *1:1 (1985), p. 6*

Authors

ROBERT ALTER is professor of Hebrew and comparative literature and chairman of the Department of Comparative Literature at the University of California, Berkeley. His books include *The World of Biblical Literature* (Basic Books, 1991), *The Art of Biblical Poetry* (Basic Books, 1985) and *The Art of Biblical Narrative* (Basic Books, 1981).

BERNHARD W. ANDERSON is professor emeritus of Old Testament studies at Princeton University and past president of the Society of Biblical Literature. He is best known for his widely used textbook, *Understanding the Old Testament* (Prentice-Hall, 1957).

RICHARD A. BATEY is W. J. Millard Professor of Religion at Rhodes College in Memphis, Tennessee. He was assistant director of the University of South Florida excavations at Sepphoris from 1984 to 1989. Batey's books include *Jesus and the Forgotten City* (Baker Book House, 1991), *Jesus and the Poor* (Harper & Row, 1972) and *The Letter of Paul to the Romans* (R. B. Sweet, 1969).

JAMES L. CRENSHAW is professor of Old Testament at Duke University Divinity School. He is currently preparing the New Century Bible commentary on Proverbs and the Anchor Bible volume on Joel. Crenshaw's books include *Ecclesiastes* (Westminster Press, 1987) and *Story of Faith: A Guide to the Old Testament* (Macmillan, 1986).

JOHN DOMINIC CROSSAN is professor of religious studies at DePaul University in Chicago and a founder and co-director (with Robert W. Funk) of the Westar Institute Jesus Seminar. Crossan has written a trilogy on the historical Jesus, *The Historical Jesus: The Life of a Mediterranean Jewish Peasant* (1991), *Jesus: A Revolutionary Biography* (1993) and *The Essential Jesus: Original Sayings and Earliest Images* (1994), all published by HarperSanFrancisco.

ROLAND DE VAUX was a renowned archaeologist who excavated the Qumran site. He was also editor of the scholarly journal *Revue Biblique* for 15 years, editor-in-chief of the Jerusalem Bible and editor-in-chief of Discoveries in the

Judaean Desert, the series in which the texts of the Dead Sea Scrolls are being published. De Vaux's *The Early History of Israel* (Westminster Press, 1978) is an indispensable work of biblical scholarship.

J. CHERYL EXUM is associate professor of Old Testament at Boston College and was on the translation committee of the Revised Standard Version of the Bible from 1983 to 1987. Her publications include *Tragedy and Biblical Narrative: Arrows of the Almighty* (Cambridge University Press, 1992) and *Signs and Wonders: Biblical Texts in Literary Focus* (Scholars Press, 1989).

ISRAEL FINKELSTEIN is senior lecturer at Bar-Ilan University (Israel) and a leading Israeli archaeologist. He is co-editor of *From Nomadism to Monarchy: Archaeological and Historical Aspects of Early Israel* (Biblical Archaeology Society/Israel Exploration Society/Yad Yitshak Ben-Tsevi, 1994) and author of *The Archaeology of the Israelite Settlement* (Israel Exploration Society, 1988).

DAVID NOEL FREEDMAN is Arthur F. Thurnau Professor of Biblical Studies at the University of Michigan and general editor of the new Anchor Bible series. His many publications include *The Unity of the Hebrew Bible* (University of Michigan Press, 1991) and *Pottery, Poetry, and Prophecy* (Eisenbrauns, 1981).

R. DAVID FREEDMAN is former director of the Religious Studies program at the University of California, Davis. Among his publications is "'Put Your Hand Under My Thigh'–The Patriarchal Oath," *BAR* (May/June 1976).

RICHARD ELLIOTT FRIEDMAN, professor of Hebrew and comparative literature at the University of California, San Diego, is author of the popular *Who Wrote the Bible?* (Harper & Row, 1988), *The Exile and Biblical Narrative* (Scholars Press, 1981) and *Introduction to the Hebrew Bible* (Doubleday, forthcoming).

KENNETH R. R. GROS LOUIS is chancellor of Indiana University, Bloomington, and the author of the two-volume *Literary Interpretations of Biblical Narrative* (Abingdon Press, 1972, 1982).

RONALD S. HENDEL is associate professor in the Department of Religious Studies at Southern Methodist University, in Dallas, Texas. He is the author of *The Epic of the Patriarch: The Jacob Cycle and the Narrative Traditions of Canaan and Israel* (Scholars Press, 1987) and many other publications.

PHILIP J. KING is an archaeologist and professor of biblical studies at Boston College and has directed excavations of many sites, including Tell er-Rumeith, Jordan (1967), Tell Taanach, West Bank (1968), Tell Gezer, Israel (1968-1969), Tell el-Hesi, Israel (1970-1971, 1973) and Wadi el-Jubah, North Yemen (1984).

P. KYLE McCARTER, JR., is the William Foxwell Albright Professor of Biblical and Ancient Near Eastern Studies at the Johns Hopkins University in Baltimore,

Maryland. His many publications include commentaries on 1 and 2 Samuel in the Anchor Bible series published by Doubleday.

ALAN R. MILLARD is Rankin Reader in Hebrew and Ancient Semitic Languages at the University of Liverpool, England, and the author of *Treasures from Bible Times* (Lion, 1985) and *Discoveries from the Time of Jesus* (Lion, 1990).

PAMELA J. MILNE is associate professor in the Religious Studies Department at the University of Windsor, Ontario. Her publications include *Vladimir Propp and the Study of Structure in Biblical Narratives* (Almond/Sheffield Academic Press, 1988).

HARVEY MINKOFF, editor, is professor of linguistics at Hunter College in New York City and the author of nine books, including *Visions and Revisions* (Prentice-Hall, 1990) and *Exploring America: Perspectives on Critical Issues* (Harcourt Brace, forthcoming). Minkoff works in many languages, including French, Spanish, Hebrew, Latin, Yiddish and Aramaic.

LAWRENCE E. STAGER is Dorot Professor of the Archaeology of Israel at Harvard University, director of the Harvard Semitic Museum and director of the Leon Levy Expedition to Ashkelon.

PHYLLIS TRIBLE is Baldwin Professor of Sacred Literature at Union Theological Seminary in New York. Her publications include *Texts of Terror: Literary-Feminist Readings of Biblical Narratives* (Fortress Press, 1984) and *God and the Rhetoric of Sexuality* (Fortress Press, 1978).

Endnotes

PART I
Introduction
(pages 2-4)

1. James L. Kugel, "The Bible in the University" in *The Hebrew Bible and Its Interpreters*, ed. William H. Propp, Baruch Halpern and David Noel Freedman, Biblical and Judaic Studies 1 (Winona Lake, IN: Eisenbrauns, 1990), p. 145.

2. G. Ernest Wright, *God Who Acts: Biblical Theology as Recital* (London: SCM, 1952), p. 128.

3. Rolf Rendtorff, "Must 'Biblical Theology' Be Christian Theology?" *BR* 4:3 (1988).

4. See Hemchand Gossai, "The Old Testament among Christian Theologians," *BR* 6:1 (1990).

5. Henry O. Thompson, "Why Christians Should Bother with the Old Testament," *BR* 5:1 (1989); an excerpt from this article is reprinted on pp. 27-30 in this volume.

6. Simon Greenberg, in the foreword to Nahum M. Sarna, *Understanding Genesis: The Heritage of Biblical Israel* (New York: Schocken Books, 1966), p. xiv.

1. Crenshaw
(pages 5-13)

"Ecclesiastes: Odd Book In" first appeared in **BR** *October 1990.*

1. Verse citations refer to the traditional Hebrew text. See, for example, the New Jewish Publication Society translation (Philadelphia, 1985).

2. See Philip J. King, "The Great Eighth Century," *BR* 5:4 (1989).

3. Frank Crusemann, "Die unveranderbare Welt: Uberlegungen zur 'Krisis der Weisheit' beim Prediger (Kohelet)," in *Der Gott der kleinen Leute*, ed. Willy Schottroff and Wolfgang Stegemann (Munich: Kaiser, 1979), pp. 80-104. Published in English as *The God of the Lowly*, trans. Matthew J. O'Connell (Maryknoll, NY: Orbis Books, 1984).

4. Michael V. Fox, "Frame-Narrative and Composition in the Book of Qohelet," *Hebrew Union College Annual* 48 (1977), pp. 83-106.

5. James A. Loader (in *Polar Structures in the Book of Qohelet*, Beihefte zur Zeitschrift für die alttestamentliche Wissenschaft 152 [Berlin/New York: de Gruyter, 1979]) works out an elaborate theory of binary opposites throughout the book.

6. R. Norman Whybray, "Qoheleth, Preacher of Joy," *Journal for the Study of the Old Testament* 23 (1982), pp. 87-98; and a more recent commentary, *Ecclesiastes*, New Century Bible (Grand Rapids, MI: Eerdmans, 1989).

7. Graham Ogden, *Qoheleth* (Sheffield: JSOT Press, 1987), pp. 48, 59-60, 137-138, 160, 213.

8. Philippe Rouillard, "The Figure of Job in the Liturgy: Indignation, Resignation or Silence?" in *Job and the Silence of God*, ed. Christian Doquoc and Casiano Floristan (New York: Seabury Press, 1983), pp. 8-12; Terence W. Tilley, "God and the Silencing of Job," *Modern Theology* 5 (1989), pp. 257-270.

Crenshaw, Afterword
(pages 14-15)

1. Thomas Wolfe, "Ecclesiasticus" in *You Can't Go Home Again* (New York/London: Harper, 1940), pp. 732-733.

2. Ernest Hemingway, *The Sun Also Rises* (New York: Charles Scribner's Sons, 1926).

3. Paul Tillich, *The New Being* (New York: Charles Scribner's Sons, 1955), p. 168.

2. Hendel
(pages 16-25)

"When God Acts Immorally" first appeared in **BR** *June 1991.*

1. Leviticus 19:18; Exodus 20:12 (see also Deuteronomy 5:16); Exodus 20:13 (also Deuteronomy 5:17).

2. Isaiah 2:24 and Micah 4:14.

3. The prophets frequently sound this theme.

4. Amos 5:21-25.

5. This position was espoused by some ancient Gnostic sects; see Birger A. Pearson, "Use, Authority and Exegesis of Mikra in Gnostic Literature" in *Mikra: Text, Translation, Reading and Interpretation of the Hebrew Bible in Ancient Judaism and Early Christianity*, ed. M.J. Mulder (Philadelphia: Fortress Press, 1988), pp. 638-641.

6. Cited in W. Neil, "The Criticism and Theological Use of the Bible, 1700-1950" in *The Cambridge History of the Bible*, vol. 3, ed. S.L. Greenslade (Cambridge, UK: Cambridge University Press, 1963-1970), pp. 250-251.

7. Neil, "Criticism and Theological Use of the Bible," p. 251.

8. Steve Allen, *On the Bible, Religion, and Morality* (Buffalo, NY: Prometheus Press, 1990).

9. For discussions of this and related topics, see John Barton, "Understanding Old Testament Ethics," *Journal for the Study of the Old Testament* (*JSOT*) 9 (1978), pp. 44-64, and "Approaches to Ethics in the Old Testament" in *Beginning Old Testament Study*, ed. J. Rogerson (Philadelphia: Westminster Press, 1982), pp. 113-130; and Jon D. Levenson, *Creation and the Persistence of Evil* (San Francisco: Harper & Row, 1988).

10. Allen, *On the Bible*, p. 63.

11. Genesis 3:22.

12. For example, Targum Pseudo-Jonathan on Genesis 4:1, perhaps implied in 1 John 3:12, and many later Jewish and Christian sources; see Louis Ginzberg, *The Legends of the Jews*, 7 vols. (Philadelphia: Jewish Publication Society, 1909-1938), vol. 1, p. 105, and vol. 5, pp. 133-134; and Neil Forsyth, *The Old Enemy: Satan and the Combat Myth* (Princeton, NJ: Princeton University Press, 1987), pp. 236-237.

13. Among ancient commentators, for example, Philo *On the Sacrifices of Abel and Cain* 52 and 72, trans. in *Philo*, vol. 2, ed. F.H. Colson and G.H. Whitaker, Loeb Classical Library (Cambridge, MA: Harvard University Press, 1929), Genesis Rabbah 22.5. Among modern commentators, see, for example, Umberto Cassuto, *A Commentary on the Book of Genesis* (Jerusalem: Magnes Press, 1961), p. 205; Ephraim A. Speiser, *Genesis*, Anchor Bible 1 (Garden City, NY: Doubleday, 1964), p. 30; Nahum M. Sarna, *Understanding Genesis: The Heritage of Biblical Israel* (New York: Schocken Books, 1966), pp. 29-30; Gordon J. Wenham, *Genesis 1-15*, Word Biblical Commentary 1 (Waco, TX: Word Books, 1987), pp. 101-102.

14. Leviticus 2:14-16 specifies that an offering of first fruits is one of several acceptable grain offerings.

15. See Saul Levin, "The More Savory Offering: A Key to the Problem of Gen. 4:3-5," *Journal of Biblical Literature* (1979), p. 85.

16. Origen *On First Principles* 4, 2.9, in *Biblical Interpretation in the Early Church*, ed. and trans. Karlfried Froehlich (Philadelphia: Fortress Press, 1984), p. 62.

17. Philo *On the Sacrifices of Abel and Cain* 3, p. 97.

18. Augustine *The City of God* 15.1.

19. See the discussion by James Barr, "The Literal, the Allegorical, and Modern Biblical Scholarship," *JSOT* 44 (1989), pp. 3-17.

20. So, with variations, Hermann Gunkel, *Genesis: Übersetzt und Erklärt*, 3d ed. (Göttingen: Vandenhoeck & Ruprecht, 1910), pp. 47-49, and *The Folktale in the Old Testament*, trans. Michael D. Rutter, Historic Texts and Interpreters in Biblical Scholarship 6 (Sheffield: Almond Press, 1987), pp. 150-151; Walther Zimmerli, *1 Mose 1-11: Urgeschichte*, 3d ed. (Zurich: Theologischer, 1967), p. 210; Speiser, *Genesis*, p. 31.

21. See, for example, the critical remarks of John Skinner, *A Critical and Exegetical Commentary on Genesis*, 2d ed., International Critical Commentary (Edinburgh: T & T Clark, 1930), pp. 112-114; and Claus Westermann, *Genesis 1-11* (Minneapolis: Augsburg, 1984), pp. 282-284.

22. For example, Gunkel, *Genesis*, p. 48; Zimmerli, *1 Mose 1-11*, pp. 226-229.

23. Exodus 18.

24. Judges 1:16, 4:11.

25. Judges 4:17, 5:24.

26. See the critical remarks of Skinner (*Critical and Exegetical Commentary*, pp. 111-115) and

Cassuto (*Commentary on Genesis*, pp. 179-183).

27. See Genesis 18:17-33 and Exodus 32:9-14.

28. Gerhard von Rad, *Genesis: A Commentary*, rev. ed., Old Testament Library (Philadelphia: Westminster Press, 1972), p. 104; see similar comments by Zimmerli, *1 Mose 1-11*, p. 212.

29. Westermann, *Genesis 1-11*, p. 296.

30. Genesis 4:15-16.

31. A notable exception is Walter Brueggemann, *Genesis* (Atlanta: John Knox Press, 1982), pp. 56-57.

32. See, for example, the critical discussions in Philip Rieff, *Freud: The Mind of the Moralist* (Garden City, NY: Doubleday, 1961), pp. 281-328; Paul Ricoeur, *Freud and Philosophy: An Essay on Interpretation* (New Haven, CT: Yale University Press, 1970), pp. 230-259, 531-551; and James S. Preus, *Explaining Religion: Criticism and Theory from Bodin to Freud* (New Haven, CT: Yale University Press, 1987), pp. 178-204.

33. Sigmund Freud, *New Introductory Lectures on Psychoanalysis* (New York: Norton, 1965), p. 163.

34. Freud, *The Future of an Illusion* (Garden City, NY: Doubleday, 1964), p. 34.

35. See the apt criticisms of Rieff, Ricoeur and Preus (note 32).

36. The J source is the earliest of the four literary strata of the Pentateuch. For an excellent introduction to these sources, see Richard Elliott Friedman, *Who Wrote the Bible?* (New York: Simon and Schuster, 1987).

37. Harold Bloom and David Rosenberg, *The Book of J* (New York: Grove Weidenfeld, 1990), pp. 305-306. For a review, see Richard Elliott Friedman, "Is Everybody a Bible Expert?" *BR* 7:2 (1991).

38. Bloom and Rosenberg, *Book of J*, p. 286.

39. Bloom and Rosenberg, *Book of J*, p. 292.

40. Bloom and Rosenberg, *Book of J*, p. 281.

41. Ricoeur, *The Symbolism of Evil* (Boston: Beacon Press, 1967), p. 317.

42. Ricoeur, *Symbolism of Evil*, p. 322.

43. Genesis 18:17-33; Exodus 32:9-14. See the fine discussion by David Noel Freedman, "Who Asks (or Tells) God to Repent?" *BR* 1:4 (1985), pp. 56-59.

44. Genesis 18:17-19.

45. Genesis 8:21, compare with Genesis 6:5-7.

46. Compare Isaiah 45:7, which ascribes the creation of good and evil to God.

Related Articles in *BR* and *BAR*

Mayer I. Gruber, "Was Cain Angry or Depressed?" *BAR* 6:6 (1980).

Joseph P. Klein, "How Job Fulfills God's Word to Cain," *BR* 9:3 (1993).

Hendel, Afterword

(pages 26-30)

1. See Robert Gordis, "Studies in the Esther Narrative," *JBL* 95 (1976), pp. 43-58, especially 49-53. The verse reads that Mordecai wrote in the name of King Xerxes "to the effect that the king had given permission to the Jews in every single city to organize themselves and to defend themselves, to wipe out, slaughter and annihilate every armed force of any people or province that was hostile to them, along with their children and women, and to plunder their personal property."

Related Articles in *BR* and *BAR*

Michael Heltzer, "The Book of Esther–Where Does Fiction Start and History End?" *BR* 8:1 (1992).

PART II

3. de Vaux

(pages 35-44)

"The Separate Traditions of Abraham and Jacob" first appeared in **BAR** *July/August 1980.*

Related Articles in *BR* and *BAR*

Thomas Aquinas Collins, "Pere De Vaux and the Old Testament," *BAR* 3:2 (1977).

Baruch Halpern, *The First Historians: The Hebrew Bible and History*, reviewed by Michael D. Coogan, *BR* 7:6 (1991).

Jacob Licht, "The Hebrew Bible Contains the Oldest Surviving History," *BR* 5:6 (1989).

Nahum M. Sarna, "Abraham in History," *BAR* 3:4 (1977).

"Scholars Face Off Over Age of Biblical Stories," *BR* 10:4 (1994).

John Van Seters, "Dating the Patriarchal Stories," *BAR* 4:4 (1978).

de Vaux, Afterword

(pages 45-47)

1. John Van Seters, *In Search of History: Historiography in the Ancient World and the Origins of Biblical History* (New Haven, CT: Yale University Press, 1983).

4. Stager
(pages 48-66)

"The Song of Deborah" first appeared in **BAR** *January/February 1989.*

1. NJV is the New Jewish Version, The Tanakh, a translation of the Hebrew Bible (Old Testament) by the Jewish Publication Society of America (Philadelphia, 1985). Translations of Bible excerpts in this article not attributed to a particular source are by the author, Lawrence E. Stager.

2. William F. Albright, *Yahweh and the Gods of Canaan* (Garden City, NY: Doubleday, 1968), p. 13; Roland de Vaux, *The Early History of Israel* (Philadelphia: Westminster Press, 1978), pp. 794-796; Michael D. Coogan, "A Structural and Literary Analysis of the Song of Deborah," *Catholic Biblical Quarterly* 40 (1978), pp. 143-166, who suggests the 11th century B.C.E. as the latest possible date of the Song of Deborah.

3. George Foot Moore, *A Critical and Exegetical Commentary on Judges* (New York: Charles Scribner's Sons, 1895), p. 133.

4. Nearly every great biblical scholar of this century and the last has pondered the difficult language of this poem, a victory ode that ranks as one of the greatest poems in Semitic literature. But no one has succeeded in understanding its overall meaning and significance for the social history of premonarchic Israel better than Moore (*Commentary on Judges*) and Max Weber (*Ancient Judaism* [1917-1919; reprint, ed. and trans. Hans H. Gerth and Don Martindale, Glencoe, IL: Free Press, 1952]). The legacy of both will be apparent throughout my discussion. Michael Coogan (see note 2) has provided a valuable stylistic analysis and felicitous translation of the Song.

5. The earliest tribal confederation of which we know may have included only 10 tribes rather than the traditional 12 known from sources later than the Song of Deborah. If we assume that Gilead is related to or identical with Gad, and Machir to Manasseh, we are still missing three tribes–Levi, Simeon and Judah. Levi is a special case; it was always a sacerdotal "tribe," similar to a religious order, which males from lay tribes could join. Levi is sometimes omitted in later tribal lists. More conspicuous by their absence are Simeon and Judah, the latter especially, because Judah is always included in later tribal lists. It seems likely that 12 became the ideal number for a confederation of tribes but that the number and composition of tribes fluctuated over time with changes in demography and geography. As fusion and fission occurred among clans, some rose to tribal status (perhaps Judah is an example after the 12th century B.C.E.) while others receded in importance (e.g., Machir, which in later genealogical lists becomes a "son" of Manasseh, now elevated to full tribal status).

6. This is in contrast to the account in Judges 4 where Zebulun and Naphtali provided all the Israelite troops.

7. Because this area became the heartland of Israel during the monarchy, and many of the Iron I settlements continued into Iron II (1000-600 B.C.E.), it seems logical to conclude that many of the Iron I settlements were also Israelite. In other words, within the general field of survey (more than 550 square miles), many sites have to be Israelite; however, at present it is difficult, if not impossible, in the absence of textual or epigraphic evidence, to say of any particular Iron I settlement in the hills that it is Israelite rather than Hivite, Jebusite or whatever. All of these settlements seemed to share a common culture of such everyday items as cooking pots and storage jars (even collar-rimmed storage jars).

My hunch is that when "ethnic" boundary markers distinguishing Israelites from Canaanites are found by archaeologists, they will relate to ideological differences, particularly in the realm of religion. Hints of these distinctions are already emerging from the pioneering work being done by zooarchaeologists Drs. Paula Wapnish and Brian Hesse in relating the presence or absence of pigs to dietary taboos, such as we find in the Hebrew Bible (for example, Brian Hesse and Paula Wapnish, "Pig Avoidance in the Iron Age," a paper presented at the American Schools of Oriental Research Annual Meeting, Boston, 1987).

8. For the most up-to-date survey statistics, see Israel Finkelstein, *The Archaeology of the Israelite Settlement* (Jerusalem: Israel Exploration Society, 1988), parts 1-2.

9. Late Bronze Age gates have been found at Megiddo, Shechem and Hazor.

10. C.H.J. de Geus, "The Importance of Archaeological Research into the Palestinian Agricultural Terraces with an Excursus on the Hebrew Word *gbi*," *Palestine Exploration Quarterly* 107 (1975), pp. 65-74.

11. Albright, *The Archaeology of Palestine* (Baltimore: Penguin, 1960), p. 113.

12. John Bright, *A History of Israel*, 2d ed.

(Philadelphia: Westminster Press, 1972), p. 213; J. Maxwell Miller, "The Israelite Occupation of Canaan" in *Israelite and Judaean History*, ed. J.H. Hayes and Miller (Philadelphia: Westminster Press, 1977), pp. 255-257; Norman K. Gottwald, *The Tribes of Yahweh: A Sociology of the Religion of Liberated Israel, 1250-1050 B.C.E.* (Maryknoll, NY: Orbis Books, 1979), pp. 655-656.

13. de Geus, "Importance of Archaeological Research," p. 69.

14. See Joseph A. Callaway, "A Visit with Ahilud," *BAR* 9:5 (1983).

15. In contrast to the central room, the stable side rooms never had hearths, ovens or cisterns. At Iron I settlements not built directly on bedrock, the floors of the central room were frequently plastered; the side rooms were usually paved with flagstones. At Ai the side rooms were sometimes entered through small, arched passageways no higher than 2.6 feet, suitable only for sheep, goats and smaller animals. For the criteria established for stables in both public and domestic contexts, see the definitive study by John S. Holladay, Jr., "The Stables of Ancient Israel: Functional Determinants of Stable Construction and the Interpretation of Pillared Building Remains of the Palestinian Iron Age" in *The Archaeology of Jordan and Other Studies*, Siegfried Horn Festschrift, ed. Lawrence T. Geraty and Lawrence Herr (Berrien Springs, MI: Andrews University Press, 1986).

16. Aharon Kempinski, "Israelite Conquest or Settlement? New Light from Tell Masos," *BAR* 2:3 (1976).

17. Abdulla M. Lutfiyya, *Baytin, A Jordanian Village: A Study of Social Institutions and Social Change in a Folk Community* (The Hague: Mouton, 1966), pp. 142-143.

18. William R. Polk, *The Opening of South Lebanon, 1788-1840: A Study of the Impact of the West on the Middle East* (Cambridge, MA: Harvard University Press, 1963), p. 8.

19. Fernand Braudel, *The Mediterranean and the Mediterranean World in the Age of Philip II*, trans. Siân Reynolds, 2 vols. (New York: Harper & Row, 1972), vol. 1, p. 74.

20. Zvi Gal, "The Settlement of Issachar: Some New Observations," *Tel Aviv* 9 (1982), pp. 79-86.

21. In the poetic account of Judges 5, the Israelite tribesmen descended upon the Canaanites from the highlands in general, not from Mount Tabor in particular. Perhaps it was the specific mention of Mount Tabor and the location of Barak's home in Kedesh-Naphtali in Judges 4, but not in the Song of Deborah (Judges 5), that led to the reduction of the number of tribes that participated in the battle to two–the Galilean contingents of Zebulun and Naphtali, tribes that were already in the north.

22. Anatoly M. Khazanov, *Nomads and the Outside World*, trans. J. Crookenden (Cambridge, UK: Cambridge University Press, 1984), p. 70.

23. Khazanov, *Nomads*, pp. 202-205.

24. Ibn Khaldûn, *The Muqaddimah: An Introduction to History*, abridged and ed. N.J. Dawood, trans. F. Rosenthal (Princeton, NJ: Princeton University Press, 1967), p. 122.

25. W. Robertson Smith, *Lectures on the Religion of the Semites* (New York: Appleton, 1889), pp. 75-76.

26. See Hershel Shanks' interview, "Avraham Biran–Twenty Years of Digging at Tel Dan," *BAR* 13:4 (1987); and John C.H. Laughlin, "The Remarkable Discoveries at Tel Dan," *BAR* 7:5 (1981).

27. Rafi Frankel's survey is cited in Finkelstein, *Israelite Settlement*, p. 97.

28. For further details, see Lawrence E. Stager, "The Archaeology of the Family in Ancient Israel," *Bulletin of the American Schools of Oriental Research* 260 (1985); "Archaeology, Ecology and Social History: Background Themes to the Song of Deborah" in *Congress Volume: Jerusalem, 1986*, ed. John A. Emerton, Vetus Testamentum Supplement 40 (Leiden/New York: Brill, 1988), pp. 221-234.

Related Articles in *BR* and *BAR*

Yohanan Aharoni, "Hazor and the Battle of Deborah–Is Judges 4 Wrong?" *BAR* 1:4 (1975).

"Yigael Yadin on Hazor, the Head of All Those Kingdoms," *BAR* 1:1 (1975).

PART III

Introduction

(pages 70-73)

1. G. Ernest Wright, *God Who Acts: Biblical Theology as Recital* (London: SCM, 1952).

2. Edward Robinson and Eli Smith, *Biblical Researches in Palestine* (Boston: Crocker & Brewster, 1841; second edition, *Biblical Researches in Palestine and the Adjacent Regions*, London: J. Murray, 1856).

Related Articles in *BR* and *BAR*

Fredric R. Brandfon, "Archaeology and the Biblical Text," *BAR* 14:1 (1988).

Thomas W. Davis, "Faith and Archaeology," *BAR* 19:2 (1993).

William G. Dever, "What Archaeology Can Contribute to an Understanding of the Bible," *BAR* 7:5 (1981).

Dever, "Archaeology and the Bible: Understanding Their Special Relationship," *BAR* 16:3 (1990).

5. King

(pages 74-84)

"Amos' Denunciation of the Marzeaḥ*" first appeared in* **BAR** *July/August 1988.*

1. H. Darrell Lance, *The Old Testament and the Archaeologist* (Philadelphia: Fortress Press, 1981), p. 48.

2. See the following articles by Hershel Shanks: "Should the Term 'Biblical Archaeology' Be Abandoned?" *BAR* 7:3 (1981); "Whither ASOR?" *BAR* 9:5 (1983); "Dever's 'Sermon on the Mound,'" *BAR* 13:2 (1987); and see the letters by William G. Dever in *BAR* 7:5 (1981) and 13:4 (1987).

3. William F. Albright, who died in 1971, was the doyen of an earlier generation of biblical archaeologists.

4. William F. Albright, "The Impact of Archaeology on Biblical Research—1966" in *New Directions in Biblical Archaeology*, ed. David Noel Freedman and Jonas Greenfield (Garden City, NY: Doubleday, 1971), pp. 3-4.

5. This example is adapted from my book *Amos, Hosea, Micah—An Archaeological Commentary* (Philadelphia: Westminster Press, 1988).

6. On this clause, see David Noel Freedman, "But Did King David Invent Musical Instruments?" *BR* 1:2 (1985).

7. Jonas Greenfield, "The *Marzeaḥ* as a Social Institution," *Acta Antiqua* (Budapest) 22 (1974), pp. 451-455; Marvin Pope, "A Divine Banquet at Ugarit" in *The Use of the Old Testament in the New*, ed. J. Efird (Durham, NC: Duke University Press, 1972), pp. 170-203, and "The Cult of the Dead at Ugarit" in *Ugarit in Retrospect*, ed. G. Young (Winona Lake, IN: Eisenbrauns, 1981), pp. 159-179.

8. See Hershel Shanks, "Ancient Ivory—The Story of Wealth, Decadence and Beauty," *BAR* 11:5 (1985).

9. Irene J. Winter, "Ivory Carving" in *Ebla to Damascus: Art and Archaeology of Ancient Syria*, ed. Harvey Weiss (Washington, DC: Smithsonian Institution Press, 1985), pp. 343-344.

10. See Vassos Karageorghis, *Salamis in Cyprus* (London: Thames and Hudson, 1969), pp. 76-98; and *Excavations in the Necropolis at Salamis*, vol. 3 (Nicosia, Cyprus: Department of Antiquities, 1973).

11. John S. Holladay, Jr., "The Stables of Ancient Israel" in *The Archaeology of Jordan and Other Studies*, ed. Lawrence Geraty and Lawrence Herr (Berrien Springs, MI: Andrews University Press, 1986), pp. 103-165.

12. Lawrence E. Stager, "The Archaeology of the Family in Ancient Israel," *Bulletin of the American Schools of Oriental Research* 260 (1985), pp. 1-35.

13. See Bathja Bayer, "The Finds That Could Not Be," *BAR* 8:1 (1982).

14. Nahman Avigad and Greenfield, "A Bronze *phiale* with a Phoenician Dedicatory Inscription," *Israel Exploration Journal* 32 (1982), pp. 118-128.

15. Stager, "The Finest Olive Oil in Samaria," *Journal of Semitic Studies* 28 (1983), pp. 241-245.

6. Batey

(pages 85-96)

"Sepphoris: An Urban Portrait of Jesus" first appeared in **BAR** *May/June 1992.*

1. Leroy Waterman, *Preliminary Report of the University of Michigan Excavations at Sepphoris, Palestine, in 1931, Leroy Waterman, Director* (Ann Arbor: University of Michigan Press, 1937), p. v. The name Sepphoris means "bird" because (according to a postbiblical source) it is perched on a hill like a bird (pp. 18, 26).

2. Sean Freyne, *Galilee from Alexander the Great to Hadrian, 323 B.C.E. to 135 C.E.: A Study of Second Temple Judaism* (Wilmington, DE: Michael Glazier/Notre Dame, IN: University of Notre Dame Press, 1980), p. 123; Josephus *The Jewish War* 2.56, and *Antiquities of the Jews* 17.271f.

3. Josephus *Life* 232.

4. Josephus *Antiquities* 18.27.

5. See Suzanne F. Singer, "The Winter Palaces of Jericho," *BAR* 3:2 (1977).

6. The report of this project has been published

in my article, "Subsurface Interface Radar at Sepphoris, Israel, 1985," *Journal of Field Archaeology* 14 (spring 1987), pp. 1-8.

7. Shirley Jackson Case, *Jesus: A New Biography* (Chicago: University of Chicago Press, 1927), p. 205f.; "Jesus and Sepphoris," *Journal of Biblical Literature* 45 (1926), p. 18.

8. Virgil *Aeneid* 1.420-429.

9. Joachim Jeremias, *The Parables of Jesus*, rev. ed., trans. S.H. Hooke (New York: Charles Scribner's Sons/London: SCM, 1963), p. 210.

10. Josephus *Antiquities* 17.319.

11. Jack P. Lewis, *The Gospel According to Matthew*, parts 1 and 2, Living Word Commentary 2 (Austin: Sweet Publishing, 1976), part 2, p. 61.

12. John R. Donahue, *The Gospel in Parable* (Philadelphia: Fortress Press, 1988), p. 75.

13. Eta Linnemann, *Jesus of the Parables* (New York: Harper & Row, 1966), p. 110.

14. Donahue, *Gospel in Parable*, p. 142; C.H. Dodd, *The Parables of the Kingdom* (London: Nisbet, 1936), p. 114.

15. Josephus *Antiquities* 18.252.

16. The image of king and God as king appear frequently in the Old Testament.

17. Richard A. Batey, "Jesus and the Theatre," *New Testament Studies* 30 (October 1984), p. 563f.; Ulrich Wilckens in Gerhard Kittel and Gerhard Friedrich, eds., *Theological Dictionary of the New Testament*, 10 vols., ed. and trans. Geoffrey W. Bromiley (Grand Rapids, MI: Eerdmans, 1964-1976), vol. 7, p. 567f.

18. F.V. Filson, *A Commentary on the Gospel According to St. Matthew* (New York: Harper, 1960), p. 93. Also Alexander Jones, *The Gospel According to St. Matthew* (New York: Sheed & Ward, 1965), p. 85; David Hill, *The Gospel of Matthew* (London: Marshall, Morgan & Scott, 1972), p. 133; Lewis, *Gospel According to Matthew*, part 1, p. 99.

19. John P. Meier, *Matthew* (Wilmington, DE: Michael Glazier, 1980), p. 58. "The classical meaning of the Greek word is 'actor in a play.' The corresponding Aramaic word means 'a profane person.' A second-century rabbi remarked acidly that 'there are ten portions of hypocrisy in the world, and nine of them are in Jerusalem,'" Sherman E. Johnson, "The Gospel According to Matthew" in *The Interpreter's Bible*, 12 vols. (New York: Abingdon Press, 1951-1957), vol. 7, p. 306.

20. Josephus *Antiquities* 15.268.

21. James F. Strange pointed out to me that the Greek word translated "street corners" (*plateion*) is plural of *plateia* or "colonnaded street." The main street of Sepphoris is referred to as *palatia* in rabbinic sources (see Berakhot 3; Y Ketubbot 1.10). Strange translates the passage in Matthew as "And when you pray, you must not be like actors, for they love to stand and pray in [public] assemblies and on the corners of the [colonnaded] streets to be seen by people." Strange stated this idea in an unpublished paper read at the annual meeting of the Society of Biblical Literature (November 20, 1988).

22. Lewis, *Gospel According to Matthew*, part 1, p. 98f. Rabbi Halafta, a first-century rabbi, made it a religious custom at Sepphoris, at the time the residence of influential priestly families, to sound a ram's horn or a trumpet after benedictions (Babylonian Talmud Rosh Hashanah 27a and Ta'anit 16b).

23. Margarete Bieber, *The History of the Greek and Roman Theater* (Princeton, NJ: Princeton University Press, 1961), p. 161.

24. The urbanization of Galilee also suggests that Jesus spoke Greek as well as Aramaic. Today, debates among New Testament scholars are turning from the question of whether or not Jesus spoke Greek to how well he spoke Greek. Careful study of the Greek text of the Gospels has led some scholars to conclude that a number of parables were composed originally in Greek rather than Aramaic. See Batey, "Jesus and the Theatre," p. 572 n. 2; Robert W. Funk, *Parables and Presence* (Philadelphia: Fortress Press, 1982), p. 28.

Related Articles in *BR* and *BAR*

Joseph A. Fitzmyer, "Did Jesus Speak Greek?" *BAR* 18:5 (1992); reprinted in *Approaches to the Bible*, vol. 1, p. 253.

Batey, Afterword

(pages 97-100)

1. William G. Dever, *Recent Archaeological Discoveries and Biblical Research* (Seattle/London: University of Washington Press, 1990).

2. Norman K. Gottwald, *The Tribes of Yahweh: A Sociology of the Religion of Liberated Israel, 1250-1050 B.C.E.* (Maryknoll, NY: Orbis Books, 1979).

3. Israel Finkelstein, *The Archaeology of the Israelite Settlement*, trans. D. Saltz (Jerusalem: Israel Exploration Society, 1988).

4. G. Ernest Wright, *God Who Acts: Biblical Theology as Recital* (London: SCM, 1952).

5. Roland de Vaux, *Ancient Israel: Its Life and Institutions*, trans. John McHugh (New York: McGraw-Hill, 1961; French original, *Les institutions de l'Ancien Testament*, 2 vols., Paris: Cerf, 1958-1960).

6. de Vaux, "On Right and Wrong Uses of Archaeology" in *Near Eastern Archaeology in the Twentieth Century: Essays in Honor of Nelson Glueck*, ed. James A. Sanders (Garden City, NY: Doubleday, 1970), pp. 64-80. See also, significantly, Wright, "What Archaeology Can and Cannot Do," *Biblical Archaeologist* (*BA*) 34 (1971), pp. 70-76, and "The 'New Archaeology'," *BA* 38 (1975), pp. 104-117.

7. Raymond E. Brown, *Recent Discoveries and the Biblical World* (Wilmington, DE: Michael Glazier, 1983).

PART IV
Introduction
(pages 102-103)

1. Harvey Minkoff, "Coarse Language in the Bible? It's Culture Shocking!" *BR* 5:2 (1989); reprinted in *Approaches to the Bible*, vol. 1, p. 275.

7. McCarter
(pages 104-113)

"Gottwald's Socio-literary Approach to the Bible" first appeared in **BR** *summer 1986.*

1. Norman K. Gottwald, *The Hebrew Bible–A Socio-Literary Introduction* (Philadelphia: Fortress Press, 1985). Inevitably, this book will be thought of as a successor to, or replacement of, Gottwald's earlier introduction, *Light to the Nations* (New York: Harper, 1959), but the distance between the two is great. A great deal has changed in Gottwald's thinking in the past quarter century.

2. Gottwald, *The Tribes of Yahweh: A Sociology of the Religion of Liberated Israel, 1250-1050 B.C.E.* (Maryknoll, NY: Orbis Books, 1979).

3. Gottwald, ed., *The Bible and Liberation* (Maryknoll, NY: Orbis Books, 1983).

4. George E. Mendenhall's most pertinent work to the present topic is "The Hebrew Conquest of Palestine," *Biblical Archaeologist* 25 (1962), pp. 66-87; reprinted with slight revisions in *The Biblical Archaeologist Reader*, vol. 3, ed. Edward F. Campbell and David Noel Freedman (Garden City, NY: Doubleday, Anchor Books, 1970), pp. 100-120. See also "Mendenhall Disavows Paternity," *BR* 2:2 (1986); reprinted on pp. 114-119 in this volume.

5. Indeed, Marx assumed that religion did not exist before the rise of the class system, and he expected it would disappear as part of the evolving social process after the resolution of the class struggle. At this point the Marxian analysis of religion seems especially weak.

6. William F. Albright, *From the Stone Age to Christianity: Monotheism and the Historical Process*, 2d ed. (Garden City, NY: Doubleday, Anchor Books, 1957).

7. Julius Wellhausen, *Prolegomena to the History of Israel*, trans. John S. Black and Alan Menzies (Edinburgh: A & C Black, 1885; reprint, Atlanta: Scholars Press, 1994).

8. Max Weber, *Ancient Judaism*, ed. and trans. Hans H. Gerth and Don Martindale (Glencoe, IL: Free Press, 1952 [1917-1919]).

9. Marvin Harris, *Cultural Materialism* (New York: Random House, 1979).

10. To be sure, the oldest *written* source, the so-called Yahwistic, or J, narrative, dates from the age of kings and serves as a "national epic" for monarchical Israel (*Hebrew Bible*, p. 137), but Gottwald considers that the underlying traditions are those of the earlier period, which he calls retribalization.

11. Since completing this review, I have spoken with colleagues at various schools where the book has been adopted as a text. All of them express some degree of concern about its length, and one or two predict that it will prove unwieldy as a classroom text. So perhaps I have underestimated this problem.

Related Articles in *BR* and *BAR*

James W. Flanagan, *David's Social Drama: A Hologram of Israel's Early Iron Age*, reviewed by Norman K. Gottwald, *BR* 7:3 (1991).

Victor H. Matthews and Don C. Benjamin, *The Social World of Ancient Israel, 1250-587 B.C.E.*, reviewed by Philip J. King, *BR* 10:5 (1994).

"Israel's Emergence in Canaan–*BR* Interviews Norman Gottwald," *BR* 5:5 (1989).

8. Anderson
(pages 114-119)

"Mendenhall Disavows Paternity of Gottwald's Marxist Theory" first appeared in **BR** *summer 1986.*

1. The following summary is adapted from my book, *Understanding the Old Testament*, 4th ed. (Englewood Cliffs, NJ: Prentice-Hall, 1986), chap. 4.

2. George E. Mendenhall, "The Hebrew Conquest of Palestine," *Biblical Archaeologist* 25 (1962), pp. 66-87; reprinted with slight revisions in *The Biblical Archaeologist Reader*, vol. 3, ed. Edward F. Campbell and David Noel Freeman (Garden City, NY: Doubleday, Anchor Books, 1970), pp. 100-120.

3. John Bright, *A History of Israel*, 2d ed. (Philadelphia: Westminster Press, 1972).

4. Norman K. Gottwald, *The Tribes of Yahweh: A Sociology of the Religion of Liberated Israel, 1250-1050 B.C.E.* (Maryknoll, NY: Orbis Books, 1979).

5. Mendenhall, "Ancient Israel's Hyphenated History" in *Palestine in Transition*, ed. David Noel Freedman and David F. Graf, The Social World of Biblical Antiquity Ser. 2 (Sheffield: Almond Press/American Schools of Oriental Research, 1983), pp. 91-92.

6. J. Maxwell Miller, *Israelite and Judean History*, Old Testament Library (Philadelphia: Westminster Press/London: SCM, 1977), p. 279.

Anderson, Afterword

(pages 120-124)

1. The camel-riding Midianites who struck at Israel in the time of Gideon, about a century after Israel's initial formation, appear to have been the first full nomads known to us in the ancient Near Eastern sources (Judges 6:1-6).

2. Robert J. Braidwood, *Prehistoric Men*, 7th ed. (Glenview, IL: Scott, Foresman, 1967), pp. 81-153. On the physical conditions that fostered the neolithic revolution in the ancient Near East, consult K.W. Butzer in *The Cambridge Ancient History*, 3d ed., vol. 1, part 1, *Prolegomena and Prehistory*, ed. I.E.S. Edwards, C.J. Gadd and N.G.L. Hammond (Cambridge, UK: Cambridge University Press, 1970), pp. 35-62.

3. J.T. Luke, "Pastoralism and Politics in the Mari Period" (Ph.D. diss., University of Michigan, 1965), pp. 23-24, citing Braidwood's studies in Iraqi Kurdistan.

4. C.A. Reed in *Prehistoric Investigations in Iraqi Kurdistan*, ed. Braidwood and B. Howe (Chicago: University of Chicago Press, 1960), pp. 129-138. For different dates on domestication but entire agreement that domestication of animals took place in settled communities, see J. Mellaart in *Cambridge Ancient History*, pp. 248-254.

5. Luke, "Pastoralism and Politics," p. 24.

6. Other kinds of nomads are artisan or merchant nomads (an example of the latter are Gypsies; perhaps we should more appropriately call this type of nomadism "group itineracy").

7. Lawrence Krader, "Pastoralism" in *International Encyclopedia of the Social Sciences*, vol. 11, p. 458.

8. It is doubtful that we can characterize any of the later major movements of population in the historic period (e.g., Akkadians, Amorites, Arameans) as mass invasions or incursions of nomads into settled regions. In addition to the already cited refutation of the Mari nomads as invaders from the desert presented by J.T. Luke (see note 3), Alfred Haldar has examined the entire range of evidence on the socioeconomic status and origins of the Amorites–including their involvement in metallurgy and merchant caravaneering–and has demolished the foundations of the hypothesis that the Amorites were pastoral nomads from the desert. See Alfred Haldar, *Who Were the Amorites?* (Leiden: Brill, 1971).

9. Thus, Sabatino Moscati, in a 1969 study, states: "There is a direction of movement constantly repeated throughout the centuries, namely, the movement from the center towards the outskirts, from the Arabian Desert towards the surrounding regions" (*The Semites in Ancient History: An Inquiry into the Settlement of the Bedouin and Their Political Establishment* [Cardiff: University of Wales Press, 1969], p. 29).

9. Finkelstein

(pages 125-138)

"Searching for Israelite Origins" first appeared in **BAR** *September/October 1988.*

1. For my discussion of the term "Israelite" in the Iron I period, see Israel Finkelstein, *The Archaeology of the Israelite Settlement* (Jerusalem: Israel Exploration Society, 1988), pp. 27-28.

2. William F. Albright, "The Israelite Conquest of Canaan in the Light of Archaeology," *Bulletin of the American Schools of Oriental Research* (*BASOR*) 74 (1939), pp. 11-23; Yigael Yadin, "The Transition from a Semi-Nomadic to a Sedentary Society in the Twelfth Century B.C.E." in *Symposia Celebrating the Seventy-fifth*

Anniversary of the Founding of the American Schools of Oriental Research, ed. Frank Moore Cross (Cambridge, MA: American Schools of Oriental Research, 1979), pp. 57-68.

3. See Albrecht Alt, "Erwägungen über die Landnahme Israeliten in Palästina," *Palästina Jahrbuch* 35 (1939), pp. 8-63; and Yohanan Aharoni, *The Archaeology of the Land of Israel* (Philadelphia: Westminster Press, 1982), pp. 153-180.

4. George E. Mendenhall, "The Hebrew Conquest of Palestine," *Biblical Archaeologist* (*BA*) 25 (1962), pp. 66-87; Norman K. Gottwald, *The Tribes of Yahweh: A Sociology of the Religion of Liberated Israel, 1250-1050 B.C.E.* (Maryknoll, NY: Orbis Books, 1979).

5. For the end of the third millennium B.C.E., see William G. Dever, "New Vistas on EB IV ("MB I") Horizon in Syria-Palestine," *BASOR* 237 (1980), pp. 35-64.

6. See Finkelstein, *'Izbet Sartah: An Early Iron Age Site near Rosh Ha'ayin, Israel*, British Archaeological Reports International Ser. 299 (Oxford: Oxford University Press, 1986), pp. 124-128.

7. G.W. Ahlström, "The Early Iron Age Settlers at Khirbet el-Msas (Tel Masos)," *Zeitschrift des deutschen Palästina-Vereins* 100 (1984), pp. 35-52; "Giloh: A Judahite or Canaanite Settlement?" *Israel Exploration Journal* (*IEJ*) 34 (1984), pp. 170-172.

8. See, for example, similarities in the pottery of 'Izbet Sartah, which was probably an Israelite village, and the pottery of Aphek, an Egypto-Canaanite urban center. Incidentally, the degree of similarity between Israelite material culture and the preceding Canaanite material culture should be evaluated only at indisputably Israelite sites and not at borderline or questionable sites such as Tel Masos.

9. Magen Broshi and R. Gophna, "Middle Bronze Age II Palestine: Settlements and Population," *BASOR* 261 (1986), pp. 73-90.

10. Adam Zertal, "The Israelite Settlement in the Hill Country of Manasseh" (Ph.D. diss., Tel Aviv University, 1986), pp. 175-200 (in Hebrew).

11. See Finkelstein, "Shiloh Yields Some, But Not All, of Its Secrets," *BAR* 12:1 (1986).

12. Finkelstein, "Summary and Conclusions: History of Shiloh from Middle Bronze Age II to Iron Age II" in "Excavations at Shiloh 1981-1984: Preliminary Report," ed. Finkelstein, *Tel Aviv* 12 (1985), pp. 159-165.

13. Rivka Gonen, "Urban Canaan in the Late Bronze Period," *BASOR* 253 (1984), pp. 61-73.

14. Zvi Gal, "The Lower Galilee in the Iron Age" (Ph.D. diss., Tel Aviv University, 1982), pp. 43-55 (in Hebrew); James A. Sauer, "*Transjordan in the Bronze and Iron Ages*: A Critique of Glueck's Synthesis," *BASOR* 263 (1986), pp. 7-8.

15. Finkelstein, "Summary and Conclusions," pp. 165-167.

16. Broshi and Gophna, "Middle Bronze Age II Palestine"; Gonen, "Urban Canaan."

17. Zertal, "Israelite Settlement," and lecture at Bar-Ilan University, 1982.

18. Piotr Bienkowski, *Jericho in the Late Bronze Age* (Warminster, UK: Aris and Phillips, 1986), pp. 127-128.

19. Benjamin Mazar, "The Middle Bronze Age in Palestine," *IEJ* 18 (1968), pp. 89-97.

20. Dever, "The MB IIC Stratification in the Northwest Gate Area at Shechem," *BASOR* 216 (1974), p. 31.

21. See Fredrik Barth, *Nomads of South Persia* (Oslo: Oslo University Press, 1961), p. 118; B. Glatzer, "Processes of Nomadization in West Afghanistan" in *Contemporary Nomadic and Pastoral Peoples: Asia and the North*, ed. Phillip C. Salzman (Williamsburg, VA: William and Mary University Press, 1982), pp. 61-63.

22. Amnon Cohen, *Palestine in the 18th Century* (Jerusalem: Magnes Press, 1973), pp. 324-327; W. Hütteroth, "The Pattern of Settlement in Palestine in the Sixteenth Century" in *Studies on Palestine during the Ottoman Period*, ed. Moshe Ma'oz (Jerusalem: Magnes Press, 1975), pp. 3-10.

23. Avshalom Shmueli, *Nomadism About to Cease* (Tel Aviv, 1980), p. 73 (in Hebrew).

24. Henk J. Franken, "Deir 'Alla, Tell" in *Encyclopedia of Archaeological Excavations in the Holy Land*, vol. 1, ed. Michael Avi-Yonah (Jerusalem: Israel Exploration Society, 1975), p. 322; Finkelstein, "Summary and Conclusions," pp. 165-167; Ephraim Stern, *Excavations at Tel Mevorakh. Part Two: The Bronze Age, Qedem* 18 (Jerusalem: Hebrew University Press, 1984), p. 36; Robert G. Boling, "Bronze Age Buildings at the Shechem High Place: ASOR Excavations at Tananir," *BA* 32 (1969), pp. 82-103. On the possibility that the Amman and Shechem structures were shrines for tribal groups, see Edward

F. Campbell and G. Ernest Wright, "Tribal League Shrines in Amman and Shechem," ibid., pp. 104-116.

25. At Shiloh, we compared the number of sheep/goat bones to the number of cattle bones to get a ratio or percentage. In Middle Bronze II and Iron I the percentage of sheep/goat bones was low and the percentage of cattle bones was high. In the Late Bronze Age, there was a dramatic increase in sheep/goat bones compared to cattle bones (which declined). The increase in sheep/goats in the Late Bronze Age is typical of a society changing to a pastoralist mode of existence. See Salo Hellwing and Moshe Sadeh, "Animal Remains: Preliminary Report" in "Excavations at Shiloh 1981-1984: Preliminary Report," ed. Finkelstein, *Tel Aviv* 12 (1985), pp. 159-165.

26. At Lachish the intramural shrine of stratum VI was built after the Fosse Temple went out of use, but it is logical to assume that there was a sanctuary on the mound at that time too. See David Ussishkin, "Lachish—Key to the Israelite Conquest of Canaan?" *BAR* 13:1 (1987), p. 28.

27. Gonen, "Burial in Canaan of the Late Bronze Age as a Basis for the Study of Population and Settlements" (Ph.D. diss., Hebrew University, 1979), pp. 229-230 (in Hebrew); Sauer, "*Transjordan in the Bronze and Iron Ages*," p. 8.

28. M. Rowton, "Enclosed Nomadism," *Journal of the Economy and Social History of the Orient* 17 (1974), pp. 14, 22.

29. Nadav Na'aman, "Eretz Israel in the Canaanite Period: The Middle and Late Bronze Ages" in *The History of Eretz Israel*, vol. 1, ed. Israel Eph'al (Jerusalem: Keter, 1982), pp. 233-241 (in Hebrew).

30. Manfred Weippert, "The Israelite 'Conquest' and the Evidence from Transjordan" in Cross, *Symposia*, pp. 12, 35; R. Giveon, *Les Bédouins Shosou des documents égyptiens* (Leiden: Brill, 1971), pp. 269-271; Donald B. Redford, "The Ashkelon Relief at Karnak and the Israel Stela," *IEJ* 36 (1986), pp. 199-200; Na'aman, "Eretz Israel," p. 240.

31. Finkelstein, *'Izbet Sartah*, pp. 5-12, 106-109, 116-121.

32. Shmueli, *Nomadism About to Cease*, pp. 83, 154-155; Motoko Katakura, *Bedouin Village* (Tokyo: University of Tokyo, 1977), p. 73; Shirley Kay, *The Bedouin* (New York: Crain Russak, 1978), p. 143.

33. See Gustav Dalman, *Arbeit und Sitte in Palästina VI* (Gütersloh: Bertelsmann, 1939), plate 12; and A. Musil, *Arabia Petraea*, vol. 3 (Vienna: A. Hölder, 1908), p. 131. See also Claude R. Conder, *Tent Work in Palestine* (London: R. Bentley and Son, 1878), p. 275.

34. See also the theory that the four-room house—the most common architectural type in the hill-country sites—developed from the shape of the nomads' tents: Aharon Kempinski, "Tel Masos," *Expedition* 20:4 (1978), p. 35; Fritz, *Tempel und Zelt* (Neukirchen: Neukirchener Verlag, 1977), pp. 60-64. On the layout of Giloh as reflecting pastoral occupation of the inhabitants, see Amihai Mazar, "Giloh: An Early Israelite Settlement Site Near Jerusalem," *Israel Exploration Journal* 31 (1981), pp. 12, 32.

35. Shmueli, *Nomadism About to Cease*; Salzman, ed., *When Nomads Settle* (New York: Praeger, 1980), pp. 1–19; Anatoli M. Khazanov, *Nomads and the Outside World* (Cambridge, UK: Cambridge University Press, 1984), pp. 200-201.

36. D.G. Bates and S.H. Lees, "The Role of Exchange in Productive Specialization," *American Anthropologist* 79 (1977), pp. 824-841.

37. J.M. Weinstein, "The Egyptian Empire in Palestine: A Reassessment," *BASOR* 241 (1981), pp. 17-22; Niels P. Lemche, *Early Israel* (Leiden: Brill, 1985), p. 423; Bienkowski, *Jericho*, p. 155.

38. At first glance, this model contradicts our theory of nomadization of the population at the end of the Middle Bronze. But the background of these periods was so different that absolute comparisons between the two inverse processes cannot be drawn, especially because urban centers continued to flourish in the lowlands of the country during the Late Bronze period. Moreover, it is possible to suggest the following sequence of events—weakening of the urban/rural communities and nomadization of large groups at the end of the Middle Bronze followed by further deterioration of the sedentary system at the end of the 13th century, forcing pastoral groups to settle down.

39. See Volkmar Fritz, "The Israelite 'Conquest,' in the Light of Recent Excavations at Khirbet el-Meshâsh," *BASOR* 241 (1981), pp. 61-73. Fritz argued that the settlers came from without, i.e., from the desert.

40. At the same time, other groups in Transjordan were undergoing a similar process of consolidation.

Related Articles in *BR* and *BAR*

Yohanan Aharoni, "The Israelite Occupation of Canaan," *BAR* 8:3 (1982).

Rudolph Cohen, "The Mysterious MB I People," *BAR* 9:4 (1983).

Aharon Kempinski, "Israelite Conquest or Settlement? New Light from Tell Masos," *BAR* 2:3 (1976).

Abraham Malamat, "How Inferior Israelite Forces Conquered Fortified Canaanite Cities," *BAR* 8:2 (1982).

Hershel Shanks, "Frank Moore Cross–An Interview, Part I: Israelite Origins," *BR* 8:4 (1992).

Yigael Yadin, "Is the Biblical Account of the Israelite Conquest of Canaan Historically Reliable?" *BAR* 8:2 (1982).

Adam Zertal, "Israel Enters Canaan–Following the Pottery Trail," *BAR* 17:5 (1991).

Finkelstein, Afterword

(pages139-141)

1. Richard A. Horsley, *Jesus and the Spiral of Violence: Popular Resistance in Roman Palestine* (San Francisco: Harper & Row, 1987).

2. Horsley and John S. Hanson, *Bandits, Prophets, and Messiahs* (Minneapolis: Winston Press, 1985).

3. Carolyn Osiek, *What Are They Saying about the Social Setting of the New Testament?* (New York: Paulist Press, 1984).

10. Millard

(pages 142-153)

"The Question of Israelite Literacy" first appeared in **BR** *fall 1987.*

1. Anthony J. Phillips, "The Ecstatics' Father" in *Words and Meanings*, ed. Peter R. Ackroyd and Barnabas Lindars (Cambridge, UK: Cambridge University Press, 1968), pp. 137-152.

2. Alan R. Millard, "The Practice of Writing in Ancient Israel," *Biblical Archaeologist* (*BA*) 35 (1972), pp. 195-198, plate 26A.

3. See Mendel Kaplan and Yigal Shiloh, "Digging in the City of David," *BAR* 5:4 (1979), p. 49.

4. Nahman Avigad, "The Epitaph of a Royal Steward from Siloam Village," *Israel Exploration Journal* (*IEJ*) 3 (1953), pp. 137-152.

5. André Lemaire, *Inscriptiones Hébraiques, I, Les Ostraca* (Paris: Cerf, 1977), p. 37; see also Ivan T. Kaufman, "The Samaria Ostraca: An Early Witness to Hebrew Writing," *BA* 45 (1982), pp. 229-239.

6. See Lemaire, "Probable Head of Priestly Scepter from Solomon's Temple Surfaces in Jerusalem," *BAR* 10:1 (1984).

7. See Rudolph Cohen, "The Fortresses King Solomon Built to Protect His Southern Border," *BAR* 11:3 (1985); and Ze'ev Meshel, "Did Yahweh Have a Consort?" *BAR* 5:2 (1979).

8. For information on Tel Masos, see Aharon Kempinski, "Israelite Conquest or Settlement? New Light from Tell Masos," *BAR* 2:3 (1976); "Is Tel Masos an Amalekite Settlement?" *BAR* 7:3 (1981); and "Conquest or Settlement? Israelite or Canaanite?" *BAR* 3:1 (1977). See also note 9.

9. For these two texts, see Lemaire, *Inscriptiones Hébraiques*, pp. 259ff., 275.

10. For example, Avigad, "Two Hebrew Inscriptions on Wine Jars," *IEJ* 22 (1972), pp. 1-5.

11. See, for example, Sean Warner, "The Alphabet: An Innovation and Its Diffusion," *Vetus Testamentum* 30 (1980), p. 89.

12. See clear examples in Emil G. Kraeling, *Brooklyn Museum Aramaic Papyri* (New Haven, CT: Yale University Press, 1953), p. 123ff., plate 21; each document bore a single seal, except for no. 10, which had two. Fourth-century papyri from Wadi Daliyeh may have had as many as seven seals; see Frank Moore Cross, "The Discovery of the Samaria Papyri," *BA* 26 (1963), pp. 111ff., 115 (fig. 3), 120 (fig. 5), and *Frank Moore Cross: Conversations with a Bible Scholar*, ed. Hershel Shanks (Washington, DC: Biblical Archaeology Society, 1994), pp. 132-135, 139 (photo). See also Avigad, *Hebrew Bullae from the Time of Jeremiah* (Jerusalem: Israel Exploration Society, 1986).

13. The situation was, of course, different in Mesopotamia and wherever cuneiform writing was inscribed on clay tablets that formed archives. But even in Assyria, papyrus was certainly used in the seventh century B.C.E. in conjunction with clay tablets. There is pictorial evidence in the painting and reliefs of two scribes, one holding a clay tablet or a hinged writing-board, the other a curling scroll, and there is written evidence in the reports of questions put to the god Shamash about "the man whose name is written on this piece of papyrus."

14. Aaron Demsky and Moshe Kochavi, "An Alphabet from the Days of the Judges," *BAR* 4:3 (1978).

15. Cf. Warner, "Alphabet," p. 88.

16. Millard, "Ugaritic and Canaanite Alphabets, Some Notes," *Ugarit-Forschungen* 11 (1979), pp. 613-616.

17. Jacob Hoftijzer and Gerrit van der Kooij, *Aramaic Texts from Deir 'Alla* (Leiden: Brill, 1976). There are now many studies of this text; see the contributions by Lemaire ("L'inscription de Balaam trouvée à Deir 'Alla: épigraphie") and Baruch Levine ("The Balaam Inscription from Deir 'Alla: Historical Aspects") in *Biblical Archaeology Today: Proceedings of the International Congress on Biblical Archaeology, Jerusalem, April 1984* (Jerusalem: Israel Exploration Society, 1985), pp. 313-325 (Lemaire), 326-339 (Levine). See also Lemaire, "Fragments from the Book of Balaam Found at Deir Alla," *BAR* 11:5 (1985).

18. "Letter from a Hebrew King?" *BAR* 6:1 (1980).

19. Yohanan Aharoni, *Arad Inscriptions*, Judean Desert Studies (Jerusalem: Israel Exploration Society, 1981), pp. 103-104; Lemaire, *Inscriptiones Hébraiques*, p. 221; cf. Yigael Yadin, "The Historical Significance of Inscription 88 from Arad: A Suggestion," *IEJ* 26 (1976), pp. 9-14; Millard, "Aramaic and Hebrew Epigraphic Notes," *Palestine Exploration Quarterly* 110 (1978), p. 26.

PART V

11. Minkoff

(pages 160-167)

"The Man Who Wasn't There: Hebrew Textual Mysteries" first appeared in **BR** *December 1990.*

1. See Geoffrey Sampson, *Writing Systems: A Linguistic Introduction* (Stanford, CA: Stanford University Press, 1985), pp. 89-92.

2. The goal of this transcription is to approximate the format of written Hebrew, so each Hebrew letter has been equated with one English letter; ' represents aleph, š represents shin, *ḥ* represents chet and so on. However, like the letter *c* in English, several Hebrew letters may represent quite distinct sounds.

3. NEB readings that differ from the traditional Hebrew text can be found in a companion volume to the NEB, Leonard H. Brockington, *The Hebrew Text of the Old Testament: The Readings Adopted by the Translators of the New English Bible* (Oxford: Oxford University Press, 1973).

4. For another example of alternate word divisions, see H. Neil Richardson, "Amos's Four Visions of Judgment and Hope," *BR* 5:2 (1989), pp. 16-21, where the traditional reading of Amos 7:4, *lrb b'š* (contend by fire), is changed to *lrbb 'š* (rain of fire).

Related Articles in *BR* and *BAR*

Dewey M. Beegle, "What Does the Bible Say? Translations Speak in Many Tongues," *BAR* 8:6 (1982).

Frederick E. Greenspahn, "Words that Occur in the Bible Only Once–How Hard Are They to Translate?" *BR* 1:1 (1985); reprinted in *Approaches to the Bible*, vol. 1, p. 286.

Harvey Minkoff, "Problems of Translations–Concern for the Text Versus Concern for the Reader," *BR* 4:4 (1988); reprinted in *Approaches to the Bible*, vol. 1, p. 266.

12. R.D. Freedman

(pages 170-174)

"Woman, a Power Equal to Man" first appeared in **BAR** *May/June 1983.*

1. See Genesis 2:4b-24; the first creation story is in Genesis 1:1-2:4a.

2. Remember that Proverbs 31:10 describes the perfect wife as *'ēšet ḥayil* (the woman of strength), which corresponds to the masculine *iš ḥayil* (the man of strength) in Genesis 47:6 and elsewhere.

3. Thus the word for "to hear" is *š-m-ʿ* in both Ugaritic and Hebrew; but the word for "youth" is *ġlm* in Ugaritic, but *ʿelem* in Hebrew.

4. Ugaritic also has the root *ġzr* (to be strong), especially in the epithet of the god Mot, *ydd il ġzr* (the beloved *hero* of El). See Patrick D. Miller, Jr., "Ugaritic *ġzr* and Hebrew *ʿzr* II," *Ugarit-Forschungen* 2 (1970), pp. 159-175.

5. They are Exodus 18:4; Hosea 13:9; Psalms 20:2, 121:1 and 2, 124:8, 146:5.

6. See Deuteronomy 33:7; Psalms 33:20, 89:20, 115:9,10 and 11; Ezekiel 12:14; Isaiah 30:5; Daniel 11:34.

7. Another example of the biblical use of both meanings of a *double entendre* can be found in Genesis 9:20-27, where Ham "saw his father's nakedness" (a euphemism for sexual intercourse, cf. Leviticus 20-17, and so meant in Genesis 9:20-27, as the curse proves, cf.

Deuteronomy 27:20), but his brothers literally "cover their father's nakedness" with a garment they carry while walking backwards. Immanuel Casanowicz collected some 500 examples of *paronomasia* (puns) in *Paronomasia in the Old Testament* (Boston: J.S. Cushing, 1894; reprint, Jerusalem: Makor, 1970/1971).

8. Other places where the phrase "bone and flesh" is used in similar ways are Judges 9:2; 2 Samuel 5:1; Chronicles 11:1; and 2 Samuel 19:13, all of which describe the intimate connection between a king and his constituents.

9. My interpretation has been anticipated in medieval Jewish Midrashim, especially the *Alfabeta d'Rabbi Akiva* and *Pirkei d'Rabbi Eliezer*.

Related Articles in *BR* and *BAR*

Adrien Janis Bledstein, "Was Eve Cursed? (or Did a Woman Write Genesis?)" *BR* 9:1 (1993).

R.D. Freedman, Afterword

(pages 175-176)

1. *The Pentateuch*, ed. Samson Raphael Hirsch, rendered into English by Isaac Levy (London: Hachinuch, 1959).

2. Tshuvoth Rashba 60, as quoted in *The Torah Anthology* by Rabbi Yaacov Culi, translated into English by Rabbi Aryeh Kaplan (New York: Maznaim, 1977).

3. Shemuel David Luzzato, as quoted in *Studies in Bereshit (Genesis)* by Professor Nehama Leibowitz, translated into English by Rabbi Aryeh Newman (Jerusalem: WZO, 1976).

PART VI

Introduction

(pages 178-181)

1. Barry N. Olshen and Yael S. Feldman, eds., *Approaches to Teaching the Hebrew Bible as Literature in Translation*, Approaches to Teaching World Literature 25 (New York: Modern Language Association, 1989).

2. David Rosenberg, ed., *Congregation: Contemporary Writers Read the Jewish Bible* (New York: Harcourt Brace Jovanovich, 1987).

3. Richard J. Coggins, *Introducing the Old Testament*, Oxford Bible Ser. (Oxford/New York: Oxford University Press, 1990).

4. Meir Sternberg, *The Poetics of Biblical Narrative: Ideological Literature and the Drama of Reading* (Bloomington, IN: Indiana University Press, 1985).

5. Northrop Frye, *The Great Code: The Bible and Literature* (New York: Harcourt Brace Jovanovich, 1982).

6. Robert Alter and Frank Kermode, eds., *The Literary Guide to the Bible* (Cambridge, MA: Harvard University Press, Belknap Press, 1987).

7. Erich Auerbach, *Mimesis: The Representation of Reality in Western Literature*, trans. Willard R. Trask (Princeton, NJ: Princeton University Press, 1953 [1946]).

8. Matthew Arnold, *Culture and Anarchy* (1869; most recent edition, ed. Samuel Lipman, New Haven, CT: Yale University Press, 1994).

9. Jonathan Culler, "The Identity of the Literary Text" in *Identity of the Literary Text*, ed. Mario J. Valdés and Owen Miller (Toronto: University of Toronto Press, 1985).

Related Articles in *BR* and *BAR*

John H. Gabel and Charles B. Wheeler, *The Bible as Literature: An Introduction*, reviewed by Marc Brettler, *BR* 5:4 (1989).

13. D.N. Freedman

(pages 182-192)

"Understanding the Book of Job" first appeared in **BR** *April 1988.*

1. The idea that Elihu speaks for Satan is affirmed in the Testament of Job, a pseudepigraphical work of the Roman period. Cf. J.H. Charlesworth, *The Old Testament Pseudepigrapha*, 2 vols. (Garden City, NY: Doubleday, 1983-1985), vol. 1, pp. 829-868, esp. 860-863, where chapters 41-43 are translated and discussed. Note especially Testament of Job 41:5, "Then Elihu, inspired by Satan, spoke out against me..."; 43:5, "Elihu, the only evil one"; and 43:17, "and the evil one Elihu." I am grateful to my student John Kutsko for calling my attention to these references in the Testament of Job.

Related Articles in *BR* and *BAR*

Lippman Bodoff, "God Tests Abraham—Abraham Tests God," *BR* 9:5 (1993).

Joseph P. Klein, "How Job Fulfills God's Word to Cain," *BR* 9:3 (1993).

14. Gros Louis

(pages 194-207)

"Gospel Versions of the Birth of Jesus" first appeared in **BR** *spring 1985.*

Related Articles in *BR* and *BAR*

David E. Aune, "The Gospels–Biography or Theology?" *BR* 6:1 (1990).

James E. Crouch, "How Early Christians Viewed the Birth of Jesus," *BR* 7:5 (1991).

John A. Darr, *On Character Building: The Reader and the Rhetoric of Characterization in Luke-Acts*, reviewed by John T. Carroll, *BR* 9:1 (1993).

H. Neil Richardson, "The Old Testament Background of Jesus as Begotten of God," *BR* 2:3 (1986).

PART VII

Introduction

(pages 212-216)

1. Robert Alter, *The Art of Biblical Narrative* (New York: Basic Books, 1981), p. 12.

2. For example, Ferdinand de Saussure, *Course in General Linguistics*, rev. ed., ed. Charles Bally and Albert Sechehaye, trans. Wade Baskin (New York: McGraw-Hill, 1959), and more recently, annotated and trans. Roy Harris (London: G. Duckworth, 1983; reprint, La Salle, IL: Open Court, 1986). See also Emile Benveniste, *Problems in General Linguistics*, trans. Mary E. Meek, Miami Linguistic Ser. 8 (Coral Gables, FL: University of Miami Press, 1971), p. 36.

3. For example, Roman Jakobson, *Selected Writings* ('s-Gravenhage: Mouton, 1962-1971), vol. 2, p. 711.

4. Jacques Derrida, *Margins of Philosophy*, trans. Alan Bass (Chicago: University of Chicago Press, 1982), p. 139.

5. For example, Hermann Gunkel, "Fundamental Problems of Hebrew Literary History" in *What Remains of the Old Testament and Other Essays*, trans. Alexander K. Dallas (New York: Macmillan, 1928); *The Legends of Genesis: The Biblical Saga and History*, trans. W.H. Carruth (New York: Schocken Books, 1964).

6. Sigmund Mowinckel, *The Psalms in Israel's Worship*, trans. D.R. Ap-Thomas, 2 vols. (New York: Abingdon Press, 1962).

7. Gerhard von Rad, "The Form-Critical Problem of the Hexateuch" in *The Problem of the Hexateuch and Other Essays*, trans. E.W.T. Dicken (New York: McGraw-Hill, 1966), pp. 3-8.

8. Kevin G. O'Connell, "Continuity and Change in Israel's Covenant with God," *BR* 1:4 (1985).

9. Gene M. Tucker, *Form Criticism of the Old Testament*, Guides to Biblical Scholarship, Old Testament Ser. (Philadelphia: Fortress Press, 1971).

10. Claude Levi-Strauss, *Structural Anthropology*, 2 vols. (English edition, New York: Basic Books, 1963-1976).

11. Vladimir Propp, *Morphology of the Folktale*, 2d rev. ed., ed. Louis A. Wagner, trans. Laurence Scott, Publications of the American Folklore Society, Bibliographical and Special Ser. 9 (Austin: University of Texas Press, 1968).

12. Edmund Leach and D. Alan Aycock, *Structuralist Interpretations of Biblical Myth* (Cambridge, UK: Cambridge University Press, 1983).

13. Jack M. Sasson, *Ruth: A New Translation with a Philological Commentary and a Formalist-Folklorist Interpretation* (Baltimore: Johns Hopkins University Press, 1979).

14. Barry N. Olshen, "Recent Literary Criticism" in *Approaches to Teaching the Hebrew Bible as Literature in Translation*, ed. Olshen and Yael S. Feldman, Approaches to Teaching World Literature 25 (New York: Modern Language Association, 1989), p. 28.

15. Isaac M. Kikawada and Arthur Quinn, *Before Abraham Was: The Unity of Genesis 1-11* (Nashville: Abingdon Press, 1985).

16. P. Kyle McCarter, Jr., "A New Challenge to the Documentary Hypothesis," *BR* 4:2 (1988); reprinted in *Approaches to the Bible*, vol. 1, p. 23.

17. *Paul Ricoeur on Biblical Hermeneutics*, ed. John Dominic Crossan, *Semeia* 4 (Missoula, MT: Scholars Press/Society of Biblical Literature, 1975).

18. Alter, *Biblical Narrative*, p. 11.

19. Alter and Frank Kermode, eds., *Literary Guide to the Bible* (Cambridge, MA: Harvard University Press, 1987), p. 15.

20. Alter, *The Art of Biblical Poetry* (New York: Basic Books, 1985).

21. Richard J. Coggins, *Introducing the Old Testament* (Oxford/New York: Oxford University Press, 1990), p. 36.

22. Leonard Thompson, "From *Tanakh* to Old Testament" in Olshen and Feldman, *Approaches*, p. 45.

23. Thompson, "From *Tanakh* to Old Testament," p. 43.

15. Crossan

(pages 217-226)

"From Moses to Jesus: Parallel Themes" first appeared in **BR** *summer 1986.*

1. Kenneth R. R. Gros Louis, "Different Ways of Looking at the Birth of Jesus," *BR* 1:1 (1985); reprinted in this volume on pp. 194-207.

2. Renée Bloch, "Quelques aspects de la figure de Moïse dans la tradition rabbinique" *Cahiers Sioniens* 8 (1954), pp. 210-285; reprinted in *Moïse, l'Homme de l'Alliance* (Paris, 1955), pp. 53-167; "Note méthodologique pour l'étude de la littérature rabbinique" *Recherches de Science Religieuse* 43 (1955), pp. 194-225. The latter article has been translated by William Scott Green and William J. Sullivan as "Methodological Note for the Study of Rabbinic Literature" in *Approaches to Ancient Judaism*, vol. 1., *Theory and Practice*, ed. W.S. Green, Brown Judaic Studies 1 (Missoula, MT: Scholars Press, 1978), pp. 51-75.

3. Bloch made two proposals for dating the series. First, she suggested a relative sequence based on the somewhat mechanical principle of "longer is later." Although this may often be correct, it is just as likely that a given author abbreviated as expanded a source. Accordingly, this sequence may have to be held in some doubt pending more detailed analysis. Second, she noted that the basic story of Moses' infancy in rabbinic writings is known from Josephus and pseudo-Philo (see below) both of whom can be dated confidently to the end of the first century C.E. Thus, we must imagine a trajectory for the extrabiblical infancy story of Moses from *at least* the second half of the first century and on into those rabbinic texts still awaiting critical analysis for both manuscripts and content.

4. *Josephus*, trans. H. St. J. Thackeray, Ralph Marcus, Allen Wikgren, Louis H. Feldman, 10 vols., Loeb Classical Library. *Jewish Antiquities*, which tells the story of Israel from the dawn of creation to the eve of the first war with Rome, is contained in vols. 4-10, and I cite by volume and page. For general background, see Harold W. Attridge, "Josephus and His Works" in *Jewish Writings of the Second Temple Period*, ed. Michael E. Stone, *Compendia Rerum Iudaicarum ad Novum Testamentum* 2.2 (Assen: Van Gorcum/Philadelphia: Fortress Press, 1984), pp. 185-232.

5. *Liber Antiquitatum Biblicarum* retells, with deletions, summaries, expansions and additions, the biblical story from Adam to the death of Saul. The book is extant only in a Latin version, usually considered a translation of a Greek version of the Hebrew original. See Guido Kisch, *Pseudo-Philo's Liber Antiquitatum Biblicarum*, Publications in Medieval Studies 10 (Notre Dame, IN: Notre Dame University Press, 1949). I cite from the translation by Montague Rhodes James, *The Biblical Antiquities of Philo*, Library of Biblical Studies (London: SPCK, 1917; revised edition, New York: Ktav, 1971). For general background, see George W.E. Nickelsburg, "The Bible Rewritten and Expanded" in Stone, *Jewish Writings*, pp. 89-156, esp. 107-110, 153.

6. Josephus *Antiquities* 4.252-253.

7. The only available copy of this text is an unedited manuscript in the Bodleian Library at Oxford (Ms. Heb d.11, Cat. No. 2797). It is composed of 388 parchment folios and contains a collection of various writings brought together by Eleazer ben Asher. There are clearly two different hands at work; compare, for example, folio 37b with 38a. One is more ancient and written in a different script on older parchment and is marginally annotated by the redactor. This includes folios 38a-46b, and it is these that I am interested in here. The second hand is in later German rabbinical script and includes all of the work except the folios just mentioned. See also Bloch, "Methodological Note," p. 73 n. 38. See also Emil Schürer, *The History of the Jewish People in the Age of Jesus Christ*, rev. and ed. Geza Vermes, Fergus Millar and Matthew Black, 3 vols. (Edinburgh: T & T Clark, 1973-1987), vol. 1, p. 117.

8. Josephus *Antiquities* 4.254-259.

9. Pseudo-Philo *Liber Antiquitatum Biblicarum* 9.2-10, in James, *Biblical Antiquities of Philo*, pp. 100-102.

10. Even though pseudo-Philo's account is more developed than the account in Josephus, it is just as likely that the latter abbreviates as that the former expands these scenes. In any case, pseudo-Philo shows that the divorce and remarriage elements were included in the story by the last quarter of the first century C.E.

11. *Sefer ha-Zikronot* 38b.12-16.

16. Friedman

(pages 227-236)

"The Cycle of Deception in the Jacob Tradition" first appeared in **BR** *spring 1986.*

1. Genesis 29:26. Several scholars have discussed this irony in various terms: Ephraim A. Speiser, *Genesis*, Anchor Bible 1 (Garden City, NY: Doubleday, 1964), p. 227; Nahum M. Sarna, *Understanding Genesis: The Heritage of Biblical Israel* (New York: Schocken Books, 1966), p. 184; Michael Fishbane, *Text and Texture* (New York: Schocken Books, 1979), p. 55 ff.; Robert Alter (citing Umberto Cassuto), "Sacred History and Prose Fiction" in *The Creation of Sacred Literature: Composition and Redaction of the Biblical Text*, ed. Richard Elliott Friedman, Near Eastern Studies 22 (Berkeley: University of California Press, 1981), p. 23. Fishbane's discussion of recompense for deception is especially interesting in parallel with what follows here.

2. The Aramaic translation (Targum), the Greek translation (Septuagint) and, recently, the New English Bible and the New Jewish Publication Society translations all read "the older," not "the firstborn," obscuring this point for their readers.

3. Friedman and Baruch Halpern, "Composition and Paronomasia in the Book of Jonah," *Hebrew Annual Review* 4 (1980), pp. 79-92.

4. Halpern, "The Uneasy Compromise Between the Israelite Source and the Biblical Historian" in *The Poet and the Historian: Essays in Literary and Historical Biblical Criticism*, ed. Friedman, Harvard Semitic Studies 26 (Chico, CA: Scholars Press, 1983), pp. 46-99.

Related Articles in *BR* and *BAR*

Arnold Ages, "Why Didn't Joseph Call Home?" *BR* 9:4 (1993).

Carl D. Evans, "The Patriarch Jacob—An 'Innocent Man,'" *BR* 2:1 (1986).

Maurice Samuel, "Joseph—the Brilliant Failure," *BR* 2:1 (1986).

Gordon Tucker, "Jacob's Terrible Burden," *BR* 10:3 (1994).

17. Alter

(pages 237-252)

"Psalms: Beauty and Poetic Structure" first appeared in **BR** *fall 1986.*

1. Yeshurun Keshet, *The Poetry of the Bible* (Tel Aviv, 1954), p. 126 (in Hebrew).

2. The Masoretic text reads, ungrammatically, *tenah*, which is presumed to mean "give." I have followed others in vocalizing the word *tunah*, which then makes good sense as "told" or "recounted."

3. Mitchell Dahood, a commentator ever alert to Ugaritic backgrounds, made the same suggestion, rather more confidently, in *Psalms I*, Anchor Bible 16 (Garden City, NY: Doubleday, 1966), pp. 50-51.

4. The phrase might mean "the outlying towns of Judea."

5. The verb occurs only here. Others render it "pass through."

6. For a discussion of the sea/land opposition in Exodus 15, see Robert Alter, *The Art of Biblical Poetry* (New York: Basic Books, 1985), pp. 87-94.

Related Articles in *BR* and *BAR*

Patrick D. Miller, Jr., *Interpreting the Psalms*, reviewed by David M. Howard, Jr., *BR* 4:3 (1988).

Nahum M. Sarna, *Songs of the Heart: An Introduction to the Book of Psalms*, reviewed by James L. Mays, *BR* 10:2 (1994).

PART VIII
Introduction

(pages 254-258)

1. Kate Millett, *Sexual Politics* (Garden City, NY: Doubleday, 1970).

2. Nina Baym, *Woman's Fiction* (Ithaca, NY: Cornell University Press, 1978).

3. Eileen Barrett and Mary Cullinan, eds., *American Women Writers: Diverse Voices in Prose since 1845* (New York: St. Martin's, 1992).

4. Sandra M. Gilbert and Susan Gubar, *The Madwoman in the Attic: The Woman Writer and the Nineteenth-Century Literary Imagination* (New Haven, CT: Yale University Press, 1984).

5. Maria Herrera-Sobek, ed., *Beyond Stereotypes: The Critical Analysis of Chicana Literature*, Studies in the Language and Literature of United States Hispanos (Binghamton, NY: Bilingual Press, 1985).

6. Gloria T. Hull, Patricia B. Scott and Barbara Smith, *All the Women Are White, All the Blacks Are Men, But Some of Us Are Brave* (Old Westbury, NY: Feminist Press, 1982).

7. Jonathan Culler, in the introduction to Mario J. Valdés and Owen Miller, eds., *Identity of the Literary Text* (Toronto: University of Toronto Press, 1985), p. 5.

8. Robert Weimann, "Textual Identity and Relationship: A Metacritical Excursion into

History" in Valdés and Miller, *Identity of the Literary Text*, p. 278.

9. Mieke Bal, "Reading as Empowerment: The Bible from a Feminist Perspective" in *Approaches to Teaching the Hebrew Bible as Literature in Translation*, ed. Barry N. Olshen and Yael S. Feldman, Approaches to Teaching World Literature 25 (New York: Modern Language Association, 1989), pp. 87-92.

10. Matilda Joslyn Gage, *Woman, Church and State: The Original Exposé of Male Collaboration against the Female Sex* (Watertown, MA: Persephone Press, 1980).

11. Elizabeth Cady Stanton, *The Woman's Bible* (New York: European Publishing Company, 1895-1898; most recent edition, Boston: Northeastern University Press, 1993); introduction reprinted in Alice S. Rossi, ed., *The Feminist Papers: From Adams to Beauvoir* (Boston: Northeastern University Press, 1988), pp. 401-406.

12. Carey A. Moore, "Judith–The Case of the Pious Killer," *BR* 6:1 (1990).

13. Ruth Adler, "Rereading Eve and Other Women: The Bible in a Women's Studies Course" in Olshen and Feldman, *Approaches*, p. 95.

14. Harvey Minkoff and Evelyn B. Melamed, "Was the First Feminist Bible in Yiddish?" *Moment* 16:3 (1991), pp. 28-33.

15. Phyllis Trible, *Texts of Terror: Literary-Feminist Readings of Biblical Narratives*, Overtures to Biblical Theology 13 (Philadelphia: Fortress Press, 1984).

18. Milne
(pages 259-269)

"Eve and Adam: A Feminist Reading" first appeared in **BR** *June 1988.*

1. According to a prevailing theory of biblical scholarship called the documentary hypothesis, the Pentateuch (the first five books of the Bible) was written at different times by several different authors and was later combined into a single narrative. To identify the sources, Bible scholars use the letters J, E, P and D. The letters stand for Yahwist (or Jehovist), Elohist, Priestly and Deuteronomist, respectively. See Joseph Blenkinsopp, "The Documentary Hypothesis in Trouble," *BR* 1:4 (1985); and P. Kyle McCarter, Jr., "A New Challenge to the Documentary Hypothesis," *BR* 4:2 (1988); both articles reprinted in *Approaches to the Bible*, vol. 1.

2. Bernard Prusak traces the development of the interpretation of Genesis 2-3 and other biblical texts in the pseudepigraphical literature in his article, "Woman: Seductive Siren and Source of Sin?" in *Religion and Sexism*, ed. Rosemary Ruether (New York: Simon and Schuster, 1974), pp. 89-116.

3. Tertullian, "On the Apparel of Women," 1.1, in *The Ante-Nicene Fathers: Translations of the Writings of the Fathers down to A.D. 325*, ed. Alexander Roberts and James Donaldson (Grand Rapids, MI: Eerdmans, 1956; reprint 1989), vol. 4, p. 14.

4. Ambrose, *Paradise* 4.24, 10.47, in *Saint Ambrose: Hexameron, Paradise, and Cain and Abel*, trans. John J. Savage, Fathers of the Church 42 (New York: Fathers of the Church Inc., 1961), pp. 301-302, 325-327.

5. Thomas Aquinas, *Summa Theologica*, part 1, question 92, article 1.

6. See Hugh R. Trevor-Roper, "Witches and Witchcraft" (parts 1 and 2) *Encounter* 28:5-6 (1967); Rosemary Ruether, "The Persecution of Witches," *Christianity and Crisis* 34 (1974), and "The *Malleus Maleficarum*: The Woman as Witch" in *Women and Religion: A Feminist Sourcebook of Christian Thought*, ed. Elizabeth A. Clark and Herbert W. Richardson (New York: Harper & Row, 1977).

7. J.A. Phillips' important and useful book, *Eve: The History of an Idea* (San Francisco: Harper & Row, 1984), traces the development of Eve's image through history.

8. See Susan Brooks Thistlethwaite, "Every Two Minutes: Battered Women and Feminist Interpretation" in *Feminist Interpretation of the Bible*, ed. Letty M. Russell (Philadelphia: Westminster Press, 1985).

9. Elizabeth Cady Stanton, *The Woman's Bible* (Seattle: Coalition Task Force on Women and Religion, 1974 [1895-1898]), pp. 24, 26.

10. Phyllis Trible, "Depatriarchalizing in Biblical Interpretation," *Journal of the American Academy of Religion* (*JAAR*) 12 (1973), pp. 39-42; "Eve and Adam: Genesis 2-3 Reread," *Andover Newton Quarterly* 13 (1973), pp. 251-258; reprinted in *Womanspirit Rising*, ed. C. Christ and J. Plaskow (New York: Harper & Row, 1979), pp. 74-83; "A Love Story Gone Awry" in *God and the Rhetoric of Sexuality* (Philadelphia: Fortress Press, 1978), pp. 72-143.

11. J. Higgins, "The Myth of Eve: Temptress," *JAAR* 44 (1976), pp. 639-647.

12. For another powerful critique of the traditional translation of *'ezer kenegdo*, see R. David Freedman, "Woman, a Power Equal to Man," *BAR* 9:1 (1983); reprinted on pp. 170-174 in this volume. Freedman argues that the phrase should be translated "a power equal to man."

13. The terminology "reformists" and "revolutionaries" is found in Carol P. Christ's review article, "The New Feminist Theology: A Review of the Literature," *Religious Studies Review* 3:4 (1977), pp. 203-212. In Phillips' study (*Eve*, p. 174), the term "liberal" most closely corresponds to "reformist."

14. Elisabeth Schüssler Fiorenza has made major contributions to this project in two books, *In Memory of Her: A Feminist Theological Reconstruction of Christian Origins* (New York: Crossroad, 1983) and *Bread Not Stone: The Challenge of Feminist Biblical Interpretation* (Boston: Beacon Press, 1984).

15. See the articles in Russell's *Feminist Interpretation*.

16. Howard N. Wallace, *The Eden Narrative*, Harvard Semitic Monographs 32 (Atlanta: Scholars Press, 1985).

17. Jerome T. Walsh, "Genesis 2:4b-3:24: A Synchronic Approach," *Journal of Biblical Literature* 96 (1977), pp. 161-177.

18. See Terence Hawkes, *Structuralism and Semiotics* (Berkeley: University of California Press, 1977), p. 17; Robert Scholes, *Structuralism in Literature: An Introduction* (New Haven, CT: Yale University Press, 1974), p. 4; and David Jobling, "Structuralism, Hermeneutics and Exegesis," *Union Seminary Quarterly Review* 34 (1974), p. 139.

19. Edmund Leach, "Levi-Strauss in the Garden of Eden: An Examination of Some Recent Developments in the Analysis of Myth," *Transactions of the New York Academy of Sciences*, ser. 2, vol. 23/4 (1961), pp. 386-96. A revised version has been reprinted in Leach, *Genesis as Myth and Other Essays* (Suffolk, UK: Richard Clay, 1971), pp. 7-23.

20. Jobling, "Myth and Its Limits in Genesis 2:4b-3:24," in *The Sense of Biblical Narrative: Structural Analyses in the Hebrew Bible II* (Sheffield: JSOT Press, 1986), pp. 17-43.

21. Jobling, "The Myth Semantics of Genesis 2:4b-3:24" in *Genesis 2 and 3: Kaleidoscopic Structural Readings*, ed. Daniel Patte, *Semeia* 18 (Chico, CA: Scholars Press/Society of Biblical Literature, 1980), p.48.

22. Trible, *Texts of Terror: Literary-Feminist Readings of Biblical Narratives*, Overtures to Biblical Theology 13 (Philadelphia: Fortress Press, 1984).

23. Conrad L'Heureux, *In and Out of Paradise* (New York: Paulist Press, 1983), pp. 76-79.

Related Articles in *BR* and *BAR*

Adrien Janis Bledstein, "Was Eve Cursed? (or Did a Woman Write Genesis?)" *BR* 9:1 (1993).

Carol Meyers, *Discovering Eve: Ancient Israelite Women in Context*, reviewed by Ross S. Kraemer, *BR* 6:4 (1990).

Carol A. Newsom and Sharon H. Ringe, eds., *The Women's Bible Commentary*, reviewed by Blake Leyerle, *BR* 9:3 (1993).

Ilona N. Rashkow, *Upon the Dark Places: Anti-Semitism and Sexism in English Renaissance Biblical Translation*, reviewed by Jane Schaberg, *BR* 8:3 (1992).

19. Exum

(pages 273-279)

"The Mothers of Israel" first appeared in **BR** *spring 1986.*

1. See, *inter alia*, Samuel Terrien, "Toward a Biblical Theology of Womanhood," *Religion in Life* 42 (1973), pp. 322-333, reprinted in Ruth T. Barnhouse and Urban T. Holmes, eds., *Male and Female: Christian Approaches to Sexuality* (New York: Seabury Press, 1976), pp. 17-27; Phyllis Trible, *God and the Rhetoric of Sexuality* (Philadelphia: Fortress Press, 1978); Frederick E. Greenspahn, "A Typology of Biblical Women," *Judaism* 32 (1983), pp. 43-50; James G. Williams, *Women Recounted: Narrative Thinking and the God of Israel* (Sheffield: Almond Press, 1982); Elisabeth Schüssler Fiorenza, *In Memory of Her: A Feminist Theological Reconstruction of Christian Origins* (New York: Crossroad, 1983); and the recent collections edited by Mary Ann Tolbert (*The Bible and Feminist Hermeneutics*, *Semeia* 28 [Chico, CA: Scholars Press/Society of Biblical Literature, 1983]), Letty M. Russell (*Feminist Interpretation of the Bible* [Philadelphia: Westminster Press, 1985]) and Adela Yarbro Collins (*Feminist Perspectives on Biblical Scholarship*, Biblical Scholarship in North America 10 [Chico, CA: Scholars Press, 1985]).

2. See, for example, Carol Meyers, "Procreation, Production, and Protection: Male-Female

Balance in Early Israel," *Journal of the American Academy of Religion* 51 (1983), pp. 569-593.

3. On point of view and for a discussion of a number of biblical women, see Adele Berlin, *Poetics and Interpretation of Biblical Narrative* (Sheffield: Almond Press, 1983).

4. John Van Seters (in *Abraham in History and Tradition* [New Haven, CT: Yale University Press, 1975], p. 193) puts it nicely: "The son to be born to her will have a destiny that will be anything but submissive and his defiance will be her ultimate vindication." Notice, however, that the mother's importance derives from her son.

5. Tanhuma, Par. Vayira 23.

Related Articles in *BR* and *BAR*

Samuel Dresner, "Rachel and Leah–Sibling Tragedy or the Triumph of Piety and Compassion?" *BR* 6:2 (1990).

Zefira Gitay, "Hagar's Expulsion–A Tale Twice-Told in Genesis," *BR* 2:4 (1986).

John H. Otwell, *And Sarah Laughed: The Status of Women in the Old Testament*, reviewed by Rivkah Harris, *BAR* 9:1 (1983).

Savina J. Teubal, *Hagar the Egyptian: The Lost Tradition of the Matriarchs*, reviewed by Ilona N. Rashkow, *BR* 8:6 (1992).

Exum, Afterword

(pages 280-284)

1. Tikva Frymer-Kensky, *In the Wake of the Goddesses: Women, Culture, and the Biblical Transformation of Pagan Myth* (New York: Macmillan, Free Press, 1992).

2. Phyllis Trible, *Texts of Terror: Literary-Feminist Readings of Biblical Narratives*, Overtures to Biblical Theology 13 (Philadelphia: Fortress Press, 1984).

3. Elisabeth Schüssler Fiorenza, *Bread Not Stone: The Challenge of Feminist Biblical Interpretation* (Boston: Beacon Press, 1984).

Related Articles in *BR* and *BAR*

Bernhard W. Anderson, "Moving beyond Masculine Metaphors," *BR* 10:5 (1994).

Anne Baring and Jules Cashford, *The Myth of the Goddess*, reviewed by Susan Ackerman, *BR* 9:6 (1993).

Carey A. Moore, "Susanna–Sexual Harassment in Ancient Babylon," *BR* 8:3 (1992).

20. Trible

(pages 285-299)

"Bringing Miriam Out of the Shadows" first appeared in **BR** *February 1989.*

1. For a comprehensive investigation of the Miriamic traditions (excluding Exodus 2:1-10), see Rita J. Burns, *Has the Lord Indeed Spoken Only Through Moses? A Study of the Biblical Portrait of Miriam*, Society of Biblical Literature Diss. Ser. 84 (Atlanta: Scholars Press, 1987). For a wide-ranging structuralist reading, see Edmund Leach, "Why Did Moses Have a Sister?" in Leach and D. Alan Aycock, *Structuralist Interpretations of Biblical Myth* (Cambridge, UK: Cambridge University Press, 1983), pp. 33-67.

2. Bible translations in this article are by the author or adapted from the RSV. A few translations come directly from the RSV and are so identified.

3. Cf. Robert B. Lawton, "Irony in Early Exodus," *Zeitschrift für die alttestamentliche Wissenschaft* 97 (1985), p. 414; J. Cheryl Exum, "'You Shall Let Every Daughter Live': A Study of Exodus 1:8-2:10" in *The Bible and Feminist Hermeneutics*, ed. Mary Ann Tolbert, *Semeia* 28 (Chico, CA: Scholars Press, 1983), pp. 74-81.

4. See recent commentaries: e.g., Martin Noth, *Exodus*, Old Testament Library (Philadelphia: Westminster Press, 1962); Umberto Cassuto, *A Commentary on the Book of Exodus* (Jerusalem: Magnes Press, 1967); Brevard S. Childs, *The Book of Exodus*, Old Testament Library (Philadelphia: Westminster Press, 1974).

5. See especially Frank Moore Cross and David Noel Freedman, "The Song of Miriam," *Journal of Near Eastern Studies* 14 (1955), pp. 237-250. Cf. Maria-Sybilla Heister, *Frauen in der biblischen Glaubensgeschichte* (Göttingen: Vandenhoeck & Ruprecht, 1984), pp. 49-50.

6. In scholarly literature, Exodus 15:1-18 is most often called the "Song of the Sea" and Exodus 15:21 the "Song of Miriam." Following Cross and Freedman (see note 5), many scholars now attribute the Song of the Sea to Miriam (not to Moses, as tradition holds) and thus designate both Exodus 15:1-18 and Exodus 15:21 the Song of Miriam. By contrast, the Song of Moses is Deuteronomy 32:1-43, and the Blessing of Moses is Deuteronomy 33:2-29.

7. On the theme of rebellion and the difficulties of source analysis, see George W. Coats, *Rebellion in the Wilderness* (Nashville: Abingdon Press, 1968).

8. On the wilderness controversies, cf. Murray Newman, *The People of the Covenant* (Nashville: Abingdon Press, 1962), pp. 72-101.

9. Coats argues that the received text focuses on Moses; see "Humility and Honor: A Moses Legend in Numbers 12" in *Art and Meaning: Rhetoric in Biblical Literature*, ed. David J.A. Clines, David M. Gunn and Alan J. Hauser, Journal for the Study of the Old Testament Supplement Ser. (JSOTSup) 19 (Sheffield: JSOT Press, 1982), pp. 97-107. Robert R. Wilson argues that prophecy was the original focus of the text in *Prophecy and Society in Ancient Israel* (Philadelphia: Fortress Press, 1980), pp. 155-156.

10. The translation comes from Cross, *Canaanite Myth and Hebrew Epic: Essays in the History of the Religion of Israel* (Cambridge, MA: Harvard University Press, 1973), pp. 203-204.

11. See David Jobling, "A Structural Analysis of Numbers 11-12" in *The Sense of Biblical Narrative: Three Structural Analyses in the Old Testament*, JSOTSup 7 (Sheffield: University of Sheffield, Department of Biblical Studies, 1978), pp. 32-33 (2d ed., 1986, pp. 37-38).

12. Cf. Aelred Cody in *A History of Old Testament Priesthood* (Rome: Pontifical Biblical Institute, 1969), pp. 150-151; Cody argues against a priestly identification of Aaron in Numbers 12.

13. See William H. Propp, "Did Moses Have Horns?" *BR* 4:1 (1988).

14. See Noth, *Numbers* (Philadelphia: Westminster Press, 1968), pp. 138-143.

15. For a helpful analysis of the priestly ascription of ritual purity to the deity, with the concomitant rejection of women, see Nancy Joy, "Throughout Your Generation Forever: A Sociology of Blood Sacrifice" (Ph.D. diss., Brandeis University, 1981).

16. See Katharine Doob Sakenfeld, "Theological and Redactional Problems in Numbers 20:2-13" in *Understanding the Word: Essays in Honor of Bernhard W. Anderson*, ed. James T. Butler et al., JSOTSup 37 (Sheffield: JSOT Press, 1985).

17. See Propp, "The Rod of Aaron and the Sin of Moses," *Journal of Biblical Literature* (March 1988), pp. 19-26; Jacob Milgrom, "Magic, Monotheism and the Sin of Moses" in *The Quest for the Kingdom of God: Studies in Honor of George E. Mendenhall*, ed. H.B. Huffmon (Winona Lake, IN: Eisenbrauns, 1983), pp. 251-265; M. Margaliot, "The Transgression of Moses and Aaron—Numbers 20:1-13," *Jewish Quarterly Review* 74 (1983), pp. 196-228.

18. See Bernhard W. Anderson, "The Song of Miriam Poetically and Theologically Considered" in Directions in Biblical Hebrew Poetry, ed. Elaine R. Follis, JSOTSup 40 (Sheffield: JSOT Press, 1987), pp. 284-296.

19. This article is adapted from a forthcoming larger study with full annotation. Publication data are not yet available.

Related Articles in *BR* and *BAR*

Bernhard W. Anderson, "Miriam's Challenge," *BR* 10:3 (1994).

"Biblical Leprosy—Is It Really?" *BR* 8:2 (1992).

George J. Brooke, "Power to the Powerless—A Long-Lost Song of Miriam," *BAR* 20:3 (1994).

Trible, Afterword

(pages 300-304)

1. Phyllis Trible, *God and the Rhetoric of Sexuality* (Philadelphia: Fortress Press, 1978).

2. Trible, *Texts of Terror: Literary-Feminist Readings of Biblical Narratives*, Overtures to Biblical Theology 13 (Philadelphia: Fortress Press, 1984).

Related Articles in *BR* and *BAR*

Clinton Bailey, "How Desert Culture Helps Us Understand the Bible—Bedouin Law Explains Reaction to Rape of Dinah," *BR* 7:4 (1991).

Marc Brettler, "On Becoming a Male Feminist Bible Scholar," *BR* 10:2 (1994).

Carey A. Moore, "Susanna—Sexual Harassment in Ancient Babylon," *BR* 8:3 (1992).

Subject Index

Scripture Index

Genesis